RUSSIANS IN THE FORMER SOVIET REPUBLICS

PAUL KOLSTOE

Russians in the Former Soviet Republics

WITH A CONTRIBUTION BY
ANDREI EDEMSKY

INDIANA UNIVERSITY PRESS

BLOOMINGTON AND INDIANAPOLIS

Printed in Hong Kong

Library of Congress Cataloging-in-Publication Data

Kolstø, Pål.
    Russians in the former Soviet republics / Paul Kolstoe : with a
contribution by Andrei Edemsky.
        p. cm.
    Includes bibliographical references and index.
    ISBN 0-253-32917-5
    1. Russians—former Soviet republics. 2. Former Soviet republics—
Ethnic relations. I. Edemsky, Andrei. II. Title.
DK35.5.K647   1995
323.1'09171'247—dc20   95-5773

1 2 3 4 5   00 99 98 97 96 95

CONTENTS

Part II

Part III

MAPS

TABLES

PREFACE

Much of the material for this book was collected during three study tours to the former Soviet Union in 1991–3: to Russia and Estonia in 1991, to Moldova and Ukraine in 1992 and to Central Asia and Kazakhstan in 1993. These travels were made possible by generous financial support from the Norwegian Research Council for the Humanities.

Thanks are also due to my indefatigable travel companion Andrei Edemsky of the Institute of Slavonic and Balkan Studies, Russian Academy of Sciences. He arranged all the meetings with representatives of local authorities, cultural organisations etc. He has also contributed to the penultimate chapter of this book.

Indispensable to the writing of this book was the conference on 'The New Russian Diaspora' in Lielupe, Latvia, on 13–15 November 1992, arranged by the Institute of History, Latvian Academy of Sciences, in cooperation with the Institute of East European and Oriental Studies, University of Oslo. Aina Antane from the Latvian side and Merethe Kvernrød from the Norwegian side carried the burden of its preparation, and are thus largely responsible for the successes it achieved.

A number of individuals have read parts of the manuscript and contributed with comments and corrections: Aadne Aasland, Bente Bergesen, Helge Blakkisrud, Ian Bremmer, Olga Brusina, Rogers Brubaker, Tor Bukkvoll, Juris Dreifelds, Peter Duncan, Alf Grannes, Victor Grebenscicov, Torbjørn Hustoft, Alla Kallas, Miroslava Lukianchikova, Alexander Motyl, Iver B. Neumann, Gerhard Simon, Jeff Sahadeo, Mikk Titma and Boris Tsilevich. A number of unfortunate mistakes and inaccuracies were weeded out and new perspectives added through their efforts. Full responsibility for the final result, of course, rests with the author.

Stavanger, Norway
January 1995

PAUL KOLSTOE

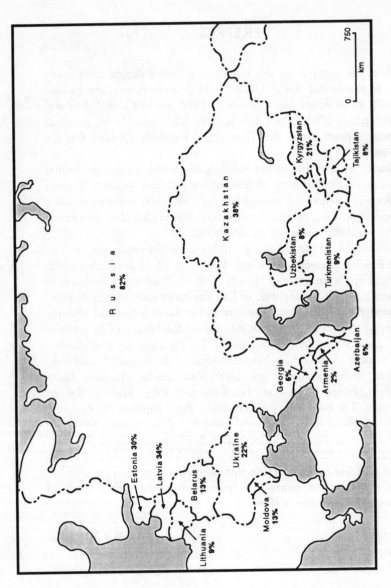

THE SUCCESSOR STATES OF THE SOVIET UNION
with % of Russians in population, 1989

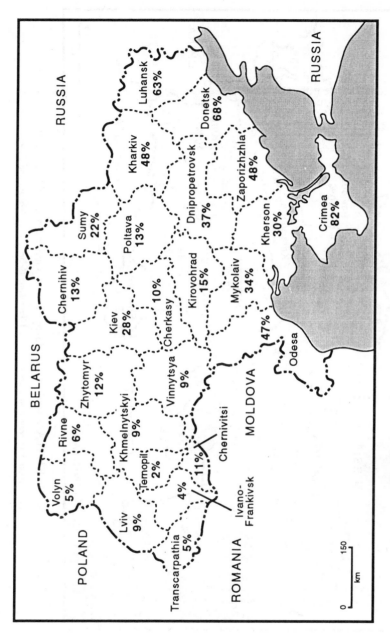

UKRAINE with % of Russian-speakers by oblast, 1989

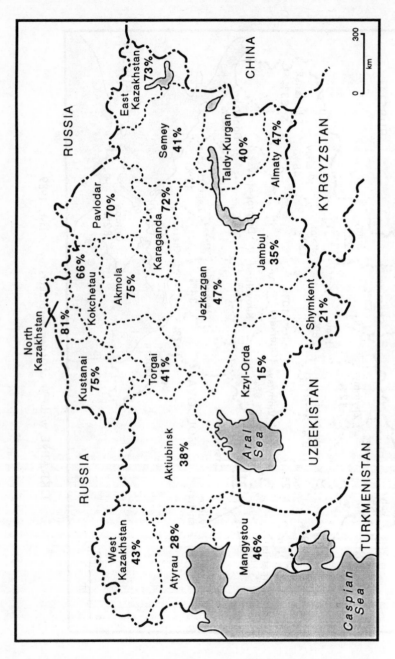

KAZAKHSTAN with % of Europeans in population by oblast, 1989
(*The major European groups are Russians, Ukrainians, Belorussians, Germans and Poles.*)

1

INTRODUCTION

'THE EMPIRE HAS COLLAPSED – WHO LIES UNDER THE DEBRIS?'[1]

The concept of a Russian diaspora

With more than 100 ethnic groups – or nationalities, as they are usually called – the Soviet Union was one of the largest multi-ethnic states in the world, and certainly the largest one in Europe. Its dissolution eliminated important minority problems, but during the same process numerous new ones were created. None of the successor states is anything near ethnically homogeneous.[2] In numerical terms the minority problems in some of them are just as big as in the former Soviet Union, or bigger.

Unlike certain other multi-ethnic states,[3] the population of the Soviet Union consisted mostly of ethnic groups rooted in a historically defined core territory. These territories provided the basis for the ethnically defined Soviet federation. However, the political frontiers did not always correspond with this ethnic map. Between the ethnic core areas there were usually 'grey zones' of ethnically mixed districts, and any attempt to draw administrative–political borders through them were bound to leave some groups on the 'wrong' side. And in modern times most Soviet nationalities have been marked by a high degree of mobility. As a result, large numbers of the titular nations in the Soviet successor states live *outside* the political unit with which they are associated (see Table 1.1A). Together they constitute a group of no less than 43 million people.[4] These groups have been

---

1. Aleksandr Tsipko, *Literaturnaia Gazeta*, no. 44 (6 November), 1991, p. 1.
2. The closest is Armenia where 93.3% of the population are ethnic Armenians.
3. The most obvious example is the United States, where the only ethnic groups with a historical territory are of course the Indians.
4. The figure of 70 million, which is cited more often, includes also the diaspora populations of the titular groups of the autonomous formations of a lower order in the Soviet Federation, the Autonomous Republics, the Autonomous Oblasts and the Autonomous Okrugs. While some of these groups have, also, ended up as residents of a new state as a result of the break-up of the Soviet Union, the vast majority of them have not. In most cases, 90–98% of the group live within

1

Introduction: 'The Empire has collapsed –
who lies under the debris?'

Table 1.1. POST-SOVIET DIASPORA GROUPS, 1989: TITULAR NATIONS OF THE SOVIET SUCCESSOR STATES RESIDING OUTSIDE THEIR POLITICAL UNIT

A. PERCENTAGES

Nationality	As % of whole group
Armenians	33.4
Tajiks	24.7
Belorussians	21.3
Kazakhs	19.7
Russians	17.4
Moldovans	16.7
Ukrainians	15.3
Uzbeks	15.2
Azeri	14.3
Kyrgyzs	11.9
Turkmens	7.0
Estonians	6.2
Latvians	4.8
Georgians	4.7
Lithuanians	4.5

B. ABSOLUTE NUMBERS

	(× 1 million)
Russians	25.30
Ukrainians	6.77
Uzbeks	2.55
Belorussians	2.13
Kazakhs	1.60
Armenians	1.54
Tajiks	1.04
Azeri	0.97
Moldovans	0.56
Kyrgyzs	0.30
Turkmens	0.19
Georgians	0.19
Lithuanians	0.14
Latvians	0.07
Estonians	0.06

Source: *Natsional'nyi sostav naseleniia SSSR*, Moscow, 1991.

the Union republic of which the autonomous unit is a part. The lowest percentage is represented by the Volga Tatars: 83%. This means that of the 4.9 million Volga Tatars who live outside the autonomous republic of Tatarstan, only 1.1 million represents a new 'diaspora' in the sense in which the word is used in this book.

transformed into the 'new diasporas' of the post-Soviet world. As a percentage of the total group, some medium-size nationalities – the Armenians and the Tajiks – have the largest diaspora populations. In this ranking the Russians are found only in fifth place. However, if we now look at the absolute numbers of the respective diasporas, the picture is radically different. As many as 25 million, or 58% of the total, are made up by the 'new Russian diaspora'. This is by far the largest minority problem created by the break-up of the Soviet Union (see Table 1.1B).

The first scholars to discuss the Russians living in the non-Russian Soviet republics as a diaspora problem seem to have been some of the participants at the colloquium on 'Ethnic Russia Today: Undergoing an Identity Crisis?' organised at Columbia University, New York, in May 1978.[5] Writing when the unitary Soviet state was still extant, they were concerned mainly with the cultural and psycho-sociological question of what kind of collective identity the Russians living in dispersion outside the RSFSR were developing.

The concept of a Russian diaspora may seem paradoxical. Some writers use the term only of those groups which possess no 'homeland' of their own anywhere in the world, such as the Jews in the period between the destruction of Jerusalem in AD 70 and the establishment of Israel in 1948. Others include ethnic communities which have co-nationals residing within a nation-state somewhere else, but only in those cases when the non-core group, in the words of John Armstrong, is 'explicitly averse to political attachment to its great society'.[6] By this criterion Armstrong excludes the English-speaking Canadians in Quebec from his diaspora concept; such a group, he believes, could more aptly be categorised as an outpost of a dominant

---

5. William Boris Kory, 'Spatial diffusion of the Russians in the USSR', in Edward Allworth (ed.) *Ethnic Russia in the USSR: the Dilemma of Dominance*, New York, 1980, pp. 285–91; Matthew Pavlovich, 'Ethnic Impact of Russian Dispersion in and Beyond the RSFSR', *ibid.*, pp. 294–305; Robert A. Lewis, 'Comment – Intensifying Russian Ethnic Identity by Dispersion', *ibid.*, pp. 306–8. (The fact that these authors used the English word 'dispersion' rather than the Greek original is immaterial.)

6. John A. Armstrong, 'Mobilized and Proletarian Diasporas', *American Political Science Review*, LXX (1976), pp. 393–408, on p. 395.

ethnic group. By implication, the Russians in the non-Russian Soviet republics would also not qualify in his terminology as a 'diaspora'.[7] Only Russian emigrants to Western Europe, America and advanced countries elsewhere would do so.[8]

Richard Marienstras defines the diaspora concept somewhat differently. In his terminology, the French-speakers in the Flemish communes of Belgium constitute a diaspora of sorts – although he believes his definition to be 'somewhat metaphorical'.[9] Similarly the Russians in the Union republics also represented diaspora communities only in a somewhat figurative sense while the Soviet Union existed. However, when it broke up, their diaspora status became political as well. This is reflected also in recent literature on the subject. In Graham Smith's excellent anthology on the nationalities question in the Soviet Union from 1990, the section on diaspora nationalities contains only two entries: the Crimean Tatars and the Jews.[10] In a sequel to this book, however, a separate chapter is also devoted to the new Russian diaspora.[11]

In the post-Soviet Russian debate the concept of 'a new Russian diaspora' is gradually gaining ground, albeit slowly. One Russian journalist believes that this slowness may be due to a certain 'superstition' among the Russian public.[12] Indeed, many Russians seem to shy away from the concept because it leaves them feeling that these people are in a sense 'cut loose' from the core group and no longer of any concern to Russia. Other observers are wary of the concept for exactly

7. In keeping with this terminology, Armstrong, in the section on diasporas in his article 'The Ethnic Scene in the Soviet Union', in Eric Goldhagen (ed.), *Ethnic Minorities in the Soviet Union*, New York, 1968, deals with Armenians, Germans and Jews but not with Russians outside Russia.
8. These communities I would prefer to call 'the old Russian diaspora'.
9. Richard Marienstras, 'On the Notion of Diaspora', in Gérard Chaliand (ed.), *Minority Peoples in the Age of Nation-States*, London, 1989, pp. 119–25, on p. 120.
10. Graham Smith (ed.), *The Nationalities Question in the Soviet Union*, London, 1990/2.
11. Aadne Aasland, 'Russians Outside Russia: The New Russian Diaspora' in Graham Smith (ed.), *The Nationalities Question in the Post-Soviet States*, London, 1994 (forthcoming).
12. Elena Iakovich, 'Russkaia diaspora', *Literaturnaia Gazeta*, no. 39 (23 September), 1992, p. 3.

the opposite reason. They suspect that it may predispose one towards irredentist thinking: what has become dispersed ought to be reassembled again under one political roof.[13] Wherever the concept is used in this book, it has none of these normative implications.

Scope and purpose of the book

The approach of the present book is above all historical and political. The objective has been to supply background material on how the Russian diaspora phenomenon has arisen and developed, as well as to analyse its effects on post-Soviet politics today. In the historical parts, an attempt is made to identify the driving forces behind the migratory patterns of the Russians seen under the tsars and the commissars, and a separate chapter discusses the social and political status of the Russians living in the non-Russian republics during the Soviet period. The common assumption that the Russians represented a privileged upper class is somewhat modified.

The contemporary post-Soviet political scene is surveyed by area. The new Russian diaspora is often referred to in the media as if it were a homogeneous group confronted with the same problems and challenges throughout. However, the *differences* between the various regions are so fundamental that any attempt to give a synoptic presentation would entail major distortions. Indeed, insofar as the term 'the new Russian diaspora' is in any sense problematical, this is because the singular definite mode which it employs obfuscates the magnitude of the differences within the group.

Chapters 5 to 9 examine the role of the diaspora Russians in the process leading up to the dissolution of the Soviet Union, as well as their status and role in the new states. The conduct and attitudes of the Russian diaspora communities are understood against the policy of the new state authorities towards the Russians, and vice versa, as an action–reaction process. While concentrating on the Russian diaspora issue, these chapters also function as general introductions both to inter-ethnic relations and to the treatment of minorities in the Soviet successor states. The interdependence of different events taking

13. E.g. Tore Lindholm at the conference on 'The New Russian Diaspora', Lielupe, Latvia, 13–15 November 1992.

part in the various different post-Soviet regions is underlined. The penultimate chapter discusses how the existence of the diaspora affects politics in the Russian Federation. The chapter was planned as an original contribution by the author's collaborator and travelling companion throughout the former Soviet Union, Andrei Edemsky, but due to illness it was turned into a 'joint venture'. Finally, I offer some policy considerations for the settlement of the Russian diaspora problem. Attention is focussed on three options: border transfers, return migration, and regimes for minority protection.

The question of what kind of collective identity/ies the Russians in the former Soviet Union will develop under the new political conditions, though a very important one, has not been directly addressed for practical reasons. Moving beyond loose generalisations and conjectures would require costly and time-consuming sociological surveys and the resources for such surveys have not been at my disposal.[14] Also, the situation of the Russians in non-Russian ethnic homelands within the Russian Federation has not been included in the study, although their problems are sometimes strongly reminiscent of those experienced by the diaspora Russians in the non-Russian successor states. A line had to be drawn somewhere, and in this study it has been drawn at the state borders of the Russian Federation.[15]

Centrality of the Russian diaspora problem in post-Soviet politics

Rogers Brubaker believes that the question of the Russian diaspora influences post-Soviet politics much more fundamentally than do the diasporas of the other successor states. While in his view these states are also potentially revisionist, and are more likely to be drawn into wars with their neighbours, 'the presence of nearly 25 million Russians in non-Russian successor states, the enormous military power of Russia, and the uniquely radical decline in status experienced both by the new Russian minorities and by key segments of Russian élites in Russia would make a revisionist Russia a potentially much graver

14. I have, however, discussed the identity dimension elsewhere, in a preliminary and theoretical fashion: Pål Kolstø, 'The new Russian diaspora – an identity of its own?', paper presented at the conference 'The new Russian diaspora', Lielupe, Latvia, 13–15 November 1992; and Pål Kolstø, 'Russkaia diaspora – sobstvennaia identichnost'?', Raduga, Tallinn, no. 11, 1993, pp. 67–75; and no. 12, pp. 68–74.
15. I hope to return to this subject in a follow-up study.

threat to the other successor states, to regional and even global security.'[16] Even more alarmed is Hélène Carrère d'Encausse. As early as in 1990, she remarked that if the diaspora Russians were prevented from being integrated into their new countries of residence, the weight of this problem 'may become particularly destabilizing, indeed even explosive'.[17]

The 145-million-strong Russian nation is generally considered the greatest collective loser from the dissolution of the Soviet state. Clearly, the Russians have benefited from the dismantling of the Communist system and the introduction of pluralist democracy just as much as the other Soviet nationalities. They were indeed also in the forefront of the democratisation process under *perestroika*. Furthermore, it can be convincingly argued that the boon of democracy could not be achieved without abandoning the empire. Seen in this perspective, the Russians may also be included among the objective beneficiaries of the break-up of the Soviet state. Even so, calculations of political loss and gain do not involve pure arithmetic but rather a question of perceptions and sentiments. Due to the historical continuity between the pre-revolutionary Russian empire and the post-revolutionary Soviet state, the distinctions between Russia, the Soviet Union and the 'Motherland' had become blurred in the mind of most Russians.[18] The Russians are the only group among the major Soviet peoples to have linked their national identity to the multinational Union to any appreciable degree. The successes and achievements of the Soviet state have been taken as a confirmation of Russian grandeur and glory. The reduction of their state to a second-rate power may well entail painful mental adjustments.

Right-wing groups in Russian politics are determined to reverse the

---

16. Rogers Brubaker, 'Nationhood and the National Question in the Soviet Union and Post-Soviet Eurasia: an Institutionalist Account', *Theory and Society*, XXIII, 1 (February 1994). pp. 47–78.

17. Hélène Carrère d'Encausse, *La gloire des nations, ou la fin de l'Empire soviétique*, Paris 1991, p. 389. Great concern is expressed also by Chauncy D. Harris, 'The New Russian Minorities: A Statistical Overview', *Post-Soviet Geography*, XXXIV (January 1993), pp. 1–27.

18. See e.g. S. Enders Wimbush, 'The Great Russians and the Soviet State: the Dilemmas of Ethnic Dominance', in Jeremy R. Azrael (ed.) *Soviet Nationality Policies and Practices*, New York, 1978, pp. 349–59; Sven Gunnar Simonsen, 'Dilemma of Dominance: Nation and Empire in Russian Nationalist Ideology', Department of Political Science, University of Oslo, 1993.

political changes of recent years and re-establish the unitary state. The
Russian diaspora plays a crucial role in their schemes. The ultimate aim of their political programmes is clearly imperial: the
re-establishment of the multi-ethnic empire. However, their line of
argument is just as clearly *national*: all ethnic Russians must be allowed
to live in the same state. If the 'empire savers'[19] – or more correctly,
'empire restorers' – were to succeed in seizing power in the Russian
Federation, they would surely attempt to use the Russian diaspora in
the same way as Hitler exploited the German populations in the
Sudetenland, Danzig, Pomerania and elsewhere – i.e. to promote territorial expansion. And conversely: if ethnic Russians in the other
Soviet successor states are discriminated against, this will create a
political climate in Russian politics favouring extremist parties. The
violent dissolution of the Yugoslav state, in which the diaspora population of the largest ethnic group, the Serbs, has likewise played a crucial
role, could be repeated.

Several Russian liberals have voiced concern that the rightists have
been allowed to monopolise the diaspora issue and exploit it for their
own sinister purposes. In 1991 the columnist Lidiia Grafova apos-
trophised the Russian democrats:

> You are too busy to be concerned about the plight of Russians who are
> becoming subjects of foreign states together with the debris of the collaps-
> ing empire, like serfs passing into the hands of a new owner when a village
> is being sold. Your opponents, however, the fervent admirers of Zhirinov-
> skii and Nevzorov, are in the meantime enlisting the support of these
> desperate souls ... Do we actually want to turn the unfortunate
> 'occupants' into a 'fifth column' yearning for the return of the empire?[20]

Possibly both the rightists and their liberal opponents exaggerate the
importance of the diaspora question for empire-restoring political programmes in Russia. Certain evidence suggests that many citizens of
the Russian Federation think that, in a time of severe economic hard-

---

19. This useful term has been coined by Roman Szporluk, 'Dilemmas of Russian
    Nationalism', *Problems of Communism*, XXXVII (July–August 1989), pp. 15–35.
    In contrast to the more conventional term 'reactionary', it is neutral on the ques-
    tion of right-wing vs left-wing politics, and also, indeed, many Russian Com-
    munists desperately cling to the multinational Soviet state. After the break-up
    of the Soviet Union, however, the concept of 'empire savers' should possibly have
    been supplanted by that of 'empire restorers'.

20. *Literaturnaia Gazeta*, no. 40, 1991, p. 2.

ships, they have enough problems of their own to deal with, and as a result are too exhausted to be concerned also with the plight of co-nationals in the other successor states. An opinion poll conducted in Russia in October 1991 showed that only 11% supported the idea of letting the diaspora Russians conduct referendums on the question of border changes whereby their areas would be joined to the Russian Federation; 12% believed that they should be provided with an opportunity to move to Russia, while the largest group, somewhat less than 40%, believed that Russia should guarantee their rights and liberties in the Soviet successor states. Apparently, the Russians in Russia preferred to help their co-nationals where they are living rather than bring about political changes that would make them fellow citizens in a common state. It is also interesting that 22.3% of the respondents thought that Russia should do nothing for the Russian diaspora: 'Let those who live in the territory of other states solve their own problems.'[21]

However, except in times of popular revolution, politics is made not by the masses but by élites, and the explosive force of the diaspora issue in Russian politics has been demonstrated by the defection of several Russian politicians, journalists and other public figures from the democratic camp because of what they see as the liberals' betrayal of the diaspora. For this reason several prominent members of Democratic Russia, the umbrella organisation which rallied Boris Yeltsin into power in 1990, later ended up in the rightist, radical National Salvation Front.

Not only in Russia but also in the other Soviet successor states, the diaspora issue is a very sensitive one. In almost all of these states, the Russians make up the largest minority group, and in several cases they account for more than 70% of the non-titular population (see Table 1.2). Under such circumstances, the question of inter-ethnic relations inevitably revolves around the Russian diaspora.

During the Soviet era, the Russian diaspora justified its presence in the non-Russian republics by adopting a stance of 'internationalist' self-understanding, claiming that in a 'mature socialist society' ethnic differences no longer mattered. When the Soviet Union began to crumble, this stance was intensified and made more explicit. In the Baltics, Moldova and, to some degree, Ukraine and Central Asia, 'internationalist movements' or 'inter-movements' were created.

21. *Rossiiskaia Gazeta*, 24 October 1991.

Table 1.2. RUSSIANS IN THE SOVIET SUCCESSOR STATES, 1989

	(× 1,000)	As % of total population in Republic	As % of non-titular population in Republic
Estonia	475	30.3	78.8
Latvia	906	34.0	70.7
Lithuania	344	9.4	45.8
Belarus	1,342	13.2	59.5
Moldova	562	13.0	36.4
Ukraine	11,356	22.1	80.8
Georgia	341	6.3	21.1
Armenia	52	1.6	23.0
Azerbaijan	392	5.6	32.2
Turkmenistan	334	9.5	33.7
Tajikistan	388	7.6	20.2
Uzbekistan	1,653	8.3	29.1
Kyrgyzstan	917	21.5	45.1
Kazakhstan	6,228	37.8	62.6

Source: *Natsional'nyi sostav naseleniia SSSR*, Moscow, 1991.

Despite their name, they functioned almost exclusively as organisations for Russians or linguistically russified non-Russians. These movements cooperated closely with the Communist Party, locally and centrally, and usually with its most orthodox phalanx, since the ideological diehards were least willing of all to compromise with the new leadership in the rebellious republics. For a long time most of those political organisations of diaspora Russians linked the defence of their status as ethnic minorities in the republics not only to the territorially unified state but also to the highly discredited Soviet power and Communist ideology.

Far from all Russians in the diaspora sympathised with the inter-movements, however. Many of them were disoriented and apathetic and not politically active. Also, in the course of 1990–1, a momentous convergence of the attitudes of the Russians on the one hand and the titular nationalities in the non-Russian republics on the other took place. This fact was brought out by the referendums on national independence which were held in several of the would-be new states. While the Russian vote in these referendums varied, between 25% and 70% supported the notion of independence. A high degree of national concord on this presumably most divisive ethnic issue had thus been reached. This was a crucial factor in explaining why the dissolution of the multinational Soviet state proceeded as peacefully as it did. In most cases, however, ethnic harmony in the Soviet successor states has not been durable. When political independence had been achieved, the authorities in the new states embarked on a policy of nation-building – a perfectly common process in all modern states. Except for the Russian Federation, which like the Soviet predecessor is a multi-ethnic federation, the former Soviet republics see themselves as 'national states' or 'nation-states'. This basic but rather vague concept can have at least two very different meanings. In the West, the dominant understanding is that of a political and civic entity in which the nation is delineated on the basis of common territory, common government and, to some extent, common (political) history. There also exists, however, a rival concept of the nation as a *cultural entity*, based on common language, traditions, mores, religion etc. – in short, the *ethnic* nation. This concept has deep roots in Eastern Europe,[22] and has also been reinforced by the Soviet experience. In the culturally heterogeneous Soviet successor states, this concept clearly militates against the consolidation of stable social relations.

It would certainly be wrong to claim that the non-Russian Soviet successor states are based exclusively upon the ethnic principle. Many of them are in fact oriented towards the Western world in their search for new values, and are anxious to live up to the generally accepted Western standards set for a democracy and for a law-governed state (*Rechtstaat*). Their new state structures embody many elements taken from the civil nation-state model, but also quite a few taken from the ethnic one. In the former Soviet Union, the civic and ethnic state concepts are, as it were, living in an uneasy condition of co-habitation.

When the ethnic concept prevails, the state authorities strive to attain a maximum degree of correspondence between the political nation and the cultural nation. That is, ideally, all inhabitants should belong to the dominant (titular) ethnic group. The existence of national minorities is seen as a problem to be solved or at least marginalised – culturally, politically and demographically. This desire is reinforced by the suspicion that the minorities, especially the Russian diaspora, may be susceptible to revisionist propaganda emanating from certain circles in Moscow, and may thus represent a threat to the very existence of the state.

22. See e.g. Hans Kohn, *The Idea of Nationalism*, New York, 1946/67; Alexander J. Motyl (ed.), *Thinking Theoretically About Soviet Nationalities*, New York, 1991.

Largely in order to withstand such conformist pressure, the various Russian communities, often in conjunction with other minority groups, have called for special cultural protection. At times they have wanted this protection to be embodied in a federal arrangement. Such demands, however, have regularly been turned down by the state authorities, as well as by representatives of the titular nationality in the successor states. They see them, rightly or wrongly, as stepping stones for secession, and even for the restoration of the defunct Union. In this way the aspirations of ethnic nation-building among some non-Russian élites and the revisionist schemes among some Russians, both in Russia and in the diaspora, have worked to reinforce each other.

The dissolution of the Soviet Union has certainly differed significantly from the débâcle of the smaller, but in many respects similar, multinational federation of Yugoslavia. Only in one instance, the Dniester war of 1992, has a Russian diaspora community been involved. in a military confrontation with the political powers in a Soviet successor state. And there are no compelling reasons why post-Soviet politics sooner or later, might lead to the same degree of bloodshed as was contributed by the South Slav diaspora problems. On the other hand, a repetition of the Yugoslav scenario on post-Soviet soil cannot be excluded *a priori*. The diaspora issues created by the collapse of the Soviet colossus (first and foremost among them the Russian one) ought to be closely monitored by the international community lest it be caught off guard once more if violent conflict on a large scale should erupt.

Part I

2

GROWTH OF THE
RUSSIAN DIASPORA, 1500–1917

In a series of penetrating articles on post-Soviet-nationalities problems,[1] Rogers Brubaker has singled out the new Russian diaspora as one of the most important fields of research. Research into this particular group, he maintains, 'would begin by analyzing the central role played by state-sponsored migration in the formation, expansion, and consolidation of the Russian state and its Soviet successor'. A particular focus ought to be put on the movement of Russians into every corner of the Russian and Soviet state.[2] Picking up this challenge, this chapter attempts to assess the centrifugal migration of Russians before 1917 in its relation to the demographic policy of the state. In the next chapter the same is done for the Soviet period.

As the Great Russians were gradually differentiated from the other East Slavs in the Middle Ages, the core area of their habitation came to be the region between the Volga and Oka rivers. Under the Mongol yoke, the Russians, protected by thick forests, retained and even strengthened their religious identity as Orthodox Christians, as well as other collective cultural traits. The political consolidation of the Russian lands under one ruler, the Muscovy tsar, also gave a great impetus to cultural homogenisation.

This core territory was never inhabited exclusively by Russians. From the earliest times, Finno-Ugric and other tribes lived interspersed

---

1. Rogers Brubaker, 'Nationhood and the National Question in the Soviet Union and Post-Soviet Eurasia: an Institutionalist Account', *Theory and Society*, XXIII, no. 1 (February 1994), pp. 47–78; 'East European, Soviet, and Post-Soviet Nationalisms: A Framework for Analysis', *Research on Democracy and Society*, I, pp. 353–78; 'Political Dimensions of Migration From and Among Soviet Successor States' in Myron Weiner (ed.), *International Migration and Security*, Boulder, CO, 1993, pp. 39–64.
2. Rogers Brubaker, 'Political Dimensions', *op. cit.*

with the Slavs in the same regions. In time, however, these other groups came to be marginalised: culturally, by assimilation, and geographically, as they managed to retain a distinct identity only in some areas in the north-west and north-east. Still, before the mid-sixteenth century, the Russian state, at that time the Muscovy principality, was fairly homogeneous in ethnic, religious, and linguistic terms.

The birth of the multinational Russian empire, then, can be dated to the conquest of Kazan, the capital of the northernmost Tatar khanate, in 1552. Two years later, the middle Tatar khanate of Astrakhan was also overrun. The fall of these states opened the gateway to Siberia, and marked the beginning of an astonishing territorial expansion which continued unabatedly for almost four hundred years. The last new territories were included in the state as late as 1945.[3]

The same four centuries also witnessed a steady outward flow of Russians from the core area to the periphery. In its consistency and magnitude, this demographic expansion was no less remarkable than the political expansion of the Russian state, and yet less attention has been paid to it. While the rise of the Russian empire has been scrutinised in numerous scholarly works, the concomitant spread of the dominant ethnos in that state has often only been noticed in passing.

In one of the few Soviet attempts to address this subject, S. I. Bruk and V. M. Kabuzan have synthesised statistics for the demographic development of the Russians from 1678 to 1917.[4] They base their computations on the revisions carried out in 1719, 1782, 1795, 1815, 1834, 1850 and 1858, plus the census of 1897 – the only complete census of the Russian population conducted under the tsars. The reliability of the revisions, especially the early ones, is questionable, and the figures of Bruk and Kabuzan should be considered only as rough approximations. Moreover, for our needs, the detailed data of the 1897 census similarly suffers from some drawbacks: it did not record the ethnicity of the respondents, only their language affiliation. With these caveats, the findings of Bruk and Kabuzan are presented in Table 2.1 (see pages 16–17).

3. This assertion is, of course, based on the view that the Soviet Union represented a continuator state of the Russian empire.
4. S. I. Bruk and V. M. Kabuzan, 'Dinamika chislennosti i rasseleniia russkogo etnosa (1678–1917 gg.)', *Sovetskaia Etnografiia*, no. 4, 1982.

In 1678, no less than nine-tenths of all Russians were living in those four north-westernmost regions – Central Industrial, Central Agrarian, Northern and the Lake District – which Bruk and Kabuzan identified as the original Russian heartland. By 1917, however, the picture had been radically altered: at the time less than half of all Russians lived in these four regions. Moreover, the outward movement was also clearly accelerating. While the Russian population in Estonia and Latvia in the late eighteenth century amounted to just over 1% of the total, in 1858 it stood at 3.6% and at the turn of the century it was 4.8%. In Transcaucasia and Central Asia/Kazakhstan, the rise was even steeper: although, in these regions Russians, as late as in 1858, accounted for no more than 1% of the population, the 1897 census recorded 4.7 times as many Russians in Transcaucasia and 7.6 times as many in Central Asia. As a percentage of the whole Russian group, the number of Russians in Estonia/Latvia, Transcaucasia and Central Asia/Kazakhstan, taken together, rose from 0.1% in the eighteenth century to 0.3% in 1858, and 1.9% in 1897.[5]

Demographic changes are in principle attributable to three causes: the natural growth (the fertility–mortality balance) of each group; assimilation (ethnic reidentification from one group to another); and migration (the balance of immigration and emigration between various areas). Without going into detail on the effects of the two first factors on the historical redistribution of the Russian ethnos, it can be safely assumed that the drastic changes in the distribution of the Russian group cannot be accounted for without assuming significant centrifugal migration. This process of migration has been conditioned by a number of factors.

Export of population surplus

The Malthusian hypothesis that pre-modern man tends to breed more children than the community can sustain has never been seriously challenged.[6] In agricultural societies, the demographic pressure on the

---

5. The territorial units used by Bruk and Kabuzan only partly correspond to the units of the Soviet and post-Soviet period. Therefore, aggregate figures for the size of the Russians diaspora (understood as the Russian population living outside present-day Russian Federation) cannot be computed on the basis of them.

6. The main reason why Malthus conspicuously failed to predict the demographic development in his own society was the fact that he could not foresee the long-term consequences of the industrial revolution taking place around him.

Growth of the Russian Diaspora

Table 2.1 DISTRIBUTION OF ETHNIC RUSSIANS IN THE RUSSIAN EMPIRE, 1678–1917

A. BY REGION (×1,000)

	1678	1719	1782	1795	1834	1858	1897	1916–17
Central Industrial	3,880	4,535	5,795	6,106	7,428	8,204	10,573	13,855
Central Agrarian	1,700	2,805	4,726	5,241	7,420	8,560	11,216	14,382
Northern	644	515	689	739	900	1,105	1,521	2,006
Lake District	900	1,051	1,830	1,916	2,399	2,683	4,406	5,628
Middle Volga	462	935	1,343	1,414	1,974	2,425	3,091	3,918
Lower Volga	–	100	576	899	1,883	2,463	4,032	5,553
Northern Urals	270	561	1,412	1,626	2,572	3,553	5,052	6,101
Southern Urals	–	19	183	253	553	967	1,966	3,007
Belorussia and Lithuania	83	165	433	493	607	645	1,961	3,510
Northern Baltic	–	3	13	13	49	63	114	180
Left-Bank Ukraine	–	40	178	175	209	301	1,010	1,249
Right-Bank Ukraine	–	–	*	4	15	33	413	426
Novorossia	27	72	193	308	614	1,063	3,213	4,496
Poland	–	–	–	–	5	6	298	167
Finland	–	*	1	1	31	36	10	7
North Caucasus	–	4	17	111	279	373	1,608	2,744
Transcaucasia	–	–	–	–	4	32	261	474
Central Asia Kazakhstan	–	–	–	–	–	50	588	1,548
Siberia	154	323	693	819	1,702	2,259	4,432	7,425
Total for European Russia	7,966	10,801	17,372	19,188	26,659	32,107	48,876	64,485
Total for Russian empire	8,120	11,128	18,082	20,118	28,644	34,821	55,765	76,676

B. AS PERCENTAGE OF TOTAL POPULATION IN EACH REGION

	1678	1719	1782	1795	1834	1858	1897	1916–17
Central Industrial	97	97.7	96.5	96.2	96	95.4	97.1	97.8
Central Agrarian	93.4	90.6	87.9	87.4	87.6	86.8	87.3	86.8
Northern	92	92	90.9	91.3	90.8	90.1	90.1	89.8
Lake District	90	89.4	92	92.1	88.7	88.4	88.7	90.9
Middle Volga	51.3	59.7	64.8	63.2	62.6	62.8	59.8	59.7
Lower Volga	–	33	62.4	66.7	68.2	67.5	65.4	65.5
Northern Urals	90	90.8	84.5	84	84.8	85.1	83.9	83.2
Southern Urals	–	10.5	40.9	40.2	43.4	47.5	51.8	54.3
Belorussia and Lithuania	4	4.5	9.4	9.5	9.9	9.9	16.9	23.6
Northern Baltic	–	0.3	1.2	1.1	3.2	3.6	4.8	6.3
Left-Bank Ukraine	–	2.2	5.4	5.2	4.9	6.1	13.3	12.8
Right-Bank Ukraine	–	–	*	0.1	0.3	0.6	4.3	3.4
Novorossia	6.7	15.6	22.2	19.1	18.1	21.6	29.8	30.7
Poland	–	–	–	–	0.1	0.1	3.2	1.3
Finland	–	–	–	–	2.2	2.1	0.4	0.3
North Caucasus	–	0.7	2.5	6.9	13.2	16.9	42.5	46.9
Transcaucasia	–	–	–	–	0.2	1.0	4.7	6.3
Central Asia and Kazakhstan	–	–	–	–	–	1.0	7.6	14.3
Siberia	51.8	66.9	67.6	68.9	73.8	74.1	76.9	77.6
Total for European Russia	39.8	45.6	49.1	47.9	47.9	48.1	46.4	46.8
Total for Russian empire	40.6	40.9	44.9	43.2	42.9	43.3	43.5	44.6

* Less than 1,000
Source: S. I. Bruk and V. M. Kabuzan, 'Dinamika chislennosti i rasseleniia russkogo etnosa (1678–1917 gg.)', *Sovetskaia Etnografiia*, no. 4, 1982, p. 17.

community is relieved either through periodic epidemics or through other natural or man-made catastrophes such as wars or by emigration.

During the eighteenth and especially the nineteenth century, almost every European nation exported a substantial amount of its population surplus. The peoples along the Atlantic (and to some extent the Mediterranean) coastline primarily crossed the oceans, and headed for America, Australia and Africa. Certain peoples of the Russian empire also participated in this trans-oceanic migration, notably Jews from the Pale of Settlement, and Poles.[7] To the Russians, however, other outlets were more readily at hand. They moved east- and southwards, into the taiga of Siberia and into the steppes along the northern coast of the Black Sea and the Caspian Sea. The main driving force was basically the same in these various movements. Barbara Anderson has concluded that the rates of Russian migration to frontier areas – in contrast to migration within a settled area – has a strong positive relationship to population pressure.[8]

In the 'new' world, the European settlers in time acquired new identities. The vast stretches of ocean which separated them from their countries of origin set them apart from their co-nationals at home mentally. The Russians, however, did not lose contact with the core group in this way. While the new Russian communities naturally developed certain peculiar traits, they nonetheless formed a continuum with few internal demarcations.

State expansion

The most important reason why Russian settlers headed south and east rather than west was that in that way they did not have to leave their original state of residence. They pushed towards the outer limits of the empire but rarely crossed them; and if they did, they settled down just across the border, or in a no-man's-land. In the latter cases, they were usually soon caught up with by the state as its expansion continued.

In his famous 'Lectures on Russian History', the Russian historian Vasilii Kliuchevskii seized upon the close interrelationship between

---

7. Raymond Pearson, *National Minorities in Eastern Europe 1848–1945*, London, 1983, pp. 100ff.
8. Barbara A. Anderson, *Internal Migration During Modernization in Late Nineteenth-Century Russia*, Princeton, 1980, pp. 191ff.

state expansion and migration as an outstanding feature. 'The history of Russia is the history of a country which colonises itself. The scope for colonisation in this state expanded together with the expansion of the state territory.'[9] As Richard Pipes has commented, Kliuchevskii's catchy formula ignored the fact that the areas being colonised by the Russians, no less than the areas occupied by other Europeans, were already inhabited by other ethnic groups. Rather than colonising 'itself', Russia was colonising the lands of others.[10]

The expansion of the Russian state, then, is the second important factor promoting the migration of the Russian people and imbuing it with its peculiar character. The military feats of the Russian army greatly influenced the creation of the future Russian diaspora.[11]

However, the exact cause–effect relationship between the peasants' movement towards the periphery in search for more land and the government's drive for territorial expansion is difficult to ascertain. As Marc Raeff has pointed out, peasants do not leave records, and this side of the Russian state's activities is poorly illuminated by the existing sources. Raeff nonetheless concludes that both relationships *have* been documented: at times, the peasants were used by the government, and at other times they forced the officials' hand.[12]

The creation of the Russian Empire may be said to have consisted of three overlapping stages, each with its own characteristics. After the fall of Kazan, Russia first expanded east, then west and finally south. Roughly, these three stages fall respectively within the seventeenth and eighteenth, and the eighteenth and the nineteenth centuries. Each of them affected Russian migration in different ways.

1. In 1649 the first Russian expeditions reached the Pacific Ocean, and soon the entire northern part of the Asian continent was claimed by

9. Vasilii Kliuchevskii, *Sochineniia v 9-i tomakh*, I, Moscow, 1987, p. 50.
10. Richard Pipes, 'Reflections on the Nationality Problems in the Soviet Union', in Nathan Glazer and Daniel P. Moynihan (eds), *Ethnicity: Theory and Experience*, Cambridge, Massachusetts, 1975, pp. 453–65, on p. 455.
11. In the words of one nineteenth-century Russian observer, 'In essence, the Russian colonialising activity, as among the Romans in antiquity and among the Austrians in our times, started as military colonisation. The first settlers and representatives of Russian culture have been the military garrisons and the Cossack settlements.' G. Gins, *Pereselenie i kolonizatsiia*, I, St. Petersburg, 1913, p. 37.
12. Marc Raeff, 'Patterns of Russian Imperial Policy Toward the Nationalities', in Edward Allworth (ed.), *Soviet Nationality Problems*, New York, 1971, pp. 22–42, on p. 28.

the tsar. This expansion in time brought the Urals, Siberia, the Far East and Kazakhstan under tsarist rule. The density of the indigenous population here was low, especially in Siberia, and the Russian settlement was correspondingly large. With the partial exception of the feeble Siberian Tatar khanate, the local tribes had few organised states, and military resistance to the Russian expansion was negligible.

The Russian conquest of Siberia and Northern Kazakhstan is comparable in many ways to the inclusion of the North American plains and the Pacific coast into the United States two centuries later, during which process the indigenous peoples were marginalised with similar ease. In both cases the ethnic composition of newly won possessions was radically altered, making the European settlers the dominant group. With the exception of Kazakhstan, these early eastern acquisitions today form part of the Russian Federation. Hence, the Russians living there do not belong to the diaspora population in the sense in which that word is used in this book and they are therefore excluded from the more detailed discussion below. However, it is important to remember that when Russians both in the nineteenth century and at the beginning of the twentieth discussed questions of colonisation and migration, they often had in mind primarily Siberia and the Far East.

In the 1730s, the leader of one of the Kazakh hordes (clans) submitted to the Russians, primarily because this horde had a greater fear of its neighbours to the east and to the south. Later the relationship between the Russians and their new subjects soured several times, and in the 1780s and 1790s serious Kazakh rebellions were crushed. In 1853 the Russians consolidated their southward push by building the fortress Vernyi in southern Kazakhstan, the beginning of contemporary Almaty.[13]

2. The westward expansion of the Russian empire began with the Peace of Nystadt in 1721 after the Northern War (1709–1721), as a result of which Sweden ceded its Baltic possessions to Peter the Great. Together with the ethnic Estonians, Latvians and Lithuanians, the small Russian community in the region remained an underprivileged group, while the role of pillar of the tsarist regime was entrusted to the Baltic Germans.[14]

13. Zev Katz, 'Kazakhstan and the Kazakhs', in Zev Katz *et al.* (ed), *Handbook of Major Soviet Nationalities*, New York, 1975, p. 216.
14. A. A. Pommer, 'Russkie v Latvii. Istoricheskii ocherk. XIII-XIX veka', *Russkie v Latvii. Istoriia i sovremennost*', Riga, 1992, pp. 17–38.

The three partitions of Poland in 1772, 1793 and 1795 brought contemporary Lithuania, Belorussia, Eastern Poland and most of the Dniepr West Bank under the empire (most of East Bank Dniepr had been obtained by the Treaty of Pereiaslavl as early as in 1654). The khanate of the Crimean Tatars was destroyed in 1783. A new drive against the Ottomans wrested the last parts of the northern littoral of the Black Sea from the Porte at the Peace of Iasi in 1791.[15]

With these conquests, Russia became firmly established as a European great power, and had become a multinational East European empire on a par with the Habsburg monarchy. The new areas to the west were more densely populated than Siberia, and Russian migration into former Polish and Swedish land was consequently far more modest. The 250,000 or so Russians in Poland were mostly officers and officials who represented the central-occupation authorities.[16] In the south-west, however, the situation was different. Many of the former Ottoman possessions acquired by the tsars had been devastated by wars and nomadic raids for centuries, and were sparsely populated. Indeed, the northern coast of the Black Sea was generally known as 'Dikoe Pole' ('Savage Plain') or 'The Turkish desert'. To consolidate the new conquests, Russian migration thereto was encouraged by the authorities in St Petersburg. The region soon became known as 'Novorossia' – 'New Russia' (cf. such names as New Zealand, New York and New Orleans). Serbs, Greeks, Bulgarians, Wallachians, Moldovans and Germans were now encouraged by various systems of privileges to move to Novorossia. While Ukrainian and Russian settlers were not offered anything similar, the extent of Slavic immigration turned out to be far more massive than that witnessed with any of the other groups.[17] The Russian share of the Novorossian population rose from approximately 20% at the end of the eighteenth century to 30% in 1917.

The westward expansion of Russia was rounded off in 1812 with the conquest of the land between the Dniester and Prut rivers. This north-eastern part of Moldavia from now on became known as Bessarabia. The acquisition of this stretch of land established Russia as a Balkan state. Bessarabia was more densely populated than

15. M. S. Anderson, *The Eastern Question 1774–1923*, London, 1966, pp. 1ff.
16. Andreas Kappeler, *Russland als Vielvölkerreich*, Munich, 1992, p. 239.
17. D. I. Bagaleia, *Kolonizatsiia Novorossiiskogo kraia*, Kiev, 1889, pp. 59ff; V. M. Kabuzan, *Zaselenie Novorossii*, Moscow, 1976, pp. 133ff and 244ff.

Novorossia, and the degree of Russian migration to the region was less great.[18] In the first half of the nineteenth century, the percentage of Russians in Bessarabia remained small, about 2%. Only in the second half of the century did their relative share start to rise – to 3.7% in 1859 and 6.4% in 1897. Most of the newcomers flocked to the cities. By 1862, two-and-a-half times as many Russians were living in Bessarabian urban settlements than in the countryside – 48,000 and 19,000, respectively.

3. The southward expansion of the Russian empire can roughly be divided into two halves. The occupation of Transcaucasia and Caucasia was completed at around the middle of the nineteenth century, and at that time the conquest of Central Asia began.

A large area primarily inhabited by Christian Armenians was wrested from the Ottoman Empire in the early 1800s, and at about the same time, the Georgian princes accepted Russian overlordship as the lesser of several evils. However, the pacification of the mountainous regions further north, the abode of numerous Muslim tribes, was a much more protracted and bloody affair, and was completed only in the 1860s. For a number of reasons – high population density, the presence of old-established cultures, the lack of arable land – Russian penetration beyond the Caucasus, demographically and culturally, was relatively modest, especially in Armenia. Only with the introduction of new agricultural techniques towards the end of the century, such as mechanised irrigation, were new areas opened up to Russian settlers in Transcaucasia, especially in the eastern part. The Russian population increased markedly, both relatively and in absolute numbers. While the total population in Transcaucasia between 1886 and 1897 increased by 22%, the Russian population in the same period was more than doubled, reaching more than 220,000 – or 4.5% of the total.[19]

In Central Asia, the Russians were confronted with age-old civilisations along the old silk route. Avicenna of Bukhara, for one, had contributed to the history of thought as early as the eleventh century. In the nineteenth century, however, Bukhara and the other Central Asian emirates and khanates had entered a phase of stagnation and decay, and as a result the military resistance they put up was easily overrun by the armies of Skobelev and Kaufman.

18. See V. S. Zelenchuk, *Naselenie Bessarabii i Podnestrov'ia v XIX v.*, Kishinëv, 1979; and Zelenchuk, *Naselenie Moldavii*, Kishinëv, 1973.
19. D. I. Ismail-Zade, *Russkoe krest'ianstvo v Zakavkaz'e*, Moscow, 1982, pp. 54ff.

Russia's Caucasian and Central Asian campaigns were colonial wars similar to the wars conducted by the British, French, Italians, Belgians and other Europeans in the last century in their scramble for overseas possessions. Indeed, the Russian and British conquests on the Central Asian subcontinent, from both the north and the south, were not only similar in manner but also overlapped in time. In the last decades of the nineteenth century, the armies of those two colonial powers were inexorably approaching each other. In order to prevent another Fashoda incident, an artificial extension of the independent Afghan kingdom was agreed in 1895 to separate the two expanding empires. The close similarity between Russian and British colonial rule in Asia becomes clear when their systems of administration are compared. In both India and Russian Central Asia, the local dynasties – rajis, emirs, khans – were often allowed to keep their thrones as long as they accepted European overlordship.

Most of the local population, especially the nomads, were officially classified as allogenous (*inorodtsy*). They were not subjects of the empire in the full sense, and were for instance exempt from military service. In many matters they were ruled by their own clan chieftains under their own customary laws. The central authorities made few efforts to russify them or to raise their level of literacy, hygiene, etc.

The population density of Central Asia was not particularly high, but the precarious ecological balance in the oases and semi-deserts could not have sustained a much higher population. Nevertheless, a significant Russian immigration did take place, at least to certain areas.[20] In the first decades after 1881, most of the Russians colonists settled in the Semireche ('Seven Rivers') regions of Southern Kazakhstan, including the Chu and Issyk-Kul valleys in Kirgizia. In the agricultural regions further south, the Russian presence before the turn of the century was very limited – in the Fergana Valley, for instance, it stood at only 0.5%.[21] While only 50,000 Russians lived in Central Asia (including Kazakhstan) in 1858, forty years later the number had increased tenfold, to more than half a million. The immigration peaked during the years of the Stolypin reforms of 1907–1912, and by 1916 it had reached 1.5 million – or 14.3% of the population.

The Russians and the *inorodtsy* in Central Asia lived in separate

20. A. I. Ginzburg, *Russkoe naselenie v Turkestane*, Institut etnologii i antropologii, Russian Academy of Sciences, Moscow, 1991.
21. Kappeler, *op. cit.*, pp. 240ff.

villages, and were subject to different sets of laws. The Russian settlement was mostly treated as an ordinary settlement in heartland Russia. For certain jobs, such as railway construction, only Russians were hired. In industry, Russians were often better paid, even if they were doing the same job, as other groups,[22] and they often lived in separate suburbs in the cities – usually the newer ones. However, some of the poorer Russians also moved into the old city, where the rent was lower. Here, they got into closer contact with the indigenous population, and at times, were accepted into the local environment as 'our Russians'.

Russian settlers in Turkestan were given exemption from military service and taxes for three years, and after that time paid only half of the taxes of ordinary subjects. Moreover, they were given weapons in order to defend both themselves and the Russian state, in case of a local insurgency. According to the Russian governor of the Syr Daria province, 'every Russian settlement in the Turkestan is worth a battalion of Russian troops.'[23] A major rebellion did break out in 1916. The immediate cause behind it was the conscription of locals into the tsarist army, but pent-up tensions between the ethnic groups due to the government's head-on migration policy also played an important part. One of the main demands of the rebels was the return of confiscated land. An estimated 2,000 Russian settlers in Kazakhstan/Kirgizia, plus 3,000 in Turkestan, were massacred by the Central Asians, who were repaid in kind: a much greater number of locals perished. Entire Kirgiz villages were incinerated, and a third of the Kirgiz population fled to China.[24]

Migration restrictions and migration encouragement

For security reasons Russian state authorities were interested in, and at times actively promoted the migration of Russians to the borderlands. If the new possessions were thinly populated, this left the new borders vulnerable to foreign invasions. And if they were inhabited

22. A. I. Ginzburg, 'Russkoe naselenie v Srednei Azii', in *Sovremennoe razvitie etnicheskikh grupp Srednei Azii i Kazakhstana*, Institut etnologii i antropologii, Russian Academy of Sciences, II, Moscow, 1992, pp. 38–66, esp. p. 40.

23. A. I. Ginzburg, *Russkoe naselenie v Turkestane*, Institut etnologii i antropologii, Russian Academy of Sciences, Moscow, 1991, p. 8.

24. Hélène Carrère d'Encausse, 'The Fall of the Czarist Empire', in Edward Allworth (ed.), *Central Asia: 120 Years of Russian Rule*, London, 1989.

by ethnic groups alien and even hostile to Russian civilisation, this again was considered as a potential threat to the state. In time, the logic of incessant Russian expansion turned all Russian border areas (with insignificant exceptions) into one of these two categories. Ironically, a major threat to the Russian state had been created by the very success of its military campaigns.

Ever since the sixteenth century, the frequent rebellions, which more than once threatened the very existence of the state, had almost invariably started in the ethnically mixed periphery, not in the Russian heartland. This did not pass unnoticed in the corridors of power. One possible way to remedy this was russification of the borderland.

However, consolidation of the borders against foreign incursions and local rebellions was not the only concern influencing the tsars' migration policy. On the contrary, a number of political decisions impeded migration. In the sixteenth century, serfdom had been imposed on almost the entire Russian peasant population. This institution tied them down to the land, and in principle made it impossible to use them as an instrument of imperial consolidation. Serfdom also had the consequence of making it difficult to find enough manpower to cultivate the newly-acquired land in the periphery. Most of this land belonged to the state or the crown – at least until it was donated to some nobleman as a favour or reward. In important ways, then, serfdom was not in the interest of the tsar, and its introduction must primarily be explained as a concession to the gentry class, on whose military and administration services the regime depended.[25]

Richard Pipes sees a clear connection between the expansion of the empire and the introduction of serfdom, the latter being intended as a measure to counteract some of the undesired effects of the former. After the conquest of Kazan and Astrakhan, which opened up much of the Black Earth belt previously controlled by nomads, the peasants immediately seized the opportunity: they 'abandoned the forests in droves, poured on to the virgin soil to the east, southeast and south'.[26] The terror regime of Ivan IV, the *oprichnina*, introduced in 1564, gave, in Pipes' view, an additional impetus to peasant emigration, as well as an additional motive for reinforcing serfdom.

However, while the peasants were tied to the soil by law, this of course did not mean that they acquiesced in it. As oppression increased

25. Richard Pipes, *Russia under the Old Regime*, Harmondsworth, 1979.
26. *ibid.*, p. 101.

from generation to generation, many tried to escape by flight and the fact that this made them outlaws gave them the impetus to run away as far as possible. In the peasant folklore of the time, a rumour circulated about a faraway 'fortunate' country, sometimes located towards the Caucasus. If the fugitives could make it there, they would become free. Those who were not caught and sent home usually ended up along the southern and eastern perimeter of the empire, and called themselves 'Cossacks', meaning 'free men'. They intermarried with the locals, took over a number of their costumes and developed an identity of their own.

Set on defending their newly won freedom, they organised themselves into military-agricultural colonies. The supreme military skills of the Cossacks could be used not only in self-defence but also in offence. Several of the most dangerous peasant rebellions in Russian history were led by Cossack chieftains such as Stenka Razin and Emelian Pugachëv. Gradually, the tsars concluded that it was better to co-opt the Cossacks than try to crush them, and they started to employ them as border guards.[27]

The disparate interests of tsardom led to abrupt vacillations in its policy on migration. The tsar had to balance the interests of the gentry in Central Russia, some of whom were becoming abysmally impoverished, with those of the affluent holders of large estates in the newly acquired land on the periphery, of whom the tsar himself was the foremost. The first group demanded the retention, and even the tightening, of adscription, the latter the easing of it. In addition, several other concerns also weighed against serfdom. The enormously costly apparatus needed to keep the unfree population in place, to prevent and quell uprisings, and to search out, identify and carry home, in chains, run-away peasants was taxing resources which could have been put to better use. For instance, between 1834 and 1853 no less than 48,000 serfs of Russian and Ukrainian stock were rounded up and shipped home from Bessarabia.[28] By abolishing serfdom and legalising the status of the fugitive peasants, the tsar could both strengthen the borders and save money at the same time. However, when the long-overdue peasant liberation was carried out, in 1861,

27. Udo Gehrmann, *Das Kasakentum in Russland zu Beginn der neunziger Jahre. Historische Traditionen und Zukunftsvisionen*, Berichte des Bundesinstituts für ostwissenschaftliche und internationale Studien, 11, 1992.
28. Zelenchuk, *op. cit.*, 1979, p. 174.

the concerns of border defence and colonisation of the periphery do not seem to have been among the main motives. More important was the realisation that serfdom was perpetuating an antiquated social system which had caused the country to fall further and further behind its European neighbours in economic and military development. This had been made abundantly clear by the Crimean war of 1854–56.

Neither was a desire for larger centrifugal migration a major *effect* of the abolition of serfdom – at least, not in the short term. The liberation act was hedged about with numerous restrictions. The peasants were given their personal freedom but not the land they were tilling. This land had to be paid for by annual instalments over a period of forty-nine years. Moreover, it was not sold to the individual peasant as his personal property but to the *mir*, the peasant commune. No one was free to leave the commune unless he had cleared himself of all arrears in state and communal levies, and this was extremely difficult to achieve. Unable to meet the instalments, many peasants instead sank ever deeper into debt. In a sense, the former legal adscription was now replaced by a new economic one.

Under these circumstances, only a few wealthy peasants could migrate legally, and even they usually had little incentive to do so. One contemporary observer called the terms of the peasant emancipation a 'prohibitory system in relation to migrants'.[29] The government was afraid that a population in drift would become receptive to revolutionary ideas, and tried by various means to keep it in place. Those who left the commune without permission and headed for the borderland were termed *samovol'nye pereselentsy* – 'spontaneous' or 'irregular' settlers. For twenty years after the Emancipation, spontaneous migration, as well as preparing for it, was punishable with imprisonment from two weeks to three months. These laws, however, were often not enforced.[30] If the former bondage had been far from watertight, the new economic variety was even less so. The Liberation Edict of 1861 in fact led to a limited upsurge of migration – at least from certain areas.

An increasing number of those who left the villages headed for the cities. Most of them gravitated to Moscow, St Petersburg and other

29. Quoted in Donald W. Treadgold, *The Great Siberian Migration*, Princeton, 1957, p. 68.
30. J. William Leasure and Robert A. Lewis, 'Internal Migration in Russia in the Late Nineteenth Century', *Slavic Review*, XXVII, 3 (September 1968), pp. 375–94.

cities in Russia proper, but a considerable number also ended up as urban dwellers outside the Russian heartland. Most of the fastest-growing Russian cities were located outside the present-day borders of Russia. Between 1863 and 1897, eleven major Russian cities increased their population three times or more. Among these we find seven outside Russia proper: Kiev, Baku, Minsk, Odessa, Ekaterinoslav, Kharkov and Riga,[31] whose growth was largely due to Russian immigration. However, quite a quantity of mobilised Russian peasants stuck to their last and moved to *rural* districts in the non-Russian parts of the country.

Part of the Russian migration was carried out in the form of government-sponsored programmes. While the tsarist regime was wary of any kind of spontaneity on the part of its subjects, and distrusted any population movements which it did not control, it had fewer qualms if the migration was initiated and led by itself. In addition, many officials started to doubt the revolution-preventing value of migration restriction. Indeed, it was thought that keeping the lid on the simmering village pot could have the opposite effect. In 1880, the liberal Minister of Internal Affairs, M. T. Loris-Melikov, concluded that carefully planned and guided migration could be an important means to counteract revolutionary ferment.

The 'Temporary Regulations' of 10 July 1881 permitted migration in cases where 'the economic situation of the petitioner called for it' and where the peasant had received permission from the Ministry of Internal Affairs and from the Ministry of State Domains.[32] These rules were confirmed in the law on the 'Voluntary migration of rural inhabitants and petty bourgeoisie to state-owned land' of 13 July 1889. For the first time special agencies for assisting the actual movements of settlers were established. While encouraging a guided flow of migrants, this law still forbade *samovol'nyi* migration.

Experience had shown that many of the 'spontaneous' colonisers, for whom the essentially negative push-factor of flight from destitution was the main motive for migration, tended to adapt poorly to their new surroundings. A certain proportion of them even gave up after a while and returned home. Those who arrived under government

31. A. G. Rashin, *Naselenie Rossii za 100 let (1813–1913 gg.)*, Moscow, 1956, pp. 93ff.

32. E. M. Brusnikin, 'Pereselencheskaia politika tsarizma v kontse XIX veka', *Voprosy istorii*, 1 (January), 1965, pp. 28–38.

auspices, however, generally fared better, not only because they had a more positive motivation and better human resources but also because they were given favourable material conditions. As a rule, they were granted both tax exemption and exemption from military service for a specified period, and their land allotments were generous – well above the average among the local inhabitants. While the reasons for the state's generosity towards them varied, a conscious desire to set them apart from the indigenous population and give them a vested interest in defending the state were surely two of them.

An important factor contributing to the easing of migration restrictions was the drastic population growth in the Russian countryside in the last third of the nineteenth century. The famines of 1891–2 and 1898 forced the government to consider ever more radical means to assuage the land hunger in central Russia. One of the measures it seized upon was accelerated migration. The soundness of this policy was disputed. Critics pointed out that it addressed only the symptoms of the agricultural crisis and not its cause, the latter being Russia's outdated production methods and property arrangements. Indeed, it was argued, by easing the population pressure in the countryside without going to the roots of the problem, accelerated migration could retard economic development and this would mean the removal of one of the main impetuses for modernisation. However, most Russians who engaged in the debate acknowledged that destitute peasants could hardly be induced to adopt modern production methods by being withheld by force in the overcrowded villages.

On 6 June 1904, a new and liberalised migration law was passed, supplanting the 1889 regulations.[33] From that time on, the government explicitly favoured the migration of certain groups: those peasants, engaged in the raising of crops, who wanted to move to areas deemed by the authorities to be suitable for new settlements, and those living in areas with a severe shortage of land. These two groups were promised both governmental privileges (*l'goty*) and material assistance. The law now explicitly encouraged the resettlement of poor peasants, whereas previously migration stimuli had primarily been geared towards the medium-rich and rich peasants.

On 10 March 1906, when the dusts of the 1905 revolution had barely settled, the government decided to extend the 1904 provisions to include a number of new regions, and especially those which had

---

33. D. I. Ismail-Zade, *Russkoe krest'ianstvo v Zakavkaz'e*, Moscow, 1982, pp. 143ff.

seen mass peasant disturbances the previous year. It was hoped that an easing of the population pressure would help cool down anti-government passions. Migrants not belonging to any of the government-sponsored groups were no longer branded as *samovol'nye*. Henceforth, their movements were no longer criminalised nor were they encouraged.

The easing of the restrictions coincided with the Stolypin reforms, which severely undermined the authority of the village commune – and could indeed be seen as a part of the same reform package. The next ten years after 1906 witnessed an explosion of internal migration. More than half a million people trekked eastward each year, primarily to Siberia but also to Kazakhstan and Central Asia. Contemporary observers complained that this led to chaotic conditions since the administrative and logistical apparatus of the state could not cope with this upsurge in mobility. Tens of thousands of new arrivals in these areas could not find any land to settle on.

Slowly it was realised that a liberalised migration regimen could alleviate the demographic and political problems in central Russia only by creating new problems in the periphery. The government was accused of having a policy of migration only, while lacking one of settlement: it was primarily concerned with such problems as which groups should be allowed to go, where they should go to and how they should get there. How the migrants fared on arrival seemed to be beyond the scope of official attention.[34]

The third Duma vainly attempted to rectify this situation by introducing a number of adjustments in the system. On 2 March 1908, migration permits were made conditional on the existence of surplus land. Certain regions, such as Central Asia, were temporarily closed for migration. Then new regulations in January 1909 instituted land commissions to supervise the selection of future colonists. However, these restrictions could not be enforced, and in March 1911 movement without restraint was reintroduced.[35]

Banishment

A fourth element of tsarist policy which influenced centrifugal migration – besides territorial expansion, and the institution and subsequent

34. G. Gins, *Pereselenie i kolonizatsiia*, St. Petersburg, 1913.
35. *ibid.*, p. 2.

abolition of serfdom – was the practice of banishing undesirable population elements – primarily religious dissenters but also political rebels – to outlying provinces. More perhaps than anything else, this brings out the incongruities and contradictions inherent in the tsarist migration policy: potentially or actually subversive groups were punished by being sent to the very regions to which other disgruntled groups fled of their own accord, and to which still others were attracted by promises of special privileges! For instance, a Russian military expedition arrived in the Baltic in 1783 to search out and send home fugitive peasants, and 4,514 captives were arrested and sent east. A few years earlier, Russians in chains had been led in the opposite direction: these were participants of the Pugachëv uprising in 1773, who were exiled to Livonia.[36] To make things even more paradoxical, some of the exiles (or their descendants) were later reclassified as 'trustworthy', and special privileges were conferred on them. These inconsistencies must be understood against the background of the multinational empire. It seems as if the authorities at times hoped that if dissenters were placed in an alien cultural environment, they might develop a stronger sense of 'Russianness' than that which they had had before the banishment. And in the upshot they could undergo an identity-transformation similar to that experienced by the Cossacks: from rebels to staunch supporters of the regime.

Religious dissenters were shipped off not only to the inclement regions of Siberia and Northern Russia but also to lush Bessarabia and sunny Transcaucasia. In fact, before the twentieth century it was religious dissenters who made up the bulk of the ethnically Russian population in several non-Russian regions. Heterodoxy was more common in Russian than is often realised, and was considered a problem not only for the church but also for the state.[37] Subjects of the tsar historically affiliated with other confessions, such as the Baltic Lutherans and Polish Catholics, were left alone, but for Orthodox believers conversion to another faith was a criminal offence.

The dissenters were usually divided into two subgroups: schismatics and sectarians. The former consisted of those who professed a deviant variety of the Orthodox faith, the latter of those who rejected Orthodoxy altogether. True, the ban was not enforced at all times –

---

36. Pommer, *op. cit.*, pp. 29 and 33.
37. Frederick C. Conybeare, *Russian Dissenters*, Cambridge, Massachusetts, 1921; Sergius Bolshakoff, *Russian Nonconformity*, Philadelphia, 1950.

the eighteenth century being more liberal in this than the previous and following ones – but even at the best of times the dissenters were just barely tolerated. Many of them preferred to leave their homes of their own accord to avoid harassment, and headed for Northern Russia, the Baltics, Bessarabia, Transcaucasia and Siberia. While isolated communities eventually ended up in places as distant as Oregon, Saskatchewan and Argentina, the vast majority never left the confines of the Empire. The schismatics, dating back to the Old Believer schism in the 1660s, were by far the largest group among the dissenters, numbering several millions. The sectarians – the Dukhobors, Molokans, Khlysty, Skoptsy *et al.* – while fewer, were regarded by the authorities as more unruly and thus gave them greater anxiety.

In the first half of the nineteenth century, most of the Russians in Transcaucasia were religious sectarians, primarily Dukhobors and Molokans. The area was used as the main dumping ground for these 'undesirables' and between 1841 and 1845 5,000 sectarians arrived in the Transcaucasian region.[38] They were exiled to not-quite-pacified areas beyond the fortified Russian lines, where raids from the indigenous mountaineers were a constant and real threat. Thus, according to the reasoning of the governor-general of Novorossia, Ermolov, two goals would be achieved in one stroke: potential converts would think twice before joining these sects, while the sectarians, strict pacifists by conviction, would be forced to defend themselves in order to save their lives, and in effect to renounce a major tenet of their faith. At least the second presumption proved in part correct. Still, the Dukhobor villages did not disintegrate but instead gradually adapted to the savage environment, and remained distinct communities.

While the banishment of the sectarians to Transcaucasia should certainly be seen as a severe punishment, the involuntary religious settlers were nonetheless given certain privileges that set them apart from the locals. They were allotted considerably more land – 30 to 60 *desiatin* – although in many areas land shortage was acute. This naturally fostered anti-tsarist sentiments among the natives, and for that reason the local Russian authorities responsible for law and order in the region tried to prevent the immigration of Russians into the area. Their objec-

38. S. A. Inikova 'Vzaimootnosheniia i khoziaistvenno-kul'turnye kontakty kavkaz-skikh dukhobortsev s mestnym naseleniem', in *Dukhobortsy i molokane v Zakavkaz'e*, Institut etnologii i antropologii, Russian Academy of Sciences, Moscow, 1992.

tions, however, were overruled in St Petersburg. Russian dissenters continued to come in ever-increasing numbers, many of them voluntarily. A *ukaz* in December 1848 granted specific *l'goty* to schismatics settling in the Transcaucasian region. However, towards the end of the century, the government's Transcaucasian policy made an about-turn. Instead of using the area as a zone of punishment for religious outcasts, a new *ukaz* in 1897 now forbade non-Orthodox believers to settle there. Henceforth, migration was to serve the cause of disseminating Russian culture as well as strengthening the state.

Russian spirituality

A final factor explaining the steady outward movement of the Russians has also been suggested. It is widely believed that a traditional trait of unrootedness and restlessness among the Russians has given them a mental disposition for migration. This has been explained by reference partly to topology and partly to religion. On the endless Russian plains, the peasant has had his gaze fixed not only on the soil beneath him and the heaven above but also on the distant horizon, which has lured him. Nicholas Arseniev talked of a peculiar Russian 'nostalgia for space' which influenced the colonisers of the huge Eurasian plain as well as the Cossacks and the peasants. 'All these travellers, adventures, brigands, explorers, seekers of employment, pilgrims and colonists manifest with more or less intensity the nomadic element which plays its part in the psychology of the Russian people.'[39]

The hankering for distant places has also been seen as reflecting Russian spirituality, and more specifically the ideal of *strannichestvo*. The *strannik* is a spiritual cousin of the pilgrim; both seek salvation in travel, but while the pilgrim heads for a particular holy site or shrine, the *strannik* roams the land, drifting aimlessly about – or, as he himself would express it, wherever the Holy Ghost will lead him.[40] This attitude may be seen as an expression of the Christian idea that terrestrial life is a passage, the believer is only a visitor on this earth, and must abhor all projects for the construction of Babylonian cities. This idea forms a common spiritual heritage for both the Eastern and Western churches, dating back to the writings of St Augustine, but

39. Nicholas Arseniev, *Russian Piety*, New York, 1975, pp. 15ff.
40. S. Maksimov, *Brodiachaia Rus' Khrista-Radi*, St. Petersburg, 1877; P. Bessonov, *Kaleki (sic) perekhozhie*, Moscow, 1861.

free-wheeling wandering is nonetheless a more venerated and time-honoured expression of religious life in Russia than in the West.

The penchant for wandering was especially strong among the dissenters, and should probably be seen as an aspect of their eschatological world view and their fervent expectation of the imminent second coming of Christ.[41] However, eschatology was not an exclusive property of the Old Believers but a strong undercurrent in all Russian spirituality. Nikolai Berdiaev has stated that

> Russians have always pined for another life, for another world. They have never felt satisfied with the extant one. Eschatological longings is a part of the structure of the Russian soul. *Strannichestvo* as a typical Russian phenomenon is unknown in the West. The *strannik* wanders over the boundless Russian land, never settling down, never attaching himself to anything.[42]

Of course, the cause–effect relationship between the tendency towards otherworldliness in Russian spirituality and the actual and preferred life conditions of the individual Russian may have been the reverse of what Berdiaev suggested. Forced to take to the highway in order to escape cruel landlords, the Russian serf rationalised his action by means of a religious doctrine. A less reductionistic explanation would be that the material life conditions of the Russian peasant and the religious universe in which he lived were two independent forces both of which predisposed him to rootlessness, wandering and centrifugal migration.

It seems that the effects of serfdom on the mentality of the Russian peasant have been profound. It imbued him with a completely different set of values from those of the West European free farmer. For the latter, attachment to the soil – his own – was a virtue on which he prided himself, while to the former this very attachment was a loathsome burden. The vagabond, despised in the West, was not only respected in Russia but even envied. It seems safe to conclude that of all the non-nomadic, agricultural peoples in Europe, the Russians have traditionally been the least sedentary.

In the nineteenth century, not only Russian political authorities but

---

41. One of the subgroups of the non-priestly branch of the Old Believers was known as the *stranniki*. See Bolshakoff, *op. cit.*, pp. 78ff.
42. Nikolai Berdiaev, *Russkaia Ideia*, Paris, 1971, p. 199.

also the Russian public took the existence of the empire for granted. The remarkable feature of Russian imperialist policy was not the body of theories put forward in defence of it but rather the conspicuous lack of interest in such justifications.[43] In the War Ministry and Foreign Ministry of nineteenth-century St Petersburg, 'might-is-right' thinking was widespread, as it was in most other European capitals. Imperialism was the order of the day, and while at least a handful of Russians had doubts about their right to subjugate fellow Slavs in Poland, few felt any qualms about the expansion of their state into Asia.

Russian imperialists seem to have been even less preoccupied than the West Europeans with elaborating excuses for their actions. As a liberal Russian expert on colonisation policies remarked in 1913, 'the unquestionable cultural needs of the local population, such as education and improved jurisprudence, are acknowledged only in passing, accidentally.'[44] To some extent this was true also for the related issue of migration. However, towards the end of the nineteenth and the beginning of the twentieth century, a growing number of authors were concerning themselves with the theoretical and practical aspects of this problem.

'Colonialism' was not a dirty word in nineteenth-century vocabulary – neither in Western Europe nor in Russia. A number of Russian scholarly works at the turn of the century discussed 'questions of colonisation' – meaning internal colonisation. For some years after 1905, even a special journal with this title was published in St. Petersburg. And indeed there were enough similarities between the Russian migratory movements and Western trans-oceanic colonisation to warrant the use of the same words to describe both phenomena.

However, those Slavophiles and other Russians who wanted instead to highlight the uniqueness of Russian solutions tried to prove that the migration of the Russians was a radically different phenomenon from the colonisation process carried out by other nations. The leading pan-Slav ideologist Nikolai Danilevskii remarked that

> the Russian people does not, as do the bees from the hives, send out swarms from its environment, forming new centres of political societies, such as the ancient Greeks did, or, in more recent times, as the Englishmen

43. S. Frederic Starr, 'Tsarist Government: The Imperial Dimension', in Jeremy R. Azrael (ed.) *Soviet Nationality Policies and Practices*, New York, 1978, p. 4.
44. Gins, *op. cit.*, p. 27.

do. Russia does not have what is called possessions, such as Rome did, or, again, as England does. The Russian state, from the times of the very first Muscovy princes, is nothing but Russia, which gradually, irrepressibly, has expanded to all sides, populating the uninhabited spaces on her borders, and forming in her own likeness the allogenous settlements which are being incorporated in the state ... Wherever Russians have moved, Moscow-Rus' has always remained the fulcrum in the life of the people.[45]

While the apologetic tendency in this quotation is obvious, Danilevskii has a point, although the will and ability of the tsarist state to russify the outlying regions ('forming them in her own likeness') was often rather weak.

In the Russian debate on migration policy which developed after 1905, when migration became a mass phenomenon, several tendencies were discernible. The leftist radicals heartily disliked migration, mainly because they feared that it might dissipate energy which could have been put to better use in the revolutionary struggle.[46] Among those who favoured migration, some focussed exclusively on the needs of the state, while others were concerned about the human dimension of migration as well. A typical representative of the *raison d'état* school was D. Pestrzhetskii,[47] who claimed that the migration of Russians to the periphery should serve one single purpose: the fortification of the state borders against foreign invasions. All other arguments, in his view, were misplaced or spurious, including the need to provide more arable land for the Russian peasants. In order to feed the admittedly growing population, it would be much more sensible to modernise agriculture (pass from a three-field to a multi-field system) and encourage the development of industry. These very modern ideas in Pestrzhetskii's writings go hand in hand with demands for a more resolute and conscious empire-building process. Against the background of Russia's recent defeat in the war against Japan, his pleas are imbued with a strong note of urgency: 'Now it is not a question of combatting the alleged land hunger but a question of to be or not to be for Great Russia.'

The Russian state should, in its own self-interest, actively promote migration with heavy investment in the building of railway and irriga-

---

45. N. Ia. Danilevskii, *Rossiia i Evropa*, St. Petersburg, 1888 (3rd edition), p. 531.
46. Treadgold, *op. cit.*, p. 186.
47. D. Pestrzhetskii, *Zaselenie Okrain*, St. Petersburg, 1908.

tion systems, as well as by instituting rationalised allotment procedures, private ownership of land etc. The borders ought to become densely populated by sturdy Slavs to avoid 'a second Mudken': 'That will be the only way to achieve victory in our inescapable future armed conflicts with the yellow race.' The admittedly anachronistic question of whether these border areas ought to be Russian in the first place if there were no Slavs living there was not addressed by Pestrzhetskii.

Rather than being an expression of tsarist state policy, Pestrzhetskii's pamphlet indicates that reasons of state security at the turn of the century played only a minor role in the Russian government's attitude towards migration. Pestrzhetskii himself deplored the fact that his viewpoints found little resonance in Russian state and society; otherwise he would probably not have bothered to write on the subject in the first place.

A different approach to the topic of migration was taken by G. Gins.[48] With reference to several French theoreticians, he distinguished between three kinds of colonial policy: subjection (*assujettissement*), self-rule (*autonomie*), and equalisation with the metropolis (*assimilation*). The third system, Gins believed, was identified as that adopted by the French, and it was this one that should be adopted by Russia also. The tsarist policy of colonisation, therefore, ought to be supplemented by a programme for the economic and cultural development of the non-Russian provinces.

What distinguished Gins's ideas was his earnest attempt to address the cultural needs of the indigenous (*tuzemnoe*) population. He agreed with Pestrzhetskii that the borderlands had to become culturally russified. However, this should be achieved not by means of migration only but also by giving local non-Russians a chance to partake in Russian culture. As a true child of his age, Gins had no doubts about Russia's cultural superiority.

> Although the differences between the Russian settlers and the Buryats and Kirgizians are not as great as between the Americans and the Indians, or between the French and the Negroes . . . not only our national self-esteem, but also the facts of reality compel us to acknowledge the great cultural superiority of the former over the latter.[49]

The Russian colonist was called to serve as a conveyor of civilisation

48. G. Gins, *op. cit.*
49. *ibid.*, p. 27.

to less fortunate people. In order to fulfil this mission, he should be distinguished by his 'energy, mobility, patience, coldbloodedness, perseverance and courage'. The ideal colonist should be a versatile jack-of-all-trades: an artisan, a carpenter, a blacksmith, a cobbler and of course an agriculturalist. Furthermore, the communities of colonists should consist not of males only but also of women. 'The local women of course cannot give the European the kind of support, comfort and care which is necessary to prevent his brutalisation and the passion for "a fast ruble", which in the colonies is so often the result of the consumption of opium, hard liquor etc.' Obviously, the Russians were no more immune to base temptations than other European settlers.

Intriguingly, the 'cultural superiority' argument was revived under Soviet rule. True, as long as Soviet historical science was dominated by the school of Mikhail Pokrovskii, the tsars' non-Russian conquests were denounced as an unmitigated evil. In 1921 even Joseph Stalin, as the commissary of the nationalities, expressed this view. From the rostrum of the 10th Party Congress he claimed:

> The policy of tsardom, of the gentry, and of the bourgeoisie, was aimed at the implanting in these regions of as many kulak elements of Russian peasant and Cossack stock as possible. These elements should be turned into trustworthy supporters of great power aspirations. The result of this policy was the gradual extinction of the local, indigenous population which was pushed into the wilderness.[50]

In the 1930s, however, Stalin himself presided over a sharp reversal in the official Soviet view. A theory of 'the lesser evil' was put forward: by being incorporated into Russia, the non-Russians had at least been saved from the evils of French and British imperialism. Finally, a theory of 'the positive good' was canonised, according to which it had been overwhelmingly advantageous to these people to become subjects of the tsar.[51]

With smaller or larger doses of jingoism, this ideology held sway in Soviet historiography right up till *perestroika*. It has affected the evaluation of centrifugal Russian migration. In 1982, two distinguished demographers claimed that 'earlier than the backward peoples the Russians were able to raise their material and cultural level.

---

50. I. V. Stalin, *Sochineniia*, V, Moscow, 1947, p. 226.
51. See e.g. Solomon M. Schwarz, 'Revising the History of Russian Colonialism', in *Foreign Affairs*, April 1952, pp. 488–93.

Russian peasants and craftsmen brought their productive skills to the backward outlying regions.'[52] As late as in 1991, another Soviet researcher claimed that 'while rightly condemning coercive colonisation, M.N. Pokrovskii failed to appreciate the objectively progressive significance of the colonisation of the periphery by Russian settlers.'[53] When the history of the Russian internal colonisation of the empire is today rewritten in the various Soviet successor states, the conclusion will no doubt be somewhat different, though not necessarily with any greater degree of nuance.

The circumstances in which the Russian diaspora came to exist clearly have an impact on its position in modern times. Rogers Brubaker's point that any investigation of the diaspora should begin with an analysis of the role played by state-sponsored migration in the formation of this group is well taken. This is to say that we should not discuss migratory patterns in economic terms only although these are indispensable. However, as Brubaker himself has pointed out, state sponsorship does not always mean promotion of migration. The Russian state sought to shape, channel and control migratory movements, now inducing, now dissuading – altering the structure of incentives and disincentives.

The main reasons for the tsarist regime's attempts to stem and impede emigration were a desire to keep the peasants attached to the soil in order to provide free or cheap labour for the gentry; the ingrained tendency of an autocratic regime to extent as much control as possible over the life of the population, including its movements; and the fear that an uprooted population might become susceptible to revolutionary propaganda. Only under intense pressure from a sudden population explosion in the late nineteenth century did the regime radically change these basic priorities.

It is tempting to speculate how many Russians would have ended up outside the Russian core area if the regime had not tried to influence the movements of its subjects in either way. While there is no final answer to this question, it is reasonable to propose that the numbers would have been no lower than they actually were in 1917. The main

---

52. Bruk and Kabuzan, *op. cit.* p. 10.
53. A. I. Ginzburg, *Russkoe naselenie v Turkestane,* Institut etnologii i antropologii, Russian Academy of Sciences, Moscow, 1991, p. 8.

migratory pressures on the population were similar to those which at the same time prompted millions of Europeans to seek their fortune in other continents, and they would have proved sufficient to sustain the same flows.

If so, was this also the case during the Soviet period?

3

MODERNISATION OR GRAND DESIGN?
RUSSIAN MIGRATION, 1917–1989

Accelerated Russian dispersion

The most important sources on migration by far are the more or less periodical censuses taken by the authorities. In the Soviet Union these were conducted in 1926, 1939, 1959, 1970, 1979 and 1989. The amount of information provided by each one varies: on some occasions relatively detailed figures were released, while on others only aggregate data were given. In a census taken in 1937, no information at all was released, probably because it revealed an appalling population decrease due to the forced collectivisation and the famine in 1932–3. For that reason one should also view with scepticism the results of the 1939 census which was clearly aimed at glossing over those losses.

Apart from the problem of the political manipulation of census results, there are also a number of technical intricacies connected with them. It is always difficult to formulate, in census questionnaires, clear and unambiguous questions which will be understood in the same sense by all respondents. This is particularly true when it comes to such evasive matters as ethnicity. Adding to the confusion, Soviet census-takers have asked different questions at different times. In 1926 the respondents were asked about their *narodnost'*, while in subsequent censuses this was changed to *natsional'nost'*. Both words mean 'nationality', but with somewhat different connotations.[1]

For many people in the Soviet Union, as elsewhere, the question of national self-awareness is difficult to answer in a straightforward and unequivocal way. People living in a multinational environment may have a dual ethnic identity, especially if they are raised in any ethnically mixed family. The Soviet census-takers, however, never allowed for more than one ethnic identity.

In 1932 a system of internal passports was introduced in which the

1. V. I. Kozlov, *Natsional'nosti SSSR. Etnodemograficheskii obzor*, Moscow, 1982 (2nd edition), p. 235. Under the tsars, no questions of ethnicity were included in the formulas, only questions of language affiliation and religion, qualities which may or may not coincide with ethnic consciousness.

'official nationality' – the *natsional'nòst* – of the carriers was registered in the so-called 'fifth point'.[2] When the citizens were handed their first passports in that year, they were free to state whatever nationality they wanted. If they later had second thoughts about their choice, it was often next to impossible to have the official nationality legally changed (although with handsome bribes much could still be accomplished). The ethnic choice made by the parents was also automatically 'inherited' by their children. Children of mixed marriages had to choose the identity of one of the parents when they reached the age of maturity at sixteen.[3]

The census-takers were not allowed to copy the information given in the passports on to their files; instead they were required to ask the respondents which nationality they subjectively felt that they belonged to. As a result, the censuses reflected ethnic change more accurately and flexibly than did the passport system. At the same time, however, there is every reason to believe that the ethnic self-awareness of most Soviet citizens was strongly influenced by the official nationality ascribed to them. The passport regime did to some extent retard the process of ethnic re-identification in the population.[4] This meant that linguistic assimilation into the Russian-language group did not automatically lead to complete russification.[5]

Censuses usually do not record diachronic change over time but instead offer only 'snaphot' pictures of the demographic situation in a country at certain arbitrarily chosen intervals and points in time. The demographers must fill in the blanks and draw lines between these fixed points on the basis of other sources of information and their general knowledge of population development. For instance, a spatial redistribution of an ethnic group showing that the percentage residing

2. See Victor Zaslavsky, *The Neo-Stalinist State*, New York, 1982, pp. 92ff; Victor Zaslavsky and Yuri Luryi, 'The Passport System in the USSR and Changes in Soviet Society', *Soviet Union/Union Sovietique*, VI, part 2 (1979), pp. 137–53.

3. See Pål Kolstø 'National Minorities in the Non-Russian Soviet Successor States', RAND report DRU-565-FF, November 1993.

4. For a thorough discussion of these problems, see Barbara A. Anderson and Brian D. Silver, 'Estimating Russification of Ethnic Identity Among Non-Russians in the USSR', *Demography*, XX, 4 (November 1983), pp. 461–89.

5. It should be remembered that this is not a uniquely Soviet phenomenon and not a result of the passport system only. In Great Britain, for instance, practically every Scotsman is linguistically Anglicised, but most still remain a strong identity as Scottish. See e.g. Anthony Birch, *Nationalism and National Integration*, London, 1989, pp. 78ff.

in Area A has gone down while the share residing in Area B has increased does not necessarily prove that a large part of the group has moved from A to B. Migration is only one of four factors influencing the size and distribution of ethnic groups, the others being fertility, mortality and ethnic re-identification. For instance, the remarkable eastward 'movement' of Jewry in Russia and the Soviet Union in the twentieth century, a movement which is evident from Soviet censuses, is the result of many factors pushing in the same direction. The westward emigration of Jews from the westernmost provinces to America and other transoceanic continents at the turn of the century was, within the confines of the Soviet Union, registered as an eastward movement by those who stayed behind. Moreover, the extermination of Jews in Belorussia and Ukraine by the Nazis produced the same result, although in this case the eastward migration that took place was probably of less significance.[6]

Complicating matters even further, the measurement units of Soviet demography have not remained constant. Within the Russian/Soviet state, there have been border adjustments between polling districts (administrative units and economic zones), and the external boundaries of the state have also fluctuated. All these factors – the political and involuntary manipulation of census results; the snapshot character of these results; the ambiguities inherent in the process of ethnic identification; and border changes – make it a formidable task for demographers to identify migratory currents in the Soviet Union with any degree of precision. Nonetheless, some have done so with impressive results.

In their pioneering work *Nationality and Population Change in Russia and the USSR, 1897–1970*, of 1976, Robert A. Lewis, Richard H. Rowland and Ralph S. Clem analysed the spatial distribution of various Soviet national groups (see Table 3.1). Using an intricate system of dissimilarity indices they measured the degrees of compactness and dispersion of each group against each other, based on the percentage of the groups residing within and outside their homelands (the various autonomous units). Without going into the details of their methodology, we can jump to one of their main conclusions, which is that an unambiguous trend towards an increased dispersion of the

---

6. The example is taken from Robert A. Lewis, Richard H. Rowland and Ralph S. Clem, *Nationality and Population Change in Russia and the USSR*, New York, 1976, pp. 238ff.

Table 3.1. RUSSIANS AS PERCENTAGE OF TOTAL REGIONAL POPULATION

	1897	1926	1926	1939	1959	1959	1970	1970	1979
	Bruk, Kabuzan	Bruk, Kabuzan	Lewis, Roland, Clem	Bruk, Kabuzan	Bruk, Kabuzan	Lewis, Roland, Clem	Bruk, Kabuzan	Lewis, Roland, Clem	Bruk, Kabuzan
1. North-west	72.4	88.5	83.9	–	86.6	86.6	86.7	86.6	91.7
2. Centre	93.3	93.5	96.0	–	94.6	94.5	94.2	94.1	–
3. Estonia	–	3.5	–	–	20.1	–	24.7	–	27.9
4. Latvia	–	8.0	–	–	26.6	–	29.8	–	32.8
5. Lithuania	–	2.6	–	–	8.5	–	8.6	–	8.9
6. *West* (=3.–5.)	5.9	–	6.3	–	–	17.1	–	19.1	–
7. Volga-Viatsk	78.5	78.5	78.4	–	76.5	76.4	75.2	75.2	75.2
8. Central Chernozem	82.0	81.8	84.3	–	95.7	96.0	96.1	96.4	95.8
9. Volga	65.0	64.6	69.4	–	68.5	75.6	67.7	75.4	67.9
10. Belorussia	5.3	4.9	5.6	4.3	8.2	8.2	10.4	10.4	11.9
11. Moldavia	8.5	8.2	11.8	7.7	10.2	10.2	11.6	11.6	12.8
12. South-west	4.9	2.9	2.3	–	5.8	6.0	6.6	6.7	7.3
13. South	19.6	26.7	19.0	–	30.9	30.9	34.0	34.0	36.3
14. Donetsk-Dniepr	18.1	11.5	14.6	–	24.9	26.1	27.9	29.1	30.1

15. North Caucasus	44.8	43.0	42.6	–	76.7	76.4	72.8	72.3	70.7
16. Georgia	–	3.6	–	8.7	10.1	–	8.5	7.9	7.4
17. Armenia	–	2.3	–	4.0	3.2	–	2.7	–	2.3
18. Azerbaijan	–	9.6	–	16.5	13.6	10.2	10.0	–	7.9
19. *Transcaucasia* (=16.–18.)	4.3	–	5.7	–	–	–	–	–	–
20. Urals	72.4	81.0	73.3	–	79.9	73.3	80.7	73.2	81.1
21. West Siberia	84.1	79.6	77.4	–	84.9	85.3	86.9	87.6	86.9
22. East Siberia	66.6	73.4	72.8	–	83.1	80.4	84.3	81.3	84.4
23. Far East	43.6	50.9	47.2	–	77.5	81.2	80.6	84.9	81.1
24. Kazakhstan	16.0	21.2	22.0	40.3	42.5	42.7	42.4	42.4	40.8
25. Uzbekistan	–	5.2	–	11.5	13.7	–	12.5	–	10.8
26. Turkmenistan	–	7.4	–	18.6	17.3	–	14.5	–	12.6
27. Tajikistan	–	0.6	–	9.1	13.3	–	11.9	–	10.4
28. Kyrgyzstan	–	11.6	–	20.8	30.2	–	29.2	–	25.9
29. *Central Asia* (=25.–28.)	2.2	–	5.8	–	–	16.4	–	15.1	–
30. *Total*	–	46.9	47.0	–	52.4	54.6	53.4	53.4	52.4

Sources: Robert A. Lewis, Richard H. Rowland and Ralph S. Clem, *Nationality and Population Change in Russia and the USSR*, New York, 1976, p. 216; and S. I. Bruk and V. M. Kabuzan, 'Dinamika chislennosti i rasseleniia russkikh posle Velikoi Oktiabrskoi sotsialisticheskoi revoliutsii', *Sovetskaia Etnografiia*, LVI, 5 (September–October 1982), p. 7.

Russian group has taken place during the twentieth century. Between 1897 and 1970 the Russian population outside the area of the RSFSR increased by more than 15 million. As a result, more than 21 million Russians now resided in the fourteen non-Russian republics. Russians comprised nearly one-fifth of the total population in these republics in 1970.[7] The percentage of Russians living in the traditional regions of Russian settlement (the Centre, Central Black Earth Zone, Urals, Volga, North-west and Volga-Viatsk) went steadily down, from 25.6% in 1897 to 20.5% in 1959, and to 19.5% in 1970. At the same time, the percentage of Russians living in the Eastern regions (defined as Siberia, the Far East, Kazakhstan and Central Asia) went up, from 3.0% in 1897 to 6.1% in 1926, and to 7.6% in 1959. In short, a significant eastward movement of the centre of gravity of the Russian population took place.

Part of this shift is clearly attributable to factors other than migration – in particular, regional differences in the number of war losses. The two world wars took a heavier toll of human lives in the western regions of the Soviet Union, which were theatres of military operations, than in the eastern parts. In addition, the assimilation of non-Russians into the Russian group seems to have pulled in the same direction. Russification has primarily affected smaller ethnic groups in Siberia and the Ural-Volga region, as well as culturally kindred groups living outside their 'own' republic – such as Ukrainians and Belorussians in Siberia, Northern Caucasus and Central Asia.[8] Nonetheless, it is the distinct centrifugal migration of Russians from west to east, and from the heartland to the periphery, that is unquestionably the main factor behind the large Russian population shift.

This conclusion is also reached by other researchers. In a sequel to their study of the pre-revolutionary Russian population, S. I. Bruk and V. M. Kabuzan examined the dynamics of the growth and distribution of the Russian nationality since the October Revolution.[9] Their analysis included data from the 1979 census, and thus represented an update compared to the Lewis–Rowland–Clem study. They found that by 1979 the total number of Russians living outside the RSFSR

7. Lewis, Rowland and Clem, *op. cit.*, 1976, p. 203.
8. See Anderson and Silver, *op. cit.*
9. S. I. Bruk and V. M. Kabuzan, 'Dinamika chislennosti i rasseleniia russkikh posle Velikoi Oktiabrskoi sotsialisticheskoi revoliutsii', *Sovetskaia etnografiia*, LVI, 5, (September–October 1982), pp. 3–20.

had risen to 23.87 million – or 17.4% of the whole Russian group found in the Soviet Union. While the total Russian population rose between 1917 and 1979 by 180%, the number of Russians living *outside* the RSFSR in the same period increased by no less than 370%. In 1917, Russians in Ukraine amounted to 4.2% of the Russian group as a whole and in 1979 this figure had risen to 7.6%. Spectacular increases took place also both in Kazakhstan (up from 1.6% to 4.4%) and in Uzbekistan (up from 0.3% to 1.2%). The Russian population in other areas rose to significant percentages of the total population in their respective republics, but as a percentage of the Russian group as a whole these diaspora communities remained relatively small.

Adjusting both for natural increase and for various assimilatory movements, Bruk and Kabuzan estimated that in 1979 approximately half of the Russian population in other Union republics (12 million people) consisted of those who immigrated during the Soviet period, as well as their children. Such figures have prompted Hélène Carrère d'Encausse to pronounce the Russians 'preeminently a nomadic people'.[10]

Russian migration into the Baltics began immediately after the incorporation of these areas into the Soviet Union, and soon attained considerable proportions. About 400,000 Russians and 100,000 other immigrants arrived in Latvia between 1945 and 1959. The peak period is believed to be 1947–9. During those three years, approximately 180,000 immigrants also arrived in Estonia. In this country, the Russian share of the population had reached 20.1% by 1959 and 27.9% by 1979. Corresponding figures for Latvia were 26.6% and 32.8% respectively. In the inter-war period the figures had been in single digits in both centuries: 3.5% in Estonia and 8.0% in Latvia in 1926. Put differently, the Russian presence increased by more than 500% and 300%, respectively, in the course of three decades. In Lithuania, by contrast, the Russian presence remained much more modest and stable: 8.5% in 1959, and 8.9% twenty years later.[11]

---

10. Hélène Carrère d'Encausse, *Decline of an Empire: The Soviet Socialist Republics in Revolt*, New York, 1980, p. 71.

11. Bruk and Kabuzan, *op. cit.*; Gerhard Simon, *Nationalism and Policy towards the Nationalities in the Soviet Union*, Boulder, CO, 1986/91; Rein Taagepera and Romuldas J. Misiunas, *The Baltic States*, London, 1983, pp. 104ff; Tõnu Parming, 'Population Changes in Estonia, 1935–1970', *Population Studies*, XXVI (March 1972), pp. 53–78; Juris Dreifelds, 'Immigration and Ethnicity in Latvia', *Journal of Soviet Nationalities*, I (Winter 1990–1), pp. 43–81; Dzintra Bungs, 'Migration

The previous chapter showed the centrifugal movement of Russians to be an important demographic factor under the tsars – and increasingly so towards the turn of the century. In general, therefore, the increase of the Russian population outside the RSFSR under Communism represents continuation rather than change in the demographic processes. Indeed, in the first decade after the revolution, migration in the Soviet Union conformed remarkably to the pattern of population movements in the late nineteenth century, in terms of both the numbers and the destinations involved.[12] However, while later the directions of the population currents also remained basically the same, a distinct *acceleration* in the outward movement of Russians took place.

The greatest quantitative jump was between the 1926 and 1939 censuses. During those years, which encompassed the two first five-year plans, the number of Russians living outside the RSFSR increased from 5.1 to 9.3 million, or by 82% – an astonishing change. As a percentage of the total Russian population this represented a rise from 8.6% to 14.9%.[13] Not all the republics, however, were affected by this upsurge of Russian migration in the 1930s. In Belorussia the percentage of Russians actually declined, and this would possibly have also been the result in Ukraine but for the great famine of 1932–3, which took its heaviest toll among the rural (i.e. ethnically Ukrainian) population.[14]

Even more impressive than the increase of the Russian diaspora at large was the growth of the Russian population in the non-Russian cities. Since the beginning of our century, migrating Russians, with few exceptions, have been settling in urban areas. This qualitative change was first noticeable during the first phase of Russian industrialisation in the 1890s, but it became more distinct in the Soviet period.

to and from Latvia', *Report on the USSR*, II (14 September 1990), pp. 27–33; Riina Kionka, 'Migration to and from Estonia', *Report on the USSR*, II (14 September 1990), pp. 20–4; Saulius Girnius, 'Migration to and from Lithuania', *Report on the USSR*, II (14 September 1990), pp. 25–7.

12. J. William Leasure and Robert A. Lewis, 'Internal Migration in Russia in the Late Nineteenth Century', *Slavic Review*, XXVII, 3, (September 1968); J. William Leasure and Robert A. Lewis, 'Internal Migration in Russia in the USSR: 1897–1926', *Demography*, IV, 2 (1967), pp. 479–96; V. Moiseenko, 'Migratsiia naseleniia po dannym vsesoiuznoi perepisi 1926 g.', in *Kuda i zachem iedut liudi*, Moscow, 1979, pp. 47–58.

13. See Simon, *op. cit.*, p. 119.

14. *ibid.*, p. 120.

By 1930, rural–urban migration had decidedly replaced rural–rural migration.

Lewis, Rowland and Clem remark that 'the rate of Russian urbanisation since the turn of the century and particularly since the inception of the five year plans very probably has been surpassed by few, if any, populations in human history'.[15] If the degree of Russian urbanisation in the 1920s was comparable to that of Latin America, half a century later it had reached the level of Western Europe and Japan. Although ethnic Russians moved from the countryside to the metropolises all over the Soviet Union, the trend in the movements was particularly biased in favour of cities outside the RSFSR. Indeed, the five economic zones where Russians attained their highest levels of urbanisation were all outside this republic (Donetsk-Dnieper, Transcaucasia, Central Asia, Belorussia and the West). The Russians were not unique in this; with few exceptions, all Soviet nationalities were, and still are, more urbanised outside their homeland than they were, and are, within it.

By 1959, the Russian share of the population in a number of Kazakh cities reached well above 50%, and in the mining city of Karaganda it stood at almost three-quarters. By 1970, Russians comprised the majority of the total urban population in both Kazakhstan and Kyrgyzstan. In that year also, the level of urbanisation of Russians inside the RSFSR stood at 55.9%, while outside this republic it had reached 64.3%.[16]

Russians were attracted not only to industrial cities outside the RSFSR but also to administrative centres. In all non-Russian republics except Ukraine, Armenia and Georgia, the Russians made up a larger share of the population in the republican capital than among the total urban population. In only two regions did the Russians make up less than 25% of the urban population: in Transcaucasia and in a south-western belt stretching from Lithuania, through Belorussia, to south-west Ukraine.

In some instances, the cities in the non-Russian republics took on a Russian quality from the very beginning, for only by the arrival of Russian migrants were they transformed from drowsy provincial towns into throbbing metropolises. The Russianisation of Soviet cities outside the RSFSR acquired a self-propelling character. As more and

---

15. Lewis, Rowland and Clem, *op. cit.*, p. 141. See also Moshe Lewin, *The Gorbachev Phenomenon*, 1990.
16. Lewis, Rowland and Clem, *op. cit.*, p. 146.

Table 3.2 RUSSIANS AS PERCENTAGE OF TOTAL AND URBAN
POPULATIONS OF ECONOMIC REGIONS OUTSIDE THE RSFSR

	1897		1926		1959		1970	
	Total	Urban	Total	Urban	Total	Urban	Total	Urban
West	5.9	20.8	6.3	6.6	17.1	27.3	19.1	27.7
Belorussia	5.3	17.4	5.6	12.8	8.2	19.4	10.4	19.7
Moldavia	8.5	28.7	11.8	26.4	10.2	30.4	11.6	28.2
South-west	4.9	26.5	2.3	7.4	6.0	16.7	6.7	15.4
South	19.6	43.5	19.0	39.9	30.9	44.1	34.0	43.6
Donetsk-Dniepr	18.1	33.7	14.6	32.2	26.1	33.8	29.1	35.5
Transcaucasia	4.3	17.0	5.7	17.7	10.2	18.4	7.9	13.5
Kazakhstan	16.0	52.4	22.0	53.8	42.7	57.6	42.4	58.4
Central Asia	2.2	9.1	5.8	23.3	16.4	36.7	15.1	33.2
Non-RSFSR Total	8.5	26.4	8.6	21.1	17.8	32.0	19.0	31.4

Source: Robert A. Lewis, Richard H. Rowland and Ralph S. Clem, *Nationality and Population Change in Russia and the USSR*, New York, 1976, p. 149.

more Russians moved in, the indigenous rural population in the
republics increasingly perceived the cities in their own homeland as
'alien'. To them, moving to the capital of their own republic demanded
almost as much cultural adaptation as moving to another republic.[17]
To the new Russian arrivals, on the other hand, the degree of cultural
adaptation required in order to settle into these cities became increasingly small. Non-Russians living in these cities or moving to them
were forced by the necessities of life to acquire a command of the
Russian language.[18]

The non-Russian republics thus acquired in time a stable Russian
population, in addition to the hundreds of thousands who came and
left. By 1989 approximately 40% of the Russian diaspora had been
born in a non-Russian republic (see Table 3.3). The highest percentage
of native-born Russians could be found in Estonia (65.1%) and Azerbaijan (61.6%), and the lowest in Belarus (32.5%). In all republics
except Georgia and Belarus, the percentage of native-borns

17. See Ann Sheehy, 'Some Aspects of Regional Development in Soviet Central Asia',
    Slavic Review, XXXI (September 1972), pp. 55–63.
18. See *Literaturnaia Gazeta*, no. 40, 1991, p. 2.

Table 3.3. NATIVE-BORN AND IMMIGRANT RUSSIANS IN THE
UNION REPUBLICS, AS PERCENTAGE OF TOTAL RUSSIAN
POPULATION IN THE REPUBLICS

Republic	1979 Native-born	1979 Immigrant	1989 Native-born	1989 Immigrant
RSFSR	46.6	53.5	50.2	49.8
Estonia	33.3	66.9	65.1	34.9
Latvia	36.6	63.4	41.6	58.4
Lithuania	36.5	63.5	38.4	61.6
Belarus	34.7	65.3	32.5	67.5
Moldova	40.6	59.4	43.3	56.7
Ukraine	40.9	59.1	42.3	57.7
Georgia	43.5	56.5	41.8	58.2
Armenia	–	–	–	–
Azerbaijan	55.0	45.0	56.4	43.6
Turkmenistan	41.2	58.8	47.1	52.9
Tajikistan	36.3	63.7	43.3	56.7
Uzbekistan	44.4	55.6	48.3	51.7
Kyrgyzstan	39.3	60.7	45.3	54.7
Kazakhstan	40.3	59.7	46.8	53.2

Source: Iu.V. Arutiunian (ed.), *Russkie: Etnosotsiologicheskie Ocherki*, Moscow, 1992, p. 52.
– = no information available.

was higher in 1989 than ten years earlier, and in some instances, such
as Estonia, significantly higher.[19]

Causes of the Russian dispersion. A broad consensus on the facts of the
Russian movements in the twentieth century has been established
within the scholarly community. However, profound disagreements
riddle the question of how these migratory patterns are now to be
explained. Generally, two explanatory trends – socio-economic and

19. These figures, which are computed by researchers from the Institute of Ethnology
and Anthropology in Moscow, seem to be at odds with the findings of Anderson
and Silver, who have estimated that between 1979 and 1989 the immigration
of Russians played a greater role in demographic development in Estonia than
it did in any other Union republic. See Barbara A. Anderson and Brian D. Silver,
'The Changing Ethnic Composition of the Soviet Union', *Population and Development Review*, XV (December 1989), pp. 642–3. The Russian researchers explain
the Estonian figures by reference to both the high fertility among Russians
in Estonia and the measures taken by Estonian authorities to curtail immigration
from other republics.

ethno-political – may be distinguished. The representatives of the socio-economic tendency take as their starting point the universal processes of modernisation, and try to explain the patterns of Russian migration in the Soviet Union by employing the same methods and insights as those being used by their colleagues studying similar processes in other parts of the world. This approach dominated Western research in the 1960s and 1970s, when a new generation of Sovietologists rebelled against the then dominant theory of totalitarianism. Proponents of totalitarianism considered the Soviet Union as a case *sui generis*, and for them, the only acceptable cases of comparison were Nazi Germany and other totalitarian societies.[20] The 'post-totalitarianists', on the other hand, made a point of treating the Soviet Union, as much as possible as 'a country like any other'. They found that a number of the political, social, cultural and demographic processes which had been interpreted earlier as aspects of a highly centralised and manipulative regime only could be explained just as well if one assumed instead that the same mechanisms and dynamics were at work in Soviet as in Western society.

The proponents of the alternative, ethno-political approach do not completely reject the insights of the modernist school. In fact, they often explicitly or implicitly draw on them. However, they claim at the same time that the machinations of a wellnigh omnipotent centre had a considerable influence on social processes, including migration, in the Soviet Union. They find it hard to believe that economic rationality or universal social dynamics alone can account for the drastic redistributions of Soviet nationalities. For instance, if hundreds of thousands of Russians ended up in the Baltic republics after the Second World War, fundamentally altering the ethnic structure in that region, then there must have been a grand design behind these movements.

The representatives of the ethno-political tendency do not always agree among themselves on which objectives the Soviet leaders wanted to achieve through an active migratory policy. Some see it as having been a deliberate plan to eradicate the ethnic identities of all Soviet citizens in a 'melting pot' process, while others claim to have detected a covert but tenacious russification strategy. In the first case, it was believed that the final objective was a de-nationalised 'Soviet man',

20. Richard Sakwa, *Soviet Politics*, London, 1989, Ch. 9.

while in the second case it is held that the ultimate objective was to form all Soviet citizens in the Russian mould.

There is a third explanation, which may be called the *security argument*, which also belongs to that category of explanations which interprets Russian migration into the republics basically as centrally manipulated. Large numbers of Russians and other Slavs were, according to this theory, sent to certain republics in which the ethnic group comprising the titular nation was considered unreliable in order to provide the Kremlin with trustworthy local administrators and to stifle dissent. This argument is particularly relevant to the Baltic states and other regions incorporated into the Soviet Union after the Second World War. However, it fails to explain the absence of large-scale Russian migration into western Ukraine and Lithuania – also flagrantly refractory anti-Soviet regions.

Both the socio-economic and the ethno-political schools of thought have important strengths and weaknesses, and neither one of them can be said to have been definitively falsified by any of the arguments or material advanced by the other. To some extent, I believe, it is possible to appreciate the insights provided by both positions. However, insofar as they contradict each other, the student of Soviet demography and population policy has to decide which approach appears more convincing and fruitful.

This choice has consequences for our understanding not only of the history of the Russian diaspora but also of the contemporary situation of this group. In the post-Soviet debate, those Russians living outside the Russian Federation are frequently referred to as 'agents' (active accomplices) or alternatively as 'hostages' (passive victims)[21] of the Soviet Empire. Such characteristics are explicitly or implicitly based on certain assumptions concerning both the driving forces behind the movements of the Russian diaspora and the role of these forces in Soviet nation-building. Whether the Russians were sent to the non-Russian republics on a political mission or simply to make a living is also widely believed to have a bearing on which status they ought to be accorded in the post-Soviet successor states.

Unfortunately, the socio-economic and the ethno-political interpretation of Soviet migration have developed very much in isolation from each other. This is particularly true of their explanations of

21. See e.g. Denis Dragunskii, 'Zalozhniki imperii', *Literaturnaia Gazeta*, 20 November 1991, p. 2.

Russian migration into the non-Russian republics. In the following sections of this chapter, we examine the main arguments put forward by both interpretations, and will try to see if they can stand the test of exposure to the rival line of reasoning.

Lewis, Rowland and Clem clearly represent the socio-economic approach. Lewis, for instance, has claimed that 'there are no unique "communist" demographic processes ... Demographic processes are largely related to socio-economic conditions, rather than to the types of government under which they develop. In short the problems of the USSR cannot properly be understood solely through studying the USSR.'[22] Naturally, many political decisions of government, especially those concerned with regional patterns of industrial development, have indirect effects on migratory patterns. However, in the Soviet Union, according to Lewis, these decisions did not add up to an ethnically motivated policy of migration.

According to the socio-economic approach, the single most important factor explaining the outward movement of the Russians in our century is the *modernisation* process. In the 20th century, this universal phenomenon has been studied in detail by a number of economists, historians and political scientists, and important regularities have been discovered. The modernisation process started in Europe, and has since spread to all other continents. It has been shown that the *timing* of the initial modernisation phase fundamentally influences its subsequent character. Therefore, the modernisation process in the Third World proceeds in a way radically different from the modernisation process in Europe.

Applying this insight to multinational societies, Lewis, Rowland and Clem found that certain ethnic groups tend to modernise earlier than others, and that whichever groups reach modernity first tend to make use of their lead to consolidate their position, and are reluctant to share the benefits accruing from it with groups that modernise only later. The reasons for early modernisation are primarily of two kinds, cultural and political: either there is a culturally conditioned disposition

---

22. Robert A. Lewis 'The Mixing of Russians and Soviet Nationalities and its Demographic Impact', in Edward Allworth (ed.), *Soviet Nationality Problems*, New York, 1971, pp. 117–67, on p. 118. See also Lewis, Rowland and Clem, *Nationality and Population Change, op. cit.*, p. 87: 'Generally speaking, the distribution and redistribution patterns of the nationality groups have not been the product of governmental policies directly aimed at their creation.'

for social mobilisation or there is a political role in the state which provides advantageous preconditions for such mobilisation – or there is a combination of these two factors.

Some ethnic cultures tend to be 'achievement-orientated', Lewis, Rowland and Clem believe. They admit that this concept is difficult to define, but think that is has nonetheless proved its fruitfulness. A classic example of an achievement group is represented by the Jews in the United States. The most important *political* factor influencing modernisation is membership of the dominant ethnic group within the state – the 'state-bearing nation'. In tsarist Russia and the Soviet Union this group was the Russians.

The uneven pace of modernisation affects population change in two different ways: through population growth and through migration.

> The majority of population growth within the last two centuries has resulted from the declines in mortality associated with the early stages of modernization. This fact suggests that the timing of declines in mortality within a multinational state would be critical, since those groups that experienced declines in mortality first would be the first to experience rapid population growth. In turn, rapid population growth, assuming a static agricultural technology and intensive land use, results in outmigration.[23]

Emigration from overpopulated rural areas can take different forms: migration to cities, migration to other rural areas or international migration. The main feature of modernisation migration is a movement from the countryside to the cities. This, as we have seen, is what has characterised the demographic movements of the Russians in our own century.

The high natural rate of population growth among the Russians both in the nineteenth and early twentieth centuries clearly contributed to the strong outward movement of this group. This growth was a result not of increased fertility but of decreased mortality – especially among infants. Due to higher hygienic standards, more Russians now reached procreation age. This is what one would expect of a modernising nationality. Only in the later phases of modernisation do birth control and decreased fertility lead to a lower natural rate of population increase relative to less modernised groups.

A seemingly major problem with the Lewis–Clem–Rowland model

---

23. Lewis, Rowland and Clem, *Nationality and Population Change, op. cit.*, p. 87.

is the fact that several large ethnic groups in the Soviet Union in the twentieth century have undergone significant modernisation without any concomitant outward migration from their homelands. This is true of, among others, the Armenians and the Georgians. The authors believe, however, that they can account for this phenomenon too, without deviating from the modernisation model. They point out that the growth of the Transcaucasian cities has proceeded at more or less the same pace and at more or less the same time as the rise in the educational and hygienic level of the Transcaucasian nations. At the time when these ethnic groups got caught up in the whirlwind of modernisation, urban job opportunities were being opened up in their own republics, and as a result they did not have to leave their home regions in order to make a career. This circumstances, Lewis, Clem and Rowland believe, can also account for the insignificant trickle of Russians to Transcaucasian cities in the twentieth century: sufficient numbers of indigenous élites were available to fill the urban jobs created there, and consequently the need to import labour from outside did not arise. From this observation, these writers hypothesise a general regularity: 'The relative importance of Russians in the urban centres of non-Russian areas might be inversely related to the relative level of advancement of the indigenous group.'[24]

When this hypothesis was tested mathematically on the Soviet Union as a whole a certain but not very strong degree of correspondence was found. What in particular undermined the hypothesis was the demographic development in the Baltic region. Latvians and Estonians are highly modernised groups, and yet despite this the Russians have been moving since the Second World War into the cities of Estonia and Latvia in precipitous numbers. In Lithuania, however, the opposite was the case. Lithuanians have till recently scored low on most modernisation indices; for instance, their level of formal education has been lower than that of all major Soviet nationalities, except the Moldovans. We should therefore expect a high level of Russian immigration into Lithuania, but the number of Russians in Lithuanian cities has remained low – less than 10%, in fact. This situation is doubly remarkable since it contrasts sharply to the state of affairs found in the two northernmost Baltic republics.

Rather than abandon their 'inverse correlation' hypothesis, Lewis, Roland and Clem tried to account in some way for these Baltic anomalies. The explanation that they came up with was related to the different rates of population growth among the various different ethnic groups. In the twentieth century Latvians and Estonians, for instance, have experienced extremely low natural population increases. In marked contrast to the Transcaucasian situation, urbanisation in Estonia and Latvia has clearly outpaced the ability of the indigenous groups to fill the expanding urban labour market. In Latvia and Estonia, the local labour force, while highly qualified, has not been large enough. In Central Asia, on the other hand, precisely the opposite has been the case: the local labour force, while abundant in number has *not* been sufficiently qualified to fill the new urban jobs. In both cases, this has led to a large influx of Russians.

As concerns their 'Lithuanian predicament', Lewis, Roland and Clem remarked that in recent years the Lithuanians have been modernising rapidly. In the 1960s, their educational level rose faster than in any other republic nationality. Therefore, the demand for Russians was substantial. In addition, the fact that the Lithuanian population was growing more rapidly than the Latvian and Estonian populations meant that the need for Russians in the Lithuanian SSR, compared to the Latvian and Estonian republics, was now reduced. When Lewis, Roland and Clem tested the inverse-correlation hypothesis a second time, excluding the three Baltic republics, they found a high degree of correspondence.

The linking of the migratory movements of Russians in the twentieth century to modernisation represents a self-contained theory, or rather a cluster of theories. But how does it correspond with our general knowledge of the way the Soviet system worked? We know that Soviet leaders since the days of Stalin tried to operate the economy, and indeed society at large, according to ready-made 'plans'. Their faith in the ability to manipulate movements of large groups was also demonstrated in their practice of reinforcing a weak sector on the 'labour front' by 'throwing in' additional cadres. We also know that in spite of the internationalist ideology of Marxism which he officially adhered to, Stalin was clearly hung up on the issue of ethnicity. Among the many domestic enemies he claimed to have unmasked were certain ethnic groups. During, and immediately after, the Second World War, entire nationalities were collectively accused of having collaborated with the Nazis, and as a punishment, were deported to the eastern parts of the country.[25] In addition, more than 200,000

25. Aleksandr M. Nekrich, *The Punished Peoples*, New York, 1978.

Balts, a million Poles and many others had to go the same way. In these instances, the connection between movements of ethnic groups and Soviet government policies is indisputable. But should these cases be seen as evidence of any general policy of ethnically motivated migration?

Mikk Titma and Nancy B. Tuma believe so. In their monograph *Migration in the Former Soviet Union*[26] they claim

> Since the 1960s, the main target of the interior policy [of the USSR] has been the Sovietization and formation of a unified Soviet people. The USA was an analogue in the formation of such a society. To form the Soviet people, an extensive internal migration was necessary to obtain a 'melting pot' effect. Since there was an issue of historically shaped nations, that owned a determined territory, it was necessary to mix them with other nations.

In the 1960s, Titma and Tuma believe two 'strategic decisions' concerning migration policy were taken in the Kremlin. The first concerned the introduction of the melting-pot ideal, the second the establishment of the Russian language as the state language.[27] They claim that the latter decision should be seen as one particular expression of the conscious policy of russification that was based on Russian chauvinist positions. Titma and Tuma understand the expression 'strategic decisions' not in a metaphorical sense but quite literally. They admit that their hypothesis cannot by substantiated by reference to specific documents, but they nonetheless maintain that 'while these top secret documents are still unpublished, . . . there's no doubt that they exist.'

These two assertions – that the Soviet leadership pursued a melting-pot strategy and that they tried to russify the non-Russians – take on a very different status from the point of view of Soviet self-understanding. The second claim clearly contradicts the official ideology. The melting-pot hypothesis, on the other hand, may be understood as a mere reformulation of the semi-official ideal of *'slianie'* or the 'merger' of the Soviet peoples. This ideal was an ideological heritage from Lenin, but most Soviet leaders spoke little about it. This reticence was probably due to the perception by large sections

---

26. *Berichte des Bundesinstituts für ostwissenschaftliche und internationale Studien*, 22, 1992.
27. The authors do not make it clear whether they see these two decisions as being parallel or at cross purposes. The first one would presumably be aimed at the de-nationalisation of the Soviet citizens, while the second would facilitate their Russification.

of the population, Russians and non-Russians alike, that it posed a threat to their ethnic distinctiveness. Still, it was never completely abandoned, and Andropov apparently made a halfhearted attempt to breath new life into it.[28] Having said that, the Soviet leaders rarely presented this as a goal to be achieved through the physical moving around of ethnic groups. Rather, it was claimed that since all parts of the state were infused with the same Socialist culture and political system, they would come to resemble each other more and more until finally all differences vanished.[29]

According to Titma and Tuma, the main executors of the Soviet policy of russification through migration were the economic ministries. The central ministries, they maintain, had orders to mix the nationalities as much as possible. At the same time, the authors also believe that there was considerable leeway for each ministry in the execution of this policy. Each ministry therefore ought to be studied separately to determine its role in the forming of the Soviet people. In the Baltic states, for instance, the authors think that the military-industrial ministries were the most rigid in executing the russification agenda. As evidence of this belief, they point to the fact that in Estonia all Estonians were forced to leave the town of Sillamaë in the north-east of the country when an important nuclear industry was built there. 'Until Estonian independence, no Estonians were admitted to that enterprise. This enterprise was the main pump of migration in Estonia.' Here certainly, is evidence of an ethnically motived migration policy. On the other hand, it would certainly not serve to create a melting-pot. Rather than ethnic mixing, the result would be the establishment of segregated ghettos.

Titma and Tuma add that the various republican leaders could, in

---

28. See e.g. Darrell P. Hammer, 'Russian Nationalism and Soviet Politics', in Joseph L. Nogee (ed.), *Soviet Politics: Russia After Brezhnev*, New York, 1985, pp. 140ff.
29. Certain Soviet propagandists did in fact point to migration as an aspect of the merging of the Soviet peoples. In 1961, for instance, a certain P. G. Semënov claimed that 'The eradication of national-state borders within the Soviet Union is promoted also by such factors as the mobility of the population which is increasing as a result of the economic development', *Sovetskoe gosudarstvo i pravo*, XII (1961), p. 25. While this statement could be seen as evidence of an ethnically motivated migration policy, it can equally well be interpreted either as an *ex post factum* attempt to give the socialist system credit for processes which had non-political causes or as an attempt to push Soviet policy-makers in a certain direction. In any case, such claims have emanated from low-level ideologists only.

certain instances, have had an influence on migration policy. Their example is Lithuania, where local authorities managed to impose a considerable limit on immigration. Unfortunately, the authors do not explain why other republican leaders failed in this aim. As a partial explanation it is mentioned that the Lithuanian Communist Party consisted largely of ethnic Lithuanians, but this only moves the problem one step backwards, since one then has to explain why Lithuanians were able to prevent the russification of their party organisation while others Soviet nations succumbed to it.

Most Western specialists on the Soviet economy agree with Titma and Tuma that the ministries were largely in charge of running the economy. However, it is also widely believed that the main objective of Soviet ministerial bureaucrats was to achieve a maximum of plan fulfilment at a minimum cost.[30] For that reason, they located new plants where infrastructures were already good, so that they did not have to invest in the construction of new ones. This not very far-sighted policy put a premium on investment in the Baltic states, even if labour was scarce there and Russian workers had to be shipped in.[31] Whether we assume that the ministries were guided either by a conscious motive of ethnic mixing or by economic calculations alone, the expected result would therefore be the same.

The ethno-political approach to the study of Soviet migration is in a sense redundant, because if socio-economic factors are sufficient to explain the movement of Russians to other republics, there is no need to find secret Politburo documents concerning migration policy. This is not the same as saying that such documents do not or 'cannot' exist. To make this clearer, a parallel can be drawn with Soviet policy on religion. Most studies on religious life in the Soviet Union have indicated that the level of religious consciousness among Soviet citizens was more or less the same as in other industrialised societies, but lower than in traditional societies. Sociologists of religion believe that secularisation is related first and foremost to both modernisation and urbanisation. They claim that deliberate efforts to retard secularisation by means of evangelisation, or to speed it up by means of atheist propaganda, have little effect (Peter L. Berger even suggests, tongue-in-

---

30. See e.g. Alec Nove, *The Soviet Economic System*, London, 1980/4, Ch. 3.
31. See also the findings of I. S. Koropeckyj, Leslie Dienes and Gertrude Schroeder on Soviet industrial location policies, as summarised by Lewis, Rowland and Clem, *op. cit.*, pp. 116ff.

cheek, that agitators of 'scientific atheism' in the East, on the one hand, and Christian evangelists in the West on the other 'could come together and comfort each other' for their equally big failures).[32] But even if atheist propaganda has had little effect on the world-view of Soviet citizens, this does not, of course, 'prove' that such propaganda did not take place. On the contrary, we know for a fact that it was a constant feature of Soviet reality. Similarly, a deliberate Soviet strategy involving either a 'melting-pot' or russification by means of the migration of ethnic groups – or *both* – cannot be categorically excluded, even if it also cannot be proved. But if this presumed strategy did not in fact have any noticeable effects whatsoever, in which case the migration currents would have been exactly the same without it, the hypothesis becomes rather uninteresting.

Most experts on Soviet migration policy place themselves somewhere between the positions of Lewis, Rowland and Clem, on the one hand, and Titma and Tuma on the other hand. An early and eloquent contribution to the debate was provided by Walter Kolarz's *Russia and Her Colonies*. Employing the dramatic metaphors of warfare, Kolarz saw the Russian migrants as a mighty army advancing into non-Russian territories assisted by a number of smaller satellite detachments, namely the russified diasporas of other Soviet nationalities. These groups were all 'thrown into action by the Russian colonisers for the ultimate benefit of the Russians': The more the people of Russia become intermingled and the more they are scattered through the Eurasian continent by a *planned colonization policy* the less there is danger of the rise of 'national problems' and the greater the likelihood of their absorption by Russian civilization.'[33]

This seems to place Kolarz squarely within the ethno-political camp. However, he proclaimed in the same breath that this grandiose advance into the non-Russian territories was also guided by economic necessity: 'The primary approach of the Soviet regime towards colonization is an economic and strategic, not a national Russian one.' Finally, Kolarz also pointed to a number of cultural factors which in addition promoted migration. These were quite independent of political decisions made at the top: the enthusiasm of a young generation for

32. Peter L. Berger, *The Sacred Canopy: Elements of a Sociological Theory of Religion*, New York, 1969, p. 110.
33. Walter Kolarz, *Russia and her Colonies*, London, 1952, p. 16. Emphasis added.

building and creation in a new and unknown territory; the inborn '*wanderlust*' of the Russian peasant; his hope that the collective farm statute would be less strictly applied in the distant territories, and so on. With these clarifications, Kolarz's standpoint became more nuanced – and less clear. It seems that he refused to recognise any conflict between the respective socio-economic and ethno-political interpretations of Soviet migration.

Most students of Soviet affairs acknowledge that the available evidence is insufficient for any conclusions concerning the motives and ultimate driving forces behind internal Soviet migration to be drawn. Tönu Parming admits that the russification theory remains 'speculative'.[34] And V. Stanley Vardys essentially agrees with him, despite surmising that the Russian migration to Central Asia and the Baltic republics resulted from contrived political decisions involving nation-building. In support of this hypothesis, he points to the centralised character of the Soviet system.[35]

Walker Connor goes somewhat further with the claim that while it cannot be proved that Soviet authorities actively promoted ethnic diffusion, 'it is inconceivable that such a massive and consequential redistribution of population ... could have occurred in the absence of official approval.'[36] Connor sees the presence of large groups of Russians in the non-Russian republics as an indispensable factor in the nationality policy of 'divide and rule'. That relatively few Russians have moved into Transcaucasia does not, in his view, undermine this thesis; in this area the mutually antagonistic Armenian, Azeri and Georgian groups have had sufficiently large diasporas on each other's territories to fulfil the same role. In still other areas, linguistically russified non-Russian diasporas functioned as 'surrogate Russians for the further russification of the republic in which they live.'[37]

At first glance, Connor seems to agree with Titma and Tuma – the Soviet authorities were indeed pursuing an ethnically motivated policy of migration – but on closer scrutiny, it becomes clear that he is at the same time lambasting them for *not* having had precisely such a policy.

34. Tönu Parming, 'Population Changes in Estonia, 1935–1970', *Population Studies*, XXVI (March 1972), p. 64.
35. V. Stanley Vardys, 'Geography and Nationalities in the USSR: a Commentary', *Slavic Review*, XXXI, 3 (September 1972), p. 569.
36. Walker Connor, *The National Question in Marxist–Leninist Theory and Strategy*, Princeton, 1984, p. 310.
37. *ibid.*, pp. 314–5.

In his view, they should have intervened actively in the migratory processes in order to promote the indigenisation of the Union republics, whereas instead 'the authorities have done discernibly little to combat the continuing influx of Russians into non-Russian areas. There has been no visible attempt made by the authorities to persuade Russians living outside the RSFSR to relocate in labor-shortage areas within that republic.' While superficially consonant with the Titma–Tuma analysis, Connor's devastating indictment of Soviet migration policy is based on an opposite set of presuppositions. He admits that although the Soviet government did possess the weapons necessary to control internal migration, it lacked the will to use them. Titma–Tuma, on the contrary, believe that the Soviet leaders *had* the will but were largely unable to put their schemes into effect.

In the official Soviet debate on the subject, the modernisation model was as much anathema as was the russification theory. Soviet ideologues fulminated in strong terms against Western Sovietologists who saw the presence of Russians in the non-Russian republics as the result of a deliberate settlement policy. At the same time, these same ideologues maintained that the Soviet Union was a planned society, also in this way. A collective work on Western 'falsifications' of national relations in the Soviet Union published in the immediate pre-*perestroika* era claimed that the modernisation theory had been concocted in order to denigrate Soviet economic successes by ascribing them to some universal, apolitical processes. 'According to the schemes [of the modernisation theorists], the socialist organization of society, the brotherly help of the Russian people, and the mutual aid of the Socialist nations have played no role.'[38] In their practical work, however, Soviet demographers and sociologists have leaned towards the socio-economic approach in their treatment of migratory processes in their own country.

Russian contraction. Whatever were the reasons for Russians moving out of the RSFSR into the other republics during the Soviet period, this trend did not last. The centrifugal tendency of Russian demographic movements peaked in the latter part of the 1950s. In the 1960s and 1970s, by contrast, migration no longer played a significant

---

38. *Kritika fal'sifikatsii national'nykh otnoshenii v SSSR*, Moscow, 1984, p. 216. In the Soviet Union, collective works were usually more authoritative and official than monographs published under the name of a particular researcher.

Table 3.4 AVERAGE ANNUAL PERCENTAGE CHANGE IN
RUSSIAN POPULATION, BY ECONOMIC REGION

	1959-70	1970-79	Average annual change %
North-west	1.0	1.0	0.0
Centre	0.6	0.5	−0.1
West	2.2	1.7	−0.5
Volga-Vyatsk	−0.0	+0.0	+0.0
Central Chernozem	0.3	−0.3	−0.6
Volga	1.2	0.8	−0.4
Belorussia	3.2	2.1	−1.1
Moldavia	3.1	2.2	−0.9
South-west	1.8	1.6	−0.2
South	3.0	1.8	−1.2
Donetsk-Dniepr	2.2	1.4	−0.8
North Caucasus	1.4	0.4	−1.0
Transcaucasia	0.1	−0.7	−0.8
Urals	0.9	0.5	−0.4
West Siberia	0.7	0.4	−0.3
East Siberia	1.5	1.2	−0.3
Far East	1.9	1.8	−0.1
Kazakhstan	3.0	0.9	−2.1
Central Asia	2.6	1.2	−1.4
Total	1.1	0.7	−0.4

Source: Richard H. Rowland, 'Regional Migration and Ethnic Russian Population Change in the USSR (1959-1979)', *Soviet Geography*, XXIII, 8 (October 1982), p. 571.

role in the spatial distribution of the Russian ethnic groups.[39] Richard Rowland has calculated the average annual percentage change in the Russian population by region (see Table 3.4). These figures show that in every non-Russian area the growth was lower than in the previous intercensal period, and a large amount of it was probably attributable to the natural growth of the resident Russian population.

By the late 1970s the ethnic distribution of the Soviet population appeared to have stabilised, but this was deceptive. In reality, the seeming balance of the migratory currents was marking the transition from a steady dispersion of the Russian group to a period of steady contraction. In 1979 only one non-Russian region, Transcaucasia, saw an actual decrease in the number of Russian residents. In the thirty year period 1959–89, the Russian population in Azerbaijan increased by no

39. Bruk and Kabuzan, *op. cit.*

less than 22%. Georgia, also, had seen a reduction of its Russian population between 1959 and 1970.

In the latest intercensal period, 1979–89, this trend also affected the southern tier of Soviet Central Asia: the absolute number of Russians went down in both Tajikistan, Uzbekistan and Turkmenistan, albeit slowly. However, since the population growth rate in the indigenous groups was very high, the relative weight of the Russians decreased rapidly. In Kyrgyzstan and Kazakhstan, the population growth of the Russians was still positive but very feeble.

At this time, however, a reduction in the Russian presence could not be registered in the Western republics. In Ukraine, Belarus and the Baltic republics, the Russian share of the population increased by 0.5–2.5% during the same period.[40] However, in all the other republics including the RSFSR the growth rate of the Russian population, while still positive, was now tailing off. The highest average annual growth rate was registered in Belorussia (1.7%), and the lowest in Armenia (− 3%). These figures indicate a clear difference between the Asian and the European parts of the Soviet Union. As expressed by Barbara Anderson and Brian Silver, 'the non-European republics have become less Russianized over time, while the European ones have become more Russianized.'[41]

These two writers have estimated the relative degrees of influence of the migration, natural-growth and assimilation factors on the population changes reported by the 1989 census.[42] They conclude that by that year the Russians had attained the lowest level of fertility of all the Union-republic titular nationalities. This was contrary to the common assumption that the Estonians and Latvians had an even lower level. While this had indeed been the case, Anderson and Silver found that the situation had changed by the beginning of the 1970s. Nonetheless, the Russians in these two republics continued to have higher average natural increases. This seeming paradox was explained by the different age composition of the various groups: the Russians in the Baltic republics were generally younger than the people

40. Klaus Segbers, 'Migration and Refugee Movements from the USSR: Causes and Prospects', *Report on the USSR*, II (15 November 1991), pp. 6–14.
41. Barbara A. Anderson and Brian D. Silver, 'The Changing Ethnic Composition of the Soviet Union', *Population and Development Review*, XV, 4 (December 1989), pp. 609–56, on p. 633.
42. *ibid.*

Table 3.5 RUSSIAN POPULATION INCREASE IN
SOVIET REPUBLICS, 1989

	(× 1,000)	As % of total population in Republic	As % of non-titular population in Republic	Numerical change in republic since 1979 (1979 = 100)	As % of total Russian population
Estonia	475	30.3	78.8	116.2	0.30
Latvia	906	34.0	70.7	110.2	0.62
Lithuania	344	9.4	45.8	113.5	0.24
Belarus	1,342	13.2	59.5	118.3	0.90
Moldova	562	13.0	36.4	111.1	0.40
Ukraine	11,356	22.1	80.8	108.4	7.80
Georgia	341	6.3	21.1	91.8	0.24
Armenia	452	1.6	23.0	73.3	0.04
Azerbaijan	392	5.6	32.2	82.5	0.30
Turkmenistan	334	9.5	33.7	95.6	0.23
Tajikistan	388	7.6	20.2	98.3	0.30
Uzbekistan	1,653	8.3	29.1	99.3	1.10
Kyrgyzstan	917	21.5	45.1	100.5	0.63
Kazakhstan	6,228	37.8	62.6	103.9	4.30

Source: *Natsional'nyi sostav naseleniia SSSR*, Moscow, 1991

comprising titular nationalities. They had larger cohorts in the pro-
creative age group, and they therefore bred more children, even though
there were fewer children per family among the Russians than among
the titular groups.

As for migration, Anderson and Silver found that while there was
still considerable movement of Russians in and out of the various
republics, its net effect was self-cancelling. No net migration in or out
of the RSFSR could be registered. There were, however, important
differences between the various parts of the country. In Transcaucasia
the Russians were continuing to leave Georgia and Azerbaijan, as they
had done in the previous two intercensal periods, and in addition their
emigration from Armenia, barely noticeable between 1970 and 1979,
had now risen dramatically. In Central Asia and Kazakhstan, the
1979–89 intercensal period marked a clear break with the previous
trend. For the first time, immigration was supplanted by emigration
in all five republics. This trend was strongest in those areas where
relatively few Russians were living (Uzbekistan, Tajikistan and

Turkmenistan), and was less precipitous but still also appreciable in heavily russianised Kyrgyzstan and Kazakhstan.

Of the six European republics, it was Moldova that conformed to the Central European pattern, in the sense that the trend of Russian immigration in the 1980s changed there from positive to negative. In all the remaining European republics except Lithuania, a positive immigration trend continued, albeit at a slower pace. In Lithuania, the immigration rate, while never impressive, was slightly higher than in the previous intercensal period. Between 1979 and 1989, as in the previous intercensal periods, the broadest currents of Russians went to Estonia and Belorussia. In Estonia the level of Russian migration remained so high that it amounted to the largest single determinant of the population increase in the republic. In Latvia the single most important factor of population increase was the natural growth rate in the numbers of local Russians.

Significantly, the new pattern of Russian migration did not represent a general trend among all the major Soviet nationalities. While there was a slight tendency among the titular nationalities to return to their homelands between 1959 and 1970, this trend had been reversed by 1979. Between 1979 and 1989 Ukraine, Belorussia, Moldova, Georgia, Azerbaijan and all the five Central Asian republics witnessed a net emigration on the part of the titular nationality. Emigration from most republics between 1979 and 1989 was also larger than in the previous intercensal period. Only four Union republics – Estonia, Latvia, Lithuania and Armenia – did not conform to this pattern. However, with one exception, the rate of return-migration was slowly going down in these republics as well. Only in Latvia did members of the titular nationality continue to move in increasing numbers.

Theories of contraction

Any attempt to explain the creation and subsequent development of the Russian diaspora in the Soviet Union ought to be able to account for both the dispersion and the contraction of the Russian ethnic group. Alternatively, one should be able to tell why different sets of explanations must be applied in the study of these two phenomena.

Returning to the two schools of research discussed above, we may note that theorists of modernisation will explain the contraction in the same way as they explained Russian dispersion. In fact, a reversal of the Russian migratory pattern had been expected and predicted. If the early stages of modernisation lead to a higher natural growth rate, due to lower mortality, then the later stages lead to a lower rate of population increase, due to reduced fertility. In the 1970s and 1980s the Russians reached those later stages, and their birth rate went down precipitously. In addition, the various titular nationalities in the non-Russian Union republics were gradually catching up in the modernisation process. As some of them (in particular the Central Asians) were entering its first phases, they were experiencing significantly lower rates of mortality. While the birth rates of these groups, as late as in the 1940s, had not been significantly different from, and in some cases were lower than, that of the Russians,[43] they now suddenly took off and soared to dramatic heights. A yawning gap between the decreasing population growth of the Russians and the increasing growth of these groups was opening up.

Clearly, these circumstances can be made to explain the declining rate of emigration of Russians from the RSFSR: quite simply, the Russians had no population surplus to export. The Baltic situation, then, represents a greater challenge to the modernisation theory: why did the level of migration of Russians to Estonia and Latvia *not* go down in a period marked by the relative demographic stagnation of this group? A number of factors are usually thought to account for this paradox: the pull-factor of a high living standard; the low population growth rate of the Balts; and a certain inertia inherent in the migratory patterns. However, it ought to be conceded by the proponents of the socio-economic interpretation that a reversal or stagnation of Russian immigration to these areas would have been just as easy, or easier, to explain.

The net migration balance is a product of two factors: immigration and emigration. If the socio-economic approach can explain the decreasing level of immigration by Russians, can it also account for the increasing number of Russians *leaving* the non-Russian republics? To some extent, no doubt. Because of the high birth rates of the indigenous populations, the Central Asian republics were becoming densely populated – in sharp contrast to the RSFSR. As a result, more tempting job opportunities were opening up in the Russian republic, attracting applicants from among the Russian diaspora. At the same

---

43. Bruk and Kabuzan, *op. cit.*, p. 11; Hélène Carrère d'Encausse talks about a 'sudden jump in fertility, coinciding with economic and intellectual progress', *Decline of an Empire, op. cit.*, p. 67.

time, the indigenous job-seekers in Central Asia had acquired increasingly high levels of professional training. In one way they were even better qualified than the local Russians: they not only had a decent command of the Russian language but were also fluent in the native language. Hence, a more intensely competitive job environment developed in the non-Russians republics, in which the Russians were slowly falling behind.

However, in the reporting on the upsurge in Russian emigration from the non-Russian republics since the early 1980s, political and cultural explanations have frequently been given. The most common answer given by the migrants themselves is that they have been subject to increasing ethnic harassment and intolerable living conditions. Many also assert that this harassment is instigated or encouraged from above. While in the Soviet period it was mostly non-Russians in the Soviet Union who subscribed to the ethno-political theory of migration, many Russian migrants themselves now explain their move as the result of state-orchestrated campaigns, the states in question having become non-Russian Soviet successor states.

As we see in later chapters, the accelerated movement of Russians out of Central Asia and some other non-Russian areas since 1989 cannot be explained by reference to the universal dynamics of pull-factor migration alone. In many instances it has taken on the characteristics of flight rather than migration. Nevertheless, to anticipate some of our later conclusions it seems that, again in the post-Communist period, attempts by government to influence migratory patterns on the territory of the former Soviet Union are often fruitless. If any of the new states have expressed a clear desire to have parts of the Russian community evicted, they are Latvia and Estonia. Nonetheless, fewer Russians have emigrated from these countries than from Central Asia, where state authorities have made strenuous attempts to persuade the Russians to stay.[44] Population movements among the

44. In terms of size, the Russian diaspora communities in Kyrgyzstan and Latvia are very similar: 917,000 and 906,000, respectively, in 1989. In 1992 the Kyrgyzstani president, Askar Akaev, declared: 'I make no little effort to hold [the Russians] back . . . They are educated people, and a proficient specialist requires years of training. The withdrawal of the Slavs can paralyse our economy.' See *Argumenty i fakty*, 1992, no. 45. Nonetheless, in the first six months of 1992, some 47,000 persons (all ethnic groups) left Kyrgyzstan. See *Slavianskie vesti (Bishkek)*, 1992, no. 16, p. 2. In contrast, 51,000 persons left Latvia during the entire year of 1992. See Dzintra Bungs, 'Recent Demographic Changes in Latvia', *RFE/RL Research Report*, II, 50 (17 December 1993), pp.44–50.

post-Soviet states, therefore, seem to corroborate the thesis that deliberate governmental attempts to bring about ethnic mixing or de-mixing, short of such resolute measures as expulsion and the closing of borders, play a relatively limited role in the channelling of actual migratory currents.

4

RUSSIANS IN THE UNION REPUBLICS: DOMINANT NATION OR UNDERPRIVILEGED MINORITY?

Was the Russian diaspora a privileged group in the Soviet period? Most observers would answer 'yes'. Rogers Brubaker is very explicit on this point:

> Under the Soviet regime, Russians in the peripheral republics enjoyed distinct privileges and advantages. These included Russian-language schools, newspapers, and other cultural facilities and access to desirable jobs throughout the Soviet Union without having to learn the local language – institutionalized cultural support that was unavailable for other nationalities living outside their own republics. They also included less tangible advantages such as the security of belonging to the Soviet Union's dominant, state-bearing nationality.[1]

This statement succinctly sums up the almost unanimous conclusion of Western scholarship. Some Russian émigré scholars, however, have presented an alternative view. For instance, in his major study *Nomenklatura*, Mikhail Voslenskii maintained that there were no privileged groups in the Soviet Union apart from the *nomenklatura*. Recruited from various social and ethnic segments of the population, the members of this group cut their ties with their original milieux when they climbed into the political élite. The *nomenklatura* élite were therefore not so much supra-social or supra-ethnic as a de-socialised and de-nationalised.

In Voslenskii's view, the Union republics were 'semi-colonies' of the *nomenklatura*. On one crucial point they differed from traditional colonies of imperial nations, in that the dominant nation in the metropolis enjoyed no privileges in the dominions:

> The Russian inhabitants of the non-Russian republics do not enjoy any privileges. They are a national minority on which the other groups frequently vent the enmity they are feeling against the *nomenklatura* lords

---

1. Rogers Brubaker, 'L'éclatement des peuples à la chute des empires: approche historique et comparative', *Actes de la recherche en sciences sociales*, XCVIII (June 1993), p. 14.

in Moscow. True, the Russians are not directly persecuted ... but their situation is not enviable. They are no 'race of lords' but dependent people, with less possibilities than the indigenous population has.[2]

Most spokesmen of the Russian diaspora itself would dispute the proposition that they have represented a privileged group. Moreover, even some experts on the Russian diaspora who are themselves members of the titular ethnic groups of the Soviet successor states find this description to be less than accurate.[3]

In order to arrive at a meaningful answer to our question, it seems that the very concept of 'privileges' must be clarified. First, do we mean by that term some kind of formalised prerogatives, or simply better chances for advancement accruing from the social composition of this group? And secondly, 'better' than whose chances? At least three different axes of comparison are possible: (*a*) better than the Russian core group (that is, better than if they had stayed 'at home' in the RSFSR), (*b*) better than the indigenous populations as found in their republics of residence, or (*c*) better than other diaspora groups, such as Ukrainians living outside Ukraine. And finally, 'better' in what way? In political power? Material wealth? Social prestige? Means of cultural expression?

Moreover, there is no reason to assume *a priori* that the status of the Russian diaspora has been constant and uniform over time. We know that Stalin's nationality policy differed significantly from Lenin's, and again from that of Khrushchev and Brezhnev. It is only natural to expect that these differences affected the status of Russians living in the non-Russian republics. The vacillations of Soviet nationality policy and their effect on the Russian diaspora are explored below.

The period of korenizatsiia

Lenin hardly ever revealed a proclivity for Great Russian chauvinism, something which even his most virulent detractors will grant him.[4]

2. Mikhail Voslenskii, *Nomenklatura. Gospodstvuiushchii klass Sovetskogo Soiuza*, London, 1984, pp. 389ff.
3. Statement by, e.g., Ilga Apine, Latvian Academy of Sciences, Institute of Sociology and Philosophy, at the conference 'The New Russian Diaspora', Lielupe, Latvia, 13–15 November 1992.
4. Robert Conquest, *Lenin*, Glasgow, 1972/9, p. 14: Lenin was 'totally lacking in racial chauvinism'. See also Hugh Seton-Watson, 'Russian nationalism in an historical perspective' in Robert Conquest (ed.), *The Last Empire*, Stanford, 1986.

He apparently had a sincere conviction that national consciousness was a vestige from the past which should be eradicated, and the sooner the better. In addition, he was anxious that the new Soviet state should make as clean a break as possible with the tsarist past. Therefore, he attacked the national traditions and institutions associated with tsarism with special vehemence. These were primarily the institutions of the Russian people, such as Russian Orthodoxy. Moreover, Lenin advocated a theory that the nationalism of smaller peoples is always a defence mechanism against the great power chauvinism of the dominant nation. This analysis made it reasonable to assail Russian nationalism first.

In many non-Russian areas, the Communist regime relied almost exclusively on the support of the local Russians. Soon after their *coup d'état*, the Bolsheviks were confronted with a series of territorial breakaways in the provinces. Many of the new national regimes were of socialist and even Marxist orientation, but they would have nothing to do with the Russian Bolsheviks. They suspected, with good reason, that the new masters in Moscow would try to coerce them back into the fold. While the Bolsheviks had solemnly proclaimed the right of secession from the Russian state, they completely ignored this pledge in their practical politics, and by the early 1920s most of the tsars' land had been reassembled under their tutelage. In an innovative reinterpretation of the right-to-secession principle, Stalin later explained that the nations' right to self-determination was subordinate to the right of the working class to strengthen its power. 'The right of self-determination neither can nor must prevent the working class from realising its dictatorship.'[5] In many non-Russian provinces the proletariat was dominated by ethnic Russians who indeed supported the idea of a unitary state. Thus, the proletarian argument worked in favour of the centralistic principle. In any case, the Party reserved for itself the privilege of being the sole interpreter of the will of the proletariat.

However, Lenin understood that in the long run it was impossible to build Soviet power in the borderland on the support of the local Russians only. In order to secure the survival of the revolution and of the state, it was essential to woo the allegiance of the indigenous groups as well. This was done in various ways. The development of local languages and the education of the non-Russians was assiduously encouraged. This policy represented a sharp departure from the tsarist

5. Stalin, *Sochineniia*, V, Moscow, 1950, p. 265.

regime's indifference to the cultural advancement of the *inorodtsy*. In addition, representatives of the local élites were co-opted into the leadership of the republics, of the party and of the country. Taken together, these measures added up to the policy of *korenizatsiia* or 'indigenisation', of making Communism take root in the non-Russian areas. This policy was clearly detrimental to the local Russians. They felt that they had 'fought Lenin's revolution for him' in the provinces, often against organisations and military formations representing the native groups, and were now denied the enjoyment of its fruits.

A Communist writer acquainted with the Soviet Muslim regions explained:

> Not only the officialdom in the borderlands, which consists largely of officials of the old regime, but also the proletariat inhabiting those areas which actively support the revolution, consists in its majority of persons of Russian nationality. In Turkestan, for example, Russian workers thought that once the dictatorship of the proletariat had been established, it should work only for *their* benefit, as workers, and that they could fully ignore the interests of the backward agricultural and nomadic population, which had not yet reached their 'proletarian' level of consciousness.[6]

These expectations were thoroughly disappointed. In the 1920s, Russians living in the non-Russian areas were clearly among the losers by the nationality policy of the party. In the constitutions of some Union republics – namely Armenia and Georgia – the language of the titular nationality was enshrined as a 'state language'.[7] In all non-Russian areas strong pressure was put on the local Russians to learn the native language, and officials were required to do so. To facilitate communication between the various language groups in the republics, some of them had to be bilingual. Under *korenizatsiia* this was no longer expected of the non-Russians; it now had to be the Russians.[8]

In Kazakhstan, a massive allocation of land to the indigenous ethnic

6. Quoted in Richard Pipes, *The Formation of the Soviet Union: Communism and Nationalism, 1917–1923*, Cambridge MA, 1954, p. 271.
7. S. I. Iakubovskaia, *Razvitie SSSR kak soiuznogo gosudarstva*, Moscow, 1972, p. 49. Lenin repeatedly declared that he did not take to the idea of state languages, and the Soviet Union never had one. See V. I. Lenin, 'Nuzhen li ob"iazatel'nyi gosudarstvennyi iazyk?', *Polnoe sobranie sochineniia*, XXIV, Moscow, 1961 (5th edition).
8. Isabelle Kreindler, 'The Changing Status of Russian in the Soviet Union', Hebrew University of Jerusalem, Research Paper no. 37, November 1979, p. 3.

group was pursued in the early 1920s in order to reverse the effects of Russian colonisation in the late nineteenth century. Thousands of Russians and Ukrainian settlers were driven from their farms. For ten years, the region was practically closed to immigration. This was part of a larger policy of 'Kazakhstan for the Kazakhs' carried out by the Kazakh leadership. Furthermore, in some other republics, such as Ukraine and Georgia, the local Bolshevik leaders were bent on de-russifying their national territories as much as possible, not only culturally but also demographically.[9]

Some of the strangest manifestations of the indigenisation policy were apparently to be found in Belorussia. In this republic, which later required a reputation as the most docile and russified of the national homelands, a free-wheeling spree of 'Belorussification' reigned for a couple of years after 1918. In the vivid language of Nicholas Vakar:

> Belorussian nationality was declared predominant, and Belorussian the official language. Russian was banned from schools, courts, and offices – even from homes . . . The people were ordered to bring their dialects into line with the national standard, though it was itself still in the making. People who spoke in the mixed idiom were denounced as 'Muscovites' and deprived of rights. Although the Russians became the least considered minority in the state, Moscow remained undisturbed.[10]

Vakar even claims that some nationalist teachers were killed by peasants who wanted instruction for their children in Russian instead. Possibly, parts of Vakar's dramatic account must be taken with a pinch of salt.[11] In any case, the Belorussian nationalists were soon brought to order, and the language stipulations of the first Belorussian constitution of 1923 were the most liberal in the Soviet Union. No less than four languages were declared official: Belorussian, Polish, Yiddish and Russian.[12]

9. Gerhard Simon, *Nationalism and Policy Towards the Nationalities in the Soviet Union*, Boulder, CO, 1986/91, pp. 78–81. See also A. P. Kuchkin, 'Zemel'naia reforma v Kazakhstane v 1925–1927 godakh', *Voprosy istorii*, no. 9, 1954, pp. 25–34.

10. Nicholas P. Vakar, *Belorussia: the Making of a Nation*, Cambridge, MA, 1956, p. 139.

11. Another expert on Belorussia claims that Vakar's writings are interspersed with factual errors, and present a very personal view contested by recent evidence and other scholars. See Jan Zaprudnik, 'Belorussia and the Belorussians', in Zev Katz *et al.* (eds), *Handbook of Major Soviet Nationalities*, New York, 1975, p. 66. Unfortunately Zaprudnik does not say which errors he has found.

12. Iakubovskaia, *op cit.*, p. 49.

Russians in the periphery who tried to behave like masters in the old way were called to account. Expressions of 'Great Russian chauvinism' were roundly denounced in the central Soviet press. For instance, it was discovered that native workers at the construction sites of the Turkestan-Siberian railway were paid less for the same work than Russian workers. The management claimed that this was because of the lower quality of the work they performed, but this claim was not accepted in Moscow. In the oil fields and sulphur mines in Uzbekistan, it was disclosed that only a fraction of the managers knew the local language, and yet three out of every four workers were Uzbeks. Even worse, the factory-owned store sold goods to the Russians first, and only then to the natives. Russian workers also received apartments ahead of the non-Russians.[13]

It is difficult to ascertain how widespread such practices were. While many serious cases may have gone unreported, the fact that the press regularly exposed them in blistering reports probably served as a strong deterrent to potential perpetrators of ethnic discrimination. In several instances, the culprits were not only pilloried in the press but also taken to court. Some defendants received rather lenient sentences, but far from all. In 1930, a supervisor on the Turkestan-Siberian railway was sentenced to five years' imprisonment for giving Russian workers preferential treatment. In an exceptional case, even the death penalty was applied.[14]

Thus, in the 1920s it is difficult indeed to talk of any formalised, state-sanctioned privileges in connection with the Russian diaspora. The blame for any conflicts between Russians and other ethnic groups was laid squarely on the shoulders of the Russians. The theses on the nationality question adopted by the 10th Party Congress in 1921 stated that 'Great Russian communists working for the party in the borderlands frequently underestimate the significance of national peculiarities. They have grown up at a time when they belonged to a "dominant" nation, and have never experienced national suppression.'[15]

A party resolution at the 12th Party Congress in 1923 was harsher still:

13. Simon, *op. cit.*, pp. 75ff.
14. *ibid.*, p. 77.
15. *Kommunisticheskaia partiia Sovetskogo soiuza v rezoliutsiiakh i resheniiakh*, I, Moscow, 1954 (7th edition), p. 562.

In a number of national republics (Ukraine, Belorussia, Azerbaijan, Turkestan) the situation is very complicated due to the fact that a significant part of the working class – the main supporters of the Soviet power – belongs to the Great Russian nationality. In these regions the rapprochement (*smychka*) between town and country, between the working class and the peasantry, is encountering strong resistance in the form of vestiges of Great Russian chauvinism in the organs of the party as well as of the Soviets. Under these circumstances any talk about the advantages of Russian culture and the thesis that the more developed Russian culture will prevail over the cultures of the more backward peoples (the Ukrainians, the Azerbaijanis, the Uzbeks, the Kirgizians *et al.*), is nothing but an attempt to secure the supremacy of the Great Russian nation. Therefore, a resolute struggle against the vestiges of Great Russian chauvinism is the first and immediate task of our party.[16]

One of the most important features of Soviet nationality policy in the 1920s was the establishment of a federal state along ethnic lines.[17] As a consequence of this arrangement, it became possible for the first time to talk of the Russians outside the Russian heartland as a 'diaspora' group in a formal sense. The degree to which this new status was reflected in mental attitudes among the diasporians themselves is hard to gauge. Obviously it varied from area to area and from individual to individual.

The Union of Socialist Soviet Republics (USSR) was established only in 1922, but the Russian Socialist Federal Soviet Republics (RSFSR) had already been proclaimed (as a significantly smaller state than the Russian empire) in 1918. The external borders of the RSFSR were based on the ethnic principle only in a limited way. In some cases considerations of both political expediency and various military realities during the civil war played a more important role than ethnicity when the borders were drawn. Sometimes they were negotiated at peace conferences, while at other times they were first unilaterally proclaimed by the Bolsheviks and then secured by military means.

The borders with Estonia and Latvia were fixed as late as the peace conferences of Tartu (Iur'ev) and Riga in 1920. Certain border areas

---

16. *ibid.*, I, p. 713.
17. Also under the tsars, certain areas, such as Finland, Bukhara, Khiva and, for a time, Poland, had enjoyed a special status of various kinds, but this certainly did not amount to a general federalisation of the state. In the late nineteenth century such arrangements were increasingly regarded by Russian officials as intolerable anomalies to be obliterated.

with a strong Russian majority, notably the right bank of the Narva river with the town of Ivangorod (Jaanilinn) and most of the Petseri district in the south-east, were included within Estonia. In a similar way the ethnically Russian area of Pytalovo (Abrene) in turn now became part of Latvia. Of the approximately 300,000-strong Russian community resident in these two Baltic states during the inter-war years, 110,000 were living in these areas.[18] One reason for this arrangement was that the Bolshevik negotiators were in a hurry to secure a peace treaty with the Balts in order to concentrate the military might of the Red Army against the advancing Volunteer Army in the Ukraine. They also believed that the world revolution was imminent, and that this would make all border arrangements meaningless.[19] The world revolution did not materialise, however, and when the Soviets got a chance to dictate new arrangements after the incorporation of the Baltic states into the Soviet Union in 1940, these three areas were transferred in 1945 to the RSFSR.

Roman Szporluk has pointed out that all of the ephemeral Ukrainian state constructions which came into existence after the fall of the tsar were much smaller than present-day Ukraine. The authority of the Central Rada regime did not extend to the Donbas or to such cities as Odessa and Kherson. 'It was not obvious even to the nationally-conscious Ukrainians, let alone others, what exactly should be considered as Ukrainian territory.'[20] Oral communication from members of the Russian diaspora has suggested that when the Bolsheviks decided to join the mixed Russian-Ukrainian mining region of Donbas to the Ukraine SSR, this was done primarily for political reasons. Donbas could sport a genuine working class, and in contrast to western and central Ukraine, the Bolsheviks expected that they might be able to garner a substantial following there. It was hope that if Donbas were

18. S. I. Bruk and V. M. Kabuzan, 'Dinamika chislennosti i rasseleniia russkikh posle Velikoi Oktiabrskoi sotsialisticheskoi revoliutsii', *Sovetskaia etnografiia*, LVI, 5 (September–October 1982), p. 5. For somewhat different figures, see Tönu Parming, 'Population Changes in Estonia, 1935–1970', *Population Studies*, XXVI (March 1972) p. 56.

19. Oleg Sidelnikov, 'On the Separated Territories and the Russian Community in Estonia', *Survey of Baltic and Post-Soviet Politics*, Sakala Centre, Tallinn, January 1992, pp. 3–5. See also *Komsomol'skaia Pravda*, 18 March 1992.

20. Roman Szporluk, 'Russians in Ukraine and Problems of Ukrainian Identity in the USSR', in Peter J. Potichnyj (ed.), *Ukraine in the Seventies*, Oakville, 1974, p. 198.

made a part of a Ukrainian state, it would become unnecessary to export the Communist revolution to this republic 'on the bayonets'.[21] However, there could be a simpler explanation that Donbas was included in Ukraine because, despite its cultural heterogeneity, it nevertheless had an ethnically Ukrainian majority.

The Soviet Union was structured as a hierarchal federation with four levels of autonomous units: Union republics, autonomous republics, autonomous districts (*oblasts*) and national *okrugs*. In the first years of Soviet power, several border transfers were arranged among these units.[22] Some of them affected the structure of the RSFSR, and led to corresponding increases or decreases in the size of the Russian diaspora. In particular, the border between Russia and Belorussia was redrawn twice, in 1924 and 1926, each time transferring large tracts of land, including the cities of Vitebsk and Gomel, to Belorussia. A later Soviet commentary explained that this transfer was 'very important for the development of the economy of the Belorussian SSR and also raised the relative weight of the working class in the population of that republic'.[23] The transfer significantly raised the numbers involved in the Russian diaspora but apparently reduced the Belorussian diaspora even more. The Ukrainian politician Mykola Skrypnik tried to effect a similar border regulation between the RSFSR and Ukraine in those areas with a Ukrainian majority, but was rebuffed by Stalin.[24]

While there were obviously several factors that had an influence on border delineations, it nonetheless seems that in most cases consideration of the ethnic distribution of the population was a strong guiding principle. Lee Schwartz has demonstrated that in the autonomous republics and autonomous districts very few *raions* would have to be transferred to a neighbouring ethnic unit to achieve an 'optimal' correspondence between administrative and ethnic borders.[25] In his view, the fact that

21. Author's interview with Dmitrii Kolupaev in Simferopol, 20 September 1992. This information has not been confirmed by independent sources.
22. For an overview of some of them, see *Komsomol'skaia Pravda*, 8 October 1991; Julian Birch, 'Border Disputes and Disputed Borders in the Soviet Federal System', *Nationalities Papers*, XV, 1 (Spring 1987), pp. 43–70.
23. Iakubovskaia, *op. cit.*, p. 82.
24. Bohdan Nahaylo and Victor Swoboda, *Soviet Disunion: a History of the Nationalities Problem in the USSR*, London, 1990, p. 64.
25. Lee Schwartz, 'Regional Population Redistribution and National Homelands in the USSR', in Henry R. Huttenbach (ed.), *Soviet Nationality Policies: Ruling Ethnic Groups in the USSR*, London, 1990, pp. 121–61.

the titular nation in many of these units accounted for no more than 50%–70% of the total population was not a result of deliberate gerrymandering, as some researches have claimed[26] but rather should be seen as an inevitable consequence of the extreme complexities of the ethnic map. The Soviet nationalities lived (and still live) in such close relationships with each other that any attempt to create ethnic homelands was bound also to create large diaspora groups.

Below the four levels of the hierarchal federation, Soviet authorities in the 1920s experimented with an even more finely meshed net of ethnic units: national *raions* and national village soviets. Most of these units were established for ethnic groups living outside their core area – that is, for diasporas. These arrangements also included Russians outside the RSFSR. In the resolution on the nationalities question passed at the 10th Party Congress in 1921, it was stated that those national groups that lived interspersed within a compact settlement of another, larger group should be guaranteed the right to free development. Such groups, in Soviet parlance, were termed 'national minorities'. Thus, under the terms of the *korenizatsia* policy, large parts of the Russian diaspora were officially designated a 'national minority'.

In 1925, there were 343 national village soviets in the Ukraine alone, of which sixty-nine were Russian. Two years later, the latter number had risen to 292.[27] Similarly, of the ninety-three national village soviets in Belorussia in 1934, fifteen were Russian. Altogether, in the mid-1930s, there were no less than 5,300 national village soviets nationwide.[28] In addition, 250 *raions* (about 10% of the total) were designated as 'national'. Finally, in 1930, there were twenty-eight national *raions* in Ukraine, of which nine were Russian (the others were German, Bulgarian, Greek, Jewish and Polish).

Very little information about these national formations at the lowest levels has come down to us. As the historian of Soviet nationalities policy under Stalin, Gerhard Simon, points out, this is probably due to Stalin's dislike for this liberal arrangement, and indeed when these formations were abolished in the late 1930s, he tried to eradicate every last trace of them. One thing, however, is clear about these formations: they did not function as national ghettos in which only members of one

---

26. Concerning claims to that effect, see e.g. Walker Connor, *The National Question in Marxist–Leninist Theory and Strategy*, Princeton, 1984, pp. 302ff.
27. Iakubovskaia, *op cit.*, pp. 92ff.
28. Simon, *op cit.*, p. 58.

nationality were allowed to live. Rather, the designation 'national' primarily affected the language of administration and education. The Soviet historian S. I. Iakubovskaia claims that in all national villages the language of the titular group was used in official correspondence (*deloproizvodstvo*). However, Simon believes that not even this was always the case. 'Calling these village soviets national was often more name and claim than reality,' he maintains.[29]

In any case, the system of village soviets for national minorities affected rural dwellers only and not the urban population, and it was the latter to which the great majority of the Russian diaspora belonged. Official policy did not provide any special protection for this second group. On the contrary, they were expected to undergo a process of cultural marginalisation. During the 1921 Party Congress which decided to establish national *raions*, Joseph Stalin claimed: 'Obviously, even if Russian elements still dominate in Ukrainian cities, in the course of time these cities will inevitably be Ukrainianised.'[30] To substantiate this prognosis, he pointed to the ethnic transformation of Riga, which in the 1880s had been a German city but with the influx of Latvians from the countryside had been culturally Latvianised.

And certain evidence seems to show that this prognosis was to a certain extent borne out: the urban Russian population in some non-Russian republics was indeed subject to a certain process of assimilation. In 1932–3, only 4.8% of the children in Ukraine attended Russian-language schools, although Russians at that time made up 9.2% of the total population.[31] Consequently, more than half of the Russian school graduates in that republic were better trained in the language of the titular group than they were in their mother tongue.

The period of the 'Big Brother'

Despite this evidence, however, Stalin's prognosis turned out to be spectacularly wrong: the cities which he had expected to become Belorussian and Ukrainian in their culture and ethnic composition ended up regaining, in the late 1930s, their pre-revolutionary Russian

29. *ibid.*, p. 60.
30. I. V. Stalin, *Sochineniia*, V, Moscow, 1947, p. 49.
31. Simon, *op. cit.*, p. 51.

appearance.[32] This, of course, is to be explained not only by Stalin's lack of prescience but even more by the policies he pursued.

The drastic turnabout in Soviet nationality policy did set in with the death of Lenin in 1924, nor did it follow from Stalin's victory over his rivals in the Politburo, and the introduction of shock modernisation measures five years later. During the first years of Stalin's one-man rule, the policy of *korenizatsia* was continued more or less unaltered. Gerhard Simon is unequivocal that 'until about 1933, the official Party line called for repression of the Russian language, Russian cadres, and Russian culture.'[33] Only at that juncture did a radically new policy crystallise, and it was left to the non-Russians themselves to signal the change. In November 1933 the Ukrainian Central Committee declared that while Great Russian chauvinism was still a menace, the major threat now came from the bourgeois nationalism of the non-Russians. Leaders of other republics soon followed suit.[34]

Certain elements in the new policy, or rather in the preconditions for it, had been put in place earlier. One of them was the new cadre policy associated with 'the Lenin levy' (*leninskii prizyv*) introduced just after Lenin's death. Ostensibly intended to strengthen workers' share in party membership, it also had several other effects, some probably intentional while others may have been incidental. Since Russians were now clearly overrepresented among industrial workers in the peripheral republics, it was clear that the new recruitment policy, among other things, had the effect of russifying the party.

At the same time the shock industrialisation measures implemented as part of the first two five-year plans led to a new upsurge of Russian migration to the outlying regions. The Russian communities in the national republics were greatly reinforced, and their new quantitative strength was also reflected in enhanced political power. The number of Russians (and to some extent of other Slavs) in leadership positions rose rapidly. This was not necessarily a result of ethnic discrimination, because in a system of free and uninhibited competition these Russians would naturally come to occupy many of the more prestigious jobs by dint of their better-than-average education.[35]

32. Roman Szporluk, 'Nationalities and the Russian Problem in the USSR: an Historical Outline', *Journal of International Affairs*, XXVII, 1 (1973), pp. 22–40, esp. p. 30.
33. Simon, *op. cit.*, p. 6.
34. *ibid.*, p. 84.
35. Michael Rywkin, 'Central Asia and the Price of Sovietization', *Problems of Communism*, XIII (January–February 1964), pp. 7–15, on p. 10.

Gerhard Simon thinks that the numerical strengthening of the Russian diaspora was not necessarily an intended objective of the shock industrialisation process but more likely a chance effect of it. Nevertheless, Simon believes, this development fitted well into Stalin's overall strategy both for the transformation of the country and for the consolidation of his personal power. The new waves of Russian migrants had a vested interest in his 'second revolution':

> Stalin interpreted the increasing number of Russians in the national territories as a factor contributing to political stability. A newly arrived Russian upper class secured Soviet dominance. This new upper class had the violent social upheavals of the 1930s to thank for its position and this class contributed to supressing the unfulfillable aspirations and illusions of the non-Russian elites.[36]

Wherever the Russians moved in, Russian-language schools were opened and Russian-language newspapers and other facilities were established to cater for their cultural needs. This set the Russians apart from other migrant groups, who were offered nothing of a similar kind. With few exceptions they had to choose between Russian schools and schools giving education in the language of the titular nation. In most cases they chose the former. In that way they underwent a process of linguistic russification, and thus contributed to a further strengthening of the Russian cultural imprint upon the non-Russian cities.

As Table 4.1A shows, the diasporas of almost all major Soviet nationalities except the Russians were becoming somewhat less familiar with their native language with each successive census. (However, the non-Europeans clung to their titular language with remarkable resilience). The linguistic russification of diasporas affected primarily the other Slavs, the Ukrainians and the Belorussians.[37] For these nationalities a certain linguistic russification also took place among the core groups (see Table 4.1B).

This was to some degree an effect of the cultural influence of the Russian diaspora communities. To be sure, the marked differences between the linguistic situation in, for instance, Ukraine and Kazakhstan must be seen against the background of the important cultural differences between the European and Asian parts of the Soviet

36. Simon, *op. cit.*, p. 119.
37. The figures for the Balts were also very low, but in absolute numbers the diasporas of these groups were insignificant.

Table 4.1. MAJOR SOVIET NATIONALITIES CLAIMING THEIR
NATIONAL LANGUAGE AS MOTHER TONGUE (%)

A. LIVING OUTSIDE THEIR TITULAR AREA

	1959	1970	1979
Russians	99.3	99.2	99.9
Uzbeks	97.4	97.4	96.9
Tajiks	94.6	95.6	92.8
Kazakhs	95.6	95.0	92.8
Azerbaijanis	95.1	95.8	92.7
Turkmens	92.0	93.5	90.4
Kyrgyzians	92.3	91.6	84.8
Moldovans	77.7	79.1	74.3
Armenians	78.1	78.0	73.9
Georgians	73.4	71.5	67.3
Lithuanians	80.3	71.8	63.9
Latvians	53.2	51.1	55.3
Ukrainians	51.2	48.4	43.8
Belorussians	41.9	40.9	36.8
Estonians	56.6	53.5	33.3

B. LIVING INSIDE THEIR TITULAR AREA

Russians	100.0	100.0	100.0
Uzbeks	98.6	98.9	98.8
Tajiks	99.3	99.4	99.3
Kazakhs	99.2	98.9	98.6
Azerbaijanis	98.1	98.9	98.7
Turkmens	99.5	99.3	99.2
Kyrgyzians	99.7	99.7	99.6
Moldovans	98.2	97.7	96.5
Armenians	99.2	99.8	99.4
Georgians	99.5	99.4	99.4
Estonians	99.3	99.2	99.0
Lithuanians	99.2	99.5	97.9
Latvians	98.4	98.1	97.8
Ukrainians	93.5	91.4	89.1
Belorussians	93.2	90.1	83.5

Source: V. I. Kozlov, *Natsional'nosti SSSR*, Moscow, 1982, pp. 240–1. Figures for earlier years are not available.

population. Nevertheless, Ronald Wixman has demonstrated that *within* the various non-Russian republics, there was a strong correspondence between demographic russianisation (as reflected in the percentage of the total population in the various *oblasts* accounted for by ethnic Russians), and the linguistic russification of the titular nationality.[38]

A decree of March 1938 made Russian a compulsory subject in all schools throughout the Soviet Union.[39] This decree did not directly affect the Russian diaspora since they were already studying in Russian. Nonetheless, it made life easier for them. The necessity of learning the local language was at a stroke greatly diminished. Still, all inhabitants in the national republics, including Russians and other diaspora groups, were required to study the language of the titular ethnic group as a second language. The degree to which this requirement was enforced varied considerably.

The preferential treatment of the Russian language in the non-Russian republics was obviously not based on the principle that the largest non-titular group was entitled to special cultural facilities. If that was so, Ukrainian, Armenian, Azeri and Uzbek, the languages of the largest diaspora groups, should have been singled out for special treatment in Moldova, Georgia, Armenia and Tajikistan respectively. While some native-language schools and other cultural facilities for such groups were functioning at certain places and certain times, they could in no way be compared to the corresponding conditions created for the Russians. However, there is reason to believe that the special position of the Russian language was maintained in all republics not primarily in deference to the local Russians but more because it was the language of communication with the centre. By the same token, it also became the language of inter-ethnic communication in the republics.

Thus during the 1930s the Russian diaspora, as a result of several circumstances not necessarily linked to ethnic policies, undoubtedly received distinct cultural privileges compared to other diaspora groups. These privileges functioned as a magnet to other Russians and contributed to their continued emigration from the RSFSR. In general, the diaspora Russians scored high by most criteria of achievement, including professional advancement, living standards and education

38. Ronald Wixman, 'Territorial Russification and Linguistic Russianization in Some Soviet Republics', *Soviet Geography*, XXII, 10 (December 1981), pp. 667–75.
39. Isabelle Kreindler, *op. cit.*, p. 7.

higher than the Russians of the RSFSR and generally higher too than the indigenous population in the republic where they lived. This achievement, however, did not necessarily result from preferential treatment, formalised or informal. It could also reflect the fact that those Russians who were drawn into the vortex of migration usually belonged to the most ambitious and mobilised sections of the population. The same was true of the diaspora groups of other nationalities.[40] However, this description did not fit the Russian diaspora everywhere; in the Baltic states a larger-than-average percentage of the Russians were blue-collar workers and the Russian industrial worker generally remained by his lathe, and did not advance far up the social ladder.

In the immediate aftermath of the Second World War, the Russian nation was elevated to the status of 'elder brother' among the Soviet nationalities. The new party line was ushered in by Stalin's toast to the great Russian people at the victory celebration in May 1945.[41] Soon the non-Russian press overflowed with obsequious praise for the generous succour provided by the Russians for their junior brethren. In practice, this often meant that those Russians who were not so benevolent towards members of other ethnic groups could browbeat them with greater impunity than before.

Stalin's death in 1953 brought no immediate changes to the Russians in the non-Russian republics. True, Khrushchev tried to co-opt the Ukrainians as a 'second elder brother', and as a pledge of goodwill towards them transferred the Crimean peninsula from the jurisdiction of the RSFSR to that of the Ukrainian republic, although the majority of the population there was Russian.[42] By that act, the Russian diaspora was enlarged in one stroke by several hundred thousand. However, this political artifice spelt no changes for the people living

40. Robert A. Lewis, Richard H. Rowland and Ralph S. Clem, *Nationality and Population Change in Russia and the USSR*, New York, 1976; Yaroslav Bilinsky, 'Assimilation and Ethnic Assertiveness Among Ukrainians of the Soviet Union', in Erich Goldhagen (ed.), *Ethnic Minorities in the Soviet Union*, New York, 1968, pp. 152ff. Bilinsky somewhat conspiratorially conjectures that the large emigration of educated Ukrainians from the Ukrainian SSR might reflect a deliberate Soviet policy of syphoning the potential Ukrainian élite off from their native environment.

41. *Pravda*, 25 May 1945.

42 Frederick C. Barghoorn, *Soviet Russian Nationalism*, New York, 1956, pp. 56ff.

there except that they were now in principle required to study Ukrainian as a second language. Soon that requirement too was dropped.

In 1958 a major school reform was launched in the Soviet Union. While this reform touched upon a number of pedagogical issues, it was the proposed changes in the required language training in the non-Russian territories that were the most controversial. The law stipulated that in Russian schools in the non-Russians areas, the study of the republican language should be made optional. Likewise, it was proposed that pupils in the native-language schools in the Union republics and in the autonomous republics within the RSFSR should be free to drop the study of Russian if they wished. The reform was explained as being a necessary step towards giving equal opportunities to all pupils. Under the existing system, pupils in the non-Russian republics – Russians and non-Russians alike – were all studying one language more than were their coevals in the RSFSR. This gave them less time for other subjects, and it was argued that this put them at a disadvantage in the competition for access to institutions of higher learning.

Theoretically, the new system would affect Russian-speakers and the native language-speakers in the republic equally, but in practice the non-Russians could ill afford to drop the Russian course: non-Russian school graduates with top grades but with no knowledge of Russian would risk being written off as obtuse country bumpkins, and the highroad to advancement in society would be closed to them. To the Russians in the non-Russian republics, on the other hand, insufficient knowledge of the language of the titular group would be a less serious drawback.

The proposed changes in the curriculum sparked an unusually frank and open debate, in which representatives of numerous non-Russian groups expressed serious misgivings with the 1958 reform.[43] However, most of them were bullied into line, and soon all the republics except two had the new principles incorporated into their respective school laws. The two exceptions were Azerbaijan and Latvia, and in these republics purges of the political leadership were carried out soon afterwards. Most observers see these purges as a punishment for recalcitrance on the school issue.

The school reform had momentous consequences for the Russian

43. See Yaroslav Bilinsky, 'Soviet Educational Laws of 1985–9 and Soviet Nationality Policy', *Soviet Studies*, XIV (1962–3), pp. 138–57.

diaspora. As expected, the overwhelming majority of this group dropped the study of the republican language. It is true that certain evidence suggests that in some republics – Belorussia, Ukraine, Latvia and maybe some others – the language of the titular group remained a mandatory subject in Russian schools into the 1970s and even the early 1980s.[44] But whether or not this was really so, it did not change the basic thrust of the reform. Never very keen on learning the local languages in the first place, most Russians in the diaspora now lost the incentive to do so altogether when the new signals from Moscow indicated that knowledge of it was an unnecessary burden carrying few benefits. The new school system certainly made life easier for them in many ways although in another perspective it could be argued that it was clearly detrimental to them. Without a knowledge of the local language, they were in effect cut off from a deeper understanding of the dominant culture of the milieu in which they lived.

As Jonathan Pool has remarked, bilingualism is almost always asymmetrical: the members of one language group learn the language of the other group, which serves as the *lingua franca*, while the other group remains more or less monolingual.[45] However, the degree of asymmetry varies among different countries. In Canada, for instance, only one language group, the French, knows two languages to any appreciable degree. However, even in this case the English-speaker who lives in a compactly (98%) French-speaking community still has only a 70%–80% likelihood of knowing French. However, for the Russian in the Soviet Union living in a compactly non-Russian community, the situation was radically different, and the likelihood was only 5%–10%.

There were significant regional differences. While the figures for Central Asian Russians were below 5%, and in Kazakhstan even less than 1%, in Ukraine, Armenia and Lithuania approximately a third of the Russians were registered as fluent in the language of the titular nationality (see Table 4.2). There are several factors to account for

44. Roman Szporluk, 'Russians in Ukraine and Problems of Ukrainian Identity in the USSR', in Peter J. Potichnyj (ed.), *Ukraine in the Seventies*, Oakville, 1974, p. 203; Zev Katz *et al.* (eds), *Handbook of Major Soviet Nationalities*, New York, 1975, p. 68; Anatol Lieven, *The Baltic Revolution: Estonia, Latvia, Lithuania and the Path to Independence*, New Haven, 1993, pp. 185ff.

45. Jonathan Pool, 'Soviet Language Planning: Goals, Results, Options' in Jeremy R. Azrael (ed.), *Soviet Nationality Policies and Practices*, New York, 1978, pp. 223–49.

Table 4.2. LANGUAGE PROFICIENCY OF
DIASPORA RUSSIANS, 1989

	Russians with fluency in titular language (× 1,000)	Russians claiming fluency in titular language (%)	Russians claiming titular language as native tongue (× 1,000)	% of population (all ethnic groups) without fluency in titular language
Estonia	71	14.9	6	32.6
Latvia	201	22.0	10	37.7
Lithuania	129	37.5	14	14.7
Belarus	358	27.3	30	22.4
Moldova	66	11.7	3	33
Ukraine	3,905	34.0	177	22
Georgia	81	23.0	4	22.8
Armenia	17	33.0	*	4.6
Azerbaijan	56	14.5	*	13.5
Turkmenistan	8	2.3	*	25.3
Tajikistan	13	3.3	*	33.4
Uzbekistan	76	4.6	*	24.6
Kyrgyzstan	11	1.2	*	46.4
Kazakhstan	53	0.8	*	59.8

Source: *Natsional'nyi sostav naseleniia SSSR*, Moscow, 1991.
* Less than 1,000.

these differences: the cultural and linguistic proximity between Russians and the non-Russian nationality, the size and the compactness of the Russian community, the history of the Russian settlement and, finally, the status of the local population in the eyes of the Russians.[46]

The conventional view that Russians and other russophones in the Asian Union republics were almost completely unlettered in the indigenous languages should possibly be modified. The Soviet census data involved here are based on the subjective evaluation of each respondent. Some of the respondents might have a tendency to overrate their language ability, while others would tend to underestimate their skills. Furthermore, the censuses only recorded the number of people

46. Aadne Aasland, 'Russians Outside Russia: the New Russian Diaspora' in Graham Smith (ed.), *The Nationalities Question in the Post-Soviet States*, London, 1994 (forthcoming).

who claimed to be fluent (*svobodno*) in the titular language in the various republics. The percentage of those with a less perfect command of the language was not given. Some sources indicate that quite a number of Russians in the republics understood the local language at a conversational (*bytovoi*) level.[47] One source claims that in Uzbekistan 50% of the Europeans have a conversational command of Uzbek.[48] This term probably covers a multitude of nuances, down to the ability to buy vegetables at the market place without an interpreter. Unfortunately, few detailed studies of lower-level language proficiencies in the Union republics are available.

Opposition to Khrushchev's nationality policy was mounting in several republics. Besides the school reform, these controversies included several other issues which had a direct bearing on the situation of the Russian diaspora. Latvian leaders were charged with ethnic favouritism in the republican cadre policy. Apparently, Russians and other non-titular groups were being bypassed at appointments and promotions. In addition, the Latvians were accused of having opposed the immigration of Slavs into Latvian industry. Migration to the republic had indeed slowed down considerably after Stalin's death, but it was now resumed.[49] At the same time too, Kazakhstan experienced a new massive influx of Russians and Ukrainians in connection with Khrushchev's grandiose campaign for cultivation of the 'virgin soil'. To solve the country's chronic food problem Khrushchev opted for extensive rather than intensive growth, and decided to put vast stretches of virgin and fallow land in western Siberia and northern Kazakhstan under the plough. This project was resisted by the Kazakh leadership, which quickly realised that it would lead to a marked change in the ethnic composition of their republic's population. However, national opposition was brushed aside: Khrushchev decided that the Kazakh first secretary was infected by the 'the virus of nationalism'.[50] He was removed – together with his deputy, also an

47. Tudor Danii and Zinaida Gontsa: 'Russkie v Moldove', *Vocea Poporului*, 20 October 1992 (Russian edition).
48. Aleksei Arapov and Iakov Umanskii, '"Russkii vopros" v kontekste mezhnatsional'nykh otnoshenii v Uzbekistane', *Svobodnaia Mysl'*, no. 14, 1992, pp. 29–38, on p. 33.
49. Rein Taagepera and Romuldas J. Misiunas, *The Baltic States: Years of Dependence 1940–1980*, London, 1983, pp. 134ff.
50. *Khrushchev Remembers: the Last Testament*, Boston, 1974, p. 121.

ethnic Kazakh. Both were replaced by ethnic Russians, one of whom was Leonid Brezhnev.

Despite his reputed liberalism and life experience from a major non-Russian republic, Khrushchev had no patience with the national aspirations of the non-Russians. True, some of his reforms such as the establishment of regional economic councils (*sovnarkhozy*) transferred more economic power to the republics, but in his political statements he pursued the aim of unitary state-building. The new party programme adopted at the 22nd Congress in 1961 contained several sentences indicating a deliberate policy of ethnic amalgamation. It was claimed that 'the borders between the republics in the USSR are losing ever more of their significance'.[51] The first secretary of the Uzbek party organisation, Sharaf Rashidov, was used as a mouthpiece for the new party line. At a Central Committee meeting he praised the fact that the population of his republic was becoming ever more mixed in its national composition.[52] With such signals emanating from Moscow, the Russians outside the RSFSR had ever less reason to see themselves as a diaspora in the political sense.

The period of 'Mature Socialism'

It can be argued that the replacement of Khrushchev by Brezhnev affected the Russian diaspora more than the change from Stalin to Khrushchev had done. Certainly, in many ways the Brezhnev era saw a tightening of centralistic efforts. However, in nationality policy an opposite tendency gradually emerged. While there was certainly no question of a return to Lenin's *korenizatsia* policy, the pendulum nonetheless moved somewhat away from the position of the 'big brother' syndrome. At the centre of Soviet politics the Slavs were still firmly in charge, but in the republics the titular nations could now increasingly influence political decisions, at least on certain issues. The fields of culture, education and cadre policy fell more and more under republican control while economic decisions, including those which influenced migration, were still largely made in Moscow.

This change may be interpreted in two different ways. On one side, it could be argued that, as a result of a gradual decomposition and

51. *Programma KPSS (proekt)*, Moscow, 1961, p. 113.
52. Robert Conquest, *Russia After Khrushchev*, New York, 1965, p. 212; See also *Problems of Communism*, XIII, 1 (January–February 1964), p. 5.

emasculation of the Union centre under the 'stagnation', republican leaders were able to usurp ever more power in their own republics. The central leadership no longer had the strength to keep the republics as tightly reined in as before. Or, alternatively, it could be argued that a deliberate decision was taken in the Kremlin to loosen these reins in order to foster an ethnic truce based on a tacit consociated arrangement. Several Western experts lean towards the latter interpretation. Victor Zaslavsky, for one, sees the nationality policy of Brezhnev as a deliberate and remarkably successful attempt to forestall the creation of a 'potentially explosive situation, in which educated members of an ethnic minority find their social mobility blocked by the majority group'.[53]

Of all Kremlin leaders, Brezhnev was the consensus builder *par excellence*. He secured his position less by crushing opposition to his rule than by co-opting it. One of his main slogans was 'cadre stability', and indeed personnel policy was the part of policy-making that he cared most about.[54] A fruitful approach to Soviet politics in the period of 'mature socialism', then, including the nationalities aspect, could start with a study of the cadre policy.

During Brezhnev's rule the Slavs not only held their numerical strength in the upper echelons of Soviet power but even increased it somewhat.[55] This 're-russianization' at the centre was to some extent compensated for by the development in the republics, where a slow and gradual but distinct *indigenisation* of the political élite took place. While the Slavs at the end of the Stalin era had made up three-quarters of the leadership in the Central Asian republics, by the 1970s this share had dropped to a quarter only. In Tajikistan the Russians filled 13% of the leadership positions in 1980, and in Kyrgyzstan 26%. This was only a few percentage points above their share of the total population, which indicated that an informal system of affirmative action in favour of the indigenous population was in operation. Under a system of equal opportunities, higher shares for the Russians would have been expected in these republics, as a result of the educational level and age composition of the various groups. The titular nations had a much

53. Victor Zaslavsky, 'Nationalism and Democratic Transition in Postcommunist Societies', *Dædalus*, CXXI, 2 (spring 1992), pp. 97–121, on p. 103.
54. Fëdor Burlatskii, 'Brezhnev i krushenie ottepeli', *Literaturnaia Gazeta*, 14 September 1988.
55. Simon, *op. cit.*, p. 274.

more youthful population than the Slavs, with larger cohorts below working age. Ellen Jones and Fred W. Grupp saw this trend as evidence of a long-term Soviet commitment to ethnic equalisation: 'In order to promote fuller minority representation certain posts were reserved for specific minorities or numerical quotas were set for selected ethnic groups.'[56]

This pattern was also reflected in the composition of the republican Party Central Committees, and of the membership of the republican parties at large. In Tajikistan and Azerbaijan, for instance, the titular nations in 1955–72 made up 78.8% and 86% of the republican Central Committee secretariats – well above their share of the total population. Significantly, this trend was not limited to the Muslim republics but extended also to the Baltic area. The Latvians were clearly overrepresented in the political organs of their republic. Their 91.7% share of the membership of the CC Secretariat stood in sharp contrast to their 57% share of the population. In Ukraine, the titular nation was allowed virtually to monopolise republican politics. Between 1955 and 1972, ethnic Ukrainians made up no less than 93% of the republican Bureau, and a staggering 100% of the CC Secretariat (see Table 4.3) Defining 'self-administration' as the representation of the titular nation in the administration of the republic in a degree proportionate to or greater than the native percentage of the population, Grey Hodnett found that only two republics, Moldavia and Belorussia, could not be described as self-administered.[57]

Brezhnev's cadre policy could be interpreted as a 'live and let live' policy. The non-Russians were given a free hand in their various homelands as long as they did not pry into his affairs in Moscow. They had to pay lip-service to the internationalist brotherhood of the Soviet peoples and crack down on explicitly anti-regime nationalism, but within these limits they were given considerable room for manoeuvre. While the republican borders in the Khrushchevite era were losing their significance, under Brezhnev they were clearly becoming more important.

By no means did this trend spell complete freedom for the non-Russians from central oversight. As a rule some sensitive posts, such as the head of the local KGB and the second secretary in charge of personnel (often considered the *éminence grise* of the republican élite),

---

56. Ellen Jones and Fred W. Grupp, 'Modernisation and Ethnic Equalisation in the USSR', *Soviet Studies*, XXXVI, 2 (April 1984), pp. 159–84, on p. 159.
57. Grey Hodnett, *Leadership in the Soviet National Republics*, Oakville, 1979, p. 104.

Table 4.3. NATIVE OCCUPANCY OF LEADING POSITIONS, BY NATIONAL REPUBLICS, 1955–72
(as % of all incumbents)

	Titular nation 1970	CC Secretariat	First Secretary	Organisational Secretary	Agricultural Secretary	Capital gorcom Secretary	Chairman of Trade Union	Komsomol First Secretary	KGB Chairman	Presidium Council of Ministers	Chairman, Council of Ministers
Estonia	68.2	79.2	100	75	0	100	100	100	50	94.4	100
Latvia	56.8	91.7	100	50	100	100	100	100	50	75.7	100
Lithuania	80.1	77.8	100	25	75	100	100	100	100	87.0	100
Belarus	81.0	76.5	67	100	25	60	67	60	0	72.2	100
Moldova	64.6	40.8	50	20	100	100	0	20	0	41.6	100
Ukraine	74.9	100	100	100	67	50	100	100	50	86.7	100
Georgia	66.8	86.7	100	40	100	100	100	100	100	100	100
Armenia	88.6	100	100	100	100	100	100	100	17	100	100
Azerbaijan	73.8	86.0	100	33	83	100	100	100	0	88.9	100
Turkmenistan	65.6	48.6	100	25	75	80	100	100	0	51.9	100
Tajikistan	56.2	78.8	100	60	80	80	75	100	0	50.0	100
Uzbekistan	65.5	59.3	100	0	75	100	100	100	0	82.2	100
Kyrgyzstan	43.8	43.5	100	50	25	50	100	100	25	41.6	100
Kazakhstan	32.6	29.5	33	0	40	100	67	67	25	48.8	100

Sources: Grey Hodnett, *Leadership in the Soviet National Republics*, Oakville, 1979, pp. 101–2; Gerhard Simon, *Nationalism and Policy Towards the Nationalities in the Soviet Union*, Boulder CO, 1991, pp. 381ff.

were still reserved for ethnic Slavs but the Russian diaspora only benefited directly from this arrangement to a very small degree. The great majority of these watchdogs were sent in from Moscow and not recruited among the local Russian group.[58] Seweryn Bialer found only a single exception to this rule: the second secretary of the Ukrainian Central Committee in the late 1970s, one I. Z. Sokolov, had been born and raised in the republic.[59]

To the Russian diaspora the Brezhnev system mostly meant a reduced political clout. John H. Miller has tentatively argued that local Russians were at a direct *disadvantage* regarding promotion to high office in their own areas. He saw this as evidence of Moscow's wariness of potential localism or lordliness on the part of the Russian settler communities. 'The resident Russian official must watch over their interests to be sure, but must not be the sort of person who might identify too easily with them. Hence a preference for officials from ethnic Great Russia.'[60]

Although in the 1970s the Russian diaspora contained a strong segment of highly skilled professionals, its intelligentsia consisted to a very large degree of engineers, technocrats and other white-collar workers concerned with material production. In the upper echelons of other professions, such as journalism and administration, the Russians were often more poorly represented than the titular group (see Table 4.4) John Miller thinks this began as a result of differences in education opportunities and then became in time an habitual pattern.[61]

The changed 'correlation of forces' (to use a typical Soviet expression) at the top of society had repercussions at the street level. The master–servant relationship was felt to be shifting in favour of the indigenous group. Basing her research on interviews with Soviet émigrés in the late 1970s, Rasma Karklins detected new perceptions of 'nationality power' in the republics. Her informants distinguished sharply between the titular nations and 'others' – the Russians and other Russian-speakers – where power relations were concerned. In the Central Asia region, the latter groups were regularly seen as the losers.

58. Hélène Carrère d'Encausse, *Decline of an Empire*, New York, 1979, p. 153.
59. Seweryn Bialer, *Stalin's Successors: Leadership, Stability, and Change in the Soviet Union*, Cambridge, MA, 1981, p. 217.
60. John H. Miller, 'Cadres Policy in Nationality Areas: Recruitment of CPSU First and Second Secretaries in the non-Russian Republics of the USSR', *Soviet Studies*, XXIX, 1 (January 1977), pp. 3–36, on p. 23.
61. *ibid.*

Table 4.4. PROFESSIONAL COMPOSITION OF RUSSIAN
INTELLIGENTSIA IN UNION REPUBLICS, 1979:
DEVIATION FROM REPUBLICAN AVERAGE (%)

	Administrative	Production	Scientific	Arts	Miscellaneous
Estonia	− 24.7	+ 11.0	− 55.3	− 48.0	− 0.5
Latvia	− 12.9	+ 10.5	− 26.3	− 28.6	− 15.7
Lithuania	− 20.3	+ 18.7	− 42.4	− 15.8	− 25.4
Belarus	− 29.7	+ 6.9	+ 71.8	+ 58.3	− 11.1
Moldova	− 13.4	+ 18.3	+ 36.0	+ 23.5	− 21.1
Ukraine	− 9.3	+ 5.4	+ 21.8	+ 6.7	− 11.6
Georgia	− 57.2	+ 18.4	− 44.9	+ 4.3	− 21.6
Armenia	− 43.9	+ 23.8	− 19.7	− 4.6	− 14.7
Azerbaijan	− 34.4	+ 48.8	− 23.4	0	− 39.6
Turkmenistan	− 28.5	+ 32.6	+ 7.4	0	− 33.8
Tajikistan	− 23.7	+ 36.3	+ 15.5	+ 6.7	− 32.0
Uzbekistan	− 49.9	+ 52.8	− 3.0	+ 16.7	− 35.8
Kyrgyzstan	− 13.4	+ 24.2	− 3.2	− 5.9	− 26.4
Kazakhstan	− 11.1	+ 10.8	− 3.6	+ 8.3	− 14.1

Source: Iu. V. Arutiunian and L. M. Drobizheva, 'Russkie v raspadaiushchemsia soiuze',
Otechestvennaia Istoriia, no. 3, 1992, p. 5.

The quotations reproduced below of course express subjective perceptions, which may or may not correspond with the actual relationships:

'Now there are more Kazakhs everywhere, frequently one has a Kazakh
as the boss and a Russian on the second place; the Kazakhs don't understand as much and then the Russian does his work.' 'Formerly, the
Russians were putting the screw on Kazakhs, but now it is the other way
around.' 'If there was a fight between Kazakhs and Russians or Germans,
the Kazakhs would be let off without a sentence but the Russians or
Germans would be punished.' 'The Tadjiks are ahead now ... We got
there in 1959, then there was rarely a Tadjik in the police force – it was
mostly Russian – now 70 percent are Tadjiks.' From Moldavia: 'They feel
like the masters.'[62]

In contrast to such statements, Karklins found that respondents in
the Baltic republics perceived the nationality power of the local
Russians to be rising. From Estonia: 'You find more Russians in
responsible positions.' Lithuania: 'The Russians have much to say, the
Lithuanians are mostly in *sovkhozes* and *kolkhozes* [respectively state-

62. Rasma Karklins, *Ethnic Relations in the USSR: the Perspective From Below*, Boston,
1986/9, pp. 82ff.

owned and collective farms].' Latvia: 'Because more Russians come, there is a certain assimilation. There used to be only Latvians in our office ... now all documents are in Russian.'

There are many methodological problems connected with the interpretation of this material, such as correcting for the perspective and bias of the informants – as well as for their representativeness. However, Karklins's findings have been corroborated by other observers,[63] and as such they do apparently reflect important changes in the status and role of the Russian diaspora under Brezhnev. Gerhard Simon, for instance, has concluded that in the 1970s and 1980s a process similar to Western de-colonialisation was taking place.[64]

How, then, should the differences between the Central Asian and Baltic situations in Karklins's material be explained? Karklins sees them primarily as a reflection of demographic disparities. While the titular nationalities were increasing their share of the Central Asian populations, as a result of both high birth rates and the reversed migration pattern of the Slavs, the continued influx of Russians to the Baltics, combined with the low fertility of the ethnic Balts, led to a strengthening of the position of the former. Certainly, as numerous ethnic-minority regimes in world history have shown, demographic strength is not automatically translated into political power. In the Soviet case, the demographic factor which influenced perceptions of nationality power the most was apparently not so much the actual numbers of the various groups as the relative increase or decrease in their size. A comparison between Kazakhstan and the Baltics brings this out. The Kazakhs were perceived as gaining in power while the Balts were losing, despite the fact that in the 1980s the Kazakhs still made up a smaller share of their republic's population than did the Baltic nations. In contrast to them, however, the Kazakh group was rapidly growing.

One important aspect of the changing ethnic climate in the republics concerned the degree of access to higher education. Victor Zaslavsky has claimed that in many republics the titular nationality was given preferential treatment on entry into institutions of higher learning.[65] Rasma Karklins has calculated the ratios of indigenous and Russian

63. Victor Zaslavsky, 'Nationalism and Democratic Transition in Postcommunist Societies', *Dædalus, op. cit.*
64. Simon, *op. cit.*, p. 5.
65. Zaslavsky, *op. cit.*, p. 102.

students within the Union Republics. Her findings are reproduced in Table 4.6. She found a surprisingly wide range of differentiation in the Russian populations of the individual republics. In Belorussia there were 36.4 students per 1,000 Russians, while in nearby Estonia the figure was only 14.5 students. In Ukraine and Moldova the Russians were significantly overrepresented in higher education in both 1959/60 and 1969/70. In Lithuania and Latvia an earlier overrepresentation of the titular nations was followed in the 1970s by overrepresentation of the Russians. In the Central Asian region and Georgia the trend was the opposite. There the titular nations, while still behind the Russians, were nonetheless gaining on them. In Kazakhstan, however, ethnic Kazakhs were clearly ahead, both in 1959/60 and in 1969/70.[66]

As Rasma Karklins points out, these figures cannot be taken as direct evidence of ethnic discrimination or favouritism. A number of factors, such as the history, sociology and culture both of the various republics and of their respective Russian populations, play an important role. For instance, the high level of urbanisation and modernisation among the Russian diaspora would probably facilitate their making up a large share of the student mass, all other things being equal. The significant underrepresentation of Ukrainians in colleges within their own republic was not, therefore, necessarily *prima facie* evidence of an anti-Ukrainian bias in the school system, but could simply reflect instead the marked rural–urban cleavage of the republican population along ethnic lines.[67]

If the Russian share of the student mass in a particular republic was lower than might have been expected, this again did not necessarily have to be the result of behind-the-scene manipulations in the enrolment procedure. It could also reflect the fact that schools and universities in the RSFSR, especially in Moscow and Leningrad, were considered far superior to the corresponding republican institutions of learning. It seems that the highly mobile diaspora Russians often preferred, and indeed could afford, to travel to these cities to study. Still, it seems that under the unofficial quota system it was easier for the *non*-Russians than for the Russians to gain entrance even into the

---

66. Rasma Karklins, 'Ethnic Politics and Access to Higher Education: the Soviet Case', *Comparative Politics*, XVI, no. 3 (April 1984), pp. 277–94.
67. See also Ralph S. Clem, 'The Integration of Ukrainians into Modernized Society in the Ukrainian SSR', in Ralph S. Clem (ed.), *The Soviet West: Interplay between Nationality and Social Organization*, New York, 1975, pp. 60–9.

prestigious Moscow and Leningrad universities, probably because the authorities wanted to encourage a mobile inter-ethnic élite – to create a supra-ethnic, sovietised élite.

The only sure method of detecting ethnic discrimination or favouritism in the Soviet schools would be to invoke, for comparison, the grades and ethnic background of those applicants to universities and colleges who were *not* admittted. However, in the Soviet Union, as in most countries, such material is not available. Karklins therefore had to fall back on a qualitative rather than a statistical method. In her interview project among Soviet emigrants, she found that faced with the question 'Who do you think is most easily admitted to higher educational institutions?', the majority of respondents pinpointed nationality as the one decisive factor.[68]

Interviews conducted by the present author with diaspora Russians corroborate, in an even more qualitative fashion, the fact that in the 1970s and early 1980s at least some Russians in some republics felt the effects of an ethnic quota system. However, the system seems to have been relatively mild, even in Kazakhstan. The number of Kazakhs vying for admittance was apparently not so high that it severely affected the career chances of the Russians. The rigid, non-ethnic distinction between the scions of the *nomenklatura* and those lacking the correct family background seems to have been more important as a quota-regulation factor with the universities.[69]

While the Russian diaspora in the 1970s and 1980s was gradually becoming politically marginalised, it was nonetheless still seen by most observers as part of the glue which held the Soviet Union together. Typical was Walker Connor's assertion that the Russians in the republics served as 'agents of ethnic dilution . . . snuffing in advance any ethnonationally inspired dangers inherent in Lenin's policy of autonomy for compact ethnic groups by diluting the ethnic composition of the republic'.[70] Interestingly, not only Western sovietologists but also spokesmen of the Soviet regime highlighted the significance of the Russian diaspora as part of the Soviet nation-building process – although with rather different accents and epithets. In 1984 it was claimed that the Russian people played a 'particularly

---

68. Karklins, 1984, *op. cit.*, p. 288.
69. Author's interviews in Altamy, May 1993.
70. Walker Connor, *The National Question in Marxist–Leninist Theory and Strategy*, Princeton, 1984, p. 320.

Russians in the Union Republics: dominant nation or underprivileged minority?

Table 4.5. RATIO OF INDIGENOUS AND RUSSIAN STUDENTS WITHIN UNION REPUBLICS, 1959/60 AND 1969/70

	Nationality	% of total population		% of total number of students		Students per 1,000 Co-nationals in Republic	
		1959/60	1969/70	1959/60	1969/70	1959/60	1969/70
RSFSR	Russian	83	83	83	83		20.7
Estonia	Estonian	75	68	82	73	12.4	17.3
	Russian	20	25	14	22	8.0	14.5
Latvia	Latvian	62	57	65	47	10.7	14.3
	Russian	27	30	24	40	9.4	22.6
Lithuania	Lithuanian	79	80	89	84	11.0	19.0
	Russian	9	9	6	10	6.8	21.9
Belarus	Belorussian	81	81	67	64	6.1	12.2
	Russian	8	10	21	24	19.2	36.4
Moldova	Moldovan	65	65	50	59	5.1	10.1
	Russian	10	12	23	19	15.0	19.1

Ukraine	Ukrainian	77	75	62	60	8.1	15.1
	Russian	16	19	30	33	17.6	29.3
Georgia	Georgian	64	67	77	83	16.6	23.6
	Russian	10	9	10	7	13.2	14.6
Armenia	Armenian	88	89	94	96	12.3	23.7
	Russian	3	3	3	3	11.4	21.7
Azerbaijan	Azerbaijani	68	74	71	78	10.2	20.8
	Russian	14	10	15	12	10.6	23.7
Turkmenistan	Turkmen	61	66	55	65	7.9	13.4
	Russian	17	15	30	21	14.9	19.9
Tajikistan	Tajik	53	56	47	50	9.0	13.6
	Russian	13	12	23	21	17.8	26.7
Uzbekistan	Uzbek	61	65	47	57	9.5	17.2
	Russian	14	13	26	19	24.0	29.7
Kyrgyzstan	Kyrgyz	41	44	47	47	9.8	17.8
	Russian	29	30	37	35	10.2	19.8
Kazakhstan	Kazakh	30	32	41	40	11.2	18.9
	Russian	43	43	44	43	8.6	15.4

Source: Rasma Karklins, 'Ethnic Politics and Access to Higher Education: the Soviet Case', *Comparative Politics*, XVI (April 1984), p. 284.

important' role in the accelerating process of rapprochement (*sblizhenie*) among the Soviet peoples. With a mixed metaphor it was asserted that the Russians, 'as it were, are the pivot, the cementing principle, in the entire social and international community'. To substantiate this assertion, the focus was put on, *inter alia*, the great mobility of the Russians, as well as on the fact of their significant presence in all Union republics.[71]

However, in spite of this consensus across ideological dividing lines, it could, also, be argued that the opposite was the case. What looked like cement had many of the qualities of a plastic explosive. In many non-Russian republics, the Russian population element was a thorn in the side of the titular nationality. Important segments of these groups felt that the Russians were trespassing on their premises, entering without permission, and behaving not as guests but more as if they were at home. Such a sentiment made the nationality policy of Brezhnev less than perfect, and indeed prepared the ground for the ethnic uprisings witnessed under *perestroika*.

Were the Russians in the non-Russian Soviet republics an underprivileged or a privileged group? The rival descriptions by Rogers Brubaker and Mikhail Voslensky cited at the beginning of this chapter seem to present a stark choice: either – or. However, when the question is qualified for sub-periods, types of privileges and groups of comparison, the alternative becomes less clear-cut. Obviously, the status both of the Russians at large and of those living outside the RSFSR in particular fluctuated significantly over time. Under Stalin, for example, they were clearly more favoured than they had been both before and after.

Furthermore, while the Russians enjoyed cultural facilities in the non-Russian republics which were incomparably better than those offered to other diaspora groups, in the 1970s and 1980s they were still handicapped in most places over access to political power, and in some places even in their educational opportunities. In brief, during the post-Stalinist period the Russian diasporas were culturally and linguistically privileged in relation to other non-titular groups in the republics, but were usually not so privileged in relation to the titular groups. Moreover the Russians in the periphery did not as a rule enjoy

71. *Kritika fal'sifikatsii natsional'nykh otnoshenii v SSSR*, Moscow, 1984, p. 214.

any advantages different from those enjoyed by their co-nationals in the Russian republic – neither fewer nor more. In their material benefits, most were probably better off than the average Russian in the RSFSR (although there were significant variations both among and within the various diaspora groups). This circumstance, however, was most likely a reflection of their higher educational level and of their good human resources in general, not of ethnic privileges.

The prominence of Russian cultural facilities in the republics was primarily related to the special status accorded to the Russian *language* in the Soviet Union, and not to any special status granted to the Russian diaspora communities as such. The pride of place given to this language was an instrument both in the coordination of the common economic and political space of the Soviet Union and in a state-building policy aimed at the creation of a homogeneous Soviet culture.

The most important dividing line in Soviet society, namely that between the haves and the have-nots, was not related to ethnic criteria but determined by membership or non-membership of the ruling élite, the *nomenklatura*, which cut across ethnic boundaries. Although no hard data are available, there is every reason to believe that the differences in opportunities and material benefits enjoyed by a Russian member of the *nomenklatura*, on the one hand, and a Russian *non-*member of it on the other (a relationship which has not been a topic of this book) were much larger than those between Russians in general and non-Russians in general, whichever way they are calculated.

The *nomenklatura* élite can be characterised as the most sovietized segment of Soviet society (although post-Soviet history has shown that many members of this group were able to reconvert to ostensible national values and nationalist rhetoric). Although the *nomenklatura* were supra-ethnic, recruitment within the different republics was somewhat tilted towards the titular nationality. Even so, since Soviet culture was not a lowest common multiple of the cultures of all Soviet nationalities but first and foremost a derivative (or distortion) of Russian culture, sovietized non-Russians on entering the *nomenklatura* had to shed their ethnic identity more than the Russians in the RSFSR or in the other republics.

As Rogers Brubaker points out, one of the most important advantages enjoyed by those Russians living in the non-Russian republics was neither political nor material but psychological: the intangible sense of security stemming from the feeling of belonging to the (Union-wide) dominant nation. Therefore, in a final perspective, the

Russians living in the Soviet republics must be regarded as a privileged group compared to their *offspring*, who no longer enjoy the same feeling of security. Growing up in the new national states into which the Union republics have been transformed, the new generations of diaspora Russians will have fewer cultural opportunities, lower social status and, in some places, even a more precarious legal position than their parents.

Part II

5

THE STATE OF STATELESSNESS:
THE BALTICS

Dashed expectations

The dismantling of the Soviet Union started in the Baltics. The very first signals of national resistance to Soviet rule during *perestroika* emanated from Latvia in 1987.[1] In 1988 the leadership role in the independence struggle passed to Estonia: the first popular front materialised there, and as the first Union republic Estonia proclaimed its sovereignty (within the Soviet Union) on 16 November 1988. Finally, Lithuania took over the lead in the pursuit of full political independence, which all three Baltic countries eventually achieved in August 1991.

The success of the Baltic states has regularly, and not unreasonably, been explained by reference to their political culture. As a result of their geographical location, their historical integration into European culture and their political independence between the World Wars, the preconditions for a democratic – that is to say, a pluralistic, participatory and compromise-seeking – political culture seemed to be in place. The ability to mobilise extremely large sections of the population for the purposes of non-violent political action was demonstrated time and again.

For these reasons, many commentators expected that it would also be possible to develop harmonious inter-ethnic relations in the Baltic states. Certainly, the problem of building bridges among the various ethnic groups was formidable, but it was widely believed that no one in the former Soviet Union would be better able to tackle it than the Baltic populations. Both Latvia and Estonia had very liberal legislation

---

1. Juris Dreifelds, 'Latvian National Rebirth', *Problems of Communism*, XXXVIII, 4 (July–August 1989), pp. 77–95.

on minority rights in the inter-war period,[2] and adapted to modern circumstances these laws could still be of value.[3]

In the fall of 1991 Eric Rudenshiold wrote that in Latvia 'an unspoken resolve towards non-violence and moderation and a general willingness to guarantee the rights of all ethnic groups have evidently resulted in creating a moderate and less threatening environment for substantial numbers of ethnic Russians.'[4] Rudenshiold was seconded by, among others, Nils Muiznieks, who, in the fall of 1991 also expressed the belief that 'there appeared to be a willingness on the side of both the Slavs and the ethnic Latvians in Latvia to come to mutually acceptable agreements.' Conflicts between these groups were bound to surface, but 'the prospects for peaceful resolution of these conflicts appear positive, given the past lack of bloodshed in the region, the emergence of political pluralism and a vibrant independent press.'[5] Similar prognoses were made for Estonia.

Writing two years after Rudenshiold and Muiznieks, one is forced to conclude that their expectations have not been fulfilled. True, the commitment to non-violence has remained strong and unshaken in the Baltics. Not a single incident of physical molestation of Russians or other minorities has been reported – which in itself is remarkable. And the Baltic record of general human rights observance, as testified by several international reports, is good.[6] However, the issue of *political right* has been extremely controversial. In Latvia and Estonia, post-war immigrants, mostly Russians and other russophones, have had to *earn* their citizenship which other permanent residents have been granted *automatically*. The criteria according to which citizenship may be achieved are perceived by most Baltic Russians as excessively stringent. Moreover, as pointed out by international human rights monitors, authorities and officials in Latvia and Estonia have failed at times to

---

2. See Georg von Rauch, *The Baltic States: the Years of Independence: Estonia, Latvia, Lithuania 1917–1940*, London, 1974, pp. 135ff.
3. Aina Antane, 'Some Aspects of Cultural Autonomy of Minorities in Latvia 1920–1934 and Today', paper presented at the symposium 'National identity in the Baltic States and Croatia/Slovenia', Oslo, 5–6 September 1991.
4. Eric Rudenshiold, 'Ethnic Dimensions in Contemporary Latvian Politics: Focusing Forces for Change', *Soviet Studies*, XLIV, 4, 1992, pp. 609–39, on p. 613.
5. Nils Muiznieks, 'Latvia: origins, evolution, and triumph', in Ian Bremmer and Ray Taras (eds.) *Nations and Politics in the Soviet Successor States*, Cambridge, 1993, pp. 181–205, on pp. 200–1.
6. See e.g. 'Country reports on human rights practices for 1992', report submitted by the US Department of State, February 1993.

respect the criteria which they themselves have made, or have agreed as part of international treaties.[7]

By the end of 1993 animosity and mutual distrust between the Russians and the titular nations in Latvia and Estonia, as shown in the press and in public discourse, had reached appalling levels. It is true that at this time certain signs, particularly in Estonia, were pointing towards both a nascent ethnic harmonisation process and an earnest search for a *modus vivendi* from both sides. However, many close observers of Baltic affairs still regarded the prospects for tolerable inter-ethnic relations in these countries as unfavourable.[8]

During the independence struggle expectations for inter-ethnic harmony in Lithuania were somewhat lower. Many observers pointed out that between the World Wars this country had abandoned democracy much earlier than its northern neighbours. The uncompromising rhetoric of Sajudis in its dealings with Moscow also indicated that 'fight-or-die', 'all-or-nothing' attitudes were more prevalent in this republic. Nevertheless, inter-ethnic relations developed somewhat more smoothly than feared, at least with the Russian population.

There are certainly important differences between Estonia and Latvia in their history, culture, demography and contemporary situation. However, the parallels and points of contact are so numerous that separate treatments of the Russian question in these two countries would inevitably lead to tedious repetitions. They are therefore treated together here, while Lithuania is dealt with separately at the end. The chapter explores the vicissitudes of inter-ethnic relations in the Baltics up to the autumn of 1993, and seeks to uncover the roots of the deteriorations – without, however, extrapolating future trends.

7. Asbjørn Eide, 'Human Rights Aspects of the Citizenship Issues in Estonia and Latvia. Based on Available Material and Visit 3–7 February 1992. At the Request of the European Bank for Reconstruction and Development. Progress Report', 11 March 1992; 'Violations by the Latvian Department of Citizenship and Immigration', *Helsinki Watch*, V, 19, (October 1993).

8. 'The internal pressures and the logic of internal political development lead Estonia and particularly the even more divided Latvia towards a catastrophe', believed a former member of the Latvian parliament, Alex Grigorievs. See his 'The Baltic Predicament', Chr. Michelsen Institute, Bergen, Norway, unpublished manuscript, December 1993. Grigorievs is a former leading member of the Latvian popular front, and today is highly critical of the Latvian parliament's treatment of the citizenship issue.

Peculiarities of the Baltic ethnic scene

Demographically, the Russians' share of the total population in Estonia and Latvia is higher than in all the other former Soviet republics except Kazakhstan. In 1989, they constituted 30.3% and 34.0%, respectively, in absolute numbers 475,000 and 900,000. As pointed out in Chapter 3, this situation is radically different from the inter-war period, when the Russian minorities in both countries amounted to less than 10% of the total. In addition, Latvians and Estonians in recent years have had extremely low population growth.[9] As a combined result of these developments, the ethnic Latvian share of the population in Latvia dropped from 75.5% in 1939 to 51.8% in 1989. And in Estonia, while the Estonians constituted no less than 90% in 1940 they made up only 61.5% in 1989. This situation, though dramatic, was not absolutely unique. The demographic development of Kazakhstan led to an even more drastic decline in the titular nation's share of the population.

Culturally, the Baltic area is probably the only part of the former Soviet Union where the Russians are liable to feel confronted by a culture which many of them would regard as equal or even superior to their own.[10] In higher education, journalism and cultural life, the native languages in these countries have been more intensely exploited than in any other republics, with the possible exception of Georgia and Armenia. The level of performance in all these fields has been high. But in spite of their impressive historical record as successful guardians of their languages and cultures, many Balts see their small national cultures as extremely vulnerable and even threatened with extinction. They see Russian culture, the Russian language and the Russian demographic presence as the main threats to their cultural survival.

In general, the Russians have considered the Balts as fellow Europeans with a significant amount of common cultural heritage. They see the cultural difference between themselves and the locals as much smaller than say, in Transcaucasia and Central Asia. Many Baltic Russians point out that their own lifestyle *has* been influenced by the habits and values of the local populations, and some even indicate that

9. 'Current Changes in Estonian Demographic Development', *Monthly Survey of Baltic and Post-Soviet Politics*, Sakala Center, Tallinn, January 1992, pp. 7–9.
10. For a discussion of the Russians' 'Baltic complex', see Iurii Abyzov, 'Ostzeiskii kompleks rossianina – i sovremennost'', *Diena* (Riga), 11 April 1992; *Diena*, 16 April 1992; *Subbotnyi den'*, 25 April 1992, p. 13; *Subbotnyi den*, 30 April 1992, p. 13.

they feel strangely out of place when visiting Moscow or other Russian cities. The Balts, on the other hand, have been more reluctant to admit the Russians into a common European culture, and have stressed among other things differences in both religion and political culture. Not infrequently, the Balts define the differences between themselves and the Russians as involving a distinction between 'Europeanness' and 'Asianness'.[11]

There are marked cleavages within the Russian community in Estonia and Latvia. Those Russians who have ancestral roots in inter-war Estonia and Latvia are better integrated in society, usually have a better command of the titular language and are more likely to have inter-married with the indigenous nationalities than post-war immi-grants.[12] The latter frequently live in all-Russian neighbourhoods, and often have minimal contact with and knowledge of the titular language and culture. While the former possess a fairly large cultural intelligentsia (or at least did in the inter-war period[13]), the share of industrial workers in the second group is higher than in other Soviet successor states. This is especially true of Estonia, where the intelligentsia found in this group usually represent the technical rather than the cultural élite. If we accept John Armstrong's distinction bet-ween *proletarian* diasporas – typically migrant workers from developing countries – and *mobilised* diasporas – with strong élites and upward social mobility – then we see that the Russians in the northern Baltic countries conform more to the first category than they do in any other Soviet successor states.[14]

The russophone Baltic communities include many more groups than just the 'passport Russians'. When the ethnic Russians and non-Russian Russian-speakers are counted together, the size of the groups rises to almost 40% in Estonia and 50% in Latvia. Many Russians heartily

11. See e.g. Anatol Lieven, *The Baltic Revolution: Estonia, Latvia, Lithuania and the Path to Independence*, New Haven, 1993, pp. 185ff.
12. Aksel Kirch, 'Russians as a Minority in Contemporary Baltic States', *Bulletin of Peace Proposals*, XXIII, 2 (1992), pp. 205–12.
13. Very many Baltic Russian intellectuals fled to the West during World War II, or were deported to Siberia after 1945. See M. Mitrofanov, 'Prichiny bessiliia russkikh', *Dünaburg* (Daugavpils), no. 117, 1992; Natalia Kasatkina, 'Istoriia russkoi diaspory Litvy (1981–1940)', paper presented at the conference 'The New Russian Diaspora', Lielupe, Latvia, 13–15 November 1992.
14. John A. Armstrong, 'Mobilized and Proletarian Diasporas', *American Political Science Review*, LXX (1976), pp. 393–408.

dislike the term 'Russian-speakers',[15] preferring to see themselves just as Russians plain and simple. The term 'Russian-speakers', they suspect, signifies a lack of cultural identity rather than any positive content. During *perestroika*, when the rediscovery of 'roots' became paramount, the lack of ethnic identity was regularly seen as a major flaw. There seems to be a strong current among the nationalities in the Baltic states after independence – titulars and non-titulars alike – towards increased ethnic awareness.

A common stereotype of the Baltic Russians is that they are boorish, dirty and drink a lot.[16] This, of course, is a gross simplification. Still, the fact that this belief is prevalent in the Baltic countries is an important factor in explaining attitudes towards the Russians there. Some members of the Baltic Russian communities even subscribe to such evaluations themselves. The Latvian intellectual Iurii Abyzov has claimed that a sense of culture (which he seems to equate with an appreciation of the fine arts) is absent among most Russian residents of the Baltics. This, in his opinion, is because they came there as agents of an expanding empire: 'We should remember that an empire always draws to its outlying areas far from its best human material.'[17] A leading spokesman of the Estonian Russians, Artur Kuznetsov, has remarked that the low educational level of a part of the Estonian Russian community has turned it into 'a lumpenized mass'[18] but in his view, this situation calls for compassion and help rather than repugnance.

Reports on the *economic* conditions of the Baltic Russian communities are often mutually contradictory. As shown in the previous chapter, there has been a general tendency to see the Russian diaspora as a materially privileged group, and many Balts insist that this holds good also for Russians in their countries. A study sponsored by the Estonian Academy of Sciences in 1992 asserted that 'in the Baltic States the immigrants had *real economic privileges* and were able to get good housing almost immediately, while the native population needed to wait for decades.'[19] Others make a different claim. Two Estonian

15. See e.g. '"Russkoiazychnye"', *Lad'ia* (Riga), no. 9, 1991.
16. See e.g. Anatol Lieven, *op. cit.*, pp. 176ff.
17. Abyzov, *op. cit.*
18. *Nezavisimaia Gazeta*, 5 November 1991.
19. Aksel Kirch, Marika Kirch and Tarmo Tuisk, *The Non-Estonian Population Today and Tomorrow: a Sociological Overview*, Tallinn, December 1992, p. 5. Emphasis in the original.

sociologists have maintained that 'average wage levels, family budgets, and appraisals as to how the family was coping with its income, were not qualitatively different between workers of different nationalities.'[20] A Western journalist based in Riga has maintained that the income and living standard of the Russians are 'on the average lower than those of the Balts themselves'.[21] Obviously, somebody has got it wrong.

Most probably, the living standard among the Baltic Russians has varied. Housing in the Soviet Union was often achieved through the workplace, and a large proportion of the Russians in the Baltics were employed either by all-Union ministries or by the Soviet Army, both of which built their own housing complexes. The standard that they could offer their employees differed greatly – some brought in so many migrant workers that they could not accommodate all of them decently. Certain Latvian nationalists claim that the Russians must now be induced to leave their country because their shoddy dormitories represent a threat to the sanitation and security of their neighbourhood.

The major *political* difference between the Baltic republics and other Soviet successor states is the independent statehood enjoyed by Estonia, Latvia and Lithuania between the World Wars. Indeed, from a legal point of view the term 'Soviet successor states' does not apply to them. In contrast to the other Union republics, the Baltic countries, in 1990–1, did not proclaim their independence as new states but instead resurrected and reconfirmed their former statehood. In different ways they have tried to pick up the severed threads of those social and legal structures which were disrupted by the Soviet invasion in 1940. Many post-Soviet political and legal institutions hark back to the previous period of independence. However, this does not mean that the Balts feel obliged to continue the pre-war traditions in every way. Instead, they have picked out those elements which they believe can be suitably applied to contemporary realities. In Latvia, for example, the inter-war constitution has been resuscitated but not the inter-war law on citizenship, while in Estonia the opposite has been done: a new constitution has been written, while the 1938 citizenship law has been re-enacted.

20. Klara Hallik and Marika Kirch, *On Interethnic Relations in Estonia*, Fondazione Giangiacomo Feltrinelli, 1992, p. 156. Since Marika Kirch is a co-author also of the study referred to in the previous note, she seems to be contradicting herself to some degree.
21. Lieven *op. cit.*, p. 176.

In both cases this has been done in such a way as to remove the post-war immigrants from the body politic of original citizens. They are considered illegal immigrants or occupants although the overwhelming majority of them were subjectively convinced that by migrating into the Baltics they had merely moved to another part of a country of which they were already citizens, i.e. the Soviet Union.[22] This is the single most important political feature distinguishing the Russian diaspora question in these two states from the situation in all other new states on former Soviet territory. Indeed, the status of these immigrants has become one of the most complicated and inflammable inter-ethnic problems to be found in the entire former Soviet Union. While this could arguably have been foreseen before independence, it generally was not.

Pre-independence politics in Estonia and Latvia

The Estonian and Latvian popular fronts were established in the autumn of 1988, ostensibly to muster support for Gorbachev's *perestroika* policy, but ever more plainly pursuing quite different objects from those of the Kremlin. In the first phase these were economic and cultural and in principle they could be realised within the framework of the Soviet state: republican 'self-financing', the right to use the national symbols from the inter-war period, control over the writing of their own history and, most important, greater scope for their languages in public life. During 1989 new language laws were passed in both republics that make the titular languages the official state language, and the command of it a requirement for all state employees.[23]

These demands ran counter to the interests of important segments of the Russian population. The Russian management of the Union-controlled factories had nothing to gain from such a transfer to republican jurisdiction. On their initiative the United Councils of Labour Collectives (Russian acronym OSTK) were established. These OSTK organised several work stoppages during 1989.[24] However,

---

22. 'New Citizenship Laws in the Republics of the Former USSR', *Helsinki Watch*, IV, 7, 1992, p. 9.
23. For the Estonian language law, see reprint in *Estoniia*, 7 June 1993; for the Latvian law, *Zakon Latviiskoi SSR o iazykakh*, Riga, 1989.
24. See e.g. *Moscow News*, no. 47, 1989.

these stoppages were not particularly effective: an OSTK appeal for a general strike in Estonia in August 1989 was heeded by only some 5–8% of the workforce.

In addition to the OSTK (pursuing primarily economic aims) there were also established 'international fronts' – 'interfronts' – and these were more directly concerned with political issues. These fronts called both for the retention of the Soviet Communist system and for the territorial integrity of the Soviet state. Since it was expected, (correctly, it seems), that only the Communist party would be capable of keeping the Union together, these issues were regarded as two sides of the same coin. Ethnic rights were not at this time among the rallying cries of the interfronts. The Soviet state had taught that nationalism of any kind was reactionary and harmful (this was also the general verdict of Western scholarship), and, more important, any focus on ethnic issues would be detrimental to their interests since it would serve to legitimise the Baltic campaigns for ethnic rights. Their own self-understanding, therefore, was internationalistic, ostensibly elevated above the interests of particular ethnic groups. Hence the name 'interfront' for their movements. And certainly, in one respect at least, the interfronts were genuinely supra-ethnic. While hardly any ethnic Estonians and Latvians felt attracted to them, they appealed to members of all russophone groups. Not only Russians but many Ukrainians, Belorussians, Caucasians and others also believed that their interests would be best protected by such organisations.

From the very beginning the interfronts were on the defensive. They did not set the political agenda but instead only reacted to initiatives from the popular fronts and other anti-Communist organisations, often very lamely. While the rallies of the popular fronts regularly drew hundreds of thousands of participants, the demonstrations of the interfronts were pitiful in comparison. Many Baltic Russians, like Russians in Moscow, Leningrad and elsewhere, genuinely wanted democratic reforms, and instinctively distrusted their self-designated leaders. This was especially true of the youth. Several observers have remarked that war veterans, pensioners and old people generally seemed to dominate the interfront rallies.

The rhetoric of many interfront leaders was so excessive that it repelled many Russians who might otherwise have been attracted to them. The organ of the Latvian interfront, for example, claimed that the popular fronts used criminals and the mentally ill as pile-drivers in their anti-Soviet campaigns, and such people were assigned the task of defiling Soviet memorials and the graves of Soviet soldiers. 'They are being incited by slogans such as "Let us hang the Communists before we are running out of soap to grease the rope".'[25] Anyone with even the most superficial knowledge of the Baltic independence struggle knew this to be a lie. This extreme example, while not entirely typical of the level of truthfulness found in interfront publications, was also not a complete exception.

In the autumn of 1989 the Soviet authorities finally acknowledged the existence of the secret protocols of the Ribbentrop–Molotov pact and by doing so indirectly recognised that incorporation of the Baltic states into the Soviet Union had been unlawful. This made it possible for the Balts to move away from largely cultural demands and press instead for the restoration of their inter-war statehood. In this situation it became more important than before to muster the support also of the non-titular ethnic groups. The cultural (ethnic) aspects of the independence struggle were played down while the territorial aspect (centre–periphery) and political aspect (dictatorship vs democracy) were highlighted.

On 11 March, 30 March and 4 May 1990 Lithuania, Estonia and Latvia declared their complete independence from the Soviet Union, to become effective either immediately (Lithuania) or after a certain undefined transition period (Estonia and Latvia). The Baltic leaders pressed home the message that independence would not lead to ethnic discrimination. In a joint resolution on ethnic equality, the three heads of state (Arnold Rüütel, Anatolijs Gorbunovs and Vytautas Landsbergis) confirmed their commitment to 'guarantee the rights of all residents of Estonia, Latvia and Lithuania, regardless of nationality, native language, and political and religious beliefs'.[26]

At the other side of the barricades, the trend went in the opposite direction: in the Soviet-loyalist Baltic press the controversy with the Baltic leaders was presented for the first time in ethnic terms. In

---

25. *Edinstvo* (Riga), 26 November–2 December 1990.
26. See Peter van Kricken, 'Baltics: Citizenship and Languages', unpublished ms., Stockholm, February 1993. By July 1989, the Latvian popular front had adopted an ideological platform on the nationalities question, declaring that citizenship in Latvia should be based on 'the free expression of the will of the residents, independently of their nationality, social status, or religious belief, in support of the idea of independence'. The front was ready to grant citizenship to all permanent residents (defined as ten years' residence), with no other requirements attached. See *Atmoda*, 17 July 1989.

1990 focussing on ethnic issues was still extremely rare in interfront publications. However, in the spring of 1991, when the dissolution of the Soviet Union seemed ever more imminent, some articles were printed which cautiously explored 'the Russian idea' rather than Communism as a new ideological platform.[27] In April 1991 the organ of the Latvian interfront, *Edinstvo*, printed an open letter to the RSFSR Supreme Soviet under the title 'Remember that you are Russians!' The author lashed out against the Russian deputies in the RSFSR who were allegedly indifferent to the fate of their co-nationals in the Union republics. Their callousness, it was claimed, stemmed from the fact that no one had threatened to kill their children for belonging to the Russian nation, and that their wives were not being raped in the name of 'democracy' and 'independence'.[28]

Such outbursts were flagrantly unjust not only to the Balts but also to the Russian democrats. Ever since the Russian Federation had began to exert itself as a political power in its own right, its leaders had tried to pursue a 'dual-track' policy towards the Baltics. On the one hand, it supported the national aspirations of the Balts – up to, and including, support for separate statehood. On the other hand, the Yeltsin entourage tried to secure the rights of Russians in the region. In the summer of 1990 the RSFSR began negotiations with Estonia and Latvia on matters of mutual interest, including guarantees forbidding discrimination against ethnic minorities.[29] The agreements with Estonia and Latvia were signed by the heads of state in Tallinn on 12 and 13 January 1991 – that is, at the exact time when the Soviet army was storming the television tower in Vilnius. The appearance of Boris Yeltsin at that particular moment, side by side with the Baltic leaders, showed the world that the Soviet military were not acting on behalf of the entire Russian nation, and it seems that this significantly influenced the outcome of events.[30]

The texts of the two agreements were almost identical. The contracting parties guaranteed, *inter alia*, that any person living on the

27. See e.g. *Za Rodinu*, 24 March 1991.
28. 'Vspomnite, chto vy Russkie!', *Edinstvo* (Riga), 1–7 April 1991, p. 1.
29. See interview with the chairman of the subcommittee for interrepublican affairs in the RSFSR Supreme Soviet, F. V. Shelov-Kovediaev, *Nedelia*, no. 44, 1990, p. 3; *Kommersant*, 1–8 October 1990, p. 13.
30. John Dunlop, 'Russia: confronting a loss of empire', in Ian Bremmer and Ray Taras (eds), *Nations and Politics in the Soviet Successor States*, Cambridge, 1993, pp. 43–74, esp. pp. 53ff.

territory of either Latvia (Estonia) or the RSFSR when the agreement was signed 'has the right to receive or retain citizenship in the RSFSR or the Republic of Latvia (Estonia) in accordance with his free expression of will'.[31] The agreements were ratified by both the Latvian and the Estonian sides almost immediately. The ratification process in the Russian parliament was delayed for a number of reasons – among them, the strong anti-Baltic attitudes on the part of certain deputies. The ratification was completed only a year later as regards the Estonian–Russian agreement, while the Latvian–Russian counterpart was never ratified.

The bilateral agreements were scornfully spurned both by the interfront leaders and by others who claimed to speak on behalf of the Baltic Russians.[32] Their gut hatred for Yeltsin and other Russian democrats who had embraced the cause of Baltic independence blinded them to the fact that the agreements would in fact offer them pretty good protection if they were adhered to, but the articles in the agreements which sanctioned Baltic independence seemed to them much more important. 'Russians have been deprived of their Fatherland and have become outcasts. They have only one option left: to die at the threshold of their house, defending their family and children.'[33]

However, a growing number of Baltic Russians were rejecting the arguments and positions of the interfronts. Democratically oriented Russians did not establish their own organisations but instead collaborated with the titular nationalities within the popular fronts. The fronts published Russian-language papers and other material aimed at the russophone readership. This material strongly emphasised the territorial and political character of the struggle with Moscow, and spread the fronts' message that all ethnic groups would be guaranteed equal rights when independence had been achieved. Two leading russophone popular front supporters – Artur Kuznetsov in Estonia and Vladimir Steshenko in Latvia – were appointed minister/general director of

31. 'Dogovor ob osnovakh mezhgosudarstvennykh otnoshenii Rossiiskoi Sovetskoi Federativnoi Sotsialisticheskoi Respubliki i Latviiskoi Respubliki,' *Diena* (Riga), 25 January 1991 (prilozhenie); and 'Dogovor ob osnovakh mezhgosudarstvennykh otnoshenii Rossiiskoi Sovetskoi Federativnoi Sotsialisticheskoi Respubliki i Estonskoi Respubliki', mimeograph.
32. See e.g. interview with S. Petinov, deputy to the Estonian Supreme Soviet, *Za rodinu*, 16 January 1991.
33. *Edinstvo*, 18–24 February 1991, p. 3.

nationalities questions in their countries when these posts were established.[34]

Kuznetsov later told the present author that the question of citizenship had hardly been discussed in the Estonian popular front, simply because it was taken for granted that it would be extended to everyone.[35] And indeed, if for no other reason, Estonia's ratification of the Estonian–Russian bilateral agreement apparently made this the only possible solution. Of course, the Russian democrats knew that various sections of the titular nations did not want to extend political rights to the postwar immigrants. However, it was universally believed at the time that these groups were fringe elements without any chance of influencing real politics.

The leading organisations of the national-radicals were the Congress of Estonia and the Estonian National Independence Party in Estonia, and the Latvian Citizens' Committee and the Latvian National Independence Movement in Latvia. These organisation called for a return to the inter-war condition of statehood, and regarded the existing parliaments (the republican Supreme soviets) as illegitimate since they had been elected under an occupation regime.[36] This stand, however, did not prevent them from taking part in the elections to these very organs in the spring of 1990. In these elections, which were freer than at any other time in Soviet history and more genuinely pluralistic in the Baltics than in other Soviet republics, the national-radicals fared badly. So did the Communist party and other organisations which represented the Soviet loyalist position. In both Estonia and Latvia the centrist popular fronts won landslide victories. This resulted partly from the fact that many Russians also voted for the fronts. This trend was strongest in Latvia. For instance, in the port town of Liepaja, which had a two-thirds Russian majority, the PF won five out of nine seats.[37]

The tragic events in Riga and Vilnius in January 1991 contributed strongly to a further shift in the attitudes of the Baltic Russians. The interfront leaders as well as the local Soviet military refused to take

---

34. *Baltiiskoe Vremia*, 14 February 1991, p. 1.
35. Author's interview, Tallinn, 8 November 1991.
36. 'Estonian political parties on citizenship', *Monthly review of Baltic and post-Soviet politics*, Sakala center, Tallinn, February 1992, pp. 3–6; Merethe Kvernrød, *Citizenship and Interethnic Relations in Latvia*, University of Oslo, 1993, pp. 43ff.
37. Lieven, *op. cit.*, p. 194. In Russian-dominated Daugavpils, however, they took none.

any responsibility for what had happened, claiming that the bloodshed had been provoked by the actions of the nationalist-separatists.[38] Many Russians, however, felt that the only way they could wash this blood off their own hands was by explicitly denouncing the actions of the OMONs (units of the internal ministry forces) and the Soviet military. Two of the victims on the Latvian side had actually been Slavs – one Russian and one Belorussian – and only these actually died fighting with weapons in their hands. All the other victims were spectators or television journalists killed in the crossfire.

The changing Russian attitudes were reflected in the advisory referendums on national independence held in Latvia and Estonia on 3 March 1991, when 73% and 78%, respectively, of the total population voted if favour of secession from the Soviet Union. The turnout in both republics was above 80%.[39] This meant that no less than 64.5% of all registered voters had cast their ballots in favour of independence. There are no exact data on the distribution of the Russian votes, but since the number of 'yes' votes was considerably higher than the titular nations' share of the total population, a substantial number of Russians must have voted pro-Baltic. The exact number is disputed. Estonian sources maintain that in Estonia the figure was in the range of 25%, but while this was significant, it also meant that 75% of the Russians opposed independence, either actively by voting against it or passively by abstaining from voting.[40] In Latvia estimates vary from as low as 15% to above 50%.[41] The voters there could choose between ballots showing Latvian or Russian text, and

38. See e.g. *Za Rodinu*, 16 January 1991, p. 3.
39. For a territorial breakdown, see the *Estonian Independent*, 7 March 1991, p. 3.
40. Raivo Vetik, 'The Nationality Issue in Estonia', paper presented at the symposium 'National Identity in the Baltic States and Croatia/Slovenia', Oslo, 5–6 September 1991; Rein Taagepera, 'Ethnic Relations in Estonia', *Journal of Baltic Studies*, XXIII, 2, (Summer 1992), pp. 121–32.
41. The Russian-dominated 'equal rights' faction in the Latvian parliament claimed that only 15% of the non-Latvians in Latvia voted for independence. This low figure was probably reached by including the military men which had been barred from participation. The editor of the Latvian semi-official newspaper, *Diena*, claimed 33%. For both estimates, see *Diena*, 5 March 1991, pp. 1 and 2. The Russian researcher Leon Gudkov has offered a much higher figure: 'more than half of the Russians . . . voted for complete independence.' Leon Gudkov, 'The Disintegration of the USSR and Russians in the Republics', *Journal of Communist Studies*, IX, 1 (March 1993), pp. 75–87, on p. 80. Possibly, Gudkov has in mind only those Russians who actually voted.

it is reasonable to believe that only russophones availed themselves of the Russian version. Election monitors found that well above 60% of the ballots using Russian text were cast in favour of independence.[42] In spite of the interpretation difficulties, the results of the independence poll were seen by most observers as a clear indication both of growing Russian support for Baltic independence and of the Russians' conviction that their rights would be fully respected in a free Estonia and a free Latvia.[43]

There were obviously many reasons behind the differentiated Russian vote. Russians who had lived in the Baltic region for generations, knew the local language, or were married to a Balt often had a stronger attachment to this area than they did to Russia proper.[44] Many Russians obviously also perceived the relationship between the Baltic leaders and Moscow more as a struggle between democracy and dictatorship than as a struggle between different ethnic groups.

However, economic considerations may have been decisive for many Russians when they made up their mind how to vote.[45] It was generally expected (correctly, it seems) that a successful transition to a market economy would be more likely in the Baltics than in other parts of the Soviet Union. The Baltic Russians may have calculated that if they became citizens of independent Baltic states they would be saved from the economic morass into which their ethnic brethren in Russia were rapidly sinking.[46]

---

42. Information from Frank Aarebrot, University of Bergen, Norway, coordinator of the Scandinavian Helsinki groups' team of election monitors. In Estonia, only one set of ballots with a bilingual text was printed. Similar estimates for this country, therefore, were not available.

43. See e.g. Dzintra Bungs, 'Poll Shows Majority in Latvia Endorses Independence', *Report on the USSR*, III (15 March 1991), pp. 22–4; Riina Kionka, 'Are the Baltic Laws Discriminatory'?, *Report on the USSR*, III (12 April 1991), pp. 21–4. According to Kionka, the results of the polls showed that 'the issue of Baltic independence is not an ethnic, but a political question.'

44. See, for instance, Boris Tsilevich, 'Natsional'nye gruppy Latvii: Kak naiti model' sosushchestvovaniia?', *Sovetskaia Molodež'*, 22 May 1991, p. 4.

45. See, for instance, exit-poll interviews reported in *Baltiiskoe Vremia*, 5 March 1991.

46. Similar lines of reasoning have been evidenced at other junctures of European history. For instance, a considerable number of Germans in South Schleswig in the 1950s voted for the party of the Danish minority, SSW, indirectly indicating a preference for Danish citizenship. They hope that if Schleswig were transferred to the smaller northern neighbour, the demographic and economic convulsions which the area was experiencing would become less violent. See e.g. Timothy Alan Tilton, *Nazism, Neo-Nazism and the Peasantry*, Bloomington, 1975, pp. 96ff.

As a final explanation for the voting behaviour of the Baltic Russians, there is reason to believe that many who did not particularly like the idea of Baltic independence reasoned that it was nonetheless impossible to stem the tide. By trying to obstruct the inevitable, they might be branded as enemies of a state in which they would have to continue to live. At first glance, this explanation may seem spurious; since the referendums were secret, it would be impossible for anyone to single out afterwards those individuals who had voted against independence and then deny them citizenship as a punishment. However, this did not prevent a prominent member of the Latvian parliament, Rolands Rikards, from claiming that 'the citizens of the USSR who on 3 March vote in favour of a free, democratic and independent Latvia, having by dint of their voting testified their loyalty towards the state, will become potential citizens of the Latvian Republic.'[47] This startling statement was carried on the front page of the Russian-language edition of the semi-official Latvian newspaper *Diena* on the eve of the referendum. The very fact that the Russians had been not only invited but strongly encouraged to participate in the poll was in itself also a strong signal that they were considered an integral part of the body politic. However, no citizenship law had yet been passed in either country, and one of the first major issues to appear on the political agenda after independence was precisely the question of citizenship.

Post-independence politics in Estonia and Latvia

In Estonia a change of political climate set in almost immediately after the achievement of independence in August 1991. In an official document from the city council of Tallinn produced in September 1991, post-war immigrants were referred to as 'citizens of other states'.[48] Furthermore, a new law on Land Reform which was passed by the Estonian parliament on 17 October stated that until an Estonian citizenship law had been adopted, only those persons who had been citizens of inter-war Estonia, together with their descendants, would be allowed to participate in the privatisation process.[49]

On 26 February 1992, the Estonian citizenship law of 1938, with

47. *Diena*, 2 March, 1991, p. 1.
48. *Vechernii Kur'er*, 30 September 1991.
49. 'Zakon o zemel'noi reforme', *Estoniia*, 5 November 1991.

some later amendments, was re-enacted. In the inter-war period this was considered one of the most liberal citizenship laws in the world, and in many ways it still is. All it requires is two years' residence before submitting a citizenship application and a one-year wait afterwards before an immigrant can be naturalised. This compares favourably with a number of Western countries, where the required period of residence is much longer. In addition, Estonian applicants for citizenship must document their knowledge of the state language, both orally and in writing, and swear allegiance to the Estonian constitution.[50]

However, in this re-enacted version of the Estonian law, the naturalisation clauses were being applied not only to immigrants knocking on the country's border gate asking to be let in but also to those persons who had had permanent abode in Estonia for decades. Moreover, even the children of the latter people were denied status as original citizens, even if they were born in Estonia. It was estimated that under these conditions, only about 100,000 of the 600,000 non-Estonians qualified as original citizens. Approximately 40% of the resident population were effectively disfranchised.

As interpreted by various spokesmen for the Estonian authorities, the Estonian citizenship law denies the postwar immigrants their

50. For the text of the law, see *Estoniia*, 7 June 1993. The level of language proficiency required of applicants for Estonian citizenship was fleshed out in a draft law in the autumn of 1992. Applicants would be required to know a basic Estonian vocabulary of 1,500 words, not in isolation but combined into sentences. They should show that they could discuss a topic, 'using negative and affirmative statements, asking questions, expressing commands, bans and wishes, as well as expressing opinions and suppositions, giving explanations, accurately representing various temporal relations'. In addition, the applicant should demonstrate ability to read works of literature, including classical Estonian poetry. See 'Citizenship and Language Laws in the Newly Independent States of Europe', Copenhagen, 9–10 January 1993, seminar papers. However, as these requirements were met by protests from several quarters, they were somewhat modified in February 1993, in particular for elderly people. See *Russkaia Gazeta*, 5 December 1992, p. 5; *ibid.*, 13 February 1993, p. 3. It should be noted that according to Article 7 of the Estonian citizenship law, the language requirements may be fallved 'in the cases of' stateless persons who prior to the date of application for Estonian citizenship have resided permanently in Estonia for at least ten years'. The reference in the 1938 law to 'permanent residence' is in the enabling legislation for the reenactment of the law defined as 'legal' permanent residence. This means that if (a) the citizenship law is not amended, and if (b) the post-war immigrants are granted legal residence permits, the language requirements for naturalisation will be rendered largely irrelevant sometime early in the next century.

status not only as original citizens but also as a national minority group. They claim that international law defines as 'minorities' only those who are citizens of the state in which they live. Former Soviet citizens in Estonia who are without Estonian citizenship are not stateless persons, but should be regarded instead as citizens of Russia, since it is Russia that has declared itself the successor state of the Soviet Union.[51]

In June 1992, a new Estonian constitution was adopted through a referendum in which only citizens were allowed to participate.[52] This constitution guarantees a number of rights – such as unemployment benefits, pensions, sickness and social-security benefits, and the right to conduct business – to non-citizens only 'insofar as otherwise is not stipulated by law', thus leaving the door open for future unspecified restrictions.[53]

Non-citizens are forbidden to be members of political parties, and are barred from participation in national elections. They may vote in local elections, but they may not run for office. National elections were held in September 1992. No Russians or other Russian-speakers were elected to the new parliament.[54]

In the summer of 1993 the Estonian parliament discussed a law on aliens in which the conditions for the continued existence of non-citizens in Estonia were spelled out. The draft law stipulated, *inter alia*, that a residence permit had to be renewed every five years. This law gave no guarantees that the permit would actually be renewed, and it was seen by many Russians as a law that gave the authorities an opportunity to expel them. The draft created an uproar among Russians in Estonia[55] as well as in Russia, and also caused great concern among delegates at a CSCE meeting which happened to be assembled in Helsinki at that time. Some of the most controversial requirements, such as the need to renew the residence permit every five years, were

51 Aap Neljas, in *Isamaa*, August 1992, p. 11, as summarised by Raivo Vetik, 'Ethnic Conflict and Accomodation in Post-Communist Estonia', *Journal of Peace Research*, XXX, 3 (1993), pp. 271–80, p. 277; Mart Rannut (member of the National Language Board in Estonia), 'Language and Citizenship Policy in Estonia', paper presented at the seminar on 'Citizenship and Language Laws in the Newly Independent States of Europe', Copenhagen, 9–10 January 1993, p. 5.
52 *Izvestiia*, 30 June 1992.
53 *Konstitutsiia Estonskoi Respubliki*, Tallinn, 1992, pp. 9ff (articles 28 and 319).
54 *Komsomol'skaia Pravda*, 22 September 1992.
55 'Obrashchenie Prezidiuma Predstavitel'noi Assamblei', *Estoniia*, 16 June 1993, p. 1.

amended or deleted on the recommendation of the CSCE High Commissioner for national minorities.[56]

In Latvia, heated debates on the citizenship issue took off in the immediate aftermath of the abortive August coup. Several leading politicians who had earlier defended the zero option (i.e. no formal requirements) now began to insist that postwar immigrants should have to go through a naturalisation process including a test of their Latvian language skills. In July 1991 the liberal chairman of the Human Rights Commission in the Latvian parliament, Andreis Pantelejevs, had suggested five years' residence and no language requirements for would-be citizens.[57] However, by May 1992 Pantelejevs had decidedly rejected the zero option.[58] The same was the case with the chairman of the Latvian Supreme Council, Anatolijs Gorbunovs – another strong supporter of the zero option in the pre-independence period. In March 1992, however, he suggested that the issue of citizenship ought to be decided in a referendum in which only prewar citizens should be allowed to participate. To justify this idea, he pointed to the referendum on the future of apartheid in South Africa, held in the same year, in which black people were barred from voting.[59]

In an interview in June 1991, the leader of the Latvian National Independence Movement, Visvaldis Lacis, gave an assurance that if his party came to power, non-Latvians would be allowed to have 'equal rights in the Latvian Republic', as long as they applied for citizenship in accordance with republican legislation.[60] However, by November of the same year, Lacis declared that the Russians should not be regarded as second-class citizens: rather, in a political sense, they were 'nobodies'. They should have no more rights than he himself would have if he were to take a trip to Sweden.[61] The statement caused a

56. Ann Sheehy, 'The Estonian Law on Aliens', *RFE/RL Research Report*, II, 38 (24 September 1993). For the text of the draft law, see *Molodëzh' Estonii*, 15 June 1993. For the text of final law, see *Estoniia*, 23 July 1993.
57. *Subbotnii Den*, 20 July 1991, p. 1. This proposal may be considered as a variant of the zero option. The granting of citizenship is almost always linked to 'permanent residence', and this concept must be given an operationable definition, such as, for instance, five years.
58. Author's conversation with Andrejs Pantelejevs, *Riga*, 20 May 1992.
59. *Baltic Independent*, 17–23 April 1992.
60. *Sovetskaia Molodëzh'*, 5 June, 1991, p. 2.
61. 'Vivaldis Lacis: "Vy ne grazhdane vtorogo sorta, vy nikto" ', *Sovetskaia Molodëzh'*, 11 September 1991.

sensation, and was immediately quoted in 'empire-saving' sections of the Russian press.[62]

On 15 October 1991 the Latvian parliament adopted a resolution on citizenship which stated that 'the aggregate body of Republic of Latvia citizens, in accordance with the Republic of Latvia 'Law on citizenship' of August 23, 1919, continues to exist.' In addition, the parliament adopted general guidelines for naturalisation which required sixteen years' residence for those who had not held a Latvian passport in the inter-war period, or who were direct descendants of persons who did possess such a passport. In addition, a knowledge of and loyalty to the Latvian constitution, plus proficiency in the Latvian language on a conversational level, were required.[63] With a few changes, these guidelines were incorporated into a new citizenship law which was passed on the first reading in November the same year.[64] This law, however, would have acquired legal force only if it had been adopted on a second and third reading as well, and this was not done.

The adoption of the resolution on the aggregate body of prewar citizens, combined with the failure to adopt a law on naturalisation, led to conflicting reports on whether Latvia had actually enacted a citizenship law or not. The situation made possible the development of a legal framework for Latvian political life even while the postwar immigrants continued to find themselves in a legal limbo. The latter were trying to guess which rights and freedoms they might be deprived of when a naturalisation law was finally enacted. Fears that they might, for example, be denied re-entry into the country after a sojourn abroad seemed reasonably well-founded.[65] In a Constitutional Act adopted by the Supreme Council on 10 December 1991, a number of rights were reserved for citizens, including the right to own and dispose of land and other natural resources; the freedom to reside in Latvia and return there; the right of access to state office; and the

---

62. *Politika*, 1991, no. 15, p. 2.
63. 'On the Renewal of Republic of Latvia Citizens' Rights and Fundamental Principles of Naturalisation', *Survey of Baltic and Post-Soviet Politics*, Sakala Center, Tallinn, February 1992, pp. 24–5. See also Dzintra Bungs, 'Latvia Adopts Guidelines for Citizenship', *Report on the USSR*, III (18 October 1991).
64. 'Draft law on Citizenship, Republic of Latvia', not dated. Reproduced in '*Citizenship and Language Laws in the Newly Independent States of Europe: Seminar Documents*, Copenhagen 9–10 January 1993.
65. Ibrahima Fall, 'Summary of the Report on a Fact-Finding Mission to Latvia', 27 November 1992.

right both to vote and to be elected.[66] In contrast to the Estonian situation, non-citizens in Latvia will not be allowed to vote in local elections either. Based on the October 1991 resolution on citizenship, citizens-only national elections were held in June 1993.

In November 1993 the new Latvian parliament, the 'Saiema'; discussed a naturalisation law based on a proposal drafted by the republic's largest party, the Latvian Way. It will grant citizenship to applicants who have lived in the country for ten years and speak Latvian. In addition, a system of annual naturalisation quotas is under discussion. These quotas are to be calculated as a certain percentage of the natural rate of increase of the citizen population. Since in recent years this increase has verged on the negative, the annual quotas might, as a result, become so miniscule that it will take decades or more to naturalise all those who qualify for citizenship. The explicit aim of the quota system, as defined by the draft law, is to 'ensure the development of a one-community nation-state'.[67]

In the citizenship debate in both Estonia and Latvia, the bilateral agreements with Russia have played a negligible role. Many Baltic leaders ignore them. In a conversation with the author in the spring of 1993, a prominent member of the Estonian cabinet revealed that he had never even heard of the agreement. This ignorance was made possible because the agreements are regularly overlooked in the Western debate also. In hardly any of the human rights reports written by Western expert commissions have the terms of these agreements ever been discussed.[68] Yet the attitudes and behaviour of the Baltic Russians have largely been formed by the fate of these agreements.

The Balts frequently claim that the agreements had been extorted from them under duress, and so cannot be regarded as binding. This argument obviously lets the innocent suffer for the guilty (the pressure was, of course, put on the Balts by the Soviet, not the Russian leader-

---

66. For further details on how the citizenship legislation influenced the position of the Russians in Estonia and Latvia, see Paul Kolstoe, 'National Minorities in the Non-Russian Soviet Successor States of the Former Soviet Union', *RAND Report, DRU-565-FF*, November 1993.

67. Grigorievs, *op. cit.* (note 8).

68. Jan De Meyer and Christos Rozakis, 'Human Rights in the Republic of Latvia', *Human Rights Law Journal*, XIII, 5–6 (June 1992), pp. 244–9; Raimo Pekkanen and Hans Danelius, 'Human Rights in the Republic of Estonia', *Human Rights Law Journal*, XIII, 5–6 (June 1992), pp. 236–44; Ibrahima Fall, *op. cit.*

ship). In addition, the Balts point to Article IV, Section 3, which states that the right to choose citizenship shall be exercised in accordance both with the agreement 'and with domestic legislation'. The latter clause is understood as giving the signatory states the right to adopt any citizenship law they please. The Russian view is that domestic law cannot modify the substance of the agreement commitment but can only regulate minor issues of procedure. The Norwegian human rights expert Asbjørn Eide claims that the latter view '*is much better founded in rules of interpretation of treaties*'.[69]

In Russia, the failure by Estonia and Latvia to honour their obligations under these agreements has greatly influenced Russian policy towards the Baltics.[70] In one particularly harsh statement made in October 1992, President Yeltsin indirectly linked the question of the political rights of the Baltic Russians to the withdrawal of Russian troops from the area. Since the agreement with Latvia has not been ratified by the Russian side, it cannot be used as an argument in the Russian–Latvian dispute. The agreement with Estonia, on the other hand, is frequently referred to.[71]

In May 1991, Yeltsin defended his policy towards the Baltic states by claiming that since the signing of the bilateral agreements, Latvia and Estonia had begun to amend some laws which were discriminatory towards the Russians.[72] Whether or not his claim was correct, the tendency in Estonian and Latvian legislation after August 1991 switched in the opposite direction. A clear example of this was the Latvian language law. Many of the provisions of the 1989 language law were due to enter into legal force in May 1992 but some weeks earlier substantial changes to it were made.[73] The next text was considered by many observers not as a revision but as a completely new law.[74] In the 1989 version it had been unequivocally stated that in any correspondence between a citizen and the state organs, 'the citizen chooses the language' of communication. This sentence was deleted from the amended version, and a rewritten Article 9 now stipulated that written

69. Asbjørn Eide, *op. cit.* (note 7), p. 10. Italics in the original.
70. For more details, see Chapter 10.
71. See e.g. 'Postanovlenie Verkhovnogo Soveta Rossiiskoi Federatsii o pravakh cheloveka v Estonii', *Nezavisimaia Gazeta*, 23 July 1992; *Nezavisimaia Gazeta*, 8 July 1992.
72. *Izvestiia*, 24 May 1991.
73. For the text of the law, see *Diena*, 24 April 1992.
74. Boris Tsilevich, 'Iazyk v zakone i iazyk vne zakona', *SM-Segodnia*, 15 April 1992.

replies from officials to citizens would be given in the state language. The new version of the law regulates not only the official uses of the languages but also the work of public organisations, private firms etc.[75] No less than three different state agencies were set up to monitor the application of the above language law. A failure to comply with it was to be met with prosecution, transgressors being fined a maximum of 10,000 rubles.[76] Mandatory language tests were conducted at a number of enterprises, and those failing them were to be fired.[77]

Andrejs Pantelejevs has justified the changes in the law by pointing out that the Russian-speakers had made little effort since the promulgation of the first version to learn the state language.[78] Possibly he is right, although some Latvians claim that in the fall of 1991 many Russians did actually begin to stammer forth what few Latvian words they knew.[79] Still, quite a number of Slavs admitted that they lack any motivation to take appropriate language courses.[80] Some evidently hoped that the language requirements would miraculously 'go away'. Many are industrial workers who are quite unfamiliar with bookish studies of any kind and furthermore the Estonian and Latvian governments do not provide any state-run language courses for would-be citizens or other non-Balts.

Russian attitudes after independence

After the abortive *coup d'état* in August 1991, the interfronts and other militantly pro-Communist and pro-empire organisations in the Baltics were in total disarray. Several of their leaders were arrested for actual

75. This was singled out for particular criticism by the CSCE High Commissioner on National Minorities, Max van der Stoel, in his letter to the Latvian Government of 6 April 1993.
76. 'Law on Additions to the Latvian Code on Administrative Violations Concerning the Official State Language Issues', 1 July 1992.
77. Boris Tsilevich, 'Citizenship Issue and Language Legislation in Today's Latvia: Tools for Implementation of the Ethnic Nation-State Concept', paper presented at the Conference on Citizenship and Language Laws of the Newly Independent States of Europe, Copenhagen, 9–10 January 1993.
78. Author's conversation, Riga, 20 May 1992.
79. Author's conversations in Riga, May 1992.
80. 'Russians in Estonia: Problems and Prospects', *Report Prepared by the Staff of the Commission on Security and Cooperation in Europe*, September 1992, p. 6.

or alleged coup support.[81] Others were deprived of their seats in the parliament on similar grounds. Their constituencies were disoriented and demoralised.

In addition, those non-natives who had supported Baltic independence now found themselves at a crossroads. A few Russian supporters of Baltic independence were prepared to defend the new currents in Estonian and Latvian nationality in their entirety.[82] However, the prevalent mood among Russian supporters of Baltic independence was one of disappointment and despondency.[83] Already, in November 1991, the Estonian minister for nationality questions, Artur Kuznetsov, had resigned, declaring that he could not and would not participate in the sorting of people.[84] His Latvian colleague, Vladimir Steshenko, basically shared Kuznetsov's disillusionment but tried to hold onto his job in order to defend the interests of Russian-speakers from within the prevailing structures.[85] In November 1992, however, he too gave up.[86]

During the 'stagnation period', the Latvian Russian-language youth newspaper *Sovetskaia Molodëzh'* had been known for its progressive views and editorial independence. After August 1991 it became an increasingly unrelenting critic of Latvian nationality policy, to the

---

81. *Komsomol'skaia Pravda*, 7 November 1991.

82. One of them was the Narva-based researcher Sergei Gorokhov, who was awarded Estonian citizenship for his services to the Estonian state without having to pass the language test. Also, the editor of the Russian language Estonian cultural journal *Raduga*, Alla Kallas, retained her support for Estonia's handling of the citizenship issue. See *Literaturnaia Gazeta*, no. 40, 1991, p. 2; and *Raduga*, no. 3, 1993, pp. 76–7; and a personal communication with the author.

83. See, e.g., statement by the former prominent front member Vladlen Dozortsev at the conference 'The New Russian Diaspora', Lielupe, Latvia, 13–15 November 1992; and interview with Dozortsev in *SM-Segodnia*, 15 December, 16 December and 17 December 1992. A number of disillusioned statements have been recorded also by Richard J. Krickus, 'Latvia's "Russian Question"', *RFE/RL Research Report* II, 18 (30 April 1993).

84. Author's interview, Tallinn, 8 November 1991. In January 1992, Kuznetsov took Russian citizenship, and was appointed Russian ambassador to Estonia. The appointment, however, was not accepted by Estonian authorities. They objected to it on technical grounds, as well as on the grounds that Kuznetsov had criticised Estonian policy while being a member of the Estonian government. See *Nezavisimaia Gazeta*, 7 February 1992, p. 3. Later Kuznetsov was charged with cooperation with the KGB, and disappeared from Estonian politics.

85. Author's interview, Riga, 21 May 1992.

86. *Smena* (St. Petersburg), 30 March 1993, p. 3.

point where it began to sacrifice its previous stance of non-partisanship. In December 1991 the deputy editor of *SM-Segodnia* ruefully wrote:

> Today, retired interfronters are probably gleefully exclaiming: 'We warned you, Judases! Your popular fronters will only exploit you and then throw you away. Isn't that exactly what happened!?' To state the bitter truth, this *is* what happened. It is high time to recognise our mistake. But it could not have been otherwise. Russian democrats could not rally under the militant red banner or march under the cover of an armed personnel carrier from Moscow.[87]

Similar sentiments could be found in *SM-Segodnia's* Estonian counterpart, *Molodëzh' Estonii*. In September 1992 it published an open letter from a teacher at the Tallinn pedagogical institute to her students: 'My dear students, I feel very guilty because of my emotional and optimistic forecasts about your future in independent Estonia, claiming that we russophone citizens would find our proper place in that society.'[88] She had now become convinced that they would not find this. Still, she would not recant her support for Estonian independence, or her joy at the rectification of the historical injustice done to the Estonian nation.

In the vacuum created by the ending of the interfronts, a number of Russian cultural-social organisations have sprung up in both Latvia and Estonia. However, the fragmentation and constant infighting which have become characteristic traits of political life in Russia seem to have affected the Baltic Russian organisations as well. In Estonia, the Russian Democratic Movement was set up in August 1991 with the support of the Savisaar popular front government. The Movement fully accepted Estonian as the sole state language in Estonia, but was highly critical of the Estonian citizenship law which it believed endangered civil peace and democracy in the country. It also maintained that the majority of the non-native population perceived Estonia as their homeland, and it deplored what it saw as strong psychological pressure on them to emigrate.[89]

87. Evgenii Orlov, *SM-Segodnia*, 13 December 1991, p. 1.
88. Margarita Petrova, in *Molodëzh' Estonii*, 1 September 1992.
89. 'Citizenship Law of the Republic of Estonia and the Non-native Population: Situation and Prognosis', Analytical Draft by Russian Democratic Movement of Estonia', printed in the seminar papers from the conference 'Citizenship and Language Laws in the Newly Independent States of Europe', Copenhagen, 9–10 January 1993.

Together with some other pro-democracy organisations, the Democratic Movement, in January 1993, established a Representative Assembly: a sort of quasi-parliament to represent the interests of the disenfranchised population, irrespective of their ethnic background.[90] The Assembly now serves as a kind of umbrella structure for a large number of organisations, including the Narva Labour Union Centre, the Organisation of Former Deputies to the Estonian Supreme Council, the Union of Veteran Organisations, the Union of Slavic Cultural Centres and the national cultural centres of the Jewish, Korean and Uzbek communities in Estonia. Thus it aspires to function as an organisational link between the russophone community and various authorities in Estonia, in Russia and in other states.[91] For some time the Estonian Supreme Council opposed the establishment of the Assembly, fearing the emergence of any parallel legislative body, but it did finally register it in the summer of 1993.[92]

A number of Estonian Russian organisations refused to join the Assembly, finding its profile too liberal, and instead set up a rival organisation, the Russian Council, which united only ethnic Russians (as distinct from all russophones).[93] Both organisations fielded candidates at the local elections in October 1993 and did surprisingly well. In Tallinn, a city with roughly equal-sized communities of Estonians and russophones, the parliamentary group affiliated to the Representative Assembly became the second largest caucus in the city council, with 27 out of 64 seats. In general, cities with high concentrations of Russians had a higher-than-average turnout – an indication that the supposed political apathy of Etonian Russians may be exaggerated. Also, their willingness to participate in Estonian political life within the limits imposed by the authorities may also be growing. As expressed by the new deputy speaker in the Tallinn city council, Viktor Poliakov, a Russian: 'We have had enough enmity and tension. For that reason, I am against the politicisation of our activities . . . It is necessary to find compromises, without, of course, effacing

90. The *Baltic Independent*, 22–28 January 1993, p. 7; *Nezavisimaia Gazeta*, 28 January 1993.
91. 'Ustav predstavitel'noi assamblei', typescript.
92. 'Russians in Estonia: Problems and Prospects', *op. cit.*. p. 10 (note 80).
93. *Estoniia*, 22 January 1993, p. 2; *ibid.*, 2 February 1993, pp. 1 and 3.

ourselves, without forgetting the interests of our voters, the russo-phone population.[94]

In Latvia, the Latvian Society of Russian Culture (LORK) also remained basically pro-Baltic after independence. However, it attracted only a very small part of the Russian population – and that mostly from the cultural intelligentsia. Much more critical of Latvian nationality policy was the larger organisation, the Russian Community of Latvia (ROL), which also appealed to blue-collar workers. ROL's main goal was to create a comprehensive and effective system of mutual aid, moral, spiritual and material for its members. It worked both for the preservation of the national self-awareness of the Russians and for the development of traditional Russian culture. Membership was open to Russian-speakers of all nationalities.[95] The attitude of the Latvian authorities towards ROL was ambivalent. While allowing the organisation to be registered, the minister of justice also alleged that its activities were directed against the Latvian state – although this serious charge was never substantiated.[96]

ROL attempted to run its own Russian-language technological university in order to offer higher education to students finding difficulty in studying in Latvian.[97] The community also published a readable newspaper, *The Russian Way (Russkii Put')*. However, the organisation was being eaten up from within. In September 1992 an initiative group of ROL convened a Council (Sobor) which, they hoped, would become 'a symbol of national solidarity and national dignity'.[98] This pious hope was somewhat utopian, given the fact that the initiative group had already been denounced by other ROL leaders as usurpers. The *Sobor* indeed turned out to be a rather rowdy gathering. 'The speakers tried to shout each other down from the rostrum. Shocked participants left the hall. In the end, the chairman realised that E. Smekhov had the loudest voice of all those present and was compelled to give him the floor.'[99] This report could have been dismissed as malicious anti-Russian slander, but for the fact that it was

---

94. *Estoniia*, 4 December 1993. See, also, interview with the new deputy mayor of Tallinn, Viktor Andreev, in *Estoniia*, 26 November 1993.
95. 'Ustav Russkoi obshchiny Latvii', Riga, 23 March 1991, p. 1.
96. *Russkii Put'*, 13 June 1992, p. 1; *SM-Segodnia*, 22 July, 1992.
97. *SM-Segodnia*, 3 August 1991, p. 3; *Russkii Put'*, 11 July 1992, P. 3.
98. *Russkii Put'*, 12 September 1992, p. 2.
99. *Russkii Put'*, 26 September 1992, p. 1.

published in ROL's own paper. By December 1992 ROL had for all practical purposes disintegrated.[100]

Latvian Russians who have been accepted as citizens have organised political parties to promote their interests. Some attempts have been made to create a national Russian party, but these have not won the support of the Russian voters.[101] Instead, a part of the Russian vote went in the 1993 election to 'Equal Rights', a party which grew out of the Latvian Supreme Soviet faction with the same name, and was associated with the defunct interfront. It garnered 5.8% of the vote, while the moderately left-of-centre Concord for Latvia, in which a number of Russian erstwhile popular front leaders participated, was more than twice as popular with the electorate (12%).

The question of the political loyalty of the Russian-speaking minorities has been the subject of intense controversy in the Baltic press. Many members of the titular groups claim that the Russians long for the lost Soviet empire and are unwilling to adapt to the new political realities. These groups also claim that the Russians are susceptible to imperialist propaganda from Moscow, and would become willing agents of the Russian army if there were a military conflict with Russia. In short, they are actual or potential fifth columnists. However, spokesmen for the Russians themselves maintain that the overwhelming majority of the Russians faithfully abide by Latvian and Estonian law, even when they disagree with it.[102] Any expressions of Russian empire-nostalgia have to be understood as a psychological reaction against political pressure from the titular ethnic groups.

A survey conducted in Latvia in the spring of 1992 does not give a conclusive answer to this matter. It showed that 34% of the respondents identified 'Russia' as 'my motherland' while 39% held that view of Latvia. Unadulterated imperialist attitudes could be found only among some 23%, who believed that 'historically Latvia has been a part of Russia and remains so'. The Norwegian scholar who conducted the surveys concluded that Latvian Russians tend to be quite strongly attached to Latvia, the more so the longer they have stayed in the country

100. *Megapolis-Express*, no. 47, December 1992.
101. See Irina Krumina, 'Politicheskaia aktivnost' russkikh v Latvii: Istoriia i perspektivy', paper presented to the conference 'The New Russian Diaspora', Lielupe, Latvia, 13–15 November 1992.
102. Boris Tsilevich, 'Mif o piatoi kolonne', in *Vremia Zhëstkikh Reshenii*, Riga, 1993, pp. 229–32.

and the better they speak Latvian. The majority of them did not seem to be affected by an imperial way of thinking. However, a sense of imperial identity was seen as being quite widespread among certain sub-groups of the Russian population.[103]

Regional issues

The Russian population element in Estonia and Latvia is not evenly distributed over the territory of the two states. Apart from being clearly overrepresented in the capitals, greater numbers also live in the eastern parts. The Latgale region of eastern Latvia has for centuries had a strong Slavic element both culturally and demographically with both Polish and Russian groups. In addition, the local Latvians have their own dialect, and have developed a strong regional identity.

The north-eastern Estonian towns of Kohtla-Järve, Sillamaë and Narva are respectively 77%, 97% and 96% russophone. In contrast to Latgale, most of the population here are post-war immigrants, but they are generally more rooted in Estonian soil than the Russian population in and around Tallinn. In Narva 69% of the population is either born in Estonia or has lived there for more than thirty years.[104] The chairman of the Narva city council maintained in November 1991 that the city's inhabitants see themselves as Estonians in the territorial sense (*estliandtsy*).[105] However, living in a compactly Russian community, they have largely been isolated from Estonian culture.

In the aftermath of the August coup the city councils of Daugavpils and Rezekne in Latgale and of Kohtla-Järve, Sillamaë and Narva in Estonia were dissolved, allegedly for supporting the putschists. The two Latvian cities were put under a new 'temporary authority' appointed directly by the Supreme Council in Riga. New elections were promised for February 1992, but were postponed several times and by the winter of 1994 had still not been held.[106]

In Narva and Kohtla-Järve, by contrast, fresh elections were held as early as in October 1991. To the dismay of Estonian leaders, the Narvians voted most of their former city authorities back into office

---

103. Aadne Aasland, 'Russian Ethnic Identity in Latvia – A Sociological Survey', paper presented at the conference 'The New Russian Diaspora', Lielupe, Latvia, 13–15 November 1992.

104. Kirch, Kirch and Tuisk, *op. cit.*, p. 11 (cf. note 19).

105. Author's interview with Vladimir Chuikin, Narva, 7 November 1991.

106. Author's communication with Boris Tsilevich and Aleksandr Ruchkovsky.

and relations between Narva and Tallinn consequently remained tense. Particularly galling to the Estonian leaders was the fact that the Russian leaders were former Communists. As expressed by Mart Rannut: 'As long as the statue of Lenin still stands in downtown Narva any cordial dialogue with its inhabitants is meaningless.'[107] Since only citizens may run for office under the new Estonian election law, the Narva leadership was prevented from being re-elected a second time in the local elections in October 1993.

During *perestroika* the Estonian national movement focussed sharply on the grave ecological problems in the republic – particularly those associated with the wasteful and polluting phosphorite and oil shale production. This production is in the north-eastern corner of the republic – that is, in the Russian-dominated area – and is indispensable to local industry. The local Russians would certainly like to see some cleansing equipment installed but they are afraid that the activities of the environmentalists could lead to the closure of the quarries and the ruin of their economy.[108] However, nothing has been done since independence either to close or to improve the industry, a fact which has made some Narvians and some Western observers wonder if the ecology issue was simply one of the levers used by the Estonian nationalists to break out of the Soviet Union.[109] However, in most other post-Soviet states the ecology issue has generally been relegated to the back burner after independence, primarily for reasons of economic austerity.

Some aspects of Estonian government policy have certainly hit the population of the north-east particularly hard. More than any other parts of the Estonian economy, the large Moscow-controlled factories in the region were most closely linked to the all-Union market, and they suffered severely when Estonia left the ruble zone and introduced its own hard currency. Almost all economic ties with the former Union were broken, and thousands of workers at the local textile mill

107. See, e.g., interview with Mart Rannut, general director of the Estonian language department, in *Digest* (Tallinn), no. 2, 1993, p. 4.
108. Author's interview with members of the Narva City Council, 7 November 1991.
109. Charles F. Furtado Jr and Michael Hechter, 'The Emergence of Nationalist Politics in the USSR: a Comparison of Estonia and the Ukraine', in Alexander J. Motyl (ed.), *Thinking Theoretically About Soviet Nationalities*, New York, 1992, pp. 169–203, esp. p. 182.

and electronics factory were laid off.[110] Again, this does not have to be seen as a deliberate anti-Russian policy, rather as an unfortunate effect of a market transition which happens to hit one ethnic group extremely hard. In fact, the municipal authorities in Narva, while severely critical of the policies of the Estonian government, did not present their controversy with Tallinn as involving any ethnic issue.[111]

The political leaders in Narva, Kohtla-Järve and Sillamaë wanted greater administrative autonomy within the Estonian state. In July 1991 the city councils of these three towns suggested the granting of a 'special status' to their regions, with some budgetary autonomy and 'consideration of their specific character'.[112] This initiative was flatly rejected in Tallinn. Two years later, the authorities of Narva and Sillamaë organised local referendums in which the population were asked if they favoured territorial autonomy for their area. The participants overwhelmingly gave a positive answer, but turn-out was low. A British researcher visiting Narva in March 1993 concluded that 'there seems to be a readiness to adjust and adapt on the part of Russians in Narva.'[113]

Returning to our initial question, there appears to be no clear explanation of what changed the inter-ethnic climate during the Latvian and Estonian independence struggle. But one can suggest some parts of the answer. There are elements peculiar to the Baltic situation, while others are common to post-Soviet ethnic relations in general.

1. The simplistic explanation is that ethnic groups inevitably clash whenever they are not prevented from doing so by ulterior forces (for instance, by a totalitarian regime). Theoreticians of nationalism who see ethnic conflicts primarily as the result of deep-seated cultural differences will no doubt soon write books on the dissolution of the Soviet Union to prove their theories. Certainly, they will find abundant material. At the same time, there is also considerable evidence

110. *Izvestiia*, 13 November 1992, p. 2; the *Baltic Independent*, 12 February 1993, p. 5.
111. See Philip Hanson, 'Estonia's Narva Problem, Narva's Estonian Problem', *RFE/RL Research Report*, II, 18 (30 April 1993), pp. 17–23.
112. 'The Memorandum of Chairmen of Three North East Estonian Town Councils', *Survey of Baltic and post-Soviet Politics*, Sakala Centre, Tallinn, August 1991, p. 20.
113. Hanson, *op. cit.*, p. 23.

pointing in the opposite direction. Many Balts claim that cordial cross-cultural relations at the neighbourhood level continued to exist in both Latvia and Estonia, despite the ever greater tension on the political level. Obviously, many politicians in the Baltics, as well as in other parts of the former Soviet Union, have managed to secure their political future by playing on the ethnic issue. Experts who see nationalism primarily as a result of élite manipulations will have equally good reason to think that ethnic politics in the Soviet Union vindicated their theories.[114]

2. The extremely rapid demographic changes in Latvia and Estonia have clearly contributed to the hardening of ethnic fronts by causing a situation in which two population groups have been living side by side with minimal contact and understanding. Latvian and Estonian spokesmen have never made any attempt to conceal the fact that they view this situation with great concern. The official position in both countries, however, has invariably been that this problem will be overcome by integrating most of the migrants into Estonian and Latvian society and not by expelling them. However, it is not always easy to see how the means employed by the Baltic state authorities will lead to that aim.

3. The fact that Estonia and Latvia were independent states between the World Wars has enabled the question of granting or refusing franchise to postwar immigrants to be presented as a legal-historical issue rather than an ethnic one. Certainly, the legal-historical circumstances are important. The fact that the Soviet annexation of the Baltic states in 1940 was (with a few exceptions) unrecognised by the international community strongly reinforces the legal argument. As a rule, the citizenship issue has been treated in the Estonian and Latvian legislatures as a strictly constitutional matter in which references to the ethnic dimension are scrupulously avoided. However, from time to time this dimension does arise. Article 7 in the Estonian citizenship

114. For culturalist ('neo-primordialist') explanations of nationalism, see Donald Horowitz, *Ethnic Groups in Conflict*, Berkeley, 1985; Anthony D. Smith, *National Identity*, Harmondsworth, 1991. For socio-political explanations, see Ernest Gellner, *Nations and Nationalism*, Oxford, 1983/1990; E. J. Hobsbawm, *Nations and Nationalism Since 1780: Programme, Myth, Reality*, Cambridge, 1990/1991. For Horowitz's, Smith's and Gellner's attempts to apply their theories to the Soviet nationalities scene, see their respective contributions to Alexander J. Motyl (ed.) *Thinking Theoretically About Soviet Nationalities*, New York, 1991.

law states that the residence and language requirements for citizenship may be waived for 'Estonian nationals'[115] In this context, 'nationals' can only mean *ethnic* Estonians.

4. The unsavoury activities of the interfronts, the Communist parties and their satellite organisations during the Baltic struggle for independence created much bad blood between the ethnic groups. Many Balts find it hard to accept that people who have tried to deny basic rights to others should now be entitled to such rights themselves. Still, under international law, they are so entitled.

5. The crucial drift of some centrist Baltic politicians towards more nationalist positions after independence may be explained in three ways: as a reaction against provocations from the Russian community; as a Machiavellian ploy (conciliatory statements never having been seriously meant); or as a strategy to hold on to the political initiative when the electorate was abandoning them in favour of the national radicals. For lack of evidence in support of the two first theories, the third seems more plausible.

6. Some observers have pointed out that the high language barrier between the different ethnic groups fosters both mistrust and increased polarisation. Only a fraction of the articles written in Estonian and Latvian on the ethnic question are translated into Russian, and vice versa. Very often journalists try to boost the sales of their papers by translating the most inflammatory material, while calls for moderation are deemed too 'boring' to be printed.[116]

7. The involvement of the Russian state in Baltic affairs since independence has not been conducive to inter-ethnic harmony. While Yeltsin certainly has reason to feel double-crossed by the Balts, and while, in the words of Richard Krickus, 'some Latvians may have exploited the troop issue to justify their government's failure to address "the Russian question" ',[117] the linkage of troop withdrawal to human

---

115. Later, this principle was extended to include members of ethnically kindred Finno-Ugric groups in the former Soviet Union.

116. Helen Krag, 'Det baltiske dilemma.˙ Minoritetskonflikt i Estland', in Erik André Andersen (ed.), *Minoriteternes situation og rettigheder i de baltiske lande*, Copenhagen, 1992, pp. 10–37, on pp. 24ff.

117. Krickus, *op. cit.* (note 83).

rights observance was not exactly what the Baltic Russians wanted.[118]

8. A leading Latvian intellectual has pointed to the pernicious and lasting influence of Bolshevik political culture on Baltic politics in order to explain the ethnic deadlock. This culture, often summarised in Lenin's expression 'Who [crushes] whom?', thrives on confrontation rather than compromise.[119] The point is well taken, and indicates that the problems currently faced in the Baltics may be the result more of those historical traditions and cultural traits which the indigenous and the Salvic population have in common than of those traits which separate them.

Lithuania

During *perestroika*, the Lithuanian interfront was not only ardently pro-empire and pro-Communist but also openly Stalinist. It collaborated intimately with Nina Andreeva's uncompromising Stalinist faction within the CPSU.[120] Conversely, many ordinary Lithuanians made few attempts to conceal their hatred of things Russian. Already in the 1970s Andrei Sakharov had commented that ethnic Lithuanians on the Vilnius city bus ostentatiously looked away or moved to another seat if he, as a Russian, sat down next to them.[121]

With some surprise Russian observers noted that the citizenship legislation in 'mutinous Lithuania' turned out to be more liberal than in the other Baltic states.[122] The Lithuanian law of November 1989 granted citizenship automatically to postwar immigrants, provided they applied for it within two years. If they did, they had to sign a declaration that they would obey the Lithuanian constitution. Those who failed to apply for citizenship within the stipulated deadline thus forfeited the privilege of being treated as original citizens. But if on

---

118. See, e.g., 'Memorandum of the Latvian "Civil Agreement" Group', November 1992, typescript; 'Russians in Estonia: Problems and prospects', *op. cit.* (note 80).

119. Indulis Ronis, Director of Institute of History, Latvian Academy of Sciences. Cited in Krickus, *op. cit.*, p. 34 (cf. note 83).

120. Three out of the four pages of the front's newspaper in the swan-song issue of August 1991 were devoted to Andreeva's speeches and declarations. See *Interdvizhenie Litvy*, no. 12, 1991, pp. 1–3.

121. Andrei D. Sakharov, *Memoirs*, New York, 1992, p. 435.

122. Iurii Stroganov, '"Russkii vopros" v Litve', *Rossiiskaia Gazeta*, 16 April 1992, *Izvestiia*, 6 March 1992, p. 15.

second thoughts, they decided that they wanted citizenship after all, they would be treated like any other new immigrant, of whom language skills, as well as loyalty to the constitution and ten years' residence, were required.

The Lithuanian solution to the problem of the 'fifth point' (nationality registration) in the Soviet passport system was Solomonic. A retention of this system could be interpreted as ethnic stigmatisation, while its abolition could be construed as an attempt to eradicate the ethnic distinctiveness of the minorities. Lithuania leaves it to the pass-port carrier to decide whether or not s/he wants to have a nationality registered – and if so, which one.[123]

On the other hand, the Lithuanian language law adopted in January 1989 was initially rather demanding on the non-titular nationalities, since it required all state employees (which, in a socialised economy, meant almost everyone) to learn Lithuanian within two years. Not only Russians but also many Western and Lithuanian observers found this excessive.[124] By January 1991 the learning period had been extended by several years.[125]

There were two obvious reasons for Lithuania's liberalism on the citizenship issue. First, having been adopted as early as in November 1989, several years before the achievement of real independence, the citizenship law was intended as an instrument for achieving such independence in the first place, and if for no other reason, it had to be liberal. Secondly, since the country's incorporation into the Soviet Union, the Russian share of the population has remained constant at the low level of around 10%, which is much the same as in the inter-war period. Before the war, the Russian community in Lithuania (as in Latvian and Estonia) was well integrated into society.[126] It con-sisted largely of religious and political refugees from Russia – Old

---

123. Author's interview with Natal'ia Kasatkina, co-chairwoman of the Lithuanian Russian Cultural Centre, at Lielupe, Latvia, November 1992.

124. V. Stanley Vardys, 'Lithuanian National Politics', *Problems of Communism*, XXXVIII (July–August 1989), pp. 53–76, on p. 59. See also Gytis Liulevicuis, 'Lithuania Signs Treaty with Russia', *Report on the USSR*, III (23 August 1991), p. 20; *Golos Litvy*, no. 9, 1992.

125. Riina Kionka, 'Are the Baltic Laws Discriminatory?', *Report on the USSR*, III, 1991 (14 September 1990), pp. 20–4.

126. Natal'ia Kasatkina, 'Istoriia russkoi diaspory Litvy (1981–1940)', paper presented at the conference 'The New Russian Diaspora', Lielupe, Latvia, 13–15 November 1992.

Believers from the eighteenth century and anti-Bolsheviks from the twentieth. While many of them left for the West at the time of the Soviet invasion, some have remained. Furthermore, Russians today seem better integrated in Lithuania than in most non-Slav former Soviet republics. At 37%, the proportion of Russians who speak the local language is higher in Lithuania than in any other Soviet successor state.

A third reason why relations between the Russians and the indigenous population in Lithuania have developed relatively peacefully is that most Lithuanians regard the 'Polish question' as much more acute than the Russian one. Historically, animosity between Lithuania and Poland goes deep: in the inter-war period Polish–Lithuanian relations were especially bad. Much of the illiberal energy in Lithuanian nationalism seems to have been spent in this controversy.[127]

The only part of Lithuania where Russians and other Russian-speakers are a majority of the population is the town of Snieckus, inhabited by workers at the huge Ignalina nuclear power station. They are less well integrated into Lithuanian society than their co-nationals in other parts of the country,[128] and many of Snieckus's inhabitants might well have sympathised with the interfront in 1990. It seems, however, that their attitudes changed after the 'Bloody Sunday' of 13 January 1991. In mourning over the fourteen Lithuanian casualties of the Soviet assault, the Ignalina workers on 14 January called off an economically motivated strike which had been scheduled for the following day.[129]

The Lithuanian popular front, Sajudis, had many Russian members, and published a Russian-language paper with a large readership. During the dramatic January days, the Russian Orthodox archbishop of Vilnius, Khrysostom, joined president Landsbergis in the barricaded

---

127. In contrast to the Russians, the Poles in Lithuania have a territorial basis in two compactly Polish counties in the south-east. In May 1991, they, on a unilateral basis, declared an autonomous status for their counties. Later in that year, the elected councils in the Polish districts were dissolved on the grounds of alleged anti-constitutional activities. In addition, the administrative borders were changed in such a way as to render the Poles a minority in all electoral districts. Jørn-Holm Hansen, 'Polakkene i Litauen: Statsborgere eller stammemedlemmer?', *Internasjonal Politikk* (Oslo), L, 1–2 (1992), pp. 142ff.

128. Richard Krickus, 'Lithuania: nationalism in the modern era' in Ian Bremmer and Ray Taras (eds), *Nations and Politics in the Soviet Successor States*, Cambridge, 1993, pp. 157–81, on p. 176.

129. *Report on the USSR*, 25 January 1991, p. 9.

parliament building. The next weeks and months saw a blossoming of inter-ethnic fraternity. On 29 January, an initially rather anaemic Lithuanian law on ethnic minorities was amended to give the non-Lithuanians many new rights. According to the amended law, a minority language may be used on a par with the state language in areas with 'substantial numbers of a minority with a different language'. The state also pledged to provide aid to the ethnic communities for the development of their culture and education.[130]

In a national poll on independence held on 9 February (only eleven days after the passing of the amended law on minorities), the Lithuanian legislators were rewarded with solid support from the non-titular ethnic groups. A turn-out of above 80%, and 90% 'Yes'-votes, meant that a large number of Russians supported Lithuanian independence.

Since independence in August 1991 there has been a tendency towards more restrictive legislation on minorities in Lithuania, as indeed in other Soviet successor states. A Lithuanian law on the legal status of foreigners, passed on 4 September 1991 only a fortnight after the failed coup, contained several provisions which did not conform to the standards of international law.[131] According to this law, aliens would enjoy the same rights and freedoms as citizens only insofar as the constitution and laws of Lithuania do not 'provide otherwise'. Freedom of expression was one of the liberties that they were not automatically guaranteed. This law furthermore stipulated that 'when it becomes evident that another state restricts or violates universally recognized norms of legal status of foreigners with regard to citizens of the Republic of Lithuania, the Government of the Republic of Lithuania may establish reciprocating restrictions of rights of foreigners of that state who are staying in the Republic of Lithuania.' This article turned citizens of other states into potential hostages in any crisis situation. Russians in Lithuania who had not yet acquired Lithuanian citizenship would be affected by this

---

130. 'Lithuanian Law on Ethnic Minorities', adopted on 23 November 1989, amended on 29 January 1991. The state aid, however, has for most years been rather meagre. In 1992, each ethnic community received 20,000 rubles (the equivalent of $135). See the *Baltic Observer*, 6–12 August 1992.

131. 'Law on the Legal Status of Foreigners in the Republic of Lithuania', Parliamentary Record no. 5, 4 September 1991, pp. 5–10.

proviso. This law drew harsh criticism from Western human rights experts.[132]

Since independence, discussions on ethnicity-related topics in the Russian-language Lithuanian press have mainly focussed on practical questions of adaptation and integration such as the educational system. Many Russians recognise that 'transition to the state language is inevitable and preparations for it have to be made today.'[133] Ideally, Russian students ought to be given conditions for studying which enable them to compete with Lithuanian-language students both at the time when they enter higher education and afterwards when they were look for a job. If they were allowed to take their entire education in Russian, only the first goal would be achieved, since their lack of proficiency in the state language would be a major drawback on the labour market. In many institutions of learning, special groups receiving education in Russian are established if enough students request them. In the first years of study they are given intensive language training parallel with their professional training, but in the final years they must be able to participate in regular Lithuanian classes.[134] One serious problem, however, is the endemic lack of funds, of Lithuanian-language teachers and of modern textbooks in Lithuanian for Russian-language students.[135]

The only serious organisation for the Lithuanian Russian community after independence seems to be the Russian Cultural Centre. The Centre's programmatic profile is two-pronged. Socially, it works for the integration of Russians into the Lithuanian state, as well as for their active participation in the protection of the legal, ecological and economic interests of the state. And it tries to raise the general cultural level of the Russians by encouraging them to hold on to their cultural distinctiveness – but also by exposing them to Lithuanian culture. The co-chairwoman of the Centre, T. Iasnitskaia, has said: 'Only in a common cultural field can we become equal members of society.'[136]

132. Rudolf Bernhardt and Henry Schermers, 'Lithuanian law and international human rights standards', *Human Rights Law Journal*, XIII, 5–6 (June 1992) pp. 249–56, on p. 256.
133. O. Rogov, 'Razgovor o problemakh iazyka', *Ekho Litvy*, 19 March 1992, p. 3.
134. *Ekho Litvy*, 18 March 1992, p. 3.
135. *Moskovskie Novosti*, 1991, no. 42 (20 October), pp. 9–10; *Komsomol'skaia Pravda*, 9 January 1992; *Golos Litvy*, 1992, no. 9, p. 5; *Respublika* (Vilnius), 2–8 June 1992, p. 6.
136. *Rossiiskaia Gazeta*, 16 April 1992.

6

IRREDENTISM AND SEPARATISM: MOLDOVA

In two particular ways, the situation of the Russian diaspora in Moldova differs from that of the Russians in all other Soviet successor states. First, in the inter-war period the Moldovan territory west of the river Dniester – namely, Bessarabia – belonged to the kingdom of Romania. The ethnic Moldovans speak a Romanian dialect, and many of them feel more like Romanians than Moldovans. Bessarabia represents a Romanian *irredenta*, and vocal groups on both sides of the border demand immediate unification. If that should happen, the Russians in Moldova would not be residents of a Soviet successor state like the rest of the new Russian diaspora but would end up instead as citizens of another European state, which happens to have a bad reputation for the treatment of its national minorities. Secondly, the Moldovan territory on the east bank of the Dniester, which has never belonged to Romania, declared itself in 1990 an independent state, the 'Dniester Moldovan republic' (with the Russian acronym 'PMR'), with the city of Tiraspol as capital. About 24% of the population in the PMR are Russians, who together with the 26% Ukrainians make up roughly half of the total. The Dniester republic is often considered as a concoction of Russian separatists. This is for several reasons somewhat misleading, but the impression has nonetheless been created that members of the Russian diaspora in Moldova, in contrast to all their counterparts elsewhere have managed to create their own state of sorts. The Dniestrovians are intent on defending their independence by force, and in 1991 and 1992 they fended off a number of Moldovan attempts to recapture control over the territory. In June 1992 these escalated into a full-blown war, albeit a limited one, which for all practical purposes the PMR won.[1]

Several ethnic Moldovans occupy central positions in the PMR state structure, and conversely, on the right bank, many ethnic Russians

---

1. For more details, see Paul Kolstoe and Andrei Edemsky, with Natalya Kalashnikova, 'The Dniester Conflict: Between Irrendentism and Separatism', *Europe-Asia Studies*', I, (1993), pp. 973–1000.

support the Moldovan government. Both sides will insist that the conflict between the two Moldovan regimes is essentially political and not
ethnic in character (although they strongly disagree on exactly what
political values are at stake). At the same time, the ethnic dimension
cannot be completely ignored. The Russians and, to some extent, the
Ukrainians are both clearly overrepresented in the PMR leadership,[2]
and till after the war of June 1992 the members of the post-Communist
Moldovan government in Chisinau were almost exclusively ethnic
Moldovans. Chisinau has regularly accused the PMR authorities of
maltreating ethnic Moldovans on the left bank, while the Dniestrovians for their part call attention to the allegedly dire plight of Russians
and other national minorities on the other side of the river.

The Dniester republic was proclaimed in September 1990 for a
number of reasons, but one of the more important ones was certainly
the prospect of Romanian–Moldovan unification. The Moldovan unifi-
cationists have made no bones about their intention to bring the
Dniester left bank with them into Romania. Almost all opinion polls
show that since 1991, the unification issue has not been very popular
in either of the Romanian states,[3] but many Russians are still concerned. The Moldovan government has shown no great enthusiasm
for unification, but the *irredenta* issue nonetheless remains, simply
because of the ethnic composition of the two states. The unification
in recent years of the two Vietnams and of the two Germanys provides
strong precedents.

While the reunification issue, the treatment of national minorities
in the Moldovan republic and the creation of the Dniester republic are
three separate issues, they are intricately interwoven. All, in different
ways, influence the situation of the Russian diaspora in Moldova.

The treatment of national minorities in Moldova

The population of Moldova has never been anything like mono-ethnic.
Romanians, Jews, Germans, Bulgarians and Gagauz have lived there

2. To some extent, this can be explained by the fact that they are city-dwellers possess-
   ing a political élite, while the Moldovans, to a much larger degree, live in the
   countryside, and are less politicised.
3. A survey conducted between June 1991 and February 1992 gave the political
   organisations favouring early unification a joint following oscillating between 16%
   and 33%. Vladimir Socor, 'Opinion Polling in Moldova', *RFE/RL Research
   Report*, I, 13 (27 March 1992), pp. 60–3.

side by side. In the Soviet period, the Moldovan share of the population was never above 66% in any census.[4] Most of the Russians are fairly recent immigrants: their share of the population increased from 6% in 1940 to 10.2% in 1959, and to 13% in 1989.[5] In 1992 38% of the Russians declared that they had been born in the republic, while 41% had lived there more than fifteen years.[6]

However, the Russians are not the largest diaspora group, Moldova being the only Soviet successor state other than Ukraine where Russians are outnumbered by Ukrainians. Approximately 600,000 persons have 'Ukrainian' written in their passports. The linguistic russification of the Ukrainians has been thoroughgoing and in the 1989 census 220,000 of them claimed no knowledge of Ukrainian whatsoever[7] – not surprising considering the school situation in the republic: the last Ukrainian school was closed down in 1963.

Now that they had been deprived of their own schools, the natural choice for Ukrainians was to attend Russian-language schools. This choice was also made by many of the other national minorities, including the Gagauz, the Jews and the Bulgarians. In Russian schools, these students now became fluent in Russian, while their ability to express themselves in Moldovan remained limited at best. Among the Ukrainians only 12.8% knew Moldovan as a second language, while the comparative figure for the Gagauz was as low as 4.4%. As many as ethnic 120,000 Moldovans considered Russian as their native language and half of these did not even understand Moldovan. The Russian-language group, then, included many more people than just the ethnic Russians. As a result, despite the great ethnic variety in the republic, two roughly equal language groups were in confrontation with each other: the Russian speakers and the Moldovan speakers (see Table 6.1).

Of the Russians, 11.2% declared in the 1989 census that they were fluent in Moldovan. According to a more detailed survey from 1992, as few as 6.5% claimed to have a full command of Moldovan, while 23.5% both understood the language and were able to read it. 52.5% could

4. Gerhard Simon, *Nationalism and Policy Towards the Nationalities in the Soviet Union*, Boulder, CO, 1991, p. 385 (statistical appendix).
5. Bohdan Nahaylo, 'Ukraine and Moldova: the View from Kiev', *RFE/RL Research Report*, I, 18 (1 May 1992), pp. 39–45.
6. Tudor Danii and Zinaida Gontsa, 'Russkie v Moldove', *Vocea Poporului*, 20 October 1992 (Russian edition).
7. Nahaylo, *op. cit.*

Table 6.1. COMMAND OF MOLDOVAN AND RUSSIAN
AMONG ETHNIC GROUPS IN MOLDOVA, 1989 ($\times 1,000$)

	Total	Command of Moldovan	Command of Russian
Moldovans	2,794	2,712	1,609
Ukrainians	600	86	554
Russians	562	63	560
Gagauz	153	8	123
Bulgarians	88	8	76
Jews	65	10	62
Belorussians	20	1	17
Gypsies	11	5	5
Poles	5	*	4
Total, non-titular population	1,541	190	1,261
Total	4,335	2,902	2,965

Source: *Natsional'nyi sostav naseleniia SSSR*, Moscow, 1991.
* Less than 1,000.

pick out certain phrases, while 15.5% conceded total ignorance of the
language of the titular nationality.[8] Moldovan was steadily losing
ground in most social contexts – education, publications, administration and everyday communication. The Moldovans felt that their
language was being pushed back to the countryside – where it had
come from in the first place. In the nineteenth century the towns, even
more than in the twentieth, were dominated by non-Moldovans.

Besides, the Moldovan language itself was undergoing a process of
slavification. While Moldovan is in essence a northern dialect of
Romanian, Soviet linguists tried to prove that it is a separate tongue.
The rationale for this was obviously the need to present the Moldovans
as a distinct nationality to forestall Romanian irredentist claims. Cer-
tainly, more Slavic loan words were used by Moldovans than by
Romanians further south, a tendency which increased under Soviet
rule. New technical terms were taken from Russian more or less
unchanged. By 1980, it was claimed that no less than 40% of the
Moldovan vocabulary consisted of Slavic words.[9] In addition, the
Latin script which was being used in Romania was replaced by
Cyrillic.

8. Danii and Gontsa, *op. cit.*
9. V. I. Kozlov, *Natsional'nosti SSSR*, Moscow, 1982, p. 15.

When the Popular Front of Moldova was established in June 1988, a campaign to improve the status of the Moldovan–Romanian language was one of the main rallying cries. The republican authorities did their utmost to thwart the campaign which they considered – not without reason – to be a stepping-stone for the nationalists in their attempt to throw off Communist power altogether. However, the republican leaders soon had to go along with the crowd. Taking their cue from the Baltic states, the Moldovan parliament in August and September 1989 passed a number of interrelated language laws.[10] The most important of them gave the Moldovan (Romanian) language the status of 'state language' and it was now to be written with Latin and not Cyrillic characters.

The Moldovan law-makers justified conferring the status of state language on to Moldovan as 'one of the basic preconditions for the existence of the Moldovan nation in her sovereign national-state formation'. Thus, the law introduced, as it were in passing, the concept of a Moldovan nation-state, understood in an ethnic sense. The ethnic component of the nation-state concept of Moldova would appear to be stronger than it is in any of the other Soviet successor states, with the possible exceptions of Latvia and Kyrgyzstan.

It was the language laws that triggered the first serious clashes between Moldovans and representatives of the non-titular ethnic groups during the period of *perestroika*. In itself the texts of the laws could not be considered illiberal. The introduction of the Latin script for the Moldovan language was, in a sense, an internal Moldovan affair which did not directly involve the other language groups. However, the possibility that the alphabet change might lead to Romanian–Moldovan reunification caused anxiety, which was highlighted by the law on the state language. Did this law imply that all persons living in Moldova would have to learn the Moldovan–Romanian language? A casual perusal of the law could easily enable one to conclude that it did not, for while the law somewhat nebulously declared that 'the state language will function in the political, economic, social and cultural life', it also contained a number of clauses about the rights of other language groups. The Moldovan state guaranteed the use of the Ukrainian, Russian, Bulgarian, Modern Jewish, Yiddish and the Gypsy languages, as well as the various languages of other ethnic

---

10. *Zakonodatel'nye akty Moldavskoi SSR o pridanii moldavskomu iazyku statusa gosudarstvennogo i vozvrate emu latinskoi grafiki*, Chisinau, 1990.

groups residing in the country for 'national-cultural needs'. Russian was accorded the status of 'language of interethnic communication'. It was explicitly stated that the citizens could freely use the language of their choice both at all public and private gatherings and in the sphere of local administration. Moldovan would be the working language in the central administration, but documents would be translated into Russian whenever necessary.[11] A separate law on the practical realisation of these laws allowed for the gradual introduction of the various paragraphs – in certain areas, some of them would not come into force till 1996.

On the other hand, it was also stated that the law would 'provide conditions for a genuine national-Russian and Russian-national bilingualism'. Hence, the Russians *were* required to learn the state language as a second language, if they did not know it already. The Russians could not expect things to go on as before. Indeed, the adoption of the language laws would not have made much sense if they had not been intended to change the language situation in some ways.

It soon became clear that the laws were open to different interpretations, and contained a number of loopholes. The law-makers had not aimed at creating a monolingual Moldovan society, but the meaning of such lofty words as 'guarantees' and 'safeguards' was unclear. The very vagueness of the laws made them amenable to arbitrary applications. A CPSU report from 1991 that was fairly sympathetic to the Moldovan cause concluded: 'The text of the laws is awkward, abounding with hackneyed phrases, unnecessary repetitions and inaccurate definitions ... local representatives of the new Moldovan authorities avail themselves of this situation. Without batting an eyelid they may dismiss a person from work or decide not to hire him on the grounds that he does not know Moldovan. However, the actual law provides for language attestation of the cadres only in cases where knowledge of the state language is absolutely necessary, and then in the remote future.'[12]

If the language question was a mighty rallying point for Moldovan nationalists, this was no less the case for the non-titular ethnic groups. In August and September of 1989, strikes were organised in almost all the major Moldovan cities. The driving force behind them was the United Council of Work Collectives (OSTK), an organisation which

---

11. *ibid.*, pp. 25 and 29ff.
12. 'Lingvisticheskii faktor', *Izvestiia TsK KPSS*, III, 5 (1991), pp. 133ff.

at this time appeared to be a potent force. OSTK had chapters all over the Soviet Union, and particularly in the non-Russian republics. It represented not only the workers but also, just as much, the factory managers. As in the Baltic area, the OSTK in Moldova cooperated closely with the Communist party, and defended not only the ethnic rights of the non-titular ethnic groups but also the entire political and social system of the Soviet Union itself.

The strikes in question started before the language laws had been passed by the Moldovan parliament – i.e, before anyone really knew how they would function. Thus what the strikers opposed was the actual text of the new laws, not their application. Later, however, when the laws had started to operate and some Moldovans were clearly abusing them, Russian-speakers in Moldova came to realise that many of the paragraphs, if strictly adhered to, in fact offered them pretty good protection, and it was somewhat ironically that they now referred to the hitherto opprobrious language laws when complaining against violations of their rights.[13]

Russians soon started to report that those with a command of the state language were given priority on entering both higher education and employment. In the state statistical department, for example, six out of seven promotions after the adoption of the law went to Moldovans, and out of the forty-one employees who lost their jobs in the same period, only four were ethnic Moldovans.[14] An appeal from medical workers in the republic of Moldova claimed:

> At present all administrative [medical] personnel, from the minister down to the superintendents, without exception belong to the 'indigenous' population. Russian-language physicians are required to write notes on patients and converse with them in Romanian, and use the Romanian language in all professional relations. Persons without a command of it or unable to use the Latin script are not hired even when highly qualified.[15]

Pro-Moldovan sources themselves admit that ethnic discrimination in employment has taken place, although they play down the scale of the problem, and blame it on irresponsible and overzealous individuals rather than on any deliberate government policy.[16]

---

13. See, e.g., 'Obrashchenie meditsinskikh rabotnikov Respubliki Moldovy', an appeal signed by delegates to the 1st conference of the Pirogov Association of Medical Workers, Chisinau, 27 September 1992; typescript.
14. Andrei Safonov, 'Nasha bol' ', *Literaturnaia Rossiia*, 4 October 1991.
15. 'Obrashchenie meditsinskikh rabotnikov', *op. cit.*
16. V. Malakhov, 'Ia eto videl, slyshal i pytalsia osmyslit' ', Chisinau, 1992, p. 9.

The main battle front in the language war was the schools. In 1990–1, the republican government conducted a campaign for the 'nationalisation' of the education system at all levels. The extent of the campaign is difficult to establish. An overall picture of it has to be pieced together from pro-Moldovan and pro-Russian sources, all of which tend to suppress information that does not suit their purposes. Thus, Moldovan materials tend to emphasise the actual ratio of Moldovan to Russian-language educational institutions at a given moment, without saying anything about trends and changes in that ratio.[17] On the other hand, the Russians do not gladly reveal the actual number of Russian-language schools in the republic – which is still high, but instead focus on the compulsory closures[18] which are claimed by some Russian sources to reflect a deliberate policy of assimilation.[19]

This accusation is hard to substantiate. Since many Moldovans, Ukrainians and others had in the past been attending Russian schools, it was reasonable to expect that in a period of intense national awakening, pupils from other language groups would switch to schools offering education in their mother tongue if they got the chance. A number of Ukrainian schools were now reopened, and Ukrainian students flocked to them. Since many parents in earlier times had chosen Russian schools for their offspring for career reasons, the same career argument now worked in favour of Moldovan, the new state language. At the same time, however, it also seemed that in several cases coercion was being used to make the pupils desert Russian educational institutions.

From official Moldovan sources we learn that 1,032 general-education schools in Moldova use the Moldovan language, while 429 use Russian and 132 are mixed.[20] In the main cities, however, the situation was rather different. In Chisinau, a pro-Moldovan source informs us, only four out of eighty schools taught in the state language in 1991.[21] Russian sources, on the other hand, claim that in

17. 'Zaiavlenie Parlamenta Republiki Moldova o pravovom statuse lits, prinadlezhash-chikh k etnicheskim, iazykovym i religioznym men'shinstvam', Chisinau, 26 May 1992. The actual year when these figures were compiled is not given.
18. *Vechernii Kishinëv*, 8 October 1991.
19. Viktor Vislouzov, 'Respublika Moldova: assimilatory za rabotoi', *Moskovskii Literator*, no. 31, 1992.
20. 'Zaiavlenie . . .', *op. cit.* In addition, there are, according to the same source, one Jewish school, 11 Bulgarian classes, 44 Gagauz classes and 174 Ukrainian classes.
21. Malakhov, *op. cit.*

1990–1 fifteen mixed schools in Chisinau dropped education in Russian, and that Russian-language pupils were thus required to attend other schools. Consequently, most Russian language schools in Chisinau had to run day and night classes. If this is correct, then the Russian schools were obviously closed down faster than the students were deserting them.

At the university level, the situation was even more serious. In 1991 the course on 'Russian Language and Literature' was dropped at the philological department at the Moldovan state university.[22] This drastic move reflected the redundancy of Russian teachers after the school closures, but ethnic minorities were studying less and less at other faculties as well. In 1990 the number of students in the Russian section of several faculties at Chisinau University was reduced to 40–50% of the previous level. The next year, Russians, Ukrainians, Jews, Gagauz and Bulgarians, taken together, made up no more than 11% of first-year students at the Moldovan state university[23] – in stark contrast to their share of the total population. A reasonable conclusion seems to be that although the school-nationalisation campaign was to some extent understandable, its sheer speed was bound to provoke a reaction, leaving aside the methods it used. In June 1991, a recertification of educational staff was conducted in all institutions of higher learning in the republic. In one notable case, a philologist was fired because of her 'sociopolitical activity directed against the decisions of the parliament and the government'. Some months earlier she had signed a collective letter of protest against the government's plans to close down the study of Russian philology at the university.[24]

A Moldovan law on citizenship was passed on 5 June 1991. By any standards this law must be considered liberal. While it required ten years of residence for all future applicants for citizenship, this proviso did not apply to people who already lived in the country. The law granted the right of citizenship to everyone who had permanent residence in Moldovan territory at the time when Moldovan sovereignty was proclaimed (23 June 1990), and who had a legal source of income. In addition, if they or one of their parents had been born in the territory of the state, citizenship was granted automatically.

22. *Literaturnaia Rossiia*, no. 40, 1991.
23. *Narushenie prav cheloveka v Moldavii, October 1990–October 1991. Analiticheskaia zapiska: Pravlenie obshchestva 'Memorial'*, Chisinau, 22 October 1991.
24. *Moskovskii Literator*, no. 31, 1992.

Post-war immigrants had to apply for citizenship within one year.[25] There were no language requirements for any of these groups. The possibility that Moldova would follow the Estonian and Latvian examples and deny post-war Slavic immigrants the status of original citizens was therefore excluded.

Nonetheless, the law on citizenship was controversial. It was passed at a time when the future of the Soviet Union was uncertain but when its dissolution was by no means a foregone conclusion. Moldova did not recognize the possibility of dual citizenship: to obtain Moldovan citizenship, one first had to renounce citizenship of the Soviet Union.[26] In this way, the Moldovan law-makers wanted to force the Russians down from the fence. They had to stand forth as either supporters or opponents of Moldovan statehood. The citizenship issue developed into a test of nerves: the Russians had to stake their future on the continued existence of the Soviet Union, or else renounce Soviet citizenship and thus by their own actions contribute to the downfall of the Soviet state. Those who did not apply for citizenship within one year would forfeit the privilege of being treated as original citizens. Should they, on second thoughts, decide that they did want Moldovan citizenship after all, they would be treated like any other new immigrant, who would have to show language skills, loyalty to the constitution and ten years' residence.

Russians claim a steep rise in street-level discrimination against nontitular ethnic groups, who risk being accosted by gangs of Moldovan youths chanting '*Ivan – chemodan*', or 'Ivan, pack your bags.' According to spokesmen for the Russian community, activists from the Popular Front of Moldova are especially active in the harassing of other national groups. These activists break up meetings of Russian organisations, molest Russian parliamentarians whose voting is not to their liking and even try to break into their apartments.[27] In one particularly ugly case, an eighteen-year-old Russian youth, Dima Matiushin, was beaten to death in 1990. The fact that Russian reports on ethnic discrimination invariably revolve around this same incident seems to indicate that this is the only time when ethnic brutality has resulted in a death. The Moldovan press claims that certain Russian

25. 'Zakon respubliki Moldova o grazhdanstve', Articles 2 and 3.
26. V. Mamontov, 'Russkii v Moldove', *Komsomol'skaia Pravda*, 8 August 1992.
27. Safonov, *op. cit.* (cf. note 14).

groups both in the republic and in the Russian Federation are exploiting this tragic but isolated event to stir up fear.

Ethnic Moldovan politicians considered 'soft' on the Russians are targets of nationalist fury. One such alleged 'softy' is the Moldovan president Mircea Snegur and indeed he actively tries to promote the building of a civil state in Moldova in which there would be room for all ethnic groups. Here many Moldovan nationalists see the pernicious influence of his Russian wife: how, they ask, can Snegur defend the interests of his people 'if the blood running in the veins of his wife and his children is the same as the blood in the veins of Rutskoi'?[28]

Some of the Moldovan nationalist press is clearly bordering on racism. The Russian journalist Miroslava Lukianchikova, a supporter of Snegur, has collected a bizarre array of quotations from the nationalist press. In February 1992, the Popular Front published 'Ten commandments of a Bessarabian Romanian' which warned Moldovans 'not to rush to bind your fate to a person belonging to another nation. Cross breeding improves the species of animals only, while it brings harm to humans.' Six months later another publication claimed that Russian women have brought colossal harm not only to Moldovan economy and culture but also to the entire 'genetic stock' of the republic. In *Glasul natiunei* one could read, 'The character of a person is revealed by his actions, the character of a Russian – by the blood he has drunk.' And so on.[29]

The government of Mircea Snegur has never taken action to close down or fine any of the organs of the national radicals. Apparently the authorities are afraid that such actions would only confer a martyr's crown on the radicals. The nationalists are thus enabled to continue their destabilising activities with impunity, and by so doing they add grist to the separatist mill on the left bank. The newspaper of the Tiraspol OSTK, for instance, regularly prints translations of some of the more hysterical articles in *Literatura si arta, Tara* etc. under captions such as 'Hatred is being whipped up'.[30] As so often happens, extremists on both sides feed on each other, exacerbating the situation.

28. Interview with Mircea Snegur in *Moskovskie Novosti*, 10 May 1992.
29. Miroslava Lukianchikova, 'Usloviia stanovleniia novoi russkoi diaspora v Moldove', paper presented at the seminar 'The New Russian Diaspora', Lielupe, Latvia, 13–15 November 1992. Quotations from *Glasul Natunei*, 10 April 1992; *Tara*, 4 February 1992; and *Tara*, 23 June 1992.
30. For instance, *Trudovoi Tiraspol*, 9–16 September 1992.

This also shows that what lies at the bottom of Moldova's tense inter-ethnic relations is the twin issue of unification and separatism.

The unification issue

During *perestroika*, two parallel ideas captured the imagination of the Moldovan public: the idea of creating an independent state and the idea of uniting with Romania. Although these ideas were clearly at odds with each other, this fact was regularly obscured. The Moldovan Popular Front led the struggle for political independence from Moscow,[31] but gradually the idea of Moldovan sovereignty was jettisoned, and the Front stood forth instead as the most consistent champion of unification with Romania.[32] In Romania too a movement for unification was gaining speed.

On 27 August 1991, less than a week after the collapse of the *coup d'état* in Moscow, the Moldovan parliament proclaimed the complete independence of Moldova under international law. While the establishment of a separate Moldovan statehood lessened the chances of an early reunification with Romania, the actual wording of the Declaration was ambiguous: the parliament declared that it acted 'on the cognisance of a thousand-year existence of our people and its uninterrupted statehood within the historical and ethnic boundaries of its national formation'.[33]

By 1991–2, the process of Moldovan state-building was mounting, and it was clear that the idea of unification with Romania was losing its popular appeal.[34] The pro-Romanian Popular Front was losing members and influence, but it could still count on the support of around 100 deputies in the parliament. It reacted to the changing political climate by pressing the cause of unification even further, and it demanded ever more consistently that the left bank become an integral part of Moldova. In a resolution adopted at its 3rd Congress in February 1992, the Front proclaimed that all citizens of the Moldovan state residing on the left bank had a right to obtain

---

31. See e.g. *Desteptarea (Probuzhdenie)*, Vestnik Narodnogo Fronta Moldavii, July 1989, p. 1.
32. See e.g. the article entitled 'Unification – Now!', in *Tara* (Russian edition), 11 February 1992.
33. 'Deklaratsiia o nezavisimosti Respubliki Moldova', Chisinau, 27 August 1991.
34. See Vladmir Socor, 'Why Moldova does Not Seek Reunification with Romania', *RL/RFE Research Report*, I, 5, 1992, pp. 27–33.

Romanian citizenship on a par with the residents of the right bank. 'The fact that they were not citizens of Romania before 1940 cannot be a valid ground for denying them this right, as they more than anybody else have been subject to denationalisation under tsarist and Communist repression.'[35] The question of whether the residents of the left bank actually wanted Romanian citizenship was not addressed.

One year after independence, the vast majority of the Moldovan population were opposed to unification with Romania – contrary to what most experts on nationalism had expected. The new catchphrase 'cultural Romanian-ness and political Moldovan-ness' carried the day. There were obviously several reasons for this.[36] For one thing, the democratisation process in Romanian society was slow, and many Moldovans began to fear that the political and cultural freedoms they had achieved since independence might be jeopardised by unification. In addition, Romania had little to offer in economic terms. Its living standards were lower than those of Moldova. Finally, the Moldovan state-building process was advancing, and a large number of intellectuals had got prestigious jobs in the new Moldovan state apparatus, and thus had a strong vested interest in the State's continued existence.

However, the Moldovan leadership has rejected all calls to hold a referendum on the unification issue, and been unwilling to abandon this policy option. Rather, the policy line is kept deliberately vague. Occasionally the impression is conveyed that its disagreement with the Popular Front is only a matter of tactics and timing. A statement from the Political Analysis Department of the Moldovan State Office in September 1992 said: 'Matters ought not to be rushed. Every child is born only when the foetus is mature, after its allotted time in the womb. So also with the 'child' of the Front [i.e. unification].'[37] Such analyses will neither placate the Front leaders nor allay the apprehensions of the Left Bankers.

Breaking away from Moldova

When Bessarabia was joined to Romania after the First World War, left-bank Dniestria remained under Russian or, more correctly, Soviet

35. 'Rezoliutsii III s"ezda khristiansko-demokraticheskogo narodnogo fronta', supplement to *Tara*, 25 February 1992, pp. 15ff.
36. See also Vladmir Socor, 'Why Moldova . . .', *op. cit.*
37. *Moldova Suverana, Digest*, 11 September 1992 (Russian edition).

jurisdiction. When the Soviet Union was established as a federated state in 1922, the area was included in the Ukrainian SSR. Two years later, however, it was given the status of Moldovan Autonomous Socialist Soviet Republic (MASSR), again under the Ukrainian SSR. The rationale behind this was probably not so much to protect the interests of the ethnic Moldovans in the area, who were in a clear minority (although they were given special cultural rights).[38] More important to Moscow was the desire to create a springboard for the reconquest of Bessarabia.[39]

In 1940, the Soviet acquisition of Bessarabia was made possible by the secret protocols of the Ribbentrop–Molotov pact. In June 1940, the Moldavian Socialist Soviet Republic was created as a component part of the Soviet Union. In this republic the former Romanian Bessarabia was now included – except for some parts which were included in Soviet Ukraine. To the rump of Bessarabia was added most of the area of the Moldavian ASSR on the left bank.

On Stalin's orders, entire plants and industrial institutions were moved to this republic. As a concomitant effect, the Slavic population increased considerably in both Bessarabia and on the left bank of the Dniester – but mostly in the latter region. Of the 560,000 Russians in Moldova only 156,000 (or approximately 30%) now live on the left bank. In all large Moldovan cities on both banks, Russian-speakers either predominate or at least make up a substantial minority. In all parts of the country the bulk of the Slavic population element consists of recent immigrants. However, while the newly arrived Russians in Bessarabia represented a largely new cultural element in Dniestria, they were nonetheless 'grafted into' an older local Slavic culture.

A major part of the industrial capacity of Moldova consisted of

---

38. The number of ethnic Moldovans in MASSR is unclear, as official Soviet statistics were obviously juggled. In July 1924, this group was said to constitute 14.2% of the total population, while in October of the same year the number had risen to 58%! The next year, the percentage was said to be 32, which is probably closer to the truth. See *Kazach'i Vedomosti*, no. 3, 1992.

39. The similarity with the creation of the Karelian ASSR, concocted in order to facilitate a reconquest of Finland, is evident. According to a secret report note from a Moldovan Soviet initiative group to the Central Committee of the Bolshevik party in February 1924, 'A Moldavian republic may play the same role as a political-propagandistic factor as the Belorussian republic is playing towards Poland and the Karelian republic towards Finland.' Printed in *Tara*, 11 August 1992. The authenticity of this document has not been ascertained.

Union-controlled factories located on the left bank. This region accounted for 33% of all industrial goods and 56% of all consumer goods produced in the republic as a whole.[40] When Moldova began, in 1989–90, to gain real sovereignty and the power of the central authorities was seriously shaken, it is not surprising that the Dniester technocrats and factory directors became increasingly concerned: their positions depended on retaining links with Moscow.

In January 1990, a referendum was held in Tiraspol on the question of giving the city and its surrounding county the status of an autonomous territory, self-financing and with the right of self-determination. It was announced that 90% of the voters favoured such an arrangement, a verdict there is little reason to doubt. Russian-speakers made up a clear majority in the polling districts, and in any case the economically strong Tiraspol area no doubt stood to benefit from a state of financial independence. The idea of a free economic zone might be attractive to all residents on the Dniester left bank – not just the Slavs. At the same time, it is clear that in most recent Soviet and post-Soviet referendums the people have simply tended to vote in favour of whatever arrangements have been proposed to them. Those who have controlled the wording of the question on the referendum ballot have also largely controlled the outcome.

On 2 September 1990, at the Second Extraordinary Session of the Peoples' Deputies of the Dniester Area held in the city theatre in Tiraspol, the Dniester Moldovan Soviet Socialist Republic was proclaimed as a constituent part of the Soviet Union. 'Soviet' and 'Socialist' have since been dropped from the name, but the hammer and sickle have been retained in the state emblem. No Lenin statues have been torn down in the would-be republic, and it has often been referred to as a bulwark of the Communist *nomenklatura*. Certainly fewer economic, social and symbolic changes have taken place here than elsewhere. Still, this is a somewhat simplified view. The percentage of old apparatchiks in the PMR leadership is probably not significantly higher than it is among the other post-Soviet states. But the contemporary leaders in most of these states define themselves in contrast to the old regime in Moscow, and hence present themselves as 'anti-Communist'. The 'constituting other' of the PMR leadership is not Moscow, but Chisinau. Its self-understanding is therefore the opposite of the Moldovan one: 'anti-anti-Communist'.

40. *Nezavisimaia Gazeta*, 19 September 1992.

While the Moldovan republic, as seen from Tiraspol, is based on the ethnic principle, the new Dniester republic was proclaimed as a non-national civic state. The adjective 'Moldavian' was nonetheless included in the official designation of the state to underline the continuity with the MASSR, out of respect for the largest population group, and to keep the door open for negotiations with Chisinau.[41] In conscious contrast to the language situation on the right bank, the new would-be republic was given no less than three state languages: Russian, Ukrainian and Moldovan. It is emphasised that the third language is Moldovan, not Romanian, and it is written in Cyrillic. The relationship between these three languages, however, is not equal. Russian clearly predominates in official communications. A number of local Moldovan-language newspapers have been suppressed, and now that the PMR authorities have taken over the radio transmitter in Tiraspol for broadcasting their own programmes, Chisinau radio is *de facto* jammed in large areas. While this is done for political rather than ethnic reasons, it does also contribute to the russification of the PMR society. Moreover, the implementation of the language regulations is very liberal: no-one is actually required to learn any new language. The number of PMR officials fluent in Moldovan is limited, and in practice this language policy tends to perpetuate Russian linguistic hegemony.[42] Those left-bank Moldovans who want to use the Latin alphabet are not allowed to do so. The pedagogical institute in Tiraspol has been closed down because the staff there supported the Snegur regime. Many spokesmen for the Russian community in Bessarabia recognise that the situation for ethnic and linguistic minorities in PMR is no better, and probably worse, than it is on the right bank.[43]

From 2 September 1990 Tiraspol stopped taking orders from Chisinau. As the Moldovan authorities were not in a position to enforce their decrees on the left bank, they were *de facto* independent. The reactions in Chisinau and Tiraspol towards the attempted *coup d'état* in Moscow in August 1991 were predictably different. While the actual extent and character of the Dniester area's support of the State

---

41. Author's interview with PMR state secretary Valerii Litskai, Tiraspol, 18 September 1992; interview with PMR Supreme Soviet Chairman Grigore Maracuta, *Russkii Vestnik*, 11 September 1991.

42. See, e.g., Lukianchikova, *op. cit.* (see note 29).

43. *ibid.*

Committee for Emergency remains disputed, most political leaders in Tiraspol were no doubt favourably disposed towards the would-be new masters in Moscow. This was especially true of the leadership of the OSTK. However, it should be remembered that in those turbulent days most leaders in the non-Russian republics except for those in Moldova and the Baltic states either equivocated or else gave explicit support to the putschists.

In the aftermath of the coup, the OSTK leader Igor Smirnov was arrested and incarcerated in Chisinau. This action triggered a railway blockade on the left bank – organised by a women's committee affiliated with the OSTK. Since most Moldovan transport communication with the rest of the Soviet Union run through Tiraspol-controlled territory, this effectively choked the Moldovan economy. The Moldovan authorities were forced to release Smirnov, who was soon afterwards elected president of the PMR.

In this atmosphere, military confrontations between Chisinau and Tiraspol occurred almost daily. During the spring of 1992 Cossacks from other parts of the former Soviet Union started to arrive in Tiraspol to support the regime. While the Dniester authorities denied that they had invited them, and indeed discouraged them from coming, their services were nonetheless accepted.[44] However, the long-time objectives of most Cossacks were at odds with the official policy of the Dniester leadership. While the latter defended their independence, the former wanted to restore the Russian tsarist Empire.[45]

In September 1991, the PMR erected its own Republican Guard which it planned to maintain at a level of 12,000 men. Some observers found it more than odd that this was almost exactly the same size as the Russian 14th Army stationed in the area. The commander of the 14th Army since June 1992, Aleksandr Lebed', voiced his strong support for the PMR regime on a number of occasions: he declared that the right-bank city of Bendery was an inalienable part of the PMR, and that the PMR itself was 'a small part of Russia'.[46] A Western source has indicated that a peculiar 'revolving-doors' system operates in the PMR, in which the officers of the 14th Army put on the Guard uniform whenever the occasion calls for it.[47] Russian military spokes-

44. Interview with Igor Smirnov in *Moskovskie novosti*, 3 May 1992.
45. Author's interviews in the Cossack headquarters in Tiraspol, 18 September 1992.
46. *Moskovskie novosti*, 1 July 1992.
47. Vladimir Socor, 'Russian Forces in Moldova', *RFE/RL Research Report*, I, 34 (1992), pp. 38–43.

men have pointed out, however, that apart from the most senior officers, the bulk of the 14th Army consists of local conscripts and non-local NCOs who over time have struck roots in the area. Their involvement in the conflict, while not condoned by Moscow, should according to this view be seen as an aspect of Dniester self-defence.

On 29 March 1992, the Moldovan president Mircea Snegur issued an ultimatum to the left-bank leaders, demanding full compliance with Moldovan laws. When the PMR leaders remained unyielding, martial law was declared on the entire territory of the republic, and war became a reality. Bendery was recaptured by Moldovan units on 19 June, but only for a very short time. In a lightning attack on the night of 20–21 June, the Moldovan forces were driven out within a few hours.[48] Tanks from the 14th Army crossed the bridge over the Dniester. This event appears to have been the turning point of the battle.

A cease-fire was mediated by Russia on 7 July, which has been surprisingly effective, and a bilateral agreement between Russia and Moldova was further signed on 21 July. It was agreed that the 14th Army should be gradually withdrawn from the area, and a number of economic issues of mutual concern were also addressed. A joint communiqué underlined the sovereignty, independence and territorial integrity of the Republic of Moldova. Significantly, it was guaranteed that should the status of the Republic as a state be changed at any time in the future, the population of the left bank would have the right to secede.[49] The details of a 'special status' (*osobyi status*) for the left bank were to be worked out later.

Life in the region has more or less returned to normal. The martial law imposed in March 1992 was lifted in early September of the same year, and most of the refugees had already returned to their homes by the autumn of 1992.[50] The PMR is busily building up the entire infrastructure of an independent state, with ministries and state

48. 'Weekly report', *RFE/RL Research Report*, I, 27 (1992), p. 70.
49. *Izvestiia*, 23 July 1992.
50. 'Summary Confirming the Violation of Human Rights in the Nistrian Pseudo-Republic of Moldova', 5 August 1992, signed by Alexandru Arseni, chairman of the Committee on Human Rights and National Relations in the Moldovan parliament; and interview with A. Arseni in *Vocea Poporului*, 3 November 1992, p. 3 (Russian edition).

committees, customs control and border guards.[51] A separate Dniester citizenship is even being discussed.

Attitudes and sentiments among Moldovan Russians

It seems reasonably clear that the PMR leadership has the backing of the Russian population on the left bank. On 1 December 1991 the Dniester declaration of independence was followed up by an area-wide referendum in which, according to the official report, 97.7% supported the creation of the PMR. The voter turn-out was 78%.[52] No international observers were present (since no states wanted to lend the self-designated republic any legitimacy). Charges of fraud have been put forward from the Moldovan side, but these seem to be exaggerated, although there can be no question that the referendum was conducted in a very primitive fashion. During a visit to Tiraspol in September 1992, the author was shown voting lists where the 'Yes' and 'No' votes of the residents were recorded. There were hardly any 'Noes' on the lists, but evidently all blanks had been counted as such. Thus the anonymity of the voters had been compromised by the voting procedure, and for this reason the poll should be considered as a test of opinion only.

The allegiance and attitudes of the Bessarabian Russians are obviously more divided than those of the Dniester Russians. While no referendums have been arranged in which they can express their will, evaluations of their sentiments can be made on the basis of opinion polls and certain circumstantial evidence. It is clear that a number of local Russian politicians have supported the idea of a Moldovan independent state. On 27 August 1992, fifty-two of the approximately 130 non-Moldovan deputies supported the Declaration of Independence. It is not known how many of them were Russians. (Of the 356 members of the Moldovan parliament, forty-nine were Russians.) A number of ethnic Russians also occupy positions in the Moldovan government. One of them is Viktor Grebenshchikov, General Director at the Department of Nationalities Questions, and a leading spokesman on Moldovan nationality policy. Grebenshchikov believes that the majority of Russians in Moldova opposed Moldovan independence before August 1991, but that after the dissolution of the

51. *Dnestrovskaia Pravda*, 11 September 1992.
52. *Dnestrovskaia Pravda*, 2 September 1992.

Soviet Union their attitudes changed: separate Moldovan statehood was then accepted as a lesser evil, the greater evil being unification with Romania.[53]

In May 1992, according to official Moldovan sources, 4.9% of the local administrators and four representatives in the central governmental structure were Russians, but none of them had important positions. In the new Moldovan government of national consensus created after the June war, however, representation of the non-Moldovans was significantly increased. Certain government posts were also reserved for left-bank representatives, if they had wanted to fill them. So far they have not.

Many Russians in Bessarabia feel that they are caught between the hammer and the anvil. Some sympathise with the PMR state – or at least found it hard to endorse the Moldovan decision to try to bombard the separatists into obedience in the spring of 1992, but many also fear that they could easily end up as collective hostages. As the PMR leaders remain out of reach in their entrenched republic, frustrated Moldovan nationalists in Bessarabia may begin to vent their anger by stepping-up petty discrimination against local Russians instead. Russians who complain at the treatment of minorities in Moldova risk being denounced as accomplices of the 'left bank Communists'.[54] For instance, when a prominent Ukrainian deputy in the Moldovan parliament, A. Lisetskii, insisted that in Moldova 'historically formed non-Romanian language communities' exist, he was pilloried in the paper of the Moldovan Christian-Democratic Popular Front:

> Whatever Lisetskii says and however much he and his colleagues try to create the illusion that they heed the opinion of the indigenous population in the republic and dissociate themselves from the Tiraspol separatists, they continue to represent a real threat to the very ethno-national existence of the indigenous inhabitants. This will remain true even if Transnistria should come to secede from the republic.[55]

Indeed, if the PMR should really succeed in its endeavours to create an independent state, the plight of the Bessarabian Russians may well be aggravated. Their relative share of the Moldovan population would

---

53. Author's interview with Grebenshchikov, in Chisinau, 16 September 1992.
54. For such apprehensions, see, e.g., *Literaturnaia Rossiia*, no. 34, 21 August 1992.
55. M. Brukhis, 'Nostal'giia po sovetskoi imperii i antiromynism', *Tara*, 2 September 1992.

fall, and they would possibly therefore become a vulnerable minority. Furthermore, the likelihood of a Romanian-Moldovan reunification process could increase. At least one expert thinks that a major reason behind the generally lukewarm attitude of ethnic Moldovans towards reunification is their fear of jeopardising the territorial integrity of the Moldovan state.[56] Should the Dniester area be irrevocably lost, this inhibition would be removed, and enthusiasm for reunification could increase. However, this scenario is not the only possible one. Optimists hope that as soon as the hurtful Dniester issue is removed, in some way or another, from the Moldovan political agenda, ethnic passions will gradually cool.

A leading Western expert has claimed that charges of violations of ethnic rights 'have not been endorsed by any representative group of right-bank Russians'.[57] This statement should be qualified. The 'Unity' interfront continues to issue declarations on the 'intensified propaganda of hatred towards the national minorities in Moldovan mass media'.[58] As this organisation has been driven underground and leads a semi-legal existence, it can probably not be considered as representative any more, although it did seem to be resurrected, in the summer of 1993, in a new incarnation known as 'the Russian Community' (*Obshchina*).[59] Also the 'Russian Cultural Centre', the driving force behind a rival *Obshchina*, certainly has the backing of many right-bank Russians, and its chairmen do not beat about the bush in their complaints.[60]

Most Russians in Moldova certainly believe that under present circumstances Mircea Snegur is the best Moldovan president they can hope for. They are eager to support his attempts to build a supra-ethnic Moldovan state, and are anxious not to do anything that could rock the boat for him. Nonetheless, while they recognise that there is no kind of state-orchestrated anti-Russian campaign going on in Moldova, they are not willing to exculpate either the government or the president altogether. They believe that the state authorities should have moved more forcefully to counteract the nationalist activities of the Popular Front and other organisations.

56. Vladmir Socor, 'Why Moldova . . .', *op. cit.*
57. Vladimir Socor, in *RFE/RL Research Report*, I, 47 (27 November 1992), p. 7.
58. *Russkii Pul's* no. 5, 1992, p. 3; *Den*, no. 38, 1992.
59. *Nezavisimaia Gazeta*, 31 July 1993, p. 3.
60. Author's interview with Aleksandr Belopotapov and Ivan Garev at the Russian Cultural Centre in Chisinau, 16 September 1992.

Opinion polls published in the Moldovan press reveal great differences in sentiment and attitude among Moldovan Russians. According to one survey conducted in September and October 1992 among 500 respondents on both sides of the Dniester,[61] a little more than half expressed concern over aggravated national relations in the republic. This anxiety was more pronounced in the PMR (64.4%) than on the right bank. Only 7.4% of the respondents in the PMR and only 4% in Bessarabia characterised inter-ethnic relations in the republic as 'good-neighbourly', but 63% considered that attitudes towards the Russians had deteriorated during the previous two to three years. This gloomy judgement was much more prevalent in Bessarabia (74.8%) than in the Dniester republic (43.6%).

The pollsters concluded that nostalgia for the Soviet unitary state was not widespread among Moldovan Russians, since only one respondent out of four regretted the dissolution of the Union. This attitude, however, was more than twice as common on the left bank than on the right (37.5% and 16.8%, respectively). Only 9.2% of right-bank Russians believed that the current policy of the Moldovan government actually contributed to the resolution of the nationality problems, while 22.4%, on the contrary, found that it made them worse. The rating of Russian authorities, however, was better: only 10% of the respondents found that the approach taken by the Russian Federation towards the 'near abroad' was aggravating the situation in Moldova.

Another poll reported at about the same time in a government newspaper mentioned that three out of four respondents had friends among other ethnic groups; that 64% of the Russians were acquainted with traditional Moldovan music; and that 79% of them regularly ate traditional Moldovan dishes. At the same time, 71% of the Moldovan and 90% of the Russian respondents believed that the policy of the present political leadership would only serve to increase inter-ethnic tension. Nonetheless, in November 1992, a close observer concluded that 'in spite of the complicated political, economic, and social situation, there are preconditions in Moldova for a normalisation of the socio-national climate.'[62]

In one way, the Moldovan scene is certainly unique: nowhere else will the question of unification with another European state arise. Secession, however, may be repeated elsewhere. The fact that diaspora

61. Danii and Gontsa, *op. cit.* (see note 6).
62. Lukianchikova, *op. cit.* (see note 29), p. 11.

Russians in eastern Moldova, in conjunction with other ethnic groups, have achieved what seems to amount to a political separation from an ethnically defined Soviet successor state has not passed unnoticed among other diaspora groups, and some diasporians might come to believe that they should emulate this example.[63] Furthermore, certain observers ill-disposed towards the Russian diaspora see the Dniester republic as a dangerous precedent. An article in the Moldovan government newspaper *Moldova Suverana* in October 1992 concluded that 'the metastases of the "Dniester syndrome" are Narva and Crimea.'[64]

---

63. Author's conversations with several Russian diasporians.
64. Elena Danielian, 'Pridnestrovskii sindrom', *Moldova Suverana*, 23 October 1992. Reprint from *Russkoe Slovo*, New York.

7

THE EYE OF THE WHIRLWIND:
BELARUS AND UKRAINE

The new Russian diaspora is not evenly spread across post-Soviet territory. As many as 12.5 million people, or roughly half, are concentrated in the two states of Belarus and Ukraine. Of all the Soviet successor states these are the ones closest to Russia both geographically and culturally. Here ethnic controversies have not reached the same intensity as they have in some of the more distant republics. The East Slav areas represent, as it were, an undisturbed centre in the eye of the ethnic whirlwind. This is particularly true of Belarus.

Belarus

More than any other major post-Soviet nationality, the Belorussians have been exposed to the cultural sway of their overwhelming Russian neighbour. This does not necessarily mean that the pressure emanating from Moscow has been harsher here than in the other republics. On the contrary the Soviet regime, over a long period, consciously encouraged the development of a separate Belorussian identity. Indeed, in the 1920s the leaders in Moscow were accused of having created the Belorussian nation artificially from scratch. Such recriminations were indignantly rejected by Stalin.[1]

The main cause of the precarious state of Belorussian culture, it seems, was the pre-modern structure of the economy and society, which has resulted in the absence of a strong Belorussian intelligentsia in both the nineteenth and twentieth centuries. The effects of this circumstance have been strengthened by the cultural proximity to Russia, a nation which has possessed a literary culture for centuries. It has proved very difficult to establish a full-blooded Belorussian literary language, and when the affirmative action programmes for such a language were abolished in the 1930s, it threatened to slide back into oblivion. Belorussians were abandoning their mother tongue in favour

---

1. I. V. Stalin, 'Ob ocherednykh zadachakh partii v natsional'nom voprose' (1921), *Sochineniia*, V, Moscow, 1947, p. 48.

Table 7.1 LANGUAGE PROFICIENCY AMONG BELORUSSIANS: BELORUSSIANS CLAIMING BELORUSSIAN/RUSSIAN AS THEIR NATIVE LANGUAGE

Area	Language choice	1959	1970	1979	1989
In Belorussian SSR	Belorussian	93.2	90.1	83.4	80.2
	Russian	6.8	9.8	16.4	19.7
In other Soviet republics	Belorussian	41.8	41.1	36.8	36.3
	Russian	55.6	80.6	n.a	n.a.
Total	Belorussian	84.2	80.6	n.a	70.8
	Russian	15.3	19.0	n.a	28.5

Sources: Jan Zaprudnik, 'Belorussia and the Belorussians', in Zev Katz, Rosemarie Rogers and Frederic Harned (eds), *Handbook of Major Soviet Nationalities*, New York, 1975, p. 58; *Natsional'nyi sostav naselenia SSSR*, Moscow, 1991; and information provided to the author by Aleksandr Bilyk, consultant to the Committee on Nationalities Questions in the Belorussian parliament; V. I. Kozlov, *Natsional'nosti SSSR*, Moscow 1982, p. 241.

of Russian faster than any other major Soviet nationality (see Table 7.1).[2]

The changing linguistic preferences of the Belorussians were accompanied by a shift in the language policy of Belorussian publishing houses. In 1960 425 Belorussian books were published in the republic, against 1,177 Russian ones. Eleven years later the number of Belorussian books had remained constant, while the number of Russian titles had almost doubled.[3] The situation of newspaper publishing was somewhat different. There were more Belorussian dailies than Russian ones but they usually had a narrower circulation, being intended for the more limited readerships of small rural communities.

In the 1980s Western experts predicted a steady or possibly accelerating erosion of the Belorussian nationality through assimilation into the Russian group.[4] At that time 80% of Belorussians living within their titular republic still ticked Belorussian as their native tongue, but just as many were fluent in Russian. In contrast, only a quarter of

2. Stephen L. Guthier, 'The Belorussians: National Identification and Assimilation, 1897–1970: Part I', *Soviet Studies*, XXIX, 1 (January 1977), pp. 37–61.
3. Jan Zaprudnik, 'Belorussia and the Belorussians', in Zev Katz, Rosemarie Rogers and Frederic Harned (eds) *Handbook of Major Soviet Nationalities*, New York, 1975, pp. 49–71, on p. 59.
4. Ralph S. Clem, 'Belorussians', in Graham Smith (ed.), *The Nationalities Question in the Soviet Union*, London, 1990/1992, pp. 109–22, on p. 155.

the Russians in the republic were bilingual. Of the republic's total population, 65.6% in 1989 considered Belorussian to be their mother tongue, as against 31.9% Russian. However, if we look at those who claimed fluency in Belorussian and Russian, as either a first or a second language, Russian now had a slight edge: 82.6% against 77.6%.[5] In Minsk only 20% of the inhabitants were ethnic Russians, but 53% regarded Russian as their mother tongue.[6]

However, the decline of the Belorussian language seems to have been checked by the dissolution of the Soviet Union. It has been proclaimed the sole state language, and a timetable set for gradual transition to it in education and public life. By 1 September 1995, the working language of all congresses, seminars and other public meetings will be Belorussian, and by the year 2000, educational institutions will introduce it as the language of instruction. It is not quite clear how these clauses are meant to be interpreted or implemented, since the language law also guarantees the right of free use of the Russian language and to be educated in either Belorussian or Russian.[7]

Belorussian citizenship legislation automatically regards as a citizen every person who had permanent residence in the republic at the time when the law on citizenship was first adopted.[8] In the new Belorussian passports issued in the first quarter of 1994, the fifth point of nationality has been eliminated.[9] In general, no laws or official documents seem to distinguish in any way between the titular nationality and other ethnic groups.

Russians and Russian-speakers in the republic are generally optimistic for the future of inter-ethnic relations in the republic.[10] In Russia, even the most reactionary part of the national-patriotic press, which is prone to see an affront to the Russian nation in the most innocuous utterances and actions, has kept conspicuously silent on the ethnic situation in Belorussia. If anything, for these press organs it is more

5. Computed from *Natsional'nyi sostav naseleniia SSSR*, Moscow, 1991.
6. Chauncy D. Harris, 'The New Russian Minorities: a statistical Overview', *Post-Soviet Geography*, XXXIV (January 1993), pp. 1–27, on p. 22.
7. *Sovetskaia Belorussiia*, 17 February 1993.
8. 'Zakon respubliki Belarus' o grazhdanstve respubliki Belarus'', 18 October 1991 (typescript). Dual citizenship is not allowed for.
9. *Sovetskaia Belorussiia*, 26 February 1993.
10. Spartak Pol'skii, 'Russkaia diaspora v Belarusi. Etnopoliticheskoe polozhenie', paper presented at the conference 'The New Russian Diaspora', Lielupe, Latvia, 13–15 November 1992.

important to point out the contrasts between the Belorussian scene and the treatment of their co-nationals in, for instance, the Baltic states and Moldova than it is to highlight the discomfiture which may be felt by a few Russians in Belorussia.

True, certain Belorussian nationalists do apparently try to stigmatise the Russians as fifth columnists, cultural occupiers etc.[11] Conversely, some public organisations of the Russians, such as the Slavonic Council of 'White Russia' and the Movement for Democracy, Social Progress and Justice, have emphasised the unity of the East Slav peoples to the point where they are now being accused of denying the existence of a separate Belorussian nation. Certain activists in the National-Democratic Party of Belarus have demanded that such allegedly subversive organisations be outlawed.[12] It seems, however, that these disputes barely stir the general public at all.

The only nationality-related issue capable of generating a somewhat spirited debate in Belarus is that of language. The leading Russian-language newspaper, with the antiquated name *Soviet Belorussia*, opened its columns for a discussion on the anticipated consequences of the Belorussian language law. Giving Belorussian the status of a state language, it said, 'has split the nation into two polarised camps'.[13] Both camps claim their ultimate goal to be 'real' (i.e. *reciprocal*) Belorussian–Russian bilingualism, but their views diverge widely on how this objective is to be reached. Some believe that for as long as the Belorussian literary language remains at the infant stage it could slowly wither away but for the special protection provided by its official status. 'Russian would become the basic and dominant language, which would be detrimental to the prestige of the state and nation'.[14] The latter part of this prognosis is open to dispute. Hardly anyone claims that the prestige of the Irish state or nation suffers from the fact that English rather than the Irish language is dominant. However, the first proposition – that Belorussian is likely to succumb to Russian in a system of free competition – may be accurate enough.[15]

From the opposite side, it is claimed that the country is not prepared

11. *Sovetskaia Belorussiia*, 27 March 1993, p. 2; *Politika*, no. 5 (December), 1992, p. 11.
12. *Sovetskaia Belorussiia*, 12 March 1993, p. 2.
13. Academician Aleksandr Makhnach, in *Sovetskaia Belorussiia*, 31 March 1993, p. 2.
14. *ibid*.
15. See, also, interview with the painter Mikhail Savitskii, *Sovetskaia Belorussiia*, 6 February 1993.

for a transition to Belorussian as the dominant language for at least some time. The problems are partly practical and partly psychological. Since the great majority of the textbooks used in higher education are written in Russian (even those translated from a third language), a 'Belorussification' of the school system would lead to a decline in professional standards.[16] Also, it is being asserted that it will take decades to reverse the mental effects of 'seventy years of russification' (for some reason, the dominance of Russian is usually associated with the Soviet rather than the tsarist regime). 'It is impossible to cultivate love of the Belorussian language and literature, of Belorussian history and national traditions overnight, or even in ten years', claims a reader from Gomel.[17] If it is true that appreciation of anything Belorussian has sunk to such depths, it is no wonder that some activists are redoubling their efforts to resuscitate the language before it is too late.

Ukraine

An East Slav cultural continuum.   In Ukraine, the 11 million Russians account for 22% of the total population. They live in large numbers in the north-eastern region around Kharkiv (1 million), in the eastern regions of Donetsk, Dnipropetrovsk and Luhansk (4.5 million) and in southern Ukraine, around the port cities of Odessa and Mykolaiv (1 million). In these areas they are impressive minorities, ranging from 31% to 43% of the population. In the Crimea, the 1.6 million Russians are an outright majority.[18] In comparison, the other non-titular nationalities in Ukraine are generally quite small: taken together, they account for only 5.2% of the total population. This means that four out of every five non-Ukrainians in Ukraine are Russians.

In addition, more than 4 million Ukrainians living within their 'own' republic have abandoned their mother tongue in favour of Russian: in Luhansk 33%, in Donetsk 40% and in the Crimea 47%. Also, most other nationalities in these regions belong to the russophone group – in Donetsk, for instance, 67% of the Belorussians, 79% of the Greeks and 92% of the Jews. In certain eastern oblasts, the Russians, together with other Russian-speakers, make up a solid

16. Associate professor M. Il'in at the MVVIU, in *Sovetskaia Belorussiia*, 17 February 1993.
17. Valerii Novak, in *Sovetskaia Belorussiia*, 4 February 1993.
18. *Natsional'nyi sostav naseleniia SSSR*, Moscow, 1991, pp. 78ff.

majority: in Donetsk 67% and in Luhansk 63%. Added to this, only a fraction of the Russians and other Russian-speakers in these oblasts in 1989 claimed fluency in the Ukrainian language – in Odesa 23% and in Crimea 10% – and it is not difficult to guess which language has been functioning as the medium of inter-ethnic communication.

The Russian influence is much stronger in the cities than in the countryside. In most cities in left-bank Ukraine (that is, east of the Dniepr) as well as in Odesa on the right bank, Russian and Ukrainian have to a large degree penetrated each others' vocabulary and syntax. While any attempt to reduce the Ukrainian language to a variant or 'dialect' of Russian should be dismissed as linguistic ignorance, it should nonetheless be acknowledged that in Ukraine the two languages, *have*, to a large degree, interacted functionally with each other. Indeed, a Ukrainian–Russian mixed idiom is not uncommon, especially among recent migrants from the countryside into the cities. In some areas, the two languages function as social indicators, urban and rural. In the countryside, their close proximity have induced some Russians to abandon their mother tongue in favour of Ukrainian. More than half of all Russians in the former Soviet Union who claimed a non-Russian native tongue were residents of Ukraine.[19]

There are considerable dialect differences *within* the Ukrainian language. While certain Ukrainian dialects, especially Galician and Volhynian, are almost incomprehensible to heartland Russians who have not made a special study of them, Ukrainian-speakers and Russian-speakers in left-bank Ukraine understand each other much more easily. The degree of intermarriage between these groups has also been high. Ukrainian parents who disliked a daughter's fiancé because he was a Russian were rare.[20] It would be ludicrous to claim that Russians and Ukrainians have not developed separate ethnic identities. Nonetheless, before the national awakening under *perestroika*, the distinction between the various East Slav groups in parts of eastern and southern Ukraine was in many cases academic, and was of concern only to the census-takers. Many respondents in the censuses had

19. *ibid.*; V. I. Kozlov, *Natsional'nosti SSSR*, Moscow, 1982, pp. 85 and 252. In 1970, this added up to 204,000; in 1979, it had increased to 215,000 while 10 years later it had dropped to 182,000.
20. Yaroslav Bilinsky, 'Assimilation and Ethnic Assertiveness Among Ukrainians of the Soviet Union', in Erich Goldhagen (ed.), *Ethnic Minorities in the Soviet Union*, New York, 1968. pp. 157ff.

difficulty deciding for themselves which group they actually belonged to. In the late 1960s, a Soviet ethnographer found that many collective farmers in mixed Ukrainian–Russian villages in eastern Ukraine who had declared themselves to be Russians twelve or fifteen years earlier now gave their nationality as Ukrainian.[21]

This linguistic situation precludes the kind of language controversies which arose in the Baltics and Moldova under *perestroika*. In itself this circumstance does not guarantee an absence of ethnic clashes. The Serbs, Croats and Bosnian Muslims speak almost the same tongue, but this has not prevented them from turning their country into a slaughterhouse. However, this comparison is rather misleading. In contrast to the situation found in the former Soviet Union, language is now less relevant as an ethnic marker among the South Slavs, while other markers, such as religion and history, are correspondingly more significant.

In Ukraine also there are historical and religious dividing lines within the population, but these do not usually run between the Russians and the Ukrainians. More often they cut across the various Ukrainian groups. Before *perestroika*, almost all of Ukraine had belonged to the Russian empire since the eighteenth century and some areas for much longer. The westernmost parts of Ukraine, however, developed independently as provinces of another state. Under liberal Habsburg emperors Galicia, with its capital city Lviv (Lemberg), developed into a forcing house of Ukrainian national self-consciousness – a sort of Ukrainian Piedmont.

In Transcarpathia, history took a different turn. Here a large number of the Eastern Slavs saw themselves not as standard bearers of a common Ukrainian cause but as a distinct ethnic group: the Ruthenes. Religion added to these historical differences between east and west Ukraine. The dominant confession in Ukraine is Orthodoxy – among the Ukrainians as well as among the Russians. In the former Polish and Habsburg territories, however, the majority of the Ukrainians are Catholics of the Eastern rite.

In addition to linguistic, historic and religious contrasts between eastern and western Ukraine, the two parts also differ from each other demographically. Ethnic Russians make up very low percentages of

21. L. N. Chizhikova, 'Ob etnicheskikh protsessakh v vostochnykh raionakh Ukrainy', *Sovetskaia Etnografiia*, no. 1, 1968, pp. 18–31, esp. pp. 22ff.

the population in the western oblasts (in Galicia 7%, in Volyn and Rivne 4.5%, and in Transcarpathia 3.9%) – in all, less than 350,000 people.[22] Moreover, these Russians are much more 'Russia-Russian' than their co-nationals in other parts of the country. Almost all of them arrived there after the Second World War as migrant workers or employees in the state and party apparatuses or as their dependants.[23] In general their mind-frame has been 'Soviet-Internationalist', and they are poorly integrated into the local society. Certainly, their proficiency in Ukrainian – 50–60% claimed fluency in 1989[24] – has been higher than in most other parts of Ukraine, but considering that they are living in an almost totally Ukrainophone community, this must still be regarded as low. Thus, while Russians and Ukrainians in eastern Ukraine are often hardly distinguishable, in Galicia they are mentally worlds apart. If the East Slav culture is thought of as a continuum in which the Russians and Ukrainians of Donbas both belong to the centre, the inhabitants of Galicia belong to one or the other of the two extremities of this spectrum.

The demographic and cultural differences between eastern and western Ukraine have been gradually widening. With each new Soviet census, a growing number of Ukrainians have claimed Russian as their mother tongue. Almost all of these linguistic changes took place in the east and the south, but in western Ukraine, particularly in the Lviv oblast, the trend went the opposite way, with the number of Russians and Russian-speakers decreasing, both in absolute and in relative terms. As a result, western and eastern Ukraine were drifting apart, ethnically and linguistically, with the west becoming ever less Russian and the east ever more so.[25]

The remarkable referendum. This situation did not augur well for the cause of Ukrainian independence. Indeed, in 1988 and 1989, when the Baltic states, Moldova and Transcaucasia were all in the grips of rising national ferment, Ukraine, together with Belorussia, in the 'middle',

22. *Natsional'nyi sostav naseleniia SSSR*, Moscow, 1991, pp. 78ff.
23. Information from Andrei Vasetskii, Chairman of the Russian Cultural Centre, Ivano-frankivsk.
24. *Natsional'nyi sostav naseleniia SSSR*, Moscow, 1991, p. 84.
25. Roman Szporluk, 'The Strange Politics of Lviv: an Essay in Search of an Explanation', in Zvi Gitelman (ed.) *The Politics of Nationality and the Erosion of the USSR*, London, 1992, pp. 215–31.

remained unperturbed. Only in the autumn of 1989 was the Ukrainian Popular Front 'Rukh' founded, but when Volodymyr Shcherbytskyi, 'the last Brezhnevite', was finally ousted, his place was taken by another apparatchik of a not particularly reformed brand.

In the summer of 1990, when the Declaration of the Sovereignty of Ukraine was adopted, the Communists were still firmly in charge. This document astonished many observers by its radicalism – e.g. its claim that the republic should be entitled to its own armed forces and national currency. On the nationality issue, the absence of any specific reference to the Ukrainian people in the ethnic sense was noteworthy. The document spoke instead on behalf of 'the people of Ukraine', and underscored the need to respect the 'nationality rights of all peoples'.[26] While the crucial noun 'people' (*narod*) was used ambiguously, in both a political and an ethnic sense, there could be no doubt about the main message: in contrast to the situation in some other Soviet republics, the Ukrainian law-makers were pledging to create within the confines of the Soviet Union a *civic* nation-state and not an ethnic one.

While members of some non-titular ethnic groups, notably Jews, were actively involved in 'Rukh', very few Russians joined the movement.[27] It was predominantly a Western and Kievian phenomenon, and one which made relatively feeble inroads into the russianised east and south.[28] This is not to say that these areas were not mobilised under *perestroika*, but they had other demands. These concerned the economy rather than cultural and political liberties. The Donbas miners, in tandem with their colleagues in Kuzbass and Vorkuta, organised from the summer of 1989 onwards massive and protracted strikes, which did at least as much as the national movements in the republics to bring the Gorbachev regime to its knees. While the Ukrainian miners desired economic and to some extent political changes in Moscow and Kiev, they did not call for a dismantling of the Soviet Union. The All-Union referendum on the future of the Union organised by Gorbachev on 17 March 1991 brought this out. With a republic-wide turnout of above 80% in Ukraine, 70% voted

26. 'Deklaratsiia o gosudarstvennom suverenitete Ukrainy', *Argumenty i Fakty*, no. 29, 1990.
27. Information from Andrei Vasetskii, a former member of the national Rada of 'Rukh', Russian.
28. David Marples, 'A Sociological Survey of "Rukh"', *Report on the USSR*, II (12 January), 1990, pp. 19–22.

in favour of a renewed federation.[29] As expected, the support for Gorbachev's proposal was strongest in the eastern and southern parts. At the same time the Ukrainian voters, with an even greater majority, supported the idea that the Ukrainian declaration of sovereignty should define the status of the republic in any future association. In a sense, the majority of the inhabitants of Ukraine indicated that they wanted to have it both ways: to enjoy the benefits of a continued union as well as complete control over their own produce.

In the spring of 1991 an astonishing and crucial convergence of the eastern and western Ukrainian opposition movements took place. As the political analyst Vadim Skuratovskii remarked, 'the miners, whose indifference and even hostile attitude towards the more extreme expressions of the Ukraine nationalist movement was well known, suddenly, in the course of one political season, closed ranks with it.' At political meetings on the Kiev main thoroughfare, the Kreshchatik, the yellow–blue flags of the nationalists were flying above the miners' helmets. The language spoken from the rostrum was no longer necessarily Ukrainian. A certain 'russianisation' of the idea of Ukrainian independence had taken place.[30]

The Soviet Union could probably have survived the secession of several smaller republics, but if Ukraine decided to follow suit and secede, then the centrepiece of the Union would fall out. It was thus Ukraine which held the key to the future of the Union. Despite the 1990 declaration of sovereignty, the growing animosity towards the Moscow Centre and the independence agitation in western Ukraine and Kiev, things might still not have come to a head in Ukraine had it not been for the abortive coup in August 1991. Communism was, in one stroke, discredited as a political programme, and the old *nomenklatura* establishment moved swiftly towards more nationalist positions in search of a new form of legitimacy.[31] Ukrainian independence was declared on 24 August, and confirmed by a republic-wide referendum on 1 December.

29. Roman Solchanyk, 'The Referendum in Ukraine: Preliminary Results', *Report on the USSR*, III, 13 (29 March 1991).
30. Vadim Skuratovskii, 'Russkie na Ukraine – popytka prognoza', *Nezavismaia Gazeta*, 6 March 1992, p. 5.
31. The Ukrainian party leader, Leonid Kravchuk, had appeared on the putschist-controlled central television on 19 August, and expressed understanding for the necessity of the coup. Afterwards, he had a clear interest in staying out of reach of the new leaders in Moscow.

The votes of Galicia and other western and central oblasts in this referendum were certainly to be cast in favour of independence, but a slim positive majority might not have been enough to persuade the states of the world to recognise independent Ukrainian statehood. On the other hand, a massive backing from all regions, including the russified ones, would be a different matter. The fate of the Soviet Union was thus, in a sense, placed in the hands of the russianised minority of Ukraine – which, eight-and-a-half months earlier, had voted in favour of some kind of a renewed Union.

Several public figures in Russia suggested that the results of the Ukrainian referendum should be counted oblast-wise, to give the russianised areas a chance to remain in the Soviet Union if the voters there went against independence. However, this suggestion was indignantly rejected in Kiev. In the end, the recommended procedure would not have altered the outcome anyway, since, as it turned out, every oblast supported Ukrainian national independence. In aggregate figures, indeed, 90.3% of the voters supported this idea. Figures for the russified east were: 83.3% in Donetsk, 90.3% in Dnipropetrovsk, 83.8% in Luhansk and 86.3% in Kharkiv.[32] These were impressive and momentous figures. As expected, it was the Ukrainian referendum that sealed the fate of the Soviet Union. One week later, the Commonwealth of Independent States was proclaimed on its ruins.

A nationwide turnout of 84.1% meant that more than three-quarters of the entire electorate had actively supported independence. Since the Russians make up less than one quarter of the population, theoretically a large share of them had voted 'no' or else not voted, if all the other ethnic groups had voted 'yes' en bloc. In reality, however, well over half of the Russians probably voted for independence – some sources claim as many as 70%.[33] An opinion poll taken on the eve of the referendum indicated that support for a free Ukraine was

32. Bohdan Nahaylo, 'The Birth of an Independent Ukraine', Report on the USSR, III (13 December 1991), pp. 1–5; Den', no. 28, 12–18 December 1992. However, the turn-out in these oblasts was lower than the national average. In Kharkiv, Luhansk, Donetsk and Odesa, 34.8% of the eligible voters either did not vote for independence or abstained from voting. See Jaroslaw Martyniuk, 'Ukrainian Independence and Territorial Integrity', RFE/RL Research Report, I, 13 (1992), pp. 64–8.
33. Dmitro Vidrin, 'Rosiiani v Ukraini: Pid chas referendumu, do i pislia', Politologichni Chitanniia, no. 1, 1992, pp. 237–49, on p. 238.

stronger among ethnic Russians fluent in the Ukrainian language than among linguistically russified Ukrainians.[34]

In the autumn of 1991, news about increased ethnic tensions was emanating from the Baltic states, but obviously this did not influence the Russian vote in the Ukrainian referendum. Russians living in Ukraine apparently felt that the problems of their co-nationals in the Baltics did not concern them since their situation was quite different. True, an intermovement was coming together in Donetsk at the end of 1990,[35] but it did not assume anything like the proportions of its Baltic counterparts. These circumstances were adroitly exploited by the Ukrainian leader Leonid Kravchuk who, rather than making common cause with the Balts, appealed to the Russians in his own republic by emphasising the differences between the Baltic and the Ukrainian situations:

> I want to point out that the Russians in Ukraine should not be compared with the Russians in the Baltic republics. Here they are indigenous residents, they have lived on this land for hundreds of years . . . And we will not permit any kind of discrimination against them . . . Our republic, pardon me for saying so, is not Latvia, Lithuania, Estonia, or Moldova.[36]

Since many Russians in Ukraine can date their settlements back to the period before the divergence of the Russian and Ukrainian nations, they consider themselves in a territorial sense, to be 'Ukrainians' as much as anyone else living on Ukrainian soil. Against the background of their massive demographic strength and cultural influence, the fear of forced Ukrainisation seemed unreal. The notion that Ukraine would become a 'second East Slav state', or even a 'second Russian state' enjoyed a certain popularity. And indeed, outside Galicia there was no widespread feeling among the Russians of discrimination along ethnic lines. In a poll conducted in Kiev in the autumn of 1991, only 17% claimed to have encountered such discrimination at some time.[37]

34. *Moskovskie Novosti*, no. 48, 1 December 1991, p. 5.
35. Roman Solchanyk, 'Centrifugal Movements in Ukraine on the Eve of the Independence Referendum', *Report on the USSR*, III (29 November 1991), pp. 8–13.
36. *Pravda*, 16 July 1991, as quoted in Roman Solchanyk, 'Ukraine, The (Former) Center, Russia and "Russia"', *Studies in Comparative Communism*, XXV, 1 (March 1992), pp. 31–45, on p. 38.
37. *Argumenty i Fakty*, no. 49, December 1991, p. 1.

At the same time we can assume that many of the psychological mechanisms which induced some Baltic Russians to cast their votes in favour of independence in the spring must also have been at work among the Ukrainian Russians in December. Quite a number considered the alternatives in political rather than in ethnic terms, and cast their votes not *for* 'the Ukrainian cause' but *against* the old bureaucratic centre personified by Gorbachev. By 1991 Gorbachev had become an increasingly hated figure all over the Soviet Union, and his attempts to play the 'Russians-in-Ukraine' card to salvage the Union might well have induced some of them to vote in favour of independence to spite him.[38]

Parts of Rukh's agitation for national independence had minimal appeal among the Russians, such as the extravagant claim that the people of Ukraine were on the verge of physical extinction.[39] Much more decisive for the outcome of the Russian vote was undoubtedly the widespread expectation that the chances of economic recovery were greater in an independent Ukraine than they were for a Ukraine that remained part of the Union. The Moscow-based analyst Lilia Shevtsova interpreted the voting pattern of the Russians in Ukraine as both a reaction against numerous unsuccessful attempts at collective salvation and a desire to find their own path to survival.[40]

What finally endeared Rukh's programme to many Russians was probably the claim that an independent Ukraine could perform an economic miracle. A Rukh pre-referendum pamphlet contrasted the economic potential of Ukraine with that of Italy, France, Germany and Britain. This comparison showed that on four out of seven possible counts – namely coal, iron ore, steel and sugar – Ukraine produced more goods *per capita* than any of these Western countries, but because of the colonial status of Ukraine in the Soviet Union the population

38. See, for instance, Gorbachev's warning to a Lithuanian audience in January 1990 that the existence of 15 million (sic) Russians in Ukraine should make one think twice before trying to dissolve the Union. *Pravda*, 12 January 1990, p. 1.

39. A Rukh pre-referendum pamphlet, in all seriousness, predicted that the history of the Ukrainian people might come to an end in the year 2040, if not earlier, due to low fertility, a large number of miscarriages and the imperial policy of Moscow.

40. Liliia Shevtsova, 'Kak ispol'zovat' v mirnykh tseliakh energiu raspada imperii?', *Komsomol'skaia Pravda*, 24 December 1991.

had been prevented from enjoying the fruits of this abundance.[41] The fact that the productivity of Ukrainian mines was appallingly low by Western standards was overlooked. The Rukh leader Ivan Drach asserted that in a free Ukraine the Russians would live better than they did in Moscow, Leningrad and New York.[42] While these expectations seem in retrospect to have been over-wrought and naive, it should be remembered that at the time a number of Western experts also considered Ukraine to be the Union republic outside the RSFSR with the strongest economic potential.

Post-independence conflicts. The prospect of a peaceful and smooth development of inter-ethnic relations looked, and still looks, much brighter in Ukraine than it does for most other former Soviet republics. The ethnic turmoil of Estonia, Latvia and Moldova did not reach the vast Ukrainian plain – in this Kravchuk admittedly scored points. However, it would be unduly complacent to conclude that the Ukrainian ethnic barometer is preordained to point to sunny weather forever.

Three scenarios of inter-ethnic deterioration can be envisaged. *Economically*, the living standard of the Ukrainians may continue to fall and when money runs out, love goes with it. The Russian and russianised workers in the industrialised east who supported independence expecting quick opulence may feel that the politicians in Kiev have not kept their side of the 'bargain'. Just as they went on strike earlier in order to throw off the parasitic Soviet power, they may now come to believe, equally unrealistically, that all will be well if they get rid of the new 'bloodsuckers' in Kiev. True, the political élite in Kiev is by no means exclusively ethnic Ukrainian. A number of leading politicians are ethnic Russians.[43] Still, a Ukrainian centre–periphery conflict of an essentially economic character could easily take on ethnic overtones.

Internationally, should the strained relations with Russia deteriorate

41. For instance, from Ukrainian mines, more than 2,126 kilogrammes of iron ore *per capita* were dug out each year; in Great Britain, the figure was only 4 kilos, and in Germany only 2. See 'Gromodiani Ukraini! Na referendumi 1 grudnia, golosuite TAK'.
42. Ivan Drach, 'Net, ne Malorossy!', *Literaturnaia Gazeta*, no. 15, 11 April 1990, p. 3.
43. Including the Deputy Chairman of the Supreme Rada, Vladimir Grinev, the Minister of Defence, Konstantin Morozov, and the Prosecutor General, Viktor Shishkin.

further, it might have repercussions within Ukraine itself. The Russians may be suspected of nourishing sympathy with this looming neighbour and be treated by 'true' Ukrainian patriots as potential fifth columnists. The foci of such strife would be the tugs-of-war over the Crimea, the Black Sea fleet and the Ukrainian nuclear arsenal.

Culturally, central or local authorities may carry out a linguistic and educational ukrainisation process which proceeds so fast, or goes so deep, that the Russians begin to fear for their cultural identity. This danger is emanating primarily from certain sections of the cultural intelligentsia, based in Galicia, who are bent on turning the political liberation of Ukraine into a cultural triumph for ethnic Ukrainians at the expense of other groups.

Ukrainisation. In Ukraine, as in other former Soviet republics, the indigenisation of the national culture has been primarily concerned with questions of language and education. Here, again, as in all other Soviet republics, the language of the titular group was elevated under *perestroika* to the status of 'state language'. Many Ukrainian Russians will readily accept that every citizen of an independent state ought to know the majority language, but they nonetheless fear that its special, official status may be used as a lever for holding back the others. In a state where two different languages are spoken by a third and by two-thirds of the population, the prevailing view is that no official distinction should be made between them. It is thought that both should be considered state languages or that neither of them should be. Official Ukraine sees the matter differently. As hardly any overt discrimination against Russian-speakers is felt today, the authorities find the language demands of the Russians superfluous.[44] The position of the Russian language, they contend, is firmly entrenched for decades to come even without any special protection. While not unfounded, this argument may, however, be turned on its head: if the authorities have no intention of reducing the role of Russian in public life, they should also have no reason to oppose it having official status.

Attempts to preserve the current quantitative relationship between the two languages have been branded in the Ukrainian press as 'unjust and immoral attempts to freeze the consequences of more than 300 years of russification'.[45] Many Ukrainians believe that what has been

44. 'Vyuchat li ukraintsy ukrainskii iazyk?', *Izvestiia*, 14 September 1991.
45. A. Glushchak, in *Iug* (Odesa), 18 September 1992.

brought about by coercion may now, in the name of equity, be redressed by a similar means. And Ukrainian authorities are undoubtedly determined not only to halt but also to reverse the process of linguistic russification. Under the circumstances this is both inevitable and understandable, but the crucial questions concern the means, the speed and the ultimate goals of this policy, and not the policy itself. Will the stick or the carrot be its main instrument? How will the continued existence and development of the non-titular languages be safeguarded? And at what level will the decline of the Russian language be allowed to stabilise?

The Ukrainian language law of 1989 describes Russian, together with Ukrainian and other languages, as a language of 'interethnic intercourse'.[46] This law, which went into effect on 1 January 1990, provides for a time-frame of three to five years for employees of state and public institutions to acquire a knowledge of Ukrainian (and Russian) 'to the degree needed to execute their official responsibilities'. It guarantees that in those areas where a certain national minority is actually a majority, its language may be used on a par with the Ukrainian state language in the work of the state organs and public organisations. If no national group is in a majority, the population may chose the language most convenient to them.

The surest means of influencing linguistic development in any country is the school system. Opinion polls have shown that the various language groups in Ukraine disagree over the question of which should be the main language of instruction. However, more than half of the Russians living in Ukraine agree that the teaching of Ukrainian should be mandatory in all schools, and a third of them even accept that the state language should become the main language of instruction.[47] However, the Russians resent any attempts to force them to switch to a Ukrainian-language school.

In a multilingual society, all pupils should ideally be instructed in the language with which they feel most comfortable, but in reality the choice will always be limited by factors such as the number and location of schools to choose from, the scarcity of resources and the number of pupils with the same language preferences. If the number

---

46. 'Zakon o iazykakh v Ukrainskoi SSR', *Vidomosti Verkhovnoi Radi Ukraini*, 1990, Law no. 631, pp. 59–67.
47. Jaroslaw Martyniuk, 'Attitudes Towards Language in Ukraine', *RFE/RL Research Report*, I, 37 (18 September 1992).

of pupils desiring a certain language is very small, the school authorities cannot be expected to make special arrangements for them. For
these reasons it is often very difficult to say if the failure to provide
pupils with instruction in their language of preference is the result of
unfortunate circumstances or of deliberate manipulations. Many Russians in Ukraine are convinced, apparently with good reason, that in
several instances in recent years the latter has been the case. For
instance, at the beginning of the 1992 school year, it was revealed that
only one Russian class was started at a Kiev school with 250 applicants
for Russian-language instruction.[48]

In the autumn of 1992 the Donetsk intermovement began to distri-
bute leaflets maintaining that Russian had become a 'foreign language'
in Ukraine.[49] As Table 7.2 shows, this claim was not supported by
the relevant statistics on education. In most oblasts the number of
pupils being instructed in Russian in 1992 far exceeded the numbers
who in 1989 had claimed Russain as their native language. Only in
western Ukraine were a few Russian-speakers attending Ukrainian
schools. On the other hand, the trend was certainly, and not surprisingly, towards the ukrainisation of schools. Certain Ukrainian politicians and bureaucrats are indeed actively striving to reduce Russian to
the status of 'a foreign language'. The director of the Lviv oblast
bureau of public education, Iryna Kalynets, who is also a people's
deputy, has acquired particular notoriety as a doughty champion of
educational ukrainisation. On her initiative Russian-language schools
in Lviv have been closed, against the wishes of the parents.[50] In a
programme on Ukrainian radio Kalynets has declared that Russian
should be regarded as a foreign language on a par with English and
French.[51] It is in relation to such statements that demands for the
status of state language for Russian must be seen.

Russian literature is no longer studied as a separate subject but is
included in the study of world literature. For the time being Russian
literature fills up around 25% of the curriculum of 'foreign literature'

48. Galina Remizovskaia, 'Kak ia ustraivala rebënka v russkuiu shkolu', *Kievskie
    Vedomosti*, 12 September 1992.
49. Roman Solchanyk, 'The Politics of Language in Ukraine', *RFE/RL Research
    Report*, II, 10 (5 March 1993), pp. 1–4, on p. 3.
50. Vitalii Panov, '"Reformy" pani Kalinets', *Rossia*, no. 31, (29 July–4 August
    1992).
51. Radio Ukraina, 14 July 1992, 6:50, as quoted in 'Ukraine Today, RFE/RL media
    news and features digest'.

Table 7.2. PUPILS STUDYING IN RUSSIAN IN UKRAINE

Oblast	Total population, 1989 (× 1,000)	Russians, 1989 (× 1,000)	Russophones, 1989 (× 1,000)	Russophones, 1989 (% of population)	Studying in Russian, 1992 (%)	% difference between two preceding columns
Ternopil	1,164	27	29	2.5	2.4	−0.1
Ivano-Frankivsk	1,413	57	67	4.4	4.0	−0.4
Volyn	1,058	47	54	5.1	5.1	0
Rivne	1,164	54	65	5.6	6.4	0.8
Lviv	2,727	195	240	8.8	8.1	−0.7
Transcarpathia	1,246	49	62	5	7.3	2.3
Kiev Oblast	1,934	168	210	11	15.4	4.4
Chernivitsy	941	63	99	10.5	15.7	5.2
Khmelnytskyi	1,521	88	121	8	18.5	10.5
Vinnytsya	1,921	112	168	8.6	18.7	10.1
Zhytomyr	1,538	121	185	12	23.3	21.3
Cherkasy	1,527	122	157	10	24.2	24.2
Poltava	1,749	179	231	13	25.7	12.7
Chernihiv	1,413	96	191	13	32.9	19.9
Kirovohrad	1,228	144	186	15	37.8	22.8
Kherson	1,237	249	379	30	48.3	18.3
Sumy	1,427	190	310	21.7	51.5	29.8
Mykolaiv	1,328	258	448	34	56.5	22.5
Dnipropetrovsk	3,870	936	1,440	37	68.9	31.9
Kiev City	2,572	536	1,058	41	69	28
Kharkiv	3,175	1,054	1,528	48	72	24
Odesa	2,624	719	1,235	47	73.5	26.5
Zaporizhzhia	2,074	664	1,012	48	77.3	29.3
Luhansk	2,857	1,279	1,826	63	93.3	30.3
Donetsk	5,312	2,316	3,594	68	96.7	28.7
Crimea	2,430	1,629	2,008	82	99.96	18
Total	51,542	11,355	17,081	33.1	50	16.9

Computed from: *Natsional'nyi sostav naseleniia SSSR*, Moscow, 1991, pp. 78–86; and 'Shkoly Ukrainy', *Iug* (Odessa), 20 January 1993, p. 3.

in Ukrainian schools. However, the first deputy minister of education, A. G. Pogribnoi, has explained that this is a temporary arrangement, reflecting the fact that hundreds of teachers who have specialised in this topic would otherwise have to be put on the dole. In time, as these Russian philologists retire, this percentage will be reconsidered.[52]

On cadre policy, fears of ukrainisation are strongest in the heavily russified army. Understandably, a particularly high degree of loyalty must be expected from defenders of the fatherland; what is less obvious is that their mother tongue should be regarded as a criterion of trustworthiness. A circular on the language affiliation of officers in the Carpathian military district, as reported in the paper *Moloda Galichina*, was widely interpreted as being a prelude to an ethnic purge in the army.[53]

Defence Minister Morozov has hinted that many Russian officers may have sworn allegiance to the Ukrainian army not out of sincere conviction but simply to retain their careers.[54] By prying into the hearts of men in search of hidden motives, the defence minister was in a strange way casting doubt on the validity of the military oath as such. Though a Russian himself, Morozov has been suspected of yielding to pressure from the nationalist Union of Officers of Ukraine (UUO) in most of his appointments.[55]

However, many Russians find the activities of certain nationalistic Ukrainian organisations, which have mushroomed in some areas, more disturbing than the blunders of favouritism committed by certain authorities. One of them is State Independence for Ukraine (SIU), led by the renowned dissident Ivan Kandyba. An erstwhile associate of Levko Lukianenko, Kandyba broke with his former comrade-in-arms, finding him too moderate. Kandyba claims that Ukraine should be

52. *Nezavisimost'*, 11 January 1993.
53. Defence Minister Morozov categorically denied the purge charge, but admitted that certain mistakes had been committed. See *Nezavisimost*, 5 February 1993, p. 5.
54. Reuter, 25 January 1993, as reported by *RFE/RL News Briefs*, 25–29 January 1993.
55. *Rossiiskie Vesti*, 30 December 1992. For details on UUO, see Taras Kuzio, 'Ukraine's Young Turks – the Union of Ukrainian Officers', *Jane's Intelligence Review, EUROPE*, January 1993, p. 23–6.

primarily for the Ukrainians, 'as Russia is for the Russians and France is for the French'.[56]

On behalf of the Ukrainian state, SIU lays claim to territories in the Russian Federation. The logo on the front page of its paper *Neskorena Natsia* (*Unvanquished nation*) shows a map of Ukraine which includes large tracts of Kuban and other Russian areas. The paper provides much strange reading. Three of its main bywords seem to be 'nationalism', 'struggle', and 'hatred'. In its September 1992 issue moderate Ukrainian nationalists such as Levko Lukianenko came under fire, accused of having spoken up in defence of conciliation and forgiveness. Such weakness was rebutted by a quotation from Plato: 'You must feel hatred towards the enemy even before he has done anything wrong to you.'

> We Ukrainian nationalists . . . do not belong to the weak races. Between collaborators and occupiers we see no difference. Like Satan who flees from the cross, our Little Russians [*malorosi*] will be horrified by the outburst of national anger.[57]

Even more menacing is the rightist radical Ukrainian National Assembly (UNA). Established in July 1990, it has its own paramilitary structure, the Ukrainian People's Self Defence Forces. UPSDF detachments took part in the Dniester war on the side of the PMR, and distinguished themselves with their high combat discipline. Ironically, they found themselves in this war fighting the same cause as their archenemy, the Russian nationalists. Unauthorised paramilitary detachments are prohibited in Ukraine, but this has done nothing to curtail the UPSDF's activities. Official Ukrainian spokesmen warn against overestimating the influence of the UPSDF,[58] but the opposite error should also be avoided. One political analyst believes that the UPSDF 'can and is having an impact where the population is apathetic, desires a "strong hand" . . . and the authority of the state is still weak or not being observed.'[59]

56. 'Ivan Kandyba: "Bog i Ukraina – prevyshe vsego!"', *Vecherniaia Odessa*, 12 September 1992.
57. V'iacheslav Rogoziv, 'Ukrains'ka a'lternativa', *Neskorena Natsiia*, September 1992.
58. See, e.g., interview with the Ukrainian ambassador to Russia, Volodymyr Kryzhanovskii, in *Golos*, no. 47, November 1992, p. 6.
59. Taras Kuzio, 'Ukrainian Paramilitaries', *Jane's Intelligence Review*: EUROPE, December 1992, p. 541.

Russian responses. In order to counter such tendencies a number of organisations, movements and groups have been formed with the aim of asserting the interests of the Russians and other Russian-speakers in Ukraine. Many of these groups are obviously very feeble and/or purely local. Others try to reach out to all Russians in Ukraine. Among these we find the society of Russian culture, called 'Rus'', headed by the writer V. I. Ermolova. At a republic-wide Rus' conference in Kiev in September 1992, the speakers reminded the audience:

> The majority of the so-called 'russophone population' gave their vote to L. Kravchuk, believing in his promise that they would live 'better than the Russians in Russia'. However, soon disillusionment set in. Linguistic Ukrainisation takes place in institutions and schools, and certain excesses have occurred in the cadre policy. The preconditions for squeezing Russian culture out of the life of Ukraine have been put in place.[60]

However, the Rus' delegates recognised that to some extent the Russians in Ukraine have themselves to blame for this misery. In particular, not all of them have accepted the fact of Ukrainian independence, and they fail to take active part in building the state. 'Some are not in a hurry to learn the state language.'

While Rus' itself is a cultural and not a political organisation, there are other political parties, defending the interests of the Russians, that have also come to the fore in Ukraine. The Party of Communist-Bolsheviks of Ukraine, established in February 1993, should probably be counted among them although it emphasises political and economic issues much more than ethnic ones. The Party of Slavic Unity (Ukrainian Branch), on the other hand, is concerned with ethnic questions, although it is not a Russian party in the narrow sense but instead tries to 'defend and uphold the values, traditions and interests of all the nations whose historical fate is linked to Slavic statehood'.[61]

One of the questions with which Russian organisations are most preoccupied is citizenship regulations. The Ukrainian citizenship law is a variant of the zero option. All permanent residents are eligible for citizenship, but when neither the applicant's spouse, neither parent nor a single grandparent was born in Ukraine a residence period of five

---

60. V. Gridin, '"Rus": Zhit' pod odnoi kryshe', *Iug* (Odesa), 18 September 1992; *Vecherniaia Odessa*, 18 September 1992.
61. 'Programmnye printsipy partii slavianskogo edinstva (Ukrainy)', mimeograph.

years is required.[62] In 1992, however, it was decided that all citizens now had to register with the relevant passport authorities in order to have the Ukrainian state emblem, the trident, stamped into their old Soviet passport, to confirm their acceptance of the status of Ukrainian citizens.[63] Some Russians consider this procedure to be tantamount to a declaration of loyalty, and in effect as a tightening up of the requirements for citizenship. However, the main argument used against the stamp campaign – that the trident is a fascist symbol that was used by certain Ukrainian organisations with fascist leanings during the Second World War – is really not serious.[64] More likely, the real reason behind the grudge is that some Russians are not sure if they are ready to accept their status as Ukrainian citizens. As it was put in a statement from Rus':

> Now, when the majority have seen that in practice 'independence' means the tearing apart of long-established human, cultural and economic ties, enhanced dangers of international armed conflicts, reduced access to geographic territories, curtailed chances of education and job opportunities, and other negative consequences, the supporters of the idea of 'independence' are getting fewer.[65]

What might happen to those who reject Ukrainian citizenship is not clear. Some Russians are afraid that only citizens will be allowed to buy air tickets or even stay in hotels.[66] While some of these apprehensions may be taken out of thin air, the privatisation law does in fact allow only citizens to participate in the privatisation process.[67]

The optimal solution from the Russian point of view would be the taking of dual Ukrainian-Russian citizenship. This is a standard demand of most Russian organisations, and was supported by Russia's ambassador to Ukraine, Leonid Smoliakov. The Ukrainian citizenship law does allow for dual citizenship, but only on the basis of separate

---

62. Interview with the Ukrainian ambassador to Russia, Volodymyr Kryzhanovskyi, in *Golos*, no. 47, November 1992, p. 6.
63. 'O grazhdanstve Ukrainy' *Flag Rodiny*, 19 September 1992.
64. *Federatsiia*, 18 February 1993.
65. *Iug*, 18 September 1992.
66. *Pravda*, 28 January 1993; *Flag Rodiny*, 19 September 1992.
67. Susan Stewart, 'Ukraine's Policy toward Its Ethnic Minorities', *RFE/RL Research Report*, II, 6 (10 September 1993), pp. 55–62.

agreements with each country in question.[68] No such agreement has yet been signed with Russia.

A second issue which is given high priority by Russian activists in Ukraine is the transformation of the unified structure of the state into a federal arrangement. This demand is being supported also by other ethnic groups, such as the Magyars and Ruthenes of Trascarpathia.[69] Even certain leading Ukrainian politicians and political parties have expressed some sympathy for this idea. Viacheslav Chornovil toyed with it in 1991, but later backed away. The Ukrainian Social-Democratic Party has suggested a state structure which would give a high degree of local autonomy not only to compactly settled ethnic groups but also to all the historical regions of Ukraine. Taking the German Federal Republic as a model, they propose the introduction of sixteen Ukrainian *Länder* (*Zemli*), with more or less the same prerogatives as their German counterparts.[70] The influential chairman of the Ukrainian Supreme Rada, Ivan Pliushch, indicated his support for this idea.[71]

Opponents of such ideas have countered that as long as the concept of a single Ukrainian identity is not firmly entrenched in the minds of the citizens, the question of federalisation could endanger the very existence of the state. While certain advocates of the unitary state hold out a promise of territorial autonomy at some time in the distant future,[72] others reject it out of hand. As it was claimed in *Slava i Chest'*, an organ of the Odesa Military District: 'Those who demand

68. The Ukrainian citizenship law was passed on 8 October 1991. The text of the original law was published in *Vidomosti Verkhovnoi Radi Ukraini*, no. 50, 1991, pp. 1443–51 (Law no. 791), and did not allow for dual citizenship. Later, however, the law was amended. See Susan Stewart, *op. cit.*

69. Alfred A. Reisch, 'Transcarpathia's Hungarian Minority and the Autonomy Issue', *RFE/RL Research Report*, I, 6 (1992).

70. Viktor Vovk and Aleksei Mustafin, 'Bogataia mnogoobraziem, sil'naia edinstvom', *Kievskii Sotsial-Demokrat*, no. 1, October 1991.

71. Ivan Pliushch, 'Rozumnii balans vlad – zaporuka stabil'nosti suspil'stva', *Viche*, no. 5, 1993, pp. 3–14. At the time of writing, the question of federalism is still not settled. However, certain evidence suggests that whatever the formulations that will be employed in the new constitution, the Ukrainian state structure will contain certain elements of federalism *de facto*. Well-informed observers believe that central Ukrainian authorities are inclined to allow many matters to be solved locally, and will not gratuitously impose their will on the regions. See Ian Bremmer, 'Russians as Ethnic Minorities in Ukraine and Kazakhstan', unpublished ms.

72. See M. Matsiuk, 'Unitarizm ili federalizm', *Iug*, January 1993, p. 2.

"free zones" and "free cities" are usually people without kith or kin, cosmopolitans, or simply masked enemies of Ukraine.'[73]

However, many members of the national minorities remained undeterred. In Odesa several organisations such as the Civic Movement of Odesa, Rus', the Socialist Party and Novorossia are campaigning for the establishment of a separate Novorossian region, the exact borders of which are still being debated. However, these endeavours are unlikely to be successful. Conversations with inhabitants of Odesa in September 1992 left this author with the distinct impression that most Odessians are not easily agitated by questions of ethnicity or regionalism.

Greater attention should be paid to the regionalist movement in the Donbas area, which started to gain momentum in 1993.[74] It came as a rude surprise to the Donbas miners when their buying power decreased dramatically after independence; contrary to all expectations and promises, they were faring far worse than their Russian colleagues. The Movement for the Rebirth of Donbas demanded a restructuring of the Ukrainian state on federal lines, the elevation of Russian to the status of second state language and closer integration for Ukraine into the Commonwealth of Independent States.[75]

In June 1993 the sorry performance of the Ukrainian economy triggered a wave of strikes in the major industrial centres of eastern Ukraine. The demands of the workers were not only economic but included most of the programme of the Donbas movement.[76] The call for greater economic independence was somewhat paradoxical since most of the mines were unprofitable and were being kept artificially alive only by strong injections of state subsidies from Kiev. The miners, however, not unreasonably blamed their tribulations on the disruption of economic ties within the former Soviet Union, and demanded the right to trade directly with other Soviet successor states – and primarily with Russia.

The elections to the Ukraine Supreme Rada in March 1994 revealed that eastern and western Ukraine were again drifting apart, in terms not only of preferred economic policies but also of political

---

73. *Slava i Chest'*, 10 September 1992, p. 7. 'Cosmopolitans', in a Soviet or post-Soviet context, is usually an ominous allusion to the Jews.
74. Andrew Wilson, 'The Growing Challenge to Kiev from the Donbas', *RFE/RL Research Report*, II, 33 (20 August 1993, pp. 8–13.
75. *Nezavisimaia Gazeta*, 10 February 1993.
76. *Moskovskie Novosti*, no. 30, 1993, 25 July, p. 9.

allegiances. Western Ukraine voted in more radical nationalists than before, while the resurrected Ukrainian Communist Party achieved a landslide victory in the east, campaigning on an anti-nationalist and pro-Russian ticket.

The Crimean knot.   The turmoil in eastern Ukraine is serious enough, but undoubtedly the greatest challenge to the unity of the Ukrainian state has been posed by the Crimea, whose claim to autonomy is based not so much on demographic or economic arguments as on historical and legal circumstances. The Crimea is not a part of the traditional area of Ukrainian settlements. For centuries it was the home of the Crimean Tatars, who were deported to Central Asia on Stalin's orders during the Second World War. To replace them, hundreds of thousands of Russians and a great many Ukrainians too were moved in. The Russians now comprise by far the largest ethnic group with approximately 67% of the population, while the Ukrainians are the second largest group with 25%. Nonetheless, in 1954, jurisdiction over the peninsula was transferred from the RSFSR over to the Ukrainian SSR as a kind of jubilee present to commemorate the 'reunion of Russian and Ukrainian lands' 300 years earlier.[77]

On 20 January 1991, the local Crimean authorities arranged a referendum which showed that no less than 93.3% of the voters favoured the establishment of an autonomous socialist Crimean republic within the Soviet Union, outside the Ukrainian SSR (the voter turn-out was above 80%).[78] The legalities of this referendum have been questioned, since no referendum law was in existence at the time, neither in the Soviet Union nor in Ukraine.[79] The Crimean Tatars, who had begun to return to the peninsula, boycotted it. Nonetheless, the referendum was recognised by the authorities in Kiev as

---

77. Frederick C. Barghoorn, *Soviet Russian Nationalism*, Oxford, 1956, pp. 55ff. The 'gift' version is being contested by many Ukrainians who argue that the jurisdictional transfer was politically and economically well-founded. See, e.g., a press release from the movement 'Crimea with Ukraine', *Krims'kii Visnik*, September 1992, p. 2.

78. Kathleen Mihalisko, 'The Other Side of Separatism: Crimea Votes for Autonomy', *Report on the USSR*, III, 5 (1991), pp. 36–8. The text of the referendum question was: 'Are you in favour of the resurrection of the Crimean Autonomous Soviet Socialist Republic as a subject of the USSR and a participant of the Union Treaty?'. 'Biulleten' dlia golosovaniia po referendumu o gosudarstvennom i pravovom statuse Kryma'.

79. See, e.g., *Literaturnaia Gazeta*. no. 19, 6 May 1992, p. 1.

a valid expression of the will of the Crimean population. On 12 February 1991, the Ukrainian parliament conferred on the peninsula the status of autonomous republic as the first and only autonomous formation on Ukrainian soil. An autonomous Crimean republic within the RSFSR had previously existed up till the deportation of the Crimean Tatars in the 1940s; at that time the autonomy was usually regarded as existing by virtue of the Tatars even though they made up no more than a quarter of the population. (As one of the very few autonomous formations in the Soviet Union, the Crimean ASSR did not carry the name of any titular nation.) When Crimean autonomy was resurrected in 1991, still without a titular nation in its designation, this was obviously intended as a sign of goodwill not primarily towards the Tatars but towards the dominant national group, the Russians. An additional important motive, however, was the need to defuse the mounting Russian campaign for the return of the peninsula to the jurisdiction of the RSFSR.

On 4 September 1991, the Crimean Supreme Soviet affirmed the state sovereignty of the peninsula as a constituent part of Ukraine. However, a campaign was soon launched for the holding of a new referendum in Crimea. It was argued that the Ukrainian declaration of independence had radically changed the situation; in an extant Soviet Union, autonomy for the peninsula would suffice, but it would not do so in a Ukrainian national state.[80]

In the Ukrainian referendum held on 1 December, no other region registered such a low level of support for Ukrainian national independence as did the Crimea. And even here, a slim majority of 54% of the participants actually voted 'Yes'. The turn-out was fairly low – about 60% – and in effect, the population fell into three roughly equal parts: those who supported independence, those who opposed it and those who had expressed no opinion – with a slight edge to the first group. For the champions of Crimean independence the matter remained unresolved, and the 'war of referendums' continued unabated.

The driving force behind the referendum campaign was the Republican Movement of Crimea (with the Russian acronym 'RDK'). This movement emerged in the immediate aftermath of the declaration of Ukrainian independence. Contrary to a widespread assumption, its organisers were not former apparatchiks but included, rather, some of

80. Eduard Kondratov and Viktor Filippov, 'Poluostrov Krym', *Izvestiia*, 16 October 1991.

the few individuals on the peninsula who had publicly denounced the coup attempt.[81]

According to the RDK's leader, Iurii Meshkov (a deputy to the Crimean Supreme Soviet), the desire to leave the Ukrainian state is first and foremost motivated by the emergence of aggressive Ukrainian nationalism, as incarnated in the Ukrainian National Assembly (UNA). In a conversation with the present author in September 1992, Meshkov claimed that the UNA is matched by no other political organisation in Ukraine in size and structural sophistication. He compared the political situation in Ukraine to that of Germany in the 1920s, at which time most people still contemptuously dismissed the NSDAP. The RDK is set on not repeating that mistake, particularly since the fury of the UNA, they believe, is focussed on the Crimea. 'A young nation is in need of a victory. The Crimea is a suitable victim.' Meshkov accused the official Ukraine authorities of tacit connivance with the extremists.[82] While these fears sounded sincere, the RDK leader could not give a satisfactory answer to the question why Russians in other parts of Ukraine seem to take a somewhat less alarmist view of the prospects for Ukrainian fascism.[83]

Meshkov and nine other like-minded people staged a hunger strike in downtown Simferopol in October 1991 to force the Crimean authorities to organise another referendum. The action paid off, and in November the Crimean Supreme Soviet adopted a law on referendums. On 3 February 1992 it was decided that a referendum would be organised if 10% of the adult population – or 180,000 persons – demanded it. The signatures had to be collected within two months – by 3 April – or they would be void.[84] The question on the ballot would be 'Are you in favour of an independent Republic of Crimea in alliance [*soiuz*] with other states?'[85]

The RDK immediately launched an intensive signature-collection campaign, and by the end of February had received more than 100,000. At that point, however, the campaign seemed to be running out of

81. Iurii Makeev, 'Krym: Politicheskaia karta poluostrova', *Iug* (Krasnodar), no. 39, 1992, p. 7.
82. Author's interview with Iurii Meshkov in Simferopol, September 1992.
83. Admittedly, charges of fascism in Ukrainian political leadership have been put forth, also, in Donbas and other places. See, e.g., 'Sravnivaem eto s fashizmom', *Narodnaia Pravda*, no. 41, October 1992; and Andrew Wilson, *op. cit.*, p. 9.
84. Aleksandr Chizhevskii, 'Ostrov Krym', *Nedelia*, no. 6, 1992, p. 5.
85. Information received in the RDK headquarters.

steam, until a 'Friendship Train', organised by Galician nationalists, entered the scene. The 900 participants in this symbolic tour passed through Odesa and Kherson, spreading fear among the locals, before they arrived in Sevastopol on Easter Day.[86] They then bullied their way into the closed naval city, tearing down Russian and Soviet flags and holding placards bearing inscriptions such as 'Crimea for the Ukrainians'.[87] This incident gave a tremendous boost to the RDK campaign, which, as the time-limit expired, had registered 66,000 more supporters for a new referendum than were required by the authorities.[88]

In Kiev, anxiety was on the rise. Obviously, the Ukrainian leaders could not doubt the eventual outcome of the referendum if it were to be held. They warned that it would be unconstitutional and would lead to heightened tension.[89] Ironically they were now caught in the same game that they themselves and political leaders in other republics had earlier played successfully against Gorbachev: they were advancing the very same arguments and strategies to prevent the break-up of their state as those which the former Soviet president used in the Soviet Union. They warned, *inter alia*, that political fragmentation leads to economic decline[90] (the ongoing deterioration of the Ukrainian economy could have been pointed to as evidence, but for obvious reasons this was not done). In addition, the separatists were threatened with legal persecution. On 11 October 1991 Article 62 of the Ukrainian criminal code had been amended, making 'calls for the infringement of the territorial integrity' of the state a criminal offence, carrying a penalty of three to seven years' imprisonment. As some commentators pointed out, the harshness of the Ukrainian stand on the issue was probably dictated not only by the Crimean case but perhaps even more by the possible repercussions that any concessions to the Crimeans

---

86. *Izvestiia*, 3 March 1992.
87. *Jane's Intelligence Review* (Europe), no. 19, 6 May 1992, p. 541.
88. *Literaturnaia Gazeta*, no. 19, 6 May 1992; *Moskovskie Novosti*, 31 May 1992, p. 4; *Svobodnyi Krym*, no. 14, July 1992, p. 2.
89. See, e.g. *Pravda Ukrainy*, 19 May 1992.
90. The economist Elena Kuz'minskaia, for instance, pointed out that Crimea received 100% of its steel and 90% of its energy from Ukraine. 'Bogatym stanet tol'ko s Ukrainoi', *Pravda Ukrainy*, 13 May 1992, p. 2. This could be interpreted as a veiled threat of imposing an embargo similar to the one suffered by Lithuania in the spring of 1990.

could have in other regions such as Novorossia and Donbas.[91]

Meanwhile, the Ukrainian parliament had been elaborating a law on the status of the Crimean peninsula, fleshing out the details of the autonomy granted the year before. Since Ukraine, despite this autonomy, is officially considered a unitary state, what the legislators were charged with was the task of squaring a circle. On 21 April 1992, they adopted, on the first reading, a law on 'the delineation of power between Ukraine and the Republic of Crimea'. When the law was finally passed a few days later, however, it had acquired a new title – 'On the Status of the Autonomous Republic of the Crimea' – and a somewhat new content. A leading Ukrainian legal expert, A. Matsiuk, claimed that the final text was 'largely in accordance with the initial draft', but he explained at the same time that 'in a unitary state there can be no delineation of power between the state as such and its constituent parts.' To make matters even more confusing, he went on to assert that, again in the final version of the law, Crimea was given extremely wide powers – wider powers, indeed, than those granted to any member of any other federation in the world.[92] However, one Western analyst has maintained that this law had in fact been 'extensively altered to the Crimeans' disadvantage'.[93]

A political thriller with high stakes was set in motion. The Crimeans claimed that the law on the autonomous status of Crimea had in effect reduced its statehood to nil.[94] On 5 May 1992 the Crimean parliament adopted a constitution plus a Declaration of Independence. The independence bill was passed with 118 votes against 28, and was to be confirmed by a referendum slated for 2 August. However, on the very next day, the parliament inserted a new sentence into the new constitution to the effect that the Crimean republic is a constituent part of the Ukrainian republic. The relationship between the two independent republics, the one contained within the other, should, in the view of the legislators, have been based both on a treaty and on various agreements.[95] This position was no less paradoxical than the Ukrainian concept of Ukraine as a unitary state containing an autonomous formation, and was furthermore reminiscent of the shibboleth

91. See, e.g., Iu. Kulibaba, in *Komsomol'skaia Pravda*, 29 October 1991.
92. A. Matsiuk, 'Novyi status poluostova', *Pravda Ukrainy*, 7 May 1992, p. 2.
93. Roman Solchanyk, 'The Crimean Imbroglio: Kiev and Simferopol', *RFE/RL Research Report*, I, 33 (21 August 1992), pp. 13–6, on p. 14.
94. *Krymskie Izvestiia*, 8 May 1992, p. 1.
95. *ibid.*

favoured by the Tatars of Russia in their dealings with Moscow.

The Ukrainian reaction was swift and brusquely negative.[96] Several Ukrainian parties demanded that the Crimean legislature should be dissolved, its chairman Nikolai Bagrov arrested and direct presidential rule be introduced on the peninsula. The Ukrainian National Assembly declared that Crimea would be either Ukrainian or else depopulated.[97] The Ukrainian parliament convened on 13 May and annulled the Crimean declaration of independence. The Crimean parliament was given one week to do the same, and to call off the planned referendum. A proposal from Bagrov (himself a deputy to the Ukrainian parliament) to set up a conciliatory commission was rejected.[98] On 14 May, the Ukrainian parliament increased its pressure on the peninsula by adopting, at its first reading, a law on the powers of presidential representatives in Crimea. These representatives were given wide-ranging powers.

The Ukrainian legislators issued an address to the population of Crimea which is remarkable for its intense, almost desperate language:

> Fellow countrymen! Today, our future, the fate of the people of Ukraine depends to a large extent on your good sense, self-restraint, political maturity, and worldly wisdom. The situation which is unfolding in the Crimea can lead to unpredictable consequences, to social tragedy, and to the mutilation of the fate of hundreds of thousands of people . . . But we still have a possibility to overcome all contradictions and to avoid such tragic events as have broken out in Caucasia, in the Dniestria and in other regions.[99]

The message here was clear: Ukraine was willing to go to war in order to retain its jurisdiction over the peninsula. In such a war, Russia would almost certainly be drawn in as well, in which event the Crimean drama could indeed lead to 'unpredictable consequences'.

To what extent this threat should be taken at face value, or as scare

---

96. *Pravda Ukrainy*, 8 May 1992, p. 1.
97. *Jane's Intelligence Review*, EUROPE, December 1992, p. 541.
98. 'Tak reshil ukrainskii parlament', *Pravda Ukrainy*, 15 May 1992.
99. 'Obrashchenie k naseleniu Respubliki Krym', *Pravda Ukrainy*, 19 May 1992. A direct reference to the war in Moldova had been made, also, by the Ukrainian government committee on the nationalities, which claimed that the declaration of Crimean independence could have 'unpredictable consequences'. 'This is confirmed by the events in Dniester and Nagornyi Karabakh.' See 'Zaiavlenie komiteta po delam natsional'nostei', *Pravda Ukrainy*, 8 May 1992.

tactics only, is hard to gauge. However, there is every reason to believe that the Crimeans took it deadly seriously in view of the fact that the presidium of the Crimean parliament backed down one day before the Ukrainian ultimatum expired on 19 May, and recommended that the act of independence adopted two weeks earlier be rescinded. When the Crimean parliament convened the next day it adopted, after two days of heated debate, a resolution 'On the Political Situation in Crimea' which declared that Crimean state sovereignty (within Ukraine) had been achieved by dint of the adoption of the Crimean constitution. Therefore, the Act of Proclamation of State Sovereignty of the Republic of Crimea was annulled. A moratorium was put on the planned referendum on independence. Finally the Crimean legislators appealed to their opposite numbers in Kiev to reconsider the law on presidential representatives, and to suspend the law on the autonomous status of Crimea.[100]

A meeting held in Yalta on 1 June between the heads of the Crimean and Ukrainian legislatures went a long way towards settling the dispute. The text of the joint declaration specified that Crimea is an integral part of Ukraine, and has the right both to a special economic status of its own and to independent economic, social and cultural ties with other countries. The declaration has served as a starting point for the delineation of Crimean autonomy, a process which at the time of writing has not yet been completed.

Separatist organisations on the peninsula have not ceased their activities since the Yalta meeting. On the contrary, their numbers seem to have proliferated. The RDK has joined forces with 'the Movement of 20 January' within a 'Republican Movement for the Defence of the Constitution'.[101] At the same time, the 'Crimean Voters' Movement' and the 'Russian Society of Crimea', led by Anatolii Los', have stepped up their activities.[102] The Russian Society belongs to the radical right of the Russian political spectrum and cooperates with, among others, Aleksandr Sterligov and Vladimir Zhirinovskii in Moscow.[103] In the

---

100. *Krymskie Izvestiia*, 26 May 1992, p. 1.
101. *Respublika Krym*, no. 26, September 1992, p. 3.
102. Ol'ga Pronina, '"Osen" obeshchaet byt' zharkoi', *Pravda Ukrainy*, 16 September 1992, p. 1; *Krim'skii Visnik*, September 1992, p. 3; *Krymskaia Pravda*, 19 September 1992, p. 1.
103. *Nezavisimaia Gazeta*, 12 January 1993.

early part of 1993, a Crimean 'Interfront' was also crystallising; a 'Russian Party of Crimea' was founded in February 1993.[104]

In spite of their hectic activities and numerous statements, appeals and resolutions, the initiative seems to have been lost by most of these organisations.[105] Their strength is difficult to measure. Neither the RDK nor the Russian Society have fixed memberships.[106] Furthermore, some of the energy of the separatists was being squandered on squabbles among themselves. While some were fierce anti-Communists, others desired not only independence from Ukraine but also the restoration of the Soviet socialist system.[107]

As a separate Crimean state became increasingly utopian, parts of the anti- Ukrainian lobby jettisoned this objective and started to lobby for unification with Russia (which may in any case have been the ultimate objective all along). The renaming of the RDK as the 'Russian [*Rossiiskoe*] Movement of Crimea' is indicative of this reorientation. Another dispute among the Crimean separatists concerned the methods to be used: some militants advocated armed resistance to ukrainisation, while others, refering to the carnage in former Yugoslavia, warned against letting the spirit of Mars out of the bottle.[108] Finally, a perceptible switch to more ethnic slogans took place within certain sections of the various movements, while others still insisted that the conflict with Kiev was a legal and territorial one.[109]

There are fewer pro-Ukrainian movements in Crimea than separatist ones, and the former probably have smaller memberships. Their message is: Ukraine will not let go of the peninsula, and we may as well make the best of the situation as it is. The leading anti-separatist organisation is 'Democratic Crimea' ('*DemKrym*'), with its concomitant parliamentary faction 'For Peace and Harmony'. DemKrym stems from the same anti-*nomenklatura* opposition as RDK, but after the

104. *RFE/RL News Briefs*, 22–26 February 1993, p. 12; *Nezavisimaia Gazeta*, 25 February 1993.
105. See, e.g., *Krymskaia Pravda*, 19 September 1992, p. 1.
106. Author's interviews with Iurii Meshkov and Anatolii Los' in Simferopol, 21 September 1992.
107. *Nezavisimost'*, 5 February 1993.
108. *Ibid.*, 26 February 1993.
109. Aleksandr Pilat, 'Russkaia partiia Kryma – partiia russkikh?', *Nezavisimaia Gazeta*, 25 February 1993. An analyst in the separatist newspaper *Respublika Krym* claimed that deputies with Ukrainian surnames in the Crimean legislature had betrayed the interests of the peninsula. Vladimir Pavlov, 'Krymskaia tragediia', *Respublika Krym*, no. 26, September 1992.

proclamation of Ukrainian independence their ways parted. Today DemKrym sees itself as a centrist force, with the RDK as its main opponent on the one side and Rukh as the major adversary on the other.[110] The movement is opposed to any kind of national state in the Crimea – be it Russian, Ukrainian or Tatar – and rejects a Crimean referendum on independence as playing with fire.[111] It favours a federal structure for the Ukrainian state, which marks it off from the unreservedly pro-Ukrainian but marginal movement 'Crimea with Ukraine', which supports the official Ukrainian concept of a unitary state.

If the RDK claims that independence from Ukraine is necessary culturally and politically in order to escape from ukrainisation and fascism, the position of DemKrym ultimately has economic motivation. Iurii Komov, chairman of the movement, explains:

> Political independence is ephemeral, therefore what one should go for is economic independence . . . If there is peace in the Crimea, if there is civic stability and real guarantees for investments, then a stream of such investments will come, not only from the far abroad, but also from the 'near abroad'. What took place in Moldova, on the other hand, has set that state back a century.[112]

It should be noted that tourism is one of the Crimea's most important sources of income. If production of steel or grain can still continue more or less uninterrupted in times of war, tourism dries up instantly as Croatia bitterly experienced. Presumably, the structure of the Crimean economy would predispose its inhabitants to go for concessions and compromises.

Nevertheless, the separatists scored an important victory during the elections to the office of President of Crimea in January 1994. Designed to elevate the political status of the peninsula, the establishment of this office was denounced in Kiev as unconstitutional. It should be remembered that the creation of similar executive structures in several Union republics during *perestroika* was one of the steps leading up to the dissolution of the unitary state. In the Crimean presidential elections Iurii Meshkov garnered 72.9% of the votes, against 23.4% for Nikolai

110. 'Press-Release from the 2nd. Congress of 'DemKrym', 31 May 1992; mimeograph.
111. 'Deklaratsiia namerenii obshchestvenno-politicheskogo dvizheniia "Demokraticheskii Krym"', mimeograph; *Nezavisimaia Gazeta*, 23 June 1992.
112. Author's interview with Iurii Komov, 22 September 1992.

Bagrov, the candidate of the political establishment. Bagrov was running on a less anti-Ukrainian ticket than his rival, but Meshkov had also averred during the election campaign that he would not press for Crimea's separation from Ukraine. Possibly the election results should be seen as a victory of non-*nomenklatura* forces over the old *apparat* rather than being seen in the light of the independence issue. Nevertheless, the relationship between Simferopol and Kiev clearly entered a new and probably more inflammable phase after these elections.

So far, the Crimean drama has not followed the Dniestrian script. Among the reasons for this one could possibly point to differences between Moldova and Ukraine in economic conditions, the personalities of the political leaders involved, the different roles played by the 14th Army and the Black Sea Navy, differences in political culture, and differences in size and potential military strength. However, the peaceful containment of the Crimean conflict up to the time of writing seems to owe much to sheer good luck.

8

FRIGHT AND FLIGHT:
FORMER SOVIET ASIA

The Asian parts of the former Soviet Union are divided into two parts by the Caspian Sea: Caucasia to the west and Central Asia to the east. In any chronicle of the new Russian diaspora there should also be included another division which seems more suitable on both demographic and political grounds – though less so on religious or economic grounds. The southern tier of new states – Georgia, Armenia, Azerbaijan, Turkmenistan, Tajikistan and Uzbekistan constitute in many ways a natural unit, while the two north-eastern republics, Kazakhstan and Kyrgyzstan have several common traits which set them apart from their southern neighbours. They are therefore treated separately in the next chapter.

While all successor states of the Soviet Union are experiencing serious problems in the transition to democracy, these difficulties have proved even more intractable in the six Central Asian republics than elsewhere. Deep-rooted traditions of collectivism, paternalism and authoritarianism have survived the Soviet experience and are now reasserting themselves. Most political actors in these countries, as elsewhere in the former Soviet Union, pay homage to the ideals of pluralism and individual liberties, but with a few notable exceptions this seems to be little more than keeping up appearances. Independent observers agree that the dominant political forces vying for power in most of these countries can be placed in one of two categories: either a lightly dressed-up version of Communism or Islamism of a more or less fundamentalist and more or less nationalist brand. Both groups, when in power, tend to impose strict authoritarian rule. Neither of them has succeeded, despite various attempts, in crushing the other, and the resulting political stalemate has at times erupted into civil wars. Thus political life in the area has vacillated between the two extremes of political power: stark authoritarianism and the temporary dissolution of all authority.

This situation has not been conducive to freedom of the press. In those countries with authoritarian regimes, journalism has changed little since the days of Soviet power, and the periodic lapses in the state's authority have also brought no blessings. The journalists do not know which party will gain the upper hand, and are afraid that what they write today may bring down on them the wrath of the new power-holders tomorrow.[1] Under such circumstances, the safest way out is to write about official visits, the weather and forecasts for the harvest. Ethnic topics are among those most assiduously avoided. For these reasons, combined with the fact that the author has not yet had the chance to visit more than a few of the states, the material on which the following pages are based is less plentiful and perhaps also less reliable than that on which other chapters are based.

In former Soviet Asia, demographic Russian penetration has been weaker than in all other parts of the former Soviet Union. Nowhere does the share of Russians in the total population reach 10%. The Russian communities are also, to an extreme degree, clustered in the cities. The urbanites' share of the total Russian population is everywhere above 85% and in Turkmenistan as much as 97% (see Table 8.1). During and after *perestroika* the behaviour of these communities has been strongly influenced by these circumstances. Numerically weak and excluded from the traditional, often clan-based structures of political authority, they have had few chances to influence the course of events in their republics in the way that their co-nationals have done in other regions. Instead, the common Russian reaction has been either to lie low while the storm lasts or else simply to leave.

Armenia

In some ways, Armenia does not fit well into the scheme of categorisation laid out in this chapter. Belonging as they do to an ancient Christian civilisation, many Armenians prefer to see themselves as Europeans rather than Asians – and indeed as an outpost of Christian civilisation surrounded by hostile Muslim neighbours. Moreover, the development of political life in the republic has also deviated from the typical Asian pattern. Although political authority there has been shaky, with several paramilitary units roaming the land, most political leaders have still attempted to follow the rules of democratic governance.

But in other ways Armenia fits perfectly into the present scheme: no other former Soviet republic has so low a percentage of Russians (or

1. *Rossiia*, 4–10 November 1992; 'The Media in the Countries of the Former Soviet Union', *RFE/RL Research Report*, II, 27 (2 July 1993), pp. 1–16.

Table 8.1. RUSSIANS IN FORMER SOVIET ASIA, 1989

Republic	Russian population (× 1,000)	Russian population (%)	Russian population living in the capital (× 1,000)	% of all Russians living in the capital	% of all Russians living in urban settlements
Georgia	341	6.3	10.0	36	86
Armenia	52	1.6	1.9	44	85
Azerbaijan	392	5.6	16.0	75	95
Turkmenistan	334	9.5	32	39	97
Tajikistan	388	7.6	32.0	50	94
Uzbekistan	1,653	8.3	34.0	42	95

Sources: *Natsional'nyi sostav naseleniia SSSR*, Moscow, 1991; Iu. V. Arutiunian (ed.), *Russkie: Etnosotsiologicheskie Ocherki*, Moscow, 1992, p. 25.

of other ethnic minorities for that matter, in its population. Also, the most important factor influencing the situation of the Russians, as indeed of all other citizens in the republic, has been the protracted and bloody war with Azerbaijan. As with other wars in the Asian republics, the non-indigenous population has not been directly involved. Yet caught in the middle, they have had more than their share of fear and anxiety.

When the Azeris fled from Armenia during the great ethnic de-mixing process of 1989, several thousand Russians followed in their wake. Like the Azeris, many of them ended up in Baku and other Azerbaijani cities. Representatives of the Russian refugee communities in Azerbaijan have issued some statements explaining that Russians have been persecuted in Armenia since the late 1970s. 'Under the pretext of developing national cadres, Russian schoolmasters, engineers and factory foremen were dismissed. They were also squeezed out of the executive committees of the county councils and out of those councils altogether.' It in alleged that when open hostilities between Armenians and Azeris broke out, all those who in any capacity had been friends or acquaintances of Azeris were targeted as the next victims;[2] these people included Russians.

Other sources deny that Russians have in any way been molested or disadvantaged in Armenia. It is pointed out that there is no historic

2. Statement by Valerii Abakumtsev, spokesman for the community of Russian refugees from Armenia in Azerbaijan, in *Federatsiia*, no. 5, February 1993.

animosity between the Russians and the Armenians but that on the contrary Armenians have often looked to Moscow for succour. Russian culture has made a considerable impression on this distant republic, despite the paucity of ethnic Russians living there. More than 40% of the ethnic Armenians living in Armenia in 1989 claimed fluency in Russian, a higher percentage than would be found in most former Soviet republics in Asia. During the 1990s the number of Russian-language newspapers and radio stations in Armenia has increased rather than diminished.[3]

As pointed out in Chapter 2, the first Russians to arrive beyond the Caucasian mountains were religious dissidents. Some of the communities of Russian Dukhobors and Molokans survived more or less unchanged up till the end of the 1980s. Several of them were located along the Armenian–Azerbaijani border, on both sides, and thus came under crossfire in a frighteningly literal sense. As late as in August 1992 a leader of one of the larger communities denied that they were thinking of flight,[4] but only six months later this was the only option left to them. From the Krasnosel'skii raion almost the entire community of 3,000 Molokans has left. While they had been relatively well off in their isolated villages because of their thrift and strong work ethic, they left their homesteads as beggars. They could not bring their herds and farmland with them, and the locals were not interested in buying huts with the typical huge Russian stove – particularly not in a combat zone.[5]

In Russia the religious dissenters have experienced great difficulties in holding together and continuing their traditional lifestyle. Some *kolkhozes* have been willing to accept up to about a dozen families, but it does not seem as if there is anywhere that thousands of them can be accommodated in one place. Thus it is feared that their unique culture may perish completely.

Some observers believe that the Molokan villages in Transcaucasia were broken up only because of the war. In March 1993 the journalist Aleksandr Iskandarian pointed out that the Russian communities in the Kalininskii raion in northern Armenia were still mostly in place.[6]

3. *Izvestiia*, 20 July 1992.
4. Fëdor Astakhov, to *Rossiiskaia Gazeta*, 13 August 1992, p. 7.
5. Aleksandr Iskandarian, 'Chuzhaia voina. Udastsia li spasti unikal'nuiu russkuiu obshchinu na Kavkaze?', *Rossiiskie Vesti*, 18 March 1993; see also *Rossiiskie Vesti*, 6 January 1993.
6. Iskandarian, *op. cit.*

There had been no military activities there. However, Russian ethnographers who have made a special study of these communities over a period of years believe that they would have been slowly coming to an end even without the violence. O. D. Komarova is convinced that the warfare has been 'not so much the cause as the catalyst of the mass emigration of the Russian population, which has been going on independently of them. The [military] events only speeded up the process so that it reached the crisis threshold earlier than would otherwise have been the case.' Komarova does not deny that the horrors of war – in combination with ethnic harassment, particularly on the Azerbaijani side of the border – have played their part. All the same, she concludes that the material and cultural advantages of city life are the most important factors prompting the Russian population in Transcaucasia to leave the countryside.[7] This view provides a useful reminder that the modernist perspective should not be entirely forgotten, even when political, military and cultural circumstances seem to provide an exhaustive explanation of migratory patterns.

Azerbaijan

A poll conducted in several Soviet republics in the autumn of 1990 showed that 86% of Russians in Azerbaijan were happy living in the republic, while as few as 6% stated the opposite.[8] This was the highest degree of satisfaction recorded in any of the polled republics, and it puzzled many observers since the violence committed during the Baku insurgency of January 1990 had apparently been directed not only against Armenians but against foreigners in general.[9] One explanation for the attitude of the Russians in Azerbaijan may be that, because of these very same January events, many Russians had already left the republic when the poll was taken. Those who stayed behind probably had very specific reasons for doing so.[10]

The '*Sodruzhestvo*' ('Commonwealth' or 'Friendship') society, an organisation for solidarity among the peoples of Azerbaijan with a

---

7. O. D. Komarova, 'Sovremennye migratsii naselenia iz russkikh sël Zakavkaz'ia' in V. I. Kozlov and A. P. Pavlenko (eds) *Dukhobortsy i Molokane v Zakavkaz'e*, Moscow, 1992, pp. 105–43, on pp. 107 and 119.

8. *Moscow News*, no. 5, 3–10 February 1991.

9. Elizabeth Fuller, 'Gorbachev's Dilemma in Azerbaijan', *Report on the USSR*, II (2 February 1990), pp. 14–16.

10. This interpretation has been suggested to me by Professor Hallstein Myklebost, University of Oslo.

mostly Russian membership, has adopted several resolutions condemning the Armenians' pretensions to Azerbaijani soil. Its members have declared their preparedness to work for the prosperity, independence and territorial integrity of the Azerbaijani state.[11] They deplore the involvement of Russia in Transcaucasian affairs which they believe has had an anti-Azerbaijani bent. At the same time, however, they give assurances that they are safe and well, support the regime and have few serious complaints.[12]

This message was not fundamentally altered when the Mutalibov regime was toppled and the Popular Front government of Abulfaz Elchibei took over in the spring of 1992. Russian organisations in Azerbaijan acknowledged that the Russians were leaving the republic, but they continued to maintain that this was the result of general anxiety due to the proximity of war, and not of ethnic harassment. It was emphasised that the Popular Front had several times addressed the Russian community on television, pleading with its members to stay. Sodruzhestvo had also been given air time whenever they asked for it; and regular Russian-language television programmes, while not very great in number, were still transmitted daily.

It was admitted that ethnic tensions could be found at the popular level, and they often arose in connection with housing problems. In Baku, a city with 200,000 refugees, there is a desperate lack of apartments, and empty or temporarily vacant flats were not infrequently taken over in desperation by forlorn squatters. However, Sodruzhestvo spokesmen claimed that an appeal to the Popular Front leadership was usually enough to have the occupants evicted and property returned to the rightful owners.

However, it seems that the leaders of the Russian community of Azerbaijan have gradually moved away from their unqualified support for the state authorities. In the summer of 1992 some cautious criticisms could be registered. The main complaint concerned the transition to Azeri in administration and public life. While the ultimate objectives of the Azerbaijani language policy were not questioned, the Russians were calling for a longer transition period, and for better facilities for language training.[13] In 1993 these pleas acquired a new

11. Zaur Kadymbekov, 'Khotiat li russkie voiny?', *Pravda*, 17 February 1992; 'Ikh rodina – Azerbaijan', *Bakinskii Rabochii*, 24 April 1993.
12. 'Ne zabyvaite o russkikh', *Sovetskaia Rossiia*, 29 September 1991.
13. *Rossiiskaia Gazeta*, 29 July 1992.

tone of urgency: it was now maintained that the language transition was proceeding 'with the speed of cavalry'. 'In certain places the language is being turned into an instrument of pressure ... For the Russian-language population of Azerbaijan the language problem threatens to grow into a question of to stay or not stay.'[14] However, the Russians blamed the excesses of the language policy on overzealous local bureaucrats, and not the central authorities in Baku.

In the summer of 1993 the Elchibei government was toppled, and a third post-*perestroika* regime in Azerbaijan took over. It is too early to say how the relationship of the Azerbaijani Russians to the new state authorities will develop; but it seems that the very speed of regime changes in the republic is for many Russians a considerable source of unease. It undermines respect for authorities, increases the general lawlessness and makes it possible for members of the titular ethnic group to discriminate against them more brazenly. Combined with the strains created by the continuing war with Armenia, this factor seems to be strong enough to sustain a considerable flow of Russian emigrants out of the republic.

Georgia

During the 1990s Georgia, no less than Armenia and Azerbaijan, has been ravaged by ethnic warfare, mainly in the Autonomous Oblast of South Ossetia and the Autonomous Republic of Abkhazia. Here too the Russians are being caught in the midst of conflicts in which they are not themselves involved. Their plight has been aggravated by the deteriorating relationship between Russia and Georgia. This exacerbation is somewhat surprising on two accounts: both the Russians and the Georgians are not only Christians but also belong to the same Orthodox confession; and the incumbent presidents of both countries, Boris Yeltsin and Eduard Shevardnadze, were close comrades-in-arms as late as August 1991 during the coup attempt. Nonetheless, Russian army units stationed on Georgian soil have regularly been suspected of active involvement in the Georgian civil wars on the side of the insurgents. At least one Western observer believes that Russia directly encouraged secessionist sentiments in both Abkhazia and South Ossetia with the clear-cut aim of taking over

14. Ali Naibov, 'Ne znaesh' iazyka – sobirai chemodany', *Rabochaia Tribuna*, 16 January 1993.

control of these areas and incorporating them into the Russian Republic.[15] Other experts are more inclined to give credence to Russian assurances that the Russian units in the region desperately try to keep out of the conflicts while still, of course, defending themselves when attacked.[16]

In South Ossetia, Russians make up a negligible part of the population – only 2% – while the Ossetians are by far the largest group with 66%.[17] In Abkhazia the ethnic make-up is different. Here the titular nationality is no more than 17.8% of the population, while the Georgians are largest group with 45.7%. The Russians number about 75,000, or 14.3%. This is above their republican average in Georgia, but puts them in only fourth place among the ethnic groups in Abkhazia, behind the Armenians.

As in most non-Russian areas, the Russians of Abkhazia are concentrated in urban areas. In some of the towns which Georgian troops besieged, such as Tkvarcheli, the Russian presence is significant, and the Russian-diaspora issue was prominent in Russian media reporting of this war, as well as in the Russian government's own handling of the issue.[18] Huge amounts of money were allocated for large-scale rescue operations in which Russian helicopters flew in foodstuffs and medicine and returned home with refugees. The Moscow newspaper *Megapolis-Express* speculated that by this operation the Russian government wanted both to strengthen its reputation at home and to show the national-patriotic opposition that it cared about Russians in 'the near abroad'.[19] If this was the objective, the operation apparently paid off.[20]

Spokesmen for the Russian community in Abkhazia have suggested that Russia could grant a kind of 'most favoured status' to Russian business in the area, with concessions such as special customs tariffs

15. John B. Dunlop, 'Will a Large-Scale Migration of Russians to the Russian Republic Take Place over the Current Decade?', *Working Papers in International Studies I-93-1*, Hoover Institution, January 1993, pp. 4ff.

16. Catherine Dale, 'Turmoil in Abkhazia: Russian Responses', *RFE/RL Research Report*, II, 34 (27 August 1993), pp. 48–57.

17. This ethnic homeland only, therefore, constitutes a diaspora problem for Russia in the sense that the lion's share of the Ossetian nation lives in the Russian Federation, in the North Ossetian Autonomous Republic.

18. *Moskovskii Komsomolets*, 10 October 1992.

19. *Megapolis-Express*, 17 February 1993.

20. See, for instance, the positive comments in *Federatsiia*, no. 10. February 1993.

on imports and exports. 'That would secure the economic position of the Russians here.'[21] If the Russian government were to heed such advice, it would introduce a novel principle into international trade, and possibly do a disservice to the local Russians. By singling out the Russians in other states on the basis of ethnicity and introducing a system of positive discrimination for their benefit, they would find it more difficult to protest if the authorities in the same states then started exposing them to negative discrimination on the same basis.

Russians both in Tbilisi and in other parts of Georgia which are controlled by the Georgian government tend to sympathise with the Georgian cause in the Abkhazian conflict, at least they pretend to do so. In September 1993, a public statement from 'the Russian Cultural-Educational Society' in Tbilisi laid the blame for the bloodshed squarely at the door of both the Abkhazians and those 'destructive forces in Russia who always have encouraged and supported them'.[22] At the same time, the Cultural-Educational Society appealed to constructive Russian forces for help. On 22 September it organised a mass meeting outside the Russian embassy in Tbilisi, with slogans such as 'We are for Yeltsin' and 'Russia! Defend us Russians against Russian aggression.'[23]

From available information, it is hard to gauge how far the Cultural-Educational Society is representative of the Georgian Russian population as a whole. While the conservative press in Russia insisted that Georgia was fighting an undeclared war against Russia,[24] 94% of the Russian respondents interviewed in an opinion poll in Tbilisi in May 1993 expressed the belief that Georgia was genuinely interested in good relations with Russia.[25] Such a high degree of trust in the state authorities in the country of residence may express a fear of offending

21. Iurii Gladkevich, 'Russkie v Abkhazii', *Krasnaia Zvezda*, 16 October 1992. Interview with Viktor Loginov, leader of the Russian Cultural Centre in Abkhazia, 'Slavonic House'.
22. 'Zaiavlenie russkogo kul'turno-prosvetitel'skogo obshchestva Gruzii', *Svobodnaia Gruziia*, 21 September 1993.
23. *Svobodnaia Gruziia*, 23 September 1993.
24. *Russkii Vestnik*, no. 14, April 1993, p. 4; *Literaturnaia Rossiia*, 11 June 1993, p. 2.
25. *Svodbodnala Gruziia*, 1 June 1993, pp. 1–2; *Izvestiia*, 27 May 1993. In contrast, only 84% of the Russian respondents believed that Russia was benignly disposed towards Georgia. The poll was organised by the Institute of Demography and Opinion Polls under the Georgian Academy of Sciences. Appr. 270 Russians were interviewed. The pollsters were Russian speakers.

the majority population in an extremely tense situation, or else a genuine identification with the Georgian side.[26] There is some evidence that a significant segment of the Russian community is culturally well integrated into Georgian society. The Russian-language Georgian writer Vladimir Osinskii insists that he and his co-nationals in the republic are 'internationalists', at the same time as Georgia is their fatherland.[27] Another source has claimed that 'a Russian in Georgia is not quite a Russian, not even a Russian at all':

> Having lived together for a long time, people tend to resemble each other. Like old married couples. Not only their temper, but even their appearance acquires the same traits. A Russian in Tbilisi will fight in the restaurants no less than the Georgians. He will kick up a row, and propose the same toasts as they do.[28]

In the same opinion poll, approximately two-thirds of the Russian respondents claimed that they had not been exposed to any ethnic discrimination in Georgia (which of course also meant that quite a number nevertheless felt that they had been). 59% predicted that the majority of Russians in Georgia would remain in the republic, while 28% expected that they would leave.

Tajikistan

The 388,000-strong Russian community in Tajikistan has been exposed to the same horrors of war as their co-nationals in Transcaucasia, only several times worse. In causalities and atrocities, even the Armenian–Azerbaijan tragedy pales before the Tajik civil war in the latter half of 1992. While estimates are wildly divergent, knowledgeable observers believe that between 30,000 and 50,000 people died. Few of them, it seems, were Russians, but many Russians had their houses and other property completely ruined, as well as their faith in the future. Nothing has influenced the situation of Russians in Tajikistan as much as this war and the ethnic upheavals which preceded it.

The character of the conflict is extremely complex. First and foremost, it was an internecine war between various Tajik clans and

---

26. Apart from being either wishful thinking or a correct assessment of Georgian policies.
27. *Svobodnaia Gruziia*, 21 April 1993, p. 2.
28. Nukzar Mikaladze, in *Novaia Gazeta* (Tbilisi), 1 April 1993.

regions, with the Kurgan-Tiube oblast and the Gorno-Badakhshan Autonomous oblast pitted against Kuliab and Khojent (Leninabad). In Soviet times the latter region had been favoured by the Union leadership in Moscow, and provided most of the republican *nomenklatura* members. To some extent the hostilities also followed ethnic lines. In Khojent, Uzbeks make up the considerable minority of 30.9%. In addition, many Tajiks further south suspect that some people up north are 'crypto-Uzbeks'. Traditionally, many people in the border areas have indeed been bilingual, and have had a dual Uzbek–Tajik identity.

The Tajik war could also be seen as an ideological confrontation between Soviet-type Communism and Muslim fundamentalism. It seems that Islam has been turned into a political factor in Tajikistan more rapidly and thoroughly than anywhere else in the former Soviet Union, partly because of its proximity to Afghanistan.[29] The Mujaheddin have actively supplied Tajik Islamists with weapons and ammunition across the very permeable border. In a rather incongruous alliance the Islamists have joined forces with the democrats in the Tajik opposition. For a while, these groups were strong enough to challenge the Communist regime in Dushanbe but in the end the anti-opposition forces (as they call themselves) regained power. While in the autumn of 1993 isolated pockets of resistance could still be met in remote areas, law and order had been reintroduced in most of the country. Despite promises to introduce political pluralism, the post-war regime turned out to be one of the most authoritarian in the former Soviet Union, a fact which obviously has to be seen against the background of the recent war. The opposition have been severely repressed.[30]

In a final perspective, the Tajik war may also be interpreted as an urban–rural or modernist–traditionalist controversy. Kurgan-Tiube and Gorno-Badakhshan are poor agricultural regions, while the northern oblast of Khojent is more industrially developed – although even here the economy is considerably less modern than the average elsewhere among the Soviet successor states.[31] The concentration of Russians and other Slavs in the urban areas of the Khojent oblast has

29. The Tajiks are linguistically and culturally related to the Iranians. However, with the exception of the Pamir peoples of Gorno-Badakhshan, who traditionally belong to the Ismaili rite, they are Sunni rather than Shia, and it appears that 'the Islamic revolution' is being imported more from Afghanistan than from Iran.

30. Bess Brown, 'Tajik Opposition to be Banned', *RFE/RL Research Report*, II, 14 (2 April 1992).

31. Arkadii Dubnov, in *Novoe Vremia*, no. 43, 1992, pp. 8–11.

also been relatively high. Certain towns, like the formerly semi-closed uranium-processing company town of Chkalovskii, outside Khojent city, have been almost entirely European in character. If the Russians in most Asian Soviet successor states seem to feel most secure in the capital, this is not necessarily so in Tajikistan. Here Khojent is seen by many as the safest place in Tajikistan, if such a place can be said to exist there at all.

It should come as no surprise that insofar as the Russians and other Russian-speakers in Tajikistan have sided with any of the warring parties, their sympathies have been with the anti-opposition forces. This is partly due to their ideological preferences. Igor Rotar, in the pages of *Nezavisimaia Gazeta*, has claimed: 'In general, the russophone population of Central Asia have more conservative views than the inhabitants of the Russian Federation.'[32] Interviews with Russians and other russophones in Tajikistan during May 1993 left this author with much the same impression, although in many cases such pro-Communist proclivities must be seen as a legacy of the civil war. In face of the willingness of Tajik democrats to join forces with militant Islamists, a large part of the European population in the republic reacted viscerally by becoming alienated from the ideals of democracy. In any case, the nostalgic longing for the Soviet past seems to reflect shock at the rapid and incomprehensible social changes more than any deep political convictions. They bemoan the disappearance of the unitary state more than the loss of the political ideology in which it was shrouded.

However, the Russians in Tajikistan are not sure whether there is a future for them in the republic even after the victory of the anti-opposition, and they fear that the present state of tranquillity may be deceptive. The Islamists have not conceded defeat, and large-scale hostilities may be renewed. The question for the Russians that eclipses all other concerns, is: do we stay or do we go?

By April 1993 about 300,000 or 77% had chosen to go, if we can believe the figures released by the Russian Federal Migration Service.[33] Even if these numbers are exaggerated, Tajikistan holds the uncontested post-Soviet record for emigration. Not only Europeans but also Uzbeks, and even large groups of Tajiks, have been fleeing.[34]

32. *Nezavisimaia Gazeta*, 2 June 1993.
33. Igor Rotar, 'Slaviane v Srednei Azii', *Nezavisimaia Gazeta*, 29 April 1993.
34. *Far Eastern Economic Review*, 12 November 1992.

The migration has become self-propelling: the more people who leave, the more the feeling of vulnerability spreads among those who have remained behind. This is a doubly tragic state of affairs, since most Russians do not want to go and most locals do not want them to leave. The effects of the Russian exodus are being acutely felt in a number of professions. Several branches of industry, such as the important power stations and aluminium-smelting works, are gradually being brought to a halt by the flight of key personnel. The authorities have appealed over and over to the Russian population, and held several meetings with its representatives imploring them to remain. Even the Islamist-cum-democratic alliance has made strenuous efforts to stem the flight of Russians, and forbidden anti-Russian speeches at their meetings.[35] However, such appeals are often not heeded as their constant reiteration seems to make clear. The agitated mob often sees the Europeans as aliens; indeed the term '*inorodtsy*' ('allogenes') used by tsarist officialdom to designate primitive Central Asian tribes is today, by an ironic twist of history, used of the Europeans in several Central Asian countries.[36] Many Tajiks have a warped feeling that somehow the Europeans may be a major source of their many tribulations. In a perverse sense, they are right, except that the trouble is not those Russians who stay behind but rather those who have left. Because these people are out of reach, frustrated Tajiks instead vent their fury on those who are at hand, and thus manage in spite of themselves to push out yet more people.

Russians claim to have been told in the streets: 'Russians, don't leave. You are needed here as slaves.'[37] Of course, no Tajik in his right mind would say such a thing unless he wanted to achieve exactly the opposite. Whether this has been said in so many words or not is not really the issue. The important thing is that Russians tend to interpret the gestures, stares and actions that they are being met with as expressions of such attitudes, and act accordingly. In a tragic, spiralling way, the desperation of the locals and the fright of the Russians serve to reinforce each other.

In any case, the mass exodus of the Russians antedates the civil war

35. 'Weekly Review', *RFE/RL Research Report*, I, 8 (February 1992), p. 74; *ibid.*, I, 23 (May 1992), p. 76; *ibid.*, I, 31 (July 1992), p. 78; *ibid.*, II, 17 (April 1993), p. 9.
36. See, e.g., Irina Orlova, 'Beg "inorodtsa"', *Rabochaia Tribuna*, 16 January 1993; *Den'*, no. 20, 17–23 May 1992.
37. Author's interview with Russian refugees in Moscow, October 1991.

by at least three years. The first wave of some 10,000 followed the proclamation of the Tajik language law in July 1989 which made Tajik (Farsi) the sole state language. From 1 January 1990 doctors were required to write case histories in Tajik rather than in Russian.[38] Of course, very few Europeans were able to comply with this requirement in such a short time. The demographic effects of this law have been so disastrous that in 1993 a revision which would give Russian equal status with Tajik was being contemplated.[39]

A new wave of Russian emigration also occurred after the violent turmoils in Dushanbe in February 1990. For several days there was almost complete anarchy in the city, with more than fifty people being killed. Tajik violence was not directed primarily against the Russians but rather at smaller underdog groups without deep historical roots in the area – in particular, Armenians. Many Russians, however, feared that the pogroms would lead to a general demand for the expulsion of all 'aliens'. In several places self-defence units were set up to guard European homes.

As a direct result of the events of February, the organisation 'Migratsiia' (Migration) was started. Led by the energetic people's deputy Galina Belgorodskaia, it soon became one of the most enterprising and influential Russian organisations in Central Asia.[40] Migratsiia does not actively campaign for the migration of Russians; rather, it tries to give practical help and advice to those who have already decided that they cannot or will not stay.

The problems facing the Russian emigrants are formidable. For a start, the cost of renting a removal lorry has become exorbitant; in the autumn of 1992, at a time when the average monthly salary in Tajikistan was 2,000 rubles, this cost had risen to 15,000–30,000 rubles. At the same time, the value of real estate in Dushanbe was plummeting. Houses were being sold for 25,000–30,000 rubles ('with bullets whining overhead no one will pay more').[41]

Some Russian organisations have encouraged the Europeans to stay. During the civil war representatives of the Orthodox church appeared

---

38. John Payne, 'Tadzhiks', in Graham Smith (ed.) *The Nationalities Question in the Soviet Union*, London, 1990/92, p. 320.
39. *RFE/RL Research Report*, II, 17 (April 1993).
40. *Rossiia*, 4–10 November 1992; Lidiia Grafova, 'Iskhod', *Literaturnaia Gazeta*, 18 December 1991.
41. *Pravda*, 21 October 1992. See also *Izvestiia*, 16 September 1992; *Rossiiskie Vesti*, 22 September 1992.

on Tajikistani television urging the Slavs not to panic.[42] Roman Utochkin, assistant to the parish priest of Khojent, explains: 'In Russia nobody wants us. I have been to the Russian countryside. The refrain is: "If you were born in Tajikistan, then stay there." They consider us not as Russians but as Tajikistanis.' Reports in the Western media tell of some Tajikistani Russians who had moved to Russia finding life even less bearable there and returning 'home' as a result.[43]

Tough folk who refuse to be uprooted have started the society 'Russian Community' ('*Russkaia obshchina*'). Leaders of this society have told Russian journalists that they will not leave unless the lives of their families are directly threatened. They deny that the Tajiks are particularly hard to live with but say that, on the contrary, they are easygoing and amiable people. All the same, these Russian activists believe that drastic measures will be necessary to induce the Russians to stay. Tajikistani authorities must introduce special privileges (*l'goty*) for them, including dual citizenship. In addition, Russia will have to show an active interest in the Central Asian Russians, and in particular provide them with both financial support and the capability to defend themselves by military means.[44]

During a meeting with representatives of the Russian population in Dushanbe in November 1992, the Russian foreign minister Andrei Kozyrev promised that Russia would not abandon them to their fate.[45] Russian authorities have assisted in the evacuation of thousands of refugees (of various ethnic extractions).[46] Under an agreement with the Tajikistani government, the Russian army is responsible for the defence of the border with Afghanistan. Tajik Islamists have established new strongholds on the Afghan side of the border, and on several occasions have attacked Russian border garrisons, resulting in numerous Russian soldiers being killed. The fear is spreading that Tajikistan might become for Russia another Afghan quagmire, only closer to home.

42 Author's interview with Father Zakharii and his assistant, Roman Utochkin, in Khojent, 15 May 1993.
43 'Russians Come Home to Tajikistan', *Financial Times*, 23 May 1991.
44 '"Ia nekuda ne poedu"', *Argumenty i Fakty*, no. 42, October 1992; 'Russkie ne pali dukhom', *Rossiiskaia Gazeta*, 24 December 1992.
45 *Krasnaia Zvezda*, 12 November 1992; *Vecherniaia Moskva*, no. 217, 1992.
46 *Rossiiskaia Gazeta*, 18 December 1992.

Turkmenistan

The upheavals in Tajikistan are the single most important event influencing the attitudes and actions of Russians not just in Tajikistan but also in the entire Central Asian region. Fearing a spill-over effect from the south, the Europeans in neighbouring Uzbekistan and Turkmenistan have reacted in very much the same way as their co-nationals in Tajikistan: some flee, while those who stay behind give their wholehearted support to the conservative (neo-Communist, law-and-order) regimes.

Political leaders in Turkmenistan and Uzbekistan are skillfully exploiting the 'Tajikistan syndrome'. In order both to clamp down on opposition and to strengthen their grip on society, the presidents of both states are not letting their citizens forget what has taken place south of the border. If the Russian-diaspora question in the European parts of the former Soviet Union is heavily influenced by the bloodshed in Dniester, the need in the new Asian states to avoid a repetition of the Tajik disaster is now perceived as the paramount imperative.

Whether one sees yet more carnage in Central Asia as likely or as a cynically inflated bugbear depends on one's evaluation of the character and strength of Islam in the region. Many observers have claimed that in the Soviet Union Islam was no doubt a viable and important cultural factor, but one with no potential as a political force. Some even claim that deep down the Central Asians were just as secularised as other Soviet citizens. Islam had heavily influenced the moral code and lifestyle of the Central Asians, but few people attached any specifically religious significance to the rites of passage and other rituals. However, even if is this assessment is correct for the situation under Communism, it has clearly become less so after the collapse of the Soviet Union. A revival of religion is taking place, not only in Central Asia but all over the former Soviet Union, among people of all traditions. People are flocking to places of worship in increasing numbers, curious about the forbidden fruit, seeking to fill the void left by the vanished secular ideology – or simply to escape for a while from the harsh realities of everyday life.[47]

However, even if it is revitalised, Central Asian Islam does not have to become militant. Some observers have even seen it as a potentially

---

47. For a more thorough discussion of these issues, see, e.g., Yaacov Ro'i, 'The Islamic Influence on Nationalism in Soviet Central Asia', *Problems of Communism*, XXXIX (July–August 1990), pp. 49–64. See also 'Islamskii faktor', *Rossiia*, no. 11, March 1992, p. 5.

harmonising, moderating factor. By propagating the universal Islamic brotherhood of Ummah, it could cool some of the nationalist hotheads who are at the throats of their fellow Muslims. In fact, some experts reason that Islam of a fundamentalist brand does not even have to be a greater calamity than modernist Islam. For example, the Wahhabi variant of Sunni in Saudi Arabia, even if deeply fundamentalist, can in no sense be called revolutionary or violent. Since the Central Asians are Sunni rather than Shia, Wahhibism – along with Sufism – seems to be one of the strongest revivalist currents in the area. The Saudis are actively recruiting new converts in Central Asia, and no other country has invested so much in building mosques and disseminating Muslim literature in the area. However, the Russians would hardly feel more at ease in a state run by the Saudi interpretation of the *shari'a* than they would in a country where the Iranian interpretation rules supreme.[48]

So far, the 'green peril' of Islam has been held at bay in Turkmenistan. The staid regime of President Saparmurad Niazov is thoroughly secular. Even if he does have to throw an occasional sop to the believers and the nationalists, he is still fully in charge. On 27 October 1991 Niazov arranged a referendum on national independence for the republic. As in Soviet times, the voters of Turkmenistan voted pliantly as they were told to do. With a 97.4% turn-out and as many as 94.5% voting 'Yes', it has been suggested that a large number of the Slavs in the republic, possibly even the majority, also supported independence.[49] However, the figures by themselves do not compel us to draw this conclusion. In any case, given the strongly authoritarian character of Turkmenistan politics, the results may well have been manipulated.

Be that as it may, it seems that many local Russians identify with the republic – for a number of reasons. First, a large number arrived in the 1930s and are now second- or third-generation Turkmenistanis. They are mainly employed as engineers and managers in the oil and gas production and other extraction industries. According to some reports, they have adapted well to the heat and semi-desert environment. In 1991 a journalist claimed in *Komsomol'skaia Pravda* that 'Born and raised beyond the Karakum desert, they may be considered

48. See James Critchlow, 'Islam in Fergana Valley: the Wahhabi "Threat"', *Report of the USSR*, I (8 December 1989), pp. 13–7.
49. *Nezavisimaia Gazeta*, 29 October 1991.

Russians only with significant qualifications ... On more than one occasion I have listened to surprised Turkmenistani Russians telling stories about how they felt completely out of place when they visited somewhere outside Briansk or Smolensk for the first time.'[50]

Secondly, the prospect of economic recovery seems greater in independent Turkmenistan than in the destitute neighbouring states. This comes as something of a surprise, since many indicators given in Soviet statistics showed Turkmenistan to have the lowest living standard of all the republics.[51] However, the commercial exploitation of the rich gas reserves seems to be changing that situation rapidly.

The third main factor influencing the attitudes of the Russians is the absence of any major ethnic clashes. It is true that turmoil involving ethnic slogans did take place in the capital Ashgabat (Ashkhabad) in May 1989, but that was child's play compared to the violence in other Asian republics. The Niazov regime is one of the most unreformed in the former Soviet Union and has been compared to the dictatorship of Joseph Stalin.[52] One of the very few blessings of a police state is that potential riots and pogroms are nipped in the bud. For example, it is prohibited for Turkmenistani public bodies to be organised on national or religious principles.[53]

Niazov fully understands that the good performance of Turkmenistani industry depends on his ability to persuade the Russians to stay. In 1989 he promoted a plan for bilingualism which would largely remove the need for the Russians to become fluent in Turkmen. He later backed away from this particular plan, but in September 1992 he did push through a law on Turkmenistani citizenship allowing for dual citizenship. This became one of the most liberal citizenship laws of any in force in Soviet successor states,[54] and it is claimed that it

50. A. Bushev, 'Za gran'iu druzheskikh peskov', *Komsomol'skaia Pravda*, 1 October 1991.
51. See, e.g., Boris Z. Rumer, *Central Asia, 'A tragic Experiment'*, Boston, 1989; Anette Bohr, 'Turkmenistan under Perestroika: an Overview', *Report on the USSR*, II (23 March 1990), pp. 20–9.
52. Christopher J. Panico, 'Turkmenistan Unaffected by Winds of Democratic Change', *RFE/RL Research Report*, II, 4 (22 January 1993); Bess Brown, 'Central Asia: the First year of Unexpected Statehood', *RFE/RL Research Report*, II, 1 (1 January 1993).
53. *Trud*, 14 July 1993, p. 2.
54. Kronid Liubarskii, 'Grazhdane i "sootechestvenniki"', *Novoe Vremia*, no. 5, 1993, p. 41. A bilateral agreement with Russia on dual citizenship was signed in December 1993.

'overwhelmingly favours the Russians'.[55]

In July 1992, the Russian ambassador to Turkmenistan was quoted as saying that the Russian minority were in a much better position there than in other former Soviet republics.[56] Nonetheless, Russians are leaving Turkmenistan, albeit at a moderate pace. 4% of them packed their suitcases in 1992. Igor' Rotar' explains: 'The relative stability in the republic allows the Slavs to postpone the moment of departure, in search of the optimal solution. [However], even in this prosperous republic the Slavs are feeling like aliens.'[57]

Uzbekistan

With almost 20 million inhabitants Uzbekistan is by far the most populous of the six countries surveyed in this chapter. In 1989 the Russian community numbered more than 1.5 million. Certain new industrial cities, such as Navai and Zarafshan, have a predominantly European population.

The Russian community in Uzbekistan has several chronological segments. The oldest consists of descendants of pre-revolutionary, largely peasant settlers and the second mostly of blue-collar workers who arrived during the two first five-year plans. Thirdly, the evacuation of large plants and research institutions from the fighting zones during the Second World War brought a sizeable scientific and technical intelligentsia to the republic, and while some, including Andrei Sakharov, returned to Russia after the war, quite a number remained. Finally, the last great wave of Russians to Uzbekistan arrived after the earthquake in Tashkent in 1966 to participate in the huge reconstruction programme for the city.[58]

Some Moscow-based observers take a rather dim view of the Central Asian Russian community, which is occasionally described as 'lumpenised'.[59] On the other hand, the Uzbekistani Russians, like their

55. Panico, *op. cit.*
56. 'Weekly review', *RFE/RL Research Report*, I, 32 (14 August 1992), p. 72.
57. Igor' Rotar', *op. cit.*
58. Author's conversation with Salman Fatykhov, deputy editor-in-chief of *Pravda Vostoka*, at Tashkent, 12 May 1993.
59. Timur Pulatov, 'Mass Exodus Hits Central Asia', *Moscow News*, no. 41, 1990, p. 7; O. I. Brusina, 'Russkie v Srednei Azii: "Kolonizatory" ili natsional'noe men'shinstvo?', paper presented at the conference 'The New Russian Diaspora', Lielupe, Latvia, 13–15 November 1992.

co-nationals in other Central Asian states, see themselves as more hard-working and as having higher moral standards than heartland Russians. They drink less, have a lower divorce rate and abhor the debauchery and dissipation they associate with mainland Russia. They attribute their different lifestyle partly to the healthy influence of the strict Muslim moral of the locals.

Socially, the Russians mingle little with the indigenous population. Uzbekistan has been described as a 'bifurcated society'. However, the widespread notion that the Slavs occupy its upper rungs while the 'natives' do the menial work is highly misleading. In the cities, Uzbeks hold the dominant positions in trade, government, education, journalism and culture, but they form a minority both among industrial workers and in the technical professions. Nonetheless, they still represent about 70% of all heads of industrial enterprises.[60] Some Uzbekistani Russians claim that this division of labour has worked to the benefit of both groups: 'In Uzbekistan, Russians and Uzbeks have not interfered with each other but lived according to the principle: everyone minds his own affairs.'[61] Even though there is a growing problem of unemployment, the Uzbeks and other Central Asians are in no position to take over the Russian jobs, since – as Donald Carlisle has put it – they have 'failed or chosen not to acquire the appropriate skills'.[62] It has therefore been a major concern of the Uzbekistani authorities since the collapse of the Soviet Union to persuade the Russians to stay.

The Uzbekistani constitution adopted on 8 December 1992 does not single out the ethnic Uzbeks for special treatment as a state-bearing people. The preamble refers to 'the people of Uzbekistan', an entity later defined as 'the citizens of the Republic of Uzbekistan independent of their nationality'.[63] Citizenship has been granted to everyone who was a permanent resident of Uzbekistan at the moment when the law on citizenship was passed in July 1992.[64] Members of the russophone community, however, point out that in terms of practical

60. Boris Z. Rumer, 'The Gathering Storm in Central Asia', *Orbis*, XXXVII, 1 (Winter 1993), p. 97; Olga Brusina, in private correspondence with the author.
61. Igor' Rogov, 'Bez piati minut bezhentsy?', *Literaturnaia Gazeta*, no. 40, 3 October 1990.
62. Donald S. Carlisle, 'Uzbekistan and the Uzbeks', *Problems of Communism*, XL (September–October 1991), pp. 23–44, on p. 38.
63. *Konstitutsiia Respubliki Uzbekistana*, Tashkent, 1992, pp. 8 and 10.
64. For the text of the citizenship law, see *Pravda Vostoka*, 28 July 1992.

politics the Uzbeks nonetheless function as a state-bearing people. The composition of the government and state apparatus is becoming ever more mono-ethnic.

As in Turkmenistan, the Russians in Uzbekistan have supported the political leadership and possibly also the idea of separate statehood for the country. On 29 December 1992, the successful Turkmenistani independence referendum was emulated in Uzbekistan with a similar show of popular support for independence. The turnout at the Uzbekistani referendum was 95%, and 98% voted 'Yes'.[65] In the simultaneous presidential elections, the incumbent Islam Karimov, leader of the Popular-Democratic (formerly Communist) Party, received 86%, and the opposition candidate of the Erk party 12%. The Russians were reported to have voted overwhelmingly in favour of Karimov as 'the lesser of two evils' – or as the only leader capable of restraining the nationalist opposition.[66]

Karimov is indeed according rough treatment to the Uzbek opposition – both the nationalists and those adhering to more Western-democratic values. Official registration of the leading opposition movement, 'Birlik', has been withdrawn, and in addition the more moderate break-away faction, 'Erk', is kept under constant surveillance. In December 1992 three members of the Uzbek opposition who attended a humans rights conference in Bishkek, the Kyrgyzstani capital, were arrested on Kyrgyzstani territory by officials from the Uzbekistani Ministry of Internal Affairs and brought home for questioning.[67]

But it is not only the popular movements of the titular nation that are being hounded by the authorities. Organisations of other nationalities also often fail to pass through the needle's eye of official registra-

65. 'Weekly Record of Events', *RFE/RL Research Report*, I (17 January 1992), p. 67; Aleksei Arapov and Iakov Umanskii, '"Russkii vopros" v kontekste mezhnatsional'nykh otnoshenii v Uzbekistane', *Svobodnaia Mysl'*, no. 14, 1992, pp. 29–38, on p. 33. Russians may have made up a considerable part of the approximately 7% who either did not vote or voted against independence, but no information on this is available.
66. D. Sabov and I. Cherniak, 'Russkie na fone mechetei', *Komsomol'skaia Pravda*, 4 February 1992; Author's interview with Salman Fatykhov, 12 May 1993.
67. Bess Brown, 'Central Asia: the First Year . . .', *op. cit.*, p. 32. Brown believes that this action had the potential for damaging relations between Uzbekistan and Kyrgyzstan. This is not likely, however, since the arrest had been cleared with the Kyrgyzstani authorities beforehand. See the statement made by a Kyrgyzstani spokesman in *Res Publica* (Bishkek), 16 March 1993, p. 2.

tion. In principle, the Uzbekistani law on public organisations, dating from February 1991 allows for the establishment of cultural centres for different ethnic groups. However, the reality can be quite different.

An Uzbekistani interfront was active during *perestroika*, but by 1992 it had been harassed to the point where it ceased to exist.[68] An application for the registration of a Russian cultural centre was turned down in 1991 with the explanation that the russophones in Tashkent already had all the structures and facilities they needed to develop their language, tradition and culture.[69] Another explanation which was given for the refusal might have been more truthful: 'Someone might give a drunken Uzbek 100 rubles and tell him to break the windows of the centre. When he is locked up afterwards a rumour can easily be spread that he has been wronged by the Russians. Therefore, better not give anybody the chance to make provocations.'[70]

Nonetheless, in May 1992 a 'national association of Russian culture' was registered with the Tashkent authorities.[71] The stated aim of the association is to advance the culture of the Russians and other Slavic peoples in Uzbekistan and to promote the harmonisation of inter-ethnic relations.[72] As well as cultural activities, commercial enterprises seem to be important for it. While programmatically apolitical, the association nevertheless fully supports the Karimov regime.

The language question. Karimov cannot completely ignore the nationalist currents in the population. The opposition has been able to put its imprint on certain aspects of state policy, most notably on language policy. Bilingualism in Uzbekistan has been based almost exclusively on the Russian language. Not only Russians and other Slavs but also most Tatars and Jews, as well as the sizeable Korean

68. James Critchlow, 'Uzbekistan: Underlying Instabilities', *RFE/RL Research Report*, I (7 February 1992), p. 9.
69. V. Berezovskii, 'Uzbekistan: Russkim net mesta?', *Russkii Vestnik*, no. 9, 7 May 1991, p. 15.
70. Sergei Tatur, 'Vmeste podnimat' Uzbekistan', *Zvezda Vostoka*, no. 1, 1991, p. 11.
71. The president of 'Russian culture', Vladimir Emelianov, pointed out that his society is called an 'association' rather than a 'cultural centre' with a particular reason. Cultural centres are what ethnic minorities organise. The Russians, however, do not feel like a minority, he claimed. 'They are a great people, and will remain so, even in independent Uzbekistan.' Author's interview with Vladimir Emelianov, 12 May 1993.
72. 'Ustav natsional'noi assotsiatsii "Russkaia kul'tura". Respubliki Uzbekistan', Tashkent, 1992 (typescript).

community, are russophones. However, official statistics show that knowledge of the titular language is somewhat more advanced among Russians in Uzbekistan than it is in the other Central Asian republics. In 1989, 4.6% claimed fluency in it, compared to 3.5% in Tajikistan and 1.2% in Kyrgyzstan.[73]

It is generally recognised that under Soviet rule the Uzbek language did not attain the level of an advanced modern language with a fully-fledged vocabulary for all fields. However, an American sociolinguist has challenged the prevalent view that the spread of the Russian language in the republic has been at the expense of Uzbek. Bill Fierman has claimed that 'more Uzbeks may voluntarily be reading more Russian novels than 30 years ago, but . . . Uzbeks today are also reading more *Uzbek* literature.'[74]

During *perestroika*, the main battle cry of the Birlik popular front was the need to elevate Uzbek to the status of state language. Large street rallies forced the authorities to give in on this matter, and a language law was passed in October 1989. This was the golden hour of the Uzbek opposition movement, and implementation of the law continues to be closely monitored by Uzbek nationalists. However, they are not happy with what they see. One professor of philosophy, in 1993, deplored the sluggish rate of transition to the Uzbek languages, 'without rudder or sail. Strangely, the very architects of the law do not seem to want any fundamental changes. The law has been passed – no more is needed.'[75]

Actually, the language law is relatively liberal in its requirements. It stipulates an eight-year transition period, so that only in 1997 will all the regulations become effective. It is not only in deference to the European population that this has happened; many in the Uzbek intelligentsia have also received their education in Russian, and would hardly know how to conduct their professional work in their mother tongue. They would thus find an overnight switch to Uzbek as the language of administration extremely hard. However, from below, Uzbek nationalists are impatiently stretching the interpretation

---

73. The command of Uzbek among other European groups in Uzbekistan was somewhat lower: Ukrainians, 3.5%; Germans, 2.9%; etc.
74. Bill Fierman, 'The View from Uzbekistan', *International Journal of the Sociology of Language*, XXXIII (1982), pp. 71–8, on p. 71.
75. K. Khanazarov, 'Protivorechiia sotsial'nogo progressa', *Pozitsiia* (Tashkent), III, 2 (March–April 1993), p. 15.

of the law. In May 1993 the Orthodox Archbishop Vladimir of Tashkent told the author that when he sent a letter in Russian to the Tashkent city authorities, the clerk in the reception office refused to acknowledge its receipt: he said that letters had to be written in Uzbek. However, a phone call to the offices higher up revealed that no such instructions had been issued. On the contrary, the bureaucrats had actually admitted that their own command of Uzbek was faulty, and had even asked that letters written in Uzbek should be accompanied by a Russian translation![76]

Many Russians in Uzbekistan are convinced that when the 'euphoria of independence' has passed, Russian will regain its position as a major language in Uzbek society and public life. They point to the experience of many former colonies of European powers where the language of the erstwhile colonists is still used in various capacities, and at times even enjoys official status as a state language. Furthermore, they believe that Russian will continue to be an important medium of communication among the independent Central Asia states. In fact, although the Turkic languages of Central Asia are mutually intelligible, the heads of state in the region often address each other in Russian in official correspondence.[77] Many Uzbeks might want to see Uzbek function as a Central Asian *lingua franca*, but the other Turkic groups hold back, wary of what they see as a potential Uzbek great power hegemony. English has not replaced French in former French colonies, and Russians confidently predict that neither will it replace Russian in isolated former Soviet Asia.[78] This prediction is not at all unrealistic, and may allay some fears among the russophone population of social marginalisation. At the same time, such forecasts may make them lazy about pursuing a greater proficiency in Uzbek.

Ethnic turmoil. Culturally, historically, geographically and in other ways Uzbekistan is the Central Asian state with the closest ties to Tajikistan. Fears of a spill-over from the violence in the latter is therefore felt more acutely in Uzbekistan than elsewhere. Many

---

76. Author's interview with Archbishop Vladimir of Tashkent and Central Asia, at Tashkent, 16 May 1993.
77. Author's interview with Salman Fatykhov. Fatykhov referred to a confidential letter, from president Akaev in Kyrgyzstan to his Uzbekistani colleague, informing him about the introduction of a separate Kyrgyzstani currency in May 1993.
78. Author's interview with the editors of *Molodëzh Uzbekistana* and *Tashkentskaia Pravda*, 13 May 1993.

Western experts share this apprehension,[79] which has been reinforced by a number of ethnic clashes within the republic itself. The most serious of these was the pogrom of Meskhetian Turks in the Fergana Valley in June 1989, in which more than 100 people died.

The Fergana violence caught most observers by surprise. The quarrel over the price of strawberries in the market which allegedly triggered it off should not, of course, be considered as more than the straw that broke the camel's back. There are deep underlying social and economic frustrations, especially the seemingly uncontrollable overpopulation in the area. Authorities in Moscow and Tashkent quickly claimed, on little hard evidence, that the Fergana riots were carefully planned by the Mafia, by political enemies of Gorbachev or by Uzbek nationalists.[80] As Jonathan Steele reported from the valley, the fact that no-one could explain clearly why the pogrom broke out has itself created alarm, since no-one can tell whether, and if so where or when, it might happen again.[81]

The Fergana massacre led to the first massive wave of Russian emigration. Within a year and a half, 20,000 Europeans had left the valley, although most reports had indicated that the frenzy was not directed against the Russians. Anti-Turkish, anti-Kyrgyzian, anti-Semitic and anti-Armenian abuse could be heard among the mob, but nothing anti-Russian.[82] The Russians felt that the earth was moving under their feet, that their apparent shield of immunity might easily break, and they could be the next target.

For an outsider it is difficult to measure the temperature of inter-ethnic relations in Uzbekistan. In the republican media, Uzbek as well as Russian, there is an almost complete news blackout on such touchy issues – which is explained as the result not of censorship imposed from above but of simple prudence and self-interest. The theme is 'not

79. See, e.g., interview with Martha Brill Olcott in *Slovo Kyrgyzstana*, 16 January 1993, p. 3.
80. *Pravda*, 14 October 1989, p. 2.
81. *The Guardian*, 23 October 1990.
82. This information was given by Salman Fatykhov, the deputy editor-in-chief of *Pravda Vostoka*, in interview with the author, 12 May 1993. In 1989, Fatykhov was a highly placed official in the Uzbekistani CP Central Committee, and had access to restricted informaton on the Fergana events. I have chosen to disregard information set forth in the Soviet central press to the effect that the Meskhetians had been attacked because they refused to join a pan-Islamic front to 'get rid of the Russians'. See *Krasnaia Zvezda*, 21 June 1989, as quoted by John A. Armstrong in *Problems of Communism*, XXIX (July–August 1990), p. 83.

forbidden but dangerous'. 'Look what has taken place in Tajikistan. The fact that peace and tranquillity reign here is highly appreciated by us. We do not want in any way to provoke any sort of acute conflict with our articles,' explains Aleksandr Lukimov, editor-in-chief of the leading paper, *Tashkentskaia Pravda*.[83]

Indeed, if anything, the occasional references to inter-ethnic relations in Lukimov's paper contribute to the *soothing* of passions rather than their excitation. Russians are quoted as saying that 'in Uzbekistan we have not felt and do not feel in any way out of favour . . . We should realise that we have a common destiny and are all citizens of the same country.'[84] The paper even actively participates in the rehabilitation campaign of the former republican party boss Sharaf Rashidov, who became under *perestroika* the epitome of Uzbek nepotism and venality.[85]

In Moscow the reporting process has been quite different. One particularly alarmist article appeared in *Komsomol'skaia Pravda* in February 1992, in which the paper's special correspondents to Tashkent depicted in alarming colours the plight of the Uzbekistani Russians. The writers admitted that they had not experienced any discrimination against Russians themselves, but had heard about a number of unpleasant incidents. One women alleged that she had been accosted on the street with the words: 'Go back to mother Russia.' 'The most hostility is felt from the intelligentsia and the youth, and the youth make up half of the population here,' she sighed.

Komsomol'skaia Pravda asserted that since a collective exodus by the Russians would wreak havoc with the Uzbek economy, the Russians were being held back by dubious means. Train tickets from Tashkent to Moscow cost almost twice as much as tickets in the opposite direction. Moreover, local Uzbekistani authorities were demanding extortionate prices for a stamp registering an official change of residence. 'In Uzbekistan a huge hostage system is in operation,' the Moscow reporters had been told. 'Ever more often [the local Russians]

---

83. Author's interview with Lukimov, 13 May 1993.
84. *Tashkentskaia Pravda*, 22 September 1992, p. 2.
85. The praise lavished on Rashidov by Uzbekistani Russians is not necessarily hypocritical. Apart from everything else, Rashidov is also remembered as a leading figure in the campaign for the promotion of Russian in the non-Russian republics under Khrushchev and Brezhnev. See Robert Conquest, *Russia After Khrushchev*, New York, 1965, p. 212.

anxiously ask themselves: how much longer will the authorities here feel they need us?'[86]

Obviously, the feelings of horror which *Komsomol'skaia Pravda* relayed to its readers will not be diminished by such articles but almost certainly be magnified. Local Russian journalists whom this writer met in Tashkent were bewildered and sad that their Moscow colleagues should be 'stabbing them in the back' with such reporting, all the more so as the culprit was one of the most respected Russian newspapers.[87]

Anyone writing on this subject is bound to feel in a quandary. The responses one receives concerning inter-ethnic relations in Central Asia are often contradictory, and it is difficult to assess the reliability of one's sources. Almost every Russian speaking in an official capacity will deny the existence of overt discrimination against Russians, but this is contradicted by many Western observers. Boris Rumer, for one, claims that:

> Non-natives encounter growing antagonism and menacing threats on public transportation, in public places, and at the market. It is not uncommon for them to be told on the bus, 'Get out of that seat'; it is not uncommon for them to find, in shops, clerks who pretend not to understand Russian. The non-natives also feel that they suffer discrimination in promotions and salaries.[88]

This was also the message we received from 'the man in the street'.

In a rare case of *glasnost* in the Uzbekistani press in the spring of 1991, Sergei Tatur wrote candidly on inter-ethnic relations.[89] The relationship between the various nationalities, he lamented, was like 'an exposed nerve which reacts hypersensitively however gently it is touched'. The language issue was being used as a 'harsh means of putting pressure on the European population'. Knowledge of the language and traditions of the titular nation did not lessen the sense of unease, Tatur felt. 'We are aliens and only barely tolerated ... Every Russian living in a Central Asian city asked himself long ago:

---

86. D. Sabov and I. Cherniak, 'Russkie na fone mechetei', *Komsolmol'skaia Pravda*, 4 February 1992.
87. Author's interview with the editorial staff in the political department of the newspaper *Narodnoe Slovo*, Tashkent, 13 May 1993.
88. Boris Z. Rumer, 'The Gathering Storm', *op. cit.*, p. 98.
89. Sergei Tatur, 'Vmeste podnimat' Uzbekistan', *Zvezda Vostoka*, no. 1, 1991, pp. 3–17.

do I have a future here, and do my children have a future here?'

Tatur's anguished outcry seemed to confirm *Komsomol'skaia Pravda's* version, but Tatur went on to ask himself:

> Am I being chased out of here? Has anybody at any time told me 'Beat it, go back to Russia'? Nothing of the kind has ever happened. Neither in the remote countryside nor in my native city of Tashkent has anyone ever insulted me or given me a feeling of rejection ... In so far as the countryside is any different from Tashkent it is better there. In the villages, in the high mountain pastures, and on the highways I have been met with a respect and a readiness to help which certainly is not insincere.

Yes, why should we believe Tatur's testimony more than that of any of the others? He may have had his own reasons for writing as he did . . .

Of course, there has always been a cultural gulf between the Asians and the Europeans in Central Asia – although formerly this was something to which one did not pay much attention. One reason for this seems to be that till recently the Uzbeks did not have a deep sense of ethnic self-identification. What passed for 'the Uzbek nation' was in fact a conglomerate of tribes and peoples which, only as late as the Soviet era, were moulded into a seeming unity by a conscious policy of the state.[90] Lacking a clear concept of 'us', the Uzbeks also had a hazy understanding of the corresponding concept of 'them'. Under the term of 'the Russians', they could lump together Slavs, Tatars and even Koreans on the basis of language alone.[91] In fact, most experts are inclined to believe that not only the Uzbeks but all Central Asian nations lived up till the very near past in a pristine world of pre-nationalist man.

There were two developments in particular that came together and shattered this idyll. Demographically, the much higher birth rates among the titular groups tipped the ethnic balance in the cities, which were the strongholds of European culture. Young Central Asians were pouring in from the countryside in ever-increasing numbers, demanding a place in the sun. One of the strategies used to achieve this aim was nationalism. The position of the Russians and other russophones came under threat.[92] Politically, the elevation of the Soviet republics to the status of 'nation-states' gave the indigenous groups tremendous

---

90. See, e.g., Donald Carlisle, *op. cit.*, pp. 24ff.
91. Ol'ga Vasil'eva, 'Novaia natsiia? Russkie v SSSR kak natsional'noe men'shinstvo', XX *Vek i Mir*, 7 (July 1991), p. 17.
92. Leon Gudkov, 'The Disintegration of the USSR and Russians in the Republics', *Journal of Communist Studies*, IX, 1 (March 1993), pp. 75–87.

leverage in cultural conflicts – at least, this is how it was perceived. Hitherto, abuse on the bus from a member of another ethnic group would be shrugged off or returned in kind, and that was that. Now, if the loose talker was an ethnic Uzbek, he was believed, in some sense, to have the weight of the entire state apparatus behind him. The Russian no longer dared to answer back, and at the same time was unable in his mind to shrug the insult off.

The fact remains that Russians are leaving Uzbekistan, as well as the other Central Asian republics, at a rapid rate. Since 1990, emigration from the republic, though fluctuating, seems to have been around 5% a year.[93] However, no single cause can be adduced to explain this phenomenon. For each individual the motivation may be different.

Ethnic Uzbeks claim that the phenomenon of European emigration is primarily economically motivated. The Russians are offered better jobs and expect better life opportunities in Russia.[94] Certainly the highly qualified specialists in the Russian diaspora have always been a highly mobile group that has moved a great deal among the various republics.[95] The net emigration from Central Asia is also the result of a steep decline in immigration, although this obviously does not tell the whole story. Undoubtedly, cultural factors – if not direct discrimination, then at least a strong sense of alienation and marginalisation – also contribute strongly to the Russians' deciding to go. But they also feel vulnerable because they almost completely lack any social-security 'safety net'. The indigenous Central Asians live in tight community structures: extended families in the villages and the neighbourhood institution of the *makhalla* in the city. The Russians have nothing similar, and have therefore had to rely on the state apparatus to protect their interests. Nowadays this apparatus is increasingly felt not to be working for them.[96]

In general, it is the future that worries the Russians most. This anxiety certainly includes the fear of renewed ethnic violence, as well as forebodings that the secular regime of Karimov could be replaced by

93. Igor' Rotar', 'Slaviane v Srednei Azii', *Nezavisimaia Gazeta*, 29 April 1993.
94. Author's interview with Dr Azot Ata-Merzaev, deputy headmaster at the Faculty of Sociology and Geography at the University of Tashkent.
95. See Ol'ga Vasil'eva, *op. cit.*, p. 17.
96. O. I. Brusina, 'Russkie v Srednei Azii . . .', *op. cit.*

mullahs.[97] However, there are also more practical and mundane deliberations at work. Many Russians are afraid that if they do not emigrate now, they may never have another chance. For the time being the borders between the former Soviet republics are still easy to cross, but could change. Customs control will probably be tightened, making it harder to travel with one's personal belongings. The ruble zone may also collapse, and a future separate Uzbek currency is unlikely to be recognised as legal tender in Russia. A massive wave of emigration could cause congestion in the transport system, and it is therefore better to sneak out quickly before the great rush begins. The best jobs and the best accommodation in Russia will also go to those who do not hesitate for too long. The fact that some are already leaving serves as a strong inducement for others to follow in order that families can stay together.

---

97. 'The Russians leave because they are unable to stand being blamed for all the ills and humiliations inflicted on the country. And also because they are afraid of discrimination and pogroms,' writes Igor' Rogov. *Literaturnaia Gazeta*, no. 40, 3 October 1991, p. 9. As we see, when it comes to discrimination and pogroms, the reference is to future rather than actual molestations.

9

THE QUEST FOR EURASIA: KYRGYZSTAN AND KAZAKHSTAN

The Kyrgyzs and the Kazakhs are closely related. This is shown by the strong similarities in language and custom, their common history and economy, and the way they see themselves. Soviet ethnographers used to distinguish them primarily on the topological criterion: the Kazakhs were the steppe-dwellers while the Kyrgyzs lived in the mountains. A French expert has maintained that this distinction has never been totally accepted by the people themselves.[1]

Like the Uzbeks and the Turkmens, the Kyrgyzs and the Kazakhs are turkophones and Sunni Muslims, but in many other ways they are very different from their southern neighbours. Physically they have much more markedly Mongol features. In their lifestyle the Kyrgyzs and Kazakhs are traditionally herdsmen, in contrast to the crop-growers of the oases further south. They were nomads right up till the 1930s when forced into collectives. While contemporary Kyrgyzstan, for a while, did belong to the Khokand khanate in the nineteenth century, the Kyrgyzs and Kazakhs have generally not been part of the ancient Turko-Arab cultures of Central Asia. Islam was introduced in their areas relatively late, according to two Western experts, so that the nomads remained 'only superficially Islamicised' until the eighteenth century.[2] Many Kyrgyzs and Kazakhs today claim that the hold of religion over people's minds is much less firm in these two republics that it is further south.[3]

Since *perestroika*, political developments have taken a different turn in Kyrgyzstan and Kazakhstan from what has occurred in other post-

---

1. Guy G. Imart, 'Kirgizia-Kazakhstan: a Hinge or a Fault-Line?', *Problems of Communism*, XXXIX (September–October 1990), pp. 1–13. For a long time, Soviet officialdom called the Kazakhs 'Kirgiz' and the contemporary Kyrgyz 'Kara-Kirgiz'. See Zev Katz, 'Kazakhstan and the Kazakhs', in Zev Katz et al. (eds), *Handbook of Major Soviet Nationalities*, New York, 1975, pp. 213–35, on p. 216.
2. Alexandre Bennigsen and S. Enders Wimbush, *Muslims of the Soviet Empire*, London, 1985, p. 7.
3. Author's conversations in Kyrgyzstan and Kazakhstan, May 1993.

Soviet Muslim states. The commitment to democracy in these two countries seems more serious: albeit in fits and starts, both countries are moving slowly towards a multi-party system. The Kyrgyzstani media are the freest in former Soviet Asia, and include a wide spectrum of newspapers from the most highbrow right through to a sensationalist yellow press. The Kazakh press, for its part, has relatively few restrictions although it does seem rather more subject to the inhibitions of self-censorship.

In neither Kyrgyzstan nor Kazakhstan do the present political leaders see their country as Asian plain and simple. The Kyrgyzstani president Askar Akaev has claimed on many occasions that Kyrgyzstan is, or at least should become, 'another Switzerland';[4] its 'Europeanisation' is considered a paramount goal.[5] In Kazakhstan the vista is somewhat less grandiose but maybe more realistic. Here official spokesmen portray their country not as potentially 'European' but as 'Eurasian' and as a bridge between East and West.[6] This, in a sense, Kazakhstan is already; it has the highest concentration of Russians in the former Soviet Union outside the Russian Federation – in 1989, 6.2 million or 37.8% of the total population. In addition, large numbers of some other European nationalities such as the Ukrainians, Belorussians, Germans and Poles live in the republic. In 1989 these five nationalities together made up more than half of the total population. Kyrgyzstan also is much more European in its demographic make-up than the other new states in Central Asia. In 1989 the 900,000 Russians were 21.5% of the population. If the other major European nationalities are included, these figures are 1.12 million and 26.6%.

The social make-up of the European population in Kyrgyzstan and Kazakhstan is also different from that in the neighbouring countries, although the Russian here also live mainly in the large cities, and for a time were even in a majority in the capital city of both states. Some of the most fertile land has largely been cultivated by German, Russian and Ukrainian collective farmers. The percentage of rural inhabitants

4. See, e.g., *Slovo Kyrgyzstana*, 5 February 1993, p. 2.
5. Author's interview with Salijan Jigitov, President Akaev's counsellor on nationality questions, Bishkek, May 1993. See, also, Ian Pryde, 'Kyrgyzstan: Secularism vs Islam', *The World Today*, November 1992, pp. 208–11.
6. Author's interview with K. S. Smailov, chairman of the Committee on Nationality Questions in the Kazakhstani parliament. Rather than pointing to the Trubetskoi brothers and other Russian Eurasianists of the 1920s, Smailov pointed instead to Lev Gumilëv as a main inspirer of contemporary Kazakhstani ideas on Eurasianism.

among the local Russians in 1989 is higher in Kyrgyzstan (30%) than in any other former Soviet republic, Russia included. In Kazakhstan the figure was 23%.[7]

Kyrgyzstan

The political and demographic peculiarities of Kyrgyzstan and Kazakhstan have meant that members of the Russian diaspora in these two republics are in a radically different situation from their counterparts in other parts of former Soviet Asia. Because they make up such a large share of the total population, one would expect the danger for them of social and cultural marginalisation to be minimal. Under the conditions of political pluralism which prevail in both countries, they are also in a position to organise parties and societies to defend their rights openly both in the parliament and in the press. However, whoever approaches the study of ethnic relations in Kyrgyzstan with these assumptions will be puzzled to find out that the migratory currents of Russians from Kyrgyzstan are approximately the same as from Uzbekistan: 5% in 1992.[8] Thus safety in numbers is not necessarily as decisive a factor as one might assume. To understand the situation and attitudes of the Russians in this country, it is necessary to look at other circumstances as well.

The exodus of Russians from Kyrgyzstan is a puzzle not only to the outside observer but also to many Russians in the republic. 'Who would have thought that the Russians would begin to contemplate a rapid exodus from the bastion of liberty in Central Asia!' one bewildered Kyrgyzstani Russian exclaimed in May 1993. 'And nonetheless, during the evening tea practically every Russian family is discussing only one thing: where should we go and when?'[9]

A lack of information is certainly not the reason why the phenomenon of European emigration from Kyrgyzstan is so mysterious. The

---

7. Computed from Table 1.2 in Iu. V. Arutiunian (ed.), *Russkie: Etnosotsiologicheskie Ocherki*, Moscow, 1992, p. 25.
8. Igor' Rotar', 'Slaviane v Srednei Azii', *Nezavisimaia Gazeta*, 29 April 1993. In absolute figures, 47,036 persons left Kyrgyzstan in the first 6 months of 1992, while 13,295, on the other hand, arrived. The negative balance of 33,741 persons was equal to the net level of emigration for the entire year of 1991. See *Slavianskie Vesti* (Bishkek), no. 16, August 1992, p. 2. We can safely conclude that the vast majority of the emigrants were Europeans.
9. Natal'ia Ablova, 'Chuzhie i brat'ia', *Res Publica* (Bishkek), 10 March 1993.

migration issue is discussed openly and widely in the Kyrgyzstani as well as in the Russian press.[10] In May 1993 an important article on the Slavs of Central Asia from *Nezavisimaia Gazeta* in Moscow was reprinted in the Bishkek weekly *Res Publica*, with editorial comment.[11] *Res Publica* attacked it for scaring the Russian diaspora communities with groundless stories of Islamist fundamentalism, and such like. The fact is, the editorial asserted, that 'earlier, the migrants did not try to conceal their economic interests . . . but under present conditions they may hide their true motives beneath the more honourable pretext of trying to escape from ethnic discrimination.' The paper asserted that the exodus of Slavs was a normal pull-factor type of migration which has nothing to do with flight. However, the present author got an interesting glimpse into Kyrgyzstani-style pluralism when, at a meeting with the *Res Publica* staff, he learned that some of its members 'categorically' dissociated themselves from the editorial comment published in their name. Not surprisingly, these journalists were ethnic Russians and other Europeans, while the author of the comment was a Kyrgyz.

Some Russians in Kyrgyzstan have explained the European emigration from the republic in ways which are just as simplistic as those found in the *Res Publica* editorial comment, only taking the diametrically opposite view. In August 1992 a Russian journalist was told by a Russian worker in Bishkek: 'The native people hate us. We are deprived of every one of our rights. They would like to expel all, and if we don't go, things will get even worse.'[12] For all its hysteria and one-sidedness, there is a grain of truth in such an exclamation: interethnic relations in Kyrgyzstan are deteriorating, which is certainly one reason for the accelerated European exodus. However, two other circumstances must also be mentioned: the language situation and the Kyrgyzstani nation-state concept. As a result of these factors,

10. In Kyrgyzstan: Natal'ia Ablova, *op. cit.*; 'Migratsiia russkikh', *Res Publica*, no. 7, 10 March 1992; 'Brat'ia ili vragi', *Slavianskie Vesti*, no. 15 (August 1992), p. 3; interview with V. Grinchenko, leader of the private migration office, 'Semirech'e', *Kyrgyztag-TASS*, Bishkek, 21 July 1992. In Russia: *Federatsiia*, 25 February 1993; *Kuranty*, 17 February 1993; *Moskovskii Komsomolets*, 14 January 1993; *Rossiiskaia Gazeta*, 8 June 1992, p. 3; *ibid.*, 5 September 1992; *Literaturnaia Gazeta*, no. 40, 1991, p. 2; *ibid.*, 26 August 1992; *Stolitsa*, no. 12, 1993, p. 6.
11. Igor' Rotar', 'Slaviane v Srednei Azii', *Nezavisimaia Gazeta*, 29 April 1993. Reprinted in an abridged version in *Res Publica*, 15 May 1993, p. 3.
12. An anonymous Russian quoted in *Literaturnaia Gazeta*, 26 August 1992.

a contradistinction often arises between the state-bearing titular nation and the other ethnic groups.

Ethnic tensions at the popular level.   The strained relationship between the Russians and the titular nation in Kyrgyzstan seems to have not only many different manifestations but also several independent sources. A major complaint among the Russians is discrimination in the workplace. Stories of Russians being demoted or fired from leading positions without valid reason are regularly heard, and it appears that many of them are true.[13] However, this is not necessarily a result of 'hatred of the Russians' and is more often a side-effect of the intense rivalry between various Kyrgyz clans. The northern Kyrgyz are distinctly at odds with their co-nationals from the south of the country, and both of these groups are further divided into various clans with strong internal loyalties. When the Kyrgyz fight among themselves, the Europeans are the major losers. A Russian from southern Kyrgyzstan explains:

> Every new [Kyrgyz] boss starts by freeing by every means possible the lucrative jobs [under his authority] to make room for his fellow clansmen. Without the support of his kin [*rod*] he is a nobody, and will be 'eaten up' by someone else. Who are suffering under this system? Of course, the aliens, the *inorodtsy*, that is: we, the Russians, since we have nobody high up to defend us.[14]

According to many Kyrgyzstani Russians, the ethnic tension in the republic is also to some extent a by-product of certain aspects of Kyrgyzstani democracy. Kyrgyzstan has abolished the rigid Soviet *propiska* system, which required a person to register with the authorities within three days of arriving in a new township. The *propiska* has rightly been criticised as a serious infringement of the freedom of citizens, its elimination in Kyrgyzstan seems, however, to have been badly prepared and badly executed. Experts on Kyrgyzstani affairs point out that the new freedom immediately released an avalanche of young Kyrgyzs down the mountain slopes. They poured into the cities from the remote valleys, looking for work, fun or something else. Work was not forthcoming, and the idle youngsters soon formed a

13. Iu. Blium, in *Slovo Kyrgyzstana*, 28 November 1992, p. 6.
14. V. Uleev, president of the 'Slavonic Diaspora' association, in *Res Publica*, 15 May 1993, p. 3.

reservoir of restiveness and frustration of great value to the Kyrgyz nationalists. Street crime mounted, and often took on an ethnic quality. Like the Wasp middle class in American suburbs, Russians in Kyrgyzstan began to feel that their neighbourhoods had been invaded by gangsters and hooligans with a different skin colour. Many no longer dared to go out after dusk.

There have been violent ethnic clashes in Kyrgyzstan as in the other post-Soviet Asian states. Serious riots, causing hundreds of casualities, took place in the city of Osh on the Uzbekistani border in June 1990.[15] This is a part of the country with relatively few Russians, and the victims were therefore mostly ethnic Uzbeks. But stories have circulated about atrocities committed against Russians in other places. Some people whom we met in Kyrgyzstan would offer, on condition that the tape recorder was switched off, to relate episodes they had personally experienced. However, most of the incidents of ethnic sadism had been 'elsewhere', in a distant city.[16] The inhabitants of Bishkek maintained that while the situation was still quite safe in the capital, it was much worse in the countryside. However, when we visited the 'First of May' kolkhoz in the Issyk-Kul valley, the Russian chairman denied rumours of an ethnic witch-hunt in his area. Some Russians were indeed leaving his kolkhoz, but these were recent arrivals, specialists with no strong personal ties to the country. The chairman himself was a third-generation Kyrgyzstani, and he did not intend to go anywhere.[17]

Of course, the reassurances of the kolkhoz chairman must be understood in the context of his determination to stay and make the best of the situation, but some Russians who have already left Kyrgyzstan also maintain that they met no open hostility from the indigenous population. A seventeen-year-old Russian refugee from Kyrgyzstan, interviewed in Moscow in January 1993, admitted that 'there was no specific occurrence which prompted us to leave. We simply went before it was too late. After all, it will be impossible for Russians to go on living there.'[18]

15. See Gene Huskey, 'Kyrgyzstan: the politics of demographic and economic frustration', in Ian Bremmer and Ray Taras (eds), *Nations and Politics in the Soviet Successor States*, Cambridge, 1993, pp. 398–420.
16. E.g. author's interview with journalists in *Slovo Kyrgyzstana*, May 1993.
17. Author's interview with Leonid Medvedev, at Kolkhoz 'Pervoe Maia', Anan'evo, Issyk-Kul, 18 May 1993.
18. *Moskovskii Komsomolets*, 14 January 1993.

Certainly, there is serious cause for worry. The pluralistic Kyrgyzstani society contains the full spectrum of political organisations and parties – including ultra-nationalist and racist ones, some of which are both vocal and threatening. Russians have become targets of what they see as historic falsifications. The tragedy of the 1916 uprising is presented as a 'genocide of the Kyrgyz people', and calls could be heard that what the insurgents did not achieve then, i.e. the expulsion of the Russians, should be accomplished today.[19]

In particular, the officially registered party of 'national renaissance', Asaba, has issued some alarmingly vitriolic statements. In April 1992, it declared that no such thing as the people of Kyrgyzstan exists, but only the Kyrgyz nation and representatives of other peoples in Kyrgyzstan. The land of Kyrgyzstan, the party maintained, should belong to the Kyrgyz nation only.

> In the nineteenth century the Russians occupied our land ... The occupiers took over the best and most fertile land while the Kyrgyz were forced out and pushed into the mountains. During the bloody genocide of 1916 half of the innocent nation, including women, children and old people, were brutally slaughtered. It is impossible to erase such atrocities from the memory of the people.

In conclusion, Asaba ominously declared that it was prepared to use 'all necessary means' to prevent Russia from in any way interfering in Kyrgyzstani politics to protect the Russian community there.[20]

This sinister statement elicited several protests from irate Russians and an official statement by the Ministry of Justice that the Asaba proclamation was historically false and legally unjustified, and violated several articles in the Kyrgyzstani law on public organisations. Nonetheless, official registration of Asaba was not withdrawn.

Constitutional and other legal issues.   During most of 1992 and the first months of 1993, intense controversy on the basic principles of the new constitution dominated Kyrgyzstani public debate. Before its adoption on 5 May 1993, several more or less identical drafts were published in the press,[21] all of which the majority of Russians found unsatisfac-

---

19. Author's interview with Al'bert Bogdanov, Bishkek correspondent for the BBC and Itar-TASS, May 1993.
20. The statement was first published in *Res Publica*, 28 April 1992, and later reprinted in several places. See, e.g., *Slavianskie Vesti*, no. 9, May 1992, p. 3.
21. See, e.g., *Slovo Kyrgyzstana*, 29 December 1992, p. 2.

tory. The final text embodied a compromise between an ethnic and a civic state concept which was far from clear, but there appeared to be a greater bias towards the former concept than in the constitution of any other Soviet successor state with the possible exception of Moldova. The problems start with the preamble, which contains a strong inner tension between the concept of the people (*narod*) of Kyrgyzstan and the Kyrgyz people (*natsiia*):

We, the people of Kyrgyzstan
– strive to secure the national renaissance of the Kyrgyz and to defend and develop the interests of the representatives of the other nationalities, who together with the Kyrgyz make up the people of Kyrgyzstan;
– follow the behest of our forefathers to live in unity, peace and harmony;
– confirm our adherence to human rights and the idea of a national [*natsional'naia*] statehood . . .

President Akaev has defended these formulations by claiming that a 'national renaissance' is 'an objective imperative of the contemporary world'.[22] This may be true, but these are nonetheless strange words to hear from the president not only of the ethnic Kyrgyzs but also of the entire Kyrgyzstani state. It should worry but not surprise the president that the process of establishing a homogeneous Kyrgyzstani citizenry with a shared sense of belonging to the young state is, in his own words, 'more prolonged than we would have liked'.

But however much Akaev may resort to nationalistic language, no one in Kyrgyzstan believes that he is a nationalist himself. Rather, his rhetoric is seen merely as an attempt to ride the nationalist tiger in order to keep it somehow under control. However, many observers fear that the animal may be stronger than the rider, and either take him where he does not want to go or else throw him off. Then, they fear, the genuine nationalists will take over.[23]

On several occasions Akaev has had to exert the full authority of his office in order to prevent the inclusion of blatantly nationalistic clauses in legislation. At one point, for instance, it was proposed that the constitution should stipulate that the president of the republic must

22. Akaev's speech at the Congress of Democratic Forces in Kyrgyzstan, 27 February 1993. Printed in *Slovo Kyrgyzstana*, 3 March 1993, p. 2.
23. See, e.g., *Slovo Kyrgyzstana*, 28 March 1992, p. 3.

be an ethnic Kyrgyz.[24] It was even more significant when in 1991 the legislators passed a Land Code stating that the land of Kyrgyzstan belongs to the Kyrgyz nation in the ethnic sense. Akaev used his veto twice to have this Code changed.[25]

In the legislative process, Akaev has been under pressure not only from the Kyrgyz national radicals but also from the Slavic community. Russian activists have attacked the unclear formulations in the constitutional preamble, and have asked: 'Against whom shall the rights of the other nationalities be defended? Against the Kyrgyzs? And who, then, should defend us? The Kyrgyzs?'[26] They demand that 'the unity of the people of Kyrgyzstan' should be more strongly emphasised, but at the same time they have also proposed that dual citizenship should be instituted, thus giving them a chance to be citizens of Russia and of Kyrgyzstan at the same time.[27] Arguably, such an arrangement could prejudice the establishment of the unified Kyrgyzstani citizenry which they desire.[28]

Another demand from the Slavic community in Kyrgyzstan is for proportional ethnic representation both in the government and in other organs of state power.[29] Such arrangements can already be found in some of the world's ethnically divided countries, most explicitly in Lebanon,[30] and there is nothing inherently undemocratic about them. In the post-Soviet context, however, the idea is strongly associated with the fascist-inclined programme of the deceased Russian nationalist Konstantin Smirnov-Ostashvili, who primarily wanted to restrict

24. Interview with the people's deputy Viktor Rogal'skii in *Slovo Kyrgyzstana*, 23 March 1993. Rogal'skii remarked, probably quite correctly, that the president will most certainly be a Kyrgyz also *without* this constitutional guarantee.
25. Decree of 31 August 1991. See *Slovo Kyrgyzstana*, 10 September 1991; and interview with Askar Akaev in *Argumenty i Fakty*, no. 45, 1992.
26. *Slavianskie Vesti*, no. 16, August 1992, p. 2.
27. V. V. Vishnevskii, President of the Slavonic Foundation of Kyrgyzstan, *Chuiskie Izvestiia*, 1–7 May 1993, p. 5; *Slavianskie Vesti* no. 9, May 1992, p. 2.
28. A citizenship law for the Kirgizian SSR was passed in August 1990, and of course allowed for dual citizenship in the sense that all citizens of the Soviet republics were automatically citizens of the Soviet Union. (See *Sovetskaia Kirgizia*, 4 September 1990.) Such laws from the Soviet period most Kyrgyz today consider obsolete. The new Kyrgyzstani Constitution explicitly rejects dual citizenship.
29. *Slavianskie Vesti*, 1992, no. 9, May 1992, p. 2.
30. See Theodor Hanf, 'Reducing conflict through cultural autonomy: Karl Renner's contribution', in Uri Ra'anan, Maria Mesner, Keith Armes and Kate Martin (eds), *State and Nation in Multi-ethnic Societies*, Manchester, 1991, pp. 33–52.

the access of Jews to higher offices. Proportional ethnic representation has been suggested by Russian-diaspora communities in few other Soviet successor states.[31] The reason why it has come to the fore in Kyrgyzstan is probably very simple: in few other post-Soviet countries have the prerogatives and special place of the titular nationality in official political life been more strongly emphasised. The more insistently the majority nation advances an ethnic rather than a civic state-concept, the less do the minorities believe that the state organs can be trusted to defend their interests without explicit consociational arrangements. Furthermore, only when the size of the non-titular ethnic community is relatively large as it is in Kyrgyzstan will such an arrangement give them any degree of political influence.

The language question.   The hottest issue in the Kyrgyzstani parliament as well as in public debate since independence has been the language question. No one denies that the Kyrgyz language is in a miserable state. Perhaps no other titular nation of a Soviet successor state has a less developed literary language – and it almost completely lacks appropriate terminology in a variety of technical areas. As a result, the scanty Kyrgyz intellectual élite have largely switched to Russian as their preferred medium of expression. The doyen of Kyrgyz literature, Chingiz Aitmatov, writes all his novels in Russian, and President Akaev is thoroughly steeped in Russian culture, and has a better command of Russian than Kyrgyz.[32] His vice-president Feliks Kulov, also an ethnic Kyrgyz, does not know the language of his nationality at all, and the same was true of several of the journalists whom we met. This situation fills Kyrgyz nationalists with rage. They denounce the linguistically de-nationalised élite as *mankurts* – people who have lost their ethnic identity.[33]

The concept of the *mankurt*, coined in 1982 by Aitmatov in the novel *The Day Lasts Longer than a Hundred Years*, was originally devoid of any ethnic or racist content. The novel described a Central Asian youth who had been captured in the distant past by a rival tribe and exposed to excruciating torture: a wet camel skin was glued to his head and caused indescribable pain when it dried and contracted under

31. One rare example was the Latvian interfront. See *Edinstvo* (Riga), 12–18 November 1990, p. 5.
32. *Slovo Kyrgyzstana*, 7 May 1993, p. 1.
33. See, e.g., a public statement from the 'Asaba' party, reprinted in *Slavianskie Vesti*, no. 9, May 1992, p. 3.

the scorching desert sun. The victim lost his memory, and indeed his entire personality. He no longer recognised his mother, and was turned into a zombie slave for his brutal masters.[34]

The concept of the *mankurt* has been adopted by nationalists not only in Kyrgyzstan but also in other former Soviet republics (such as Moldova and Tatarstan)[35] to denounce co-nationals who have abandoned their native tongue, married a Russian or in general anyone who is insufficiently nationalist by their standards. This polemical weapon seems to hit the mark, and the blow smarts. Some of the Kyrgyz intellectual élite do apparently accept the charge that they have betrayed their nation by adopting the Russian language, although in the existing circumstances this was the only way they could become an intellectual élite in the first place.

In 1989 a language law was adopted in the then Kirgiz SSR,[36] which defined Kirgiz as the state language, and Russian as a 'language of inter-ethnic communication', – the standard formula of the time. Today, the law is contemptuously brushed aside by Kyrgyz activists as one of the monstrosities of the Communist era; and indeed the new constitutional drafts have made no references to any 'language of inter-ethnic communication'. Instead, it was stated that the Kyrgyzstani republic would show 'state concern' for the equal and free development of all languages spoken by the country's people. The russophone community immediately demanded not only that the reference to the 'language of inter-ethnic communication' be reintroduced but also that Russian be elevated to the status of second state language.[37] Somewhat sarcastically, it was suggested that if Akaev really wanted to turn Kyrgyzstan into 'a new Switzerland', he could perhaps start by studying Swiss language policy.[38]

In the end, the pleas for a special status for Russian were rejected by the Kyrgyzstani legislators by 149 to 117 votes.[39] However, it

34. Chingiz Aitmatov, *I dol'she veka dlitsia den'*, Moscow, 1982.
35. B. Georgita, 'Politika denatsionalizatsii', *Moldova Suverena Digest*, 6 November 1992; author's interview with Khazbulat Shamsutdinov, the editor of *Vecherniaia Kazan'*, at Kazan', 4 November 1991.
36. For the text of the law, see *Vedomosti Verkhovnogo Soveta Kirgizskoi SSR*, Frunze, no. 17 (949), 1989, pp. 547–53.
37. See e.g. *Slavianskie Vesti*, no. 9, May 1992, p. 2.
38. *Slovo Kyrgyzstana*, 24 February 1993. The four official languages in Switzerland are German, French, Italian and Rheto-Romani.
39. *Svobonye Gory*, no. 32, May 1993, p. 3.

was decided to insert a new clause declaring that 'no-one can be discriminated against on the basis of not speaking or not understanding the state language' – a formula which, it was asserted, provides better protection for the linguistic minorities than any muddled references to a 'medium of inter-ethnic communication'. This may well be true, but the issue has long since left the arena of jurisprudence and been turned into a matter of trust or distrust.[40] If, as the Russians pointed out, the inclusion of the phrase 'language of inter-ethnic communication' really made no difference, why then did the representatives of the titular nation insist on having it thrown out of the legal texts? The Russians suspected that since the language law requires them to know the state language, Kyrgyzstani courts will not consider it as 'discrimination' if they are fired for their lack of fluency in it.[41]

At the time of writing, the effects of the Kyrgyzstani language law on administration and education in the republic remain unclear. Many stipulations will be effective only in 1997 and some as late as the year 2000.[42] In principle all higher education and all official correspondence are set to switch to Kyrgyz within less than a decade. But many observers fear that because of these changes, a whole generation of Kyrgyzs will end up as illiterates. There is simply no money in the state treasury to pay for the printing of Kyrgyz textbooks, especially since a brand new terminology will have to be worked out for many subjects first.[43] The Kyrgyzstani economy is in a shambles, and it appears that the country's exit from the ruble zone in May 1993 did not arrest the slump but probably aggravated it.

In anticipation of these difficulties, it was decided to establish a Russian-Kyrgyz (Slavonic) University under the joint auspices of the Kyrgyzstani and Russian governments. This university was an extremely controversial idea, and several Kyrgyz nationalist organisations protested vehemently against it.[44] This may appear strange since the main purpose of the university is to cater to the needs of the ethnic Kyrgyzs not the Russian part of the population (again we see a distinction between the various ethnic groups being made in official

40. *Slovo Kyrgyzstana*, 7 May 1993, p. 1.
41. *Slovo Kyrgyzstana*, 12 March 1993.
42. *Res Publica*, 8 May 1993, p. 1.
43. *Slovo Kyrgyzstana*, 10 March 1993; Author's interview with Al'bert Bogdanov, correspondent for the BBC and TASS, Bishkek, May 1993.
44. TASS (Bishkek), 30 September and 2 October 1992; *Komsomol'skaia Pravda*, 30 September 1992.

documents). The university is intended to offer Kyrgyz youth a first-class education, in Russian, in those special subjects for which there is particularly strong demand in the republic. It is only a secondary objective to 'satisfy the linguistic and cultural needs of the Russians and other russophone citizens'.[45] However, it seems that the very priorities of this programme are offensive to Kyrgyz nationalists since they are seen as perpetuating the existence of a russified Kyrgyz élite.

Organising the Russians for a fight or for flight?   The freedom of expression in pluralistic Kyrgyzstan, which gives all groups an opportunity to elaborate their viewpoints and arguments openly, has not brought about a genuine dialogue between the various nationalities. Rather, one gets the impression that the situation has deepened mutual mistrust by giving publicity to extremist groups. The growing polarisation of political life in Kyrgyzstan on ethnic lines is likely to be the outcome of the ongoing dual process of democratisation and 'national renaissance', and this development can only be damaging to the Russians and other minorities. This, incidentally, seems to be one of the reasons why so many Russians in Uzbekistan, Turkmenistan and other post-Soviet Asian states do not regret too much the absence of democracy. They are afraid not only of the Tajikistani but also the Kyrgyzstani scenario. From an each-man-for-himself democracy in an ethnically polarised society devoid of any minority guarantees they have nothing to gain.

However, the Russians in Kyrgyzstan have no choice. If they want to stay, they will have to play by the rules as they currently are. Some draw the conclusion that they 'have to get politicised',[46] but they also realise that a 'party of ethnic accord' rather than a narrowly 'Russian party' is what would serve their interests best.

In 1993 the leading organisations of the Russians in Kyrgyzstan were all still cultural centres or other such public societies, rather than political parties. The most important among them was the 'Slavonic Foundation' of Kyrgyzstan, the local branch of the Moscow-based 'International Slavonic Foundation of Letters and Culture'. The Kyrgyzstani body started out as a cultural centre, but it is becoming

45. 'Ukaz ob uchrezhdenii v gor. Bishkeke Kyrgyzsko-rossiiskogo (Slavianskogo) universiteta', *Slavianskie Vesti*, no. 18, October 1992, p. 2.
46. Iu. Blium, 'Gde takaia partiia?', *Slovo Kyrgyzstana*, 28 November 1992, p. 6.

increasingly involved in political and social issues.[47] One of its main objectives is the 'coordination of efforts for the legal and social protection of the diaspora'.[48] The Foundation has tried vigorously but unsuccessfully to influence the legislative process in the young Kyrgyzstani state.

The Foundation has also been helping those Russians who want to migrate to Russia. It has been criticised from within the local Russian community for performing the task with insufficient professionalism,[49] to which it has replied with obvious indignation that it does not wish to be seen as a travel bureau,[50] its primary objective being to help the Russians fight for their rights, not flee. Other Russian organisations in Kyrgyzstan, however, have fewer qualms about arranging transport for Russians leaving the republic. The Semirech'e company (*tovarishchestvo*) is suspected by some observers of trying to turn the migration issue into big business.[51]

In the southern town of Jalal-Abad the local organisation of the russophones, the 'Slavonic Diaspora',[52] explicitly discourages Russians from leaving. A public statement made by the organisation in May 1993 pointed out that many of those leaving the country have later returned. The main reason for this, Slavonic Diaspora believes, lies in the great cultural differences between heartland Russians and the Russian diaspora. 'For people who have a completely different mentality it is very difficult to adapt to a new life situation. More often than not, those who migrate to their historic fatherland are perceived as aliens.'

The leaders of 'Slavonic Diaspora' describe the inter-ethnic situation in the republic as 'basically stable'. 'We are not witnessing any massive

47. Author's interview at the Slavonic Foundation's headquarters, Bishkek, May 1993. Not only Slavs but also members of other ethnic groups are rallying around the Foundation for the defence of their interests.
48. 'Ustav Slavianskogo Fonda v Kyrgyzstane' (mimeo), adopted on 18 July 1991.
49. 'Migratsiia russkikh: Vzgliad prichastnykh k protsessu', *Res Publica*, 3–10 March 1993.
50 'Kazhdyi vybiraet dlia sebia', *Slavianskie Vesti*, 7 April 1992; *ibid.*, no. 18, October 1992, p. 2.
51. *Literaturnaia Gazeta*, 26 August 1992; interview with V. Grinchenko, leader of the private migration office 'Semirech'e', Kyrgyztag-TASS, Bishkek, 21 July 1992.
52. The originally proposed name was the 'Association of National Minorities', but a bench proposal at the founding session changed it to 'the Slavonic Diaspora'. See *Res Publica*, 15 May 1993, p. 3.

persecution or discrimination on the basis of ethnicity.' However, they believe that if the exodus of Russians is to be stemmed, substantial changes must be made to the Kyrgyzstani language policy: 'Legal articles will not compel all the Russians to learn the state language. The learning process must be gradual and consistent and start with the children.'

Kazakhstan

The Kazakh nation was more thoroughly decimated than any other major Soviet nationality during collectivisation and the ensuing famine in the 1930s. Between 1926 and 1939 the ethnic Kazakh population in the republic decreased from 3.7 to 2.3 million – that is, by an astonishing 38%.[53] This was the result partly of emigration (flight to China and Mongolia) but mostly of death by starvation and execution. In the wake of this, Kazakhstan became the only Union republic in which the titular nation was in a minority: 38% as against 40% Russians. After the great influx of Slavic settlers under the Virgin Soil programme of the 1950s, the Kazakhs' share of the population fell even further, to 30% in 1959, while the Russians' share rose to 42.4%.[54] The first secretaries of the Kazakh Communist party in the 1930s and 1950s were Europeans: F. Goloshchekin, P. Ponomarenko and L. Brezhnev.[55] Many Kazakh nationalists have therefore blamed their misfortune not only on the Communist system but also on the Russians.

In the early 1980s the Kazakhs were able to catch up with and overtake the Russians as the largest ethnic group in the republic, but in 1989 the Russians still remained the majority in a number of northern and eastern oblasts: Northern Kazakhstan (62%), Eastern Kazakhstan (66%), Karagandy (52%), Kokshetau (40%), Kustanai (44%), Pavlodar (45%) and Akmola (Tselinograd, 45%). In the capital

---

53. *Kazakhstan v Tsifrakh*, Almaty, 1993, p. 8.
54. Simon, *op. cit.*, p. 383, Table A.2.
55. If we may believe certain Russian nationalists in Kazakhstan today, Goloshchekin was not a Russian but a Russified Jew. These nationalists thus want to shift the blame for the Kazakh holocaust onto the Jews (see *Russkii Vestnik*, organ of the Russian cultural centre in Almaty, no. 1, 1992, pp. 2–3). This is to miss the point no less fundamentally than do the Kazakh nationalists. Whatever his nationality, Goloshchekin was first and foremost a Communist *apparatchik*, and acted in that capacity.

Alma-Ata (Almaty), the Kazakhs in 1989 were no more than 22% of the population, against 59% for the Russians.[56]

The Russians in Kazakhstan have the dubious distinction of being less versed in the titular language of the republic than their co-nationals in any other Union republic: less than 1% claimed fluency in 1989. This is due both to the strong concentration of Russians in many Slav-dominated areas and also to the low status of the Kazakh language in the Soviet Union. While 98.6% of the Kazakhs in 1989 claimed Kazakh as their mother tongue, Kazakh intellectuals today claim that only 60% of the Kazakh youth can read and write it fluently.[57]

Under *perestroika*, inter-ethnic relations in Kazakhstan got off to a bad start. The first sign that Gorbachev's reforms might lead to ethnic turmoil was the riot in Alma-Ata in December 1986 when the Kazakh party's first secretary, D. Kunaev, was sacked and replaced by an ethnic Russian, Gennadii Kolbin, drafted in from Moscow. To be sure, Kunaev, one of Brezhnev's cronies, had been thoroughly corrupt himself, and although his dismissal was not ethnically motivated, it was nonetheless seen by large parts of the ethnic Kazakh population as an affront to their nation and a clear breach of the unwritten rules of the Brezhnevite system of 'live-and-let-live'. Details of the riot and the crack-down after it were hushed up, and the exact number of deaths is impossible to estimate.[58]

The December tragedy, however, remained a relatively isolated event. The only other serious instance of ethnically motivated violence in the *perestroika* period took place in the town of Novyi Uzen' by the Caspian Sea in the summer of 1989, and involved various Caucasian ethnic groups and not Slavs. Shortly afterwards, Kolbin was replaced by an ethnic Kazakh, Nursultan Nazarbaev, who soon earned respect and confidence among almost all segments of the population as a judicious and skillful politician.[59] While he had made his career in the party, he was not a scion of the *nomenklatura*. He tried to champion the cause of Kazakh culture and language in Kazakhstani society without alienating the large non-titular communities.

56. Chauncy D. Harris, 'The New Russian Minorities: a Statistical Overview', *Post-Soviet Geography*, XXXIV (January 1993), pp. 1–27, on pp. 13ff.

57. A. Kaidarov, 'Esli ischeznet iazyk . . .', *Kazakhstanskaia Pravda*, 15 October 1992.

58. Martha Brill Olcott, 'Kazakhstan: a republic of minorities', in Ian Bremmer and Ray Taras (eds.) *Nations and Politics in the Soviet Successor States*, Cambridge, 1993, pp. 313–30, on p. 317.

59. *Moskovskie Novosti*, 1991, no. 50, 15 December, p. 5.

Many of the circumstances singled out in Chapter 5 to explain the confrontational ethnic policy of the Estonian and Latvian governments in the post-Soviet period are also present in Kazakhstan, and to a much higher degree: dramatic demographic upheavals in the Soviet period, a strong language barrier and plenty of reason for the ethnic Kazakhs to feel victimised. It is therefore somewhat surprising to find that a radically different ethnic policy is pursued by the Kazakh leadership from what has been seen in the Baltic. More than most other Soviet successor states the state authorities in Kazakhstan have tried to formulate a policy of inclusive civic nation-state-building.

The language question. The most formidable problem Nazarbaev had to face was the language question. In August 1989, only two months after his inauguration, a new Kazakhstani language law was passed.[60] It was probably the most liberal of the myriad of language laws passed in the Soviet Union during that year. While the first article declared the Kazakh language to be the state language, the next one added that 'In the Kazakh SSR Russian is a/the language of inter-ethnic communication.'[61] The Kazakh SSR provided for the free functioning of Russian on a par with the state language, and it was even added, somewhat paternalistically but probably quite correctly: 'It is in the interest of the representatives of all ethnic groups in the republic to know Russian.' The law also stated that in regions where a certain national group lives in compact communities, the language of that group can be elevated to the status of a local official language.

A programme for the introduction of Kazakh into the sphere of official administration was introduced in July 1990. Different timetables for transition to the state language were set up for the various oblasts. After some bickering, it was decided that Russian-dominated regions would merely have to provide Kazakh-language services by 1 January 1995; and that only by 1 January 2000 would they have to switch to a fully bilingual administration.[62] This goal, it seems, is being approached at a snail's pace, and is considered by many Kazakhstanis to be quite unrealistic.[63]

60. 'Zakon Kazakhskoi SSR o iazykakh v Kazakhskoi SSR'; mimeograph.
61. Because Russian does not have definite and indefinite articles, it is difficult to determine whether 'a' or 'the' is the correct translation.
62. Brill Olcott, *op. cit.*, p. 320.
63. Author's interview with Gennadii Tolmachëv, editor-in-chief of *Narodnyi Kongress*, Almaty, 22 May 1993.

In the spring of 1992 a large poll – including almost 1.5 million interviews – showed that 17% of all non-Kazakhs, taken together, claimed knowledge of the Kazakh language. However, the proportion among the Russians at this juncture still stood at only 2%. In several northern oblasts, hardly any efforts had been made by the local authorities to implement the language programme despite pressure from the capital. The pollsters explained this failure as a result not only of a deplorable lack of interest among the Slavs in learning Kazakh but also of the acute shortage of Kazakh teachers and textbooks.[64]

The language controversy gained fresh impetus when the drafts for a new constitution were debated in the autumn of 1992. The champions of a Kazakh-language renaissance feared that the provisions of the new language law would hardly make any impact upon the solid domination of Russian, and therefore demanded that they should be tightened. The president of the semi-official 'Kazak Tili' ('Kazakh Language') society wanted to have the reference to Russian as the 'language of inter-ethnic communication' deleted: the president thought the constitution should say no more than that 'Kazakh is the state language'.[65] Nazarbaev admitted that the phrase 'inter-ethnic communication' lacks any clear legal content; the people themselves would always decide which language they preferred to use as a *lingua franca* whenever they met, no matter what was said in the law. However, the important task here was to raise the prestige of Kazakh, not to lower the prestige of Russian – which, he pointed out, is after all one of the official languages of the United Nations.[66]

However, Nazarbaev also came under pressure from the Russian community. Russian activists complained not about the language law as such but about what they saw as 'an extremely free interpretation of the law in many ministries and departments'.[67] In December 1992 Russian medical workers in the southern city of Shymkent complained that they were threatened with exclusion – a kind of *Berufsverbot* – if they did not learn the state language. They pointed to a circular from the oblast health authorities which stated that 'where promotion to leading posts is concerned, besides the applicants' professional, practical and moral qualities, serious attention should be paid also to their

64. 'Kak izuchaiutsia iazyki', *Sovety Kazakhstana*, 22 April 1992, p. 2.
65. Kaidarov, *op. cit.*
66. *Kazakhstanskaia Pravda*, 11 November 1992, p. 1.
67. *Ibid.*, 17 September 1992, p. 2.

command of the state language.'[68] On 7 December 1992, 15,000 demonstrators in northern Kazakhstan demanded that Russian should be recognised not only as a language of inter-ethnic communication but also as a second state language.[69] However, Nazarbaev fended off the attacks from both quarters. The Kazakhstani Constitution, adopted on 28 January 1993, retains the reference to Russian as the 'language of inter-ethnic communication', and also contains a clause prohibiting the restriction of anyone's rights or freedoms on the grounds that he or she does not know either the state language or the language of inter-ethnic communication.[70] These formulations were adopted by an overwhelming majority in the legislature: 276 out of 298 votes.[71]

A special commission for the implementation and supervision of the language law was set up in April 1993, apparently to ensure both that overzealous Kazakh bureaucrats do not rush ahead of the law and that it is not sabotaged by the Russians.[72] It will not be an easy job. Unless every official document in Kazakhstan is duplicated in both Russian and Kazakh, it is hard to see how the introduction of Kazakh into administration can come about without at least some rolling back of Russian.

A Kazakhstani state ideology. Martha Brill Olcott has remarked that up till 1992 Nazarbaev tried to avoid confrontation on the ethnic issue by asserting that Kazakhstan is both a multinational society and at the same time a homeland for the ethnic Kazakhs.[73] He had, in a sense, tried to avoid making a choice between an ethnic and a civic state-concept and indeed the duality inherent in the official definition of Kazakhstan as a state was lucidly expressed by the president in a speech to a congress of the Kazak Tili society in November 1992: 'We should not forget that the sovereignty of Kazakhstan is in many ways special. First and foremost it is a peculiar synthesis of the national sovereignty

68. *Iuzhnyi Kazakhstan*, 5 December 1992.
69. 'Weekly Review', *RFE/RL Research Report*, I, 50 (18 December 1992), pp. 73–4; *Kazakhstanskaia Pravda*. 25 September 1992.
70. 'Konstitutsiia respubliki Kazakhstan, *Mysl'* (Almaty), no. 4, 1993, pp. 3–17, on p. 3.
71. *Emigratsiia* (Moscow), no. 7, February 1993, p. 3.
72. *Sovety Kazakhstana*, 6 April 1993.
73. Brill Olcott, *op. cit.*, p. 315.

of the Kazakhs and the sovereignty of the people of Kazakhstan in general as an ethnopolitical community.'[74]

Actually, this situation is not peculiar to Kazakhstan. Basically it presents the dilemma that has confronted all leaders in the post-Soviet states, only few of them have had the boldness or insight to present it so clearly. However, while Nazarbaev has certainly recognised this ambiguity in the Kazakhstani state-concept, he has not been able to overcome it. This is apparent in the new constitution. As in the constitutions of Kyrgyzstan and Uzbekistan, the constitutional preamble opens with a reference to 'We, the people [*narod*] of Kazakhstan', and many Russian Nazarbaev supporters regard these words as the most crucial part of the document.[75] Those russophones who are less happy with the present state of affairs, however, point to Article 1, which proclaims the republic of Kazakhstan as 'the form of statehood of the Kazakh nation [*natsiia*]'. Writing in a leading Moscow newspaper in August 1993, an Almaty professor claimed that 'In other words, "the people of Kazakhstan" means the ethnic Kazakhs only.'[76] This is clearly a misreading. Nonetheless, official spokesmen maintain that whatever else Kazakhstan is, it is also a national state of the Kazakhs. This is accepted and defended by liberal Kazakhstani Russians, who argue that the Russians in Kazakhstan have their historical fatherland, Russia, to fall back on, and that the Germans may go to Germany, but that the Kazakhs have only Kazakhstan. The titular nation should be entitled to certain privileges.[77]

This view is reflected in several Kazakhstani laws, and in other official documents. The law on citizenship, for instance, does not allow dual citizenship for any groups other than ethnic Kazakhs living abroad.[78] This special arrangement is defended as being necessary to redress the historic injustice done to the Kazakh nation in the Soviet period when hundreds of thousands of Kazakhs fled to China and Mongolia to escape collectivisation. It is estimated that 3.3 million

---

74. *Kazakhstanskaia Pravda*, 28 November 1992.
75. Author's interview with Gennadii Tolmachëv, editor-in-chief of *Narodnyi Kongress*, at Almaty, 22 May 1993.
76. V. Moiseev, 'Ne inostrantsy, no i ne svoi', *Rossiiskaia Gazeta*, 27 August 1993, p. 7.
77. Author's interviews with Gennadii Tolmachëv and K. S. Smailov.
78. 'Zakon o grazhdanstve respubliki Kazakhstan', *Vedomosti Verkhovnogo Soveta Kazakhskoi SSR*, no. 52, 1991, p. 81–96. See also the 'Konstitutsiia respubliki Kazakhstan', *Mysl'* (Almaty), no. 4, 1993, pp. 3–17, Article 4.

ethnic Kazakhs live outside Kazakhstan today: 1.8 million in the former Soviet Union and 1.5 million in the rest of the world.[79] These groups are granted special privileges in the law on immigration,[80] which empowers the president to stipulate strict yearly quotas of immigrants, and to set detailed guidelines on the countries from which the immigrants may come, the regions where they are free to settle, the professions in which they can be employed etc. At the same time, it is stated that 'fellow citizens who live abroad may freely return to their historic fatherland, the Republic of Kazakhstan.' 'Fellow citizens' here means 'ethnic Kazakhs' – see the citizenship law.[81] In 1992, some 30,000 Kazakhs in Mongolia availed themselves of this opportunity and moved to Kazakhstan.[82]

Some Russians claim to see a connection between the immigration of Kazakhs and the emigration of Russians. The latter are allegedly being forced out to make room for the newcomers. An article in the newspaper of the Russian supreme soviet, *Rossiiskaia Gazeta* in 1993 intimated that there was indeed such a connection.[83] However, this insinuation was refuted by the facts given in the very article itself: while 128,000 Russians left Kazakhstan in 1992, almost as many, 122,000, moved in. Still, a general ambiguity in the state concept remains. The suspicion among Russians that the balance might be tipping in favour of the Kazakh-homeland variant of the concept is nurtured also by the ongoing campaign to rename Kazakhstani towns, raions, streets etc., affecting not only cities and streets named after Communist leaders and such like but also traditional non-political Russian place-names in compactly Slavic regions.[84]

However, a step away from the 'Kazakh homeland' state concept nonetheless seemed to be taken in 1993. On 11 May, Nazarbaev convened a large conference in Almaty devoted to the question 'Does

---

79. *Sovety Kazakhstana*, 3 October 1992.
80. 'Zakon Respubliki Kazakhstan ob immigratsii', *Sovety Kazakstana*, 25 August 1992, p. 2.
81. Similar regulations may be found in the legislation of certain Western countries, namely Germany and Greece, but this does not make the principle any less ethnic.
82. *Sovety Kazakhstana*, 5 August 1993, p. 2.
83. Sergei Skorokhodov, 'My vas ne zhdali i ne derzhim', *Rossiiskaia Gazeta*, 16 September 1993. For a repudiation of such allegations, see *Kazakhstanskaia Pravda*, 3 September 1992.
84. See *Kazakhstanskaia Pravda*, 17 September 1992; *Sovety Kazakhstana*, 14 May 1993, p. 1.

Kazakhstan need a state ideology?'[85] 'Ideology' was one of the words that came to be thoroughly discredited in the former Soviet Union after the fall of Communism, and most political leaders in the successor states now shy away from it. However, Nazarbaev answered the question affirmatively. In his keynote speech to the conference, which in the old Soviet style was reproduced verbatim by all major Kazakhstani newspapers, he fleshed out the main goals and elements of the new ideology.[86] A major objective behind it, he declared, was 'to combat all chauvinism, nationalism and separatism'. This, he said, should be done by the inculcation of 'Kazakhstani patriotism':

> In the world there are quite a few states, even very prosperous ones, which contain more different nations and nationalities than we have in Kazakhstan. In these countries patriotism is especially strongly developed. A devotional attitude towards the state symbols reigns in society. For instance, at the beginning of the school day, during the swearing in of a jury or an official, and at many other events and mass gatherings the state flag is flown and the national anthem played.

Although some Kazakhstani commentators felt that this ideology smacked of the old Soviet Union,[87] clearly the prototype that Nazarbaev had in mind was the United States,[88] a multinational country in which a strong sense of political patriotism goes hand in hand with a strong non-political cultivation of 'ethnic roots'. However, it is doubtful whether Kazakhstan can really look to for a viable model to the United States, where no major ethnic group is indigenous and thus able to claim any special rights or any special attachment to the territory and the state in the way that most Kazakhs do in Kazakhstan.

Cultural organisations and political parties. The Nazarbaev regime is actively mobilising popular support in favour of Kazakhstani multinational patriotism. In the President's vision the Kazakhstani civic society ought, as it were, to consist of two tiers: a 'lower' level consisting of

---

85. 'Does Kazakhstan need state ideology?', *Kazakhstan*, 19 May 1993, p. 1.
86. *Sovety Kazakhstana*, 13 May 1993; *Znamia Truda* (Jambul), 13 May 1993; *Aziia*, May 1993.
87. *Novoe Pokolenie* (Almaty), 19 May 1993.
88. The importance of this prototype was confirmed to the author by K. S. Smailov, chairman of the Committee on Nationality Questions in the Kazakhstani parliament.

various non-political cultural centres and communities, and organised largely along ethnic lines, and a 'higher' level consisting of supra-ethnic political parties. However, only to a limited extent has this vision been realised. Most of the new political parties in Kazakhstan are basically mono-ethnic, and some cultural organisations are clearly involved in politics.[89] Nonetheless, quite a number of them are not, such as the 'Southern Kazakhstan Centre of Slavic Culture' in Shymkent.[90] The activities of this centre are aimed at the preservation and development of national self-awareness, and the national languages, culture, traditions, rituals and mores, and 'the sports of the Slavonic nationalities', and at drawing Slavs into the process of democratisation.[91] However, its counterpart in the north-eastern city of Ust-Kamenogorsk has issued statements in the right-wing Moscow press accusing the Kazakhstani authorities of establishing a mono-ethnic totalitarian state. It has also appealed to the Russian parliament not to ratify the Russian–Kazakhstani bilateral agreement signed by Yeltsin and Nazarbaev on 25 May 1992.[92]

Several public organisations, such as the nationalist Azat movement, are also engaged in political activities on the Kazakh side. Particularly disturbing to the Russians are the activities of the 'Alash' political party, which propagates a variant of Islamic fundamentalism and calls for the expulsion of all Russians from Kazakhstan.[93] Its propaganda drove some concerned Russians to establish the officially inter-ethnic but basically Slavic Edinstvo (Unity) movement as a kind of counterweight.[94]

Kazakhstani political parties and public organisations may be denied official registration (and thus effectively outlawed) if they propagate or practise racial, ethnic, social or religious intolerance, make public appeals for the violent overthrow of the constitutional regime, or

89. James Critchlow, 'Kazakhstan: the Outlook for Ethnic Relations', *RFE/RL Research Report*, I, 31 January 1992, pp. 34–9.

90. *Iuzhnyi Kazakhstan*, 10 November 1992.

91. 'Ustav Iuzhno-Kazakhstanskogo slavianskogo kul'turnogo tsentra', 11 December 1991: typescript.

92. *Russkii Vestnik* (Moscow), no. 27, 17–27 July 1992. For the text of the bilaterial agreement, see *Sovety Kazakhstana*, 23 July 1992.

93. Bess Brown, 'Kazakhstan and Kyrgyzstan on the Road to Democracy', *RFE/RL Research Report*, I, 48 (4 December 1992), pp. 20–22.

94. See, for instance, an appeal published in *Literaturnaia Rossiia*, no. 19, 27 March 1992.

challenge the territorial integrity of the Kazakhstani state.[95] Edinstvo is one of the organisations which have been denied registration, which some Russians see as evidence of a deliberate anti-Russian policy. They point out that certain Kazakh nationalist organisations such as Azat continue to operate freely.[96] To be sure, the Kazakhstani law on public organisations has not been rigorously enforced, and official tolerance of Kazakh nationalist organisations has been fairly high – although, for instance, Alash has been banned and its demonstrations disrupted (in one incident a tented camp of Kazakh nationalists set up outside the parliament building was removed). However, several Russian organisations have also benefited from the relative leniency of the Kazakhstani authorities. In Almaty the Russian cultural centre is officially registered and operates freely, although its leaders are actively engaged in right-wing politics. The monthly newspaper of the centre reprints articles from the leading reactionary Moscow newspaper *Den'*, and is distributed together with material from Aleksandr Sterligov's rightist movement *Russkii sobor*. The chairperson of the centre is open in not recognising the legitimacy of Kazakhstani statehood.[97] Nonetheless, the present author received free tickets to a concert organised by the Russian centre from an official in the Almaty city administration. The concert was devoid of political propaganda except that the stage was adorned with the yellow, black and white monarchist Russian flag.[98] The performance was of a high quality, which indicates that the centre takes its commitment to culture seriously.

A 'Russian community' (*Obshchina*) also operaties in Almaty with the blessing of the authorities. Its leaders are at loggerheads with the Russian cultural centre, although both belong to the same end of the political spectrum (the chairman, Iurii Bunakov, presented himself to the present author in plain terms as politically 'red–brown'). During the festive celebration of its official registration in September 1992, *Obshchina* received congratulatory telegrams from Russian right-wingers such as Aleksandr Prokhanov, Vasilii Belov and the editorial

95. 'Konstitutsiia respubliki Kazakhstan', *Mysl* (Almaty), no. 4, 1993, Article 55, p. 8; author's interview with deputy editor-in-chief of the Kazakhstani telegraph agency, Vladimir Akimov, at Almaty, 21 May 1993.
96. Moiseev, *op. cit.*; Iu. Kirinitsianov, in *Kazakhstanskaia Pravda*, 17 September 1992.
97. Author's interview with Nina Sidorova, at Almaty on 21 May 1993.
98. The official red–blue–white flag of the Russian Federation was, by the organiser of the concert, deemed to be masonic.

staff of *Literaturnaia Rossiia* as well as from the Almaty city administration.[99] This tolerance may be due to the fact that the community's activities are mainly concerned with mutual aid among its members rather than political lobbying.[100]

Three Cossack communities – the Ural, Orenburg and Siberian Cossacks – are historically located partly on Russian and partly on Kazakhstani territory; the Semirech'e Cossacks, on the other hand, are entirely Kazakhstan-based.[101] The reactions of the Kazakhstani authorities to certain of the Cossack societies' activities have been seen as evidence of an illiberal attitude towards their European citizens. Kazakh nationalists see these communities as 'fifth columns' whose loyalty is not towards Kazakhstan but towards Russia.[102] A statue of Ermak, the Cossack conqueror of northern Kazakhstan, has been torn down with the blessing of the authorities.[103] The Cossack communities are not allowed official registration because paramilitary formations are forbidden.[104] A court in northern Kazakhstan ruled that an organ of the Ural Cossacks should be closed down for violations of the Kazakhstani press law.[105] A Cossack meeting was broken up outside Pavlodar in the spring of 1993, and the organisers were given a token fine.[106] On the other hand, the Cossacks are not prevented from publicly donning their uniforms and their symbolic weapons in downtown Almaty.

The Nazarbaev regime apparently tries to steer a middle course between the authoritarianism of Islam Karimov in Uzbekistan and the

99. *Kazakhstanskaia Pravda*, 24 November 1992.

100. *Rossiiskaia Gazeta*, 12 January 1993.

101. Vladimir Seleznev, 'Kak zhivëtsia kazakam v blizhnem zarubezh'e', *Rossiiskie Vesti*, 18 March 1993.

102. See, e.g., *Aziia Dauysy*, no. 8, April 1993. Not only Kazakhs but also some local Russians view the activities of the Cossacks as potentially destabilising. See *Kazakhstanskaia Pravda*, 14 October 1992, p. 1. An opinion poll among youth in the north-eastern Akmonlinsk oblast during the summer of 1992 indicated that 30% were unfavourably disposed towards the Cossacks while only 8.8% were in favour. See *Sovety Kazakhstana*, 22 July 1992, p. 1.

103. *Literaturnaia Rossiia*. no. 17, 24 April 1992.

104 Author's interview with K. S. Smailov, chairman of the Committee on Questions of Language and Nationalities in the Kazakhstani Supreme Soviet, May 1993.

105. Author's interview with the deputy ataman of the Semirech'e Cossacks, Pëtr Kolomets, at Almaty, May 1993.

106. *Kazakhstanskaia Pravda*, 30 September 1992.

free-for-all liberalism of Akaev in Kyrgyzstan. While Karimov keeps the lid on the nationalist kettle so tightly that he risks a major explosion if the temperature inside rises any further, and while Akaev lets off so much nationalist steam that the country becomes clouded in it, Nazarbaev seems to allow the various semi-politicised cultural centres to function as safety valves, without letting them get out of control. However, the fate of Edinstvo suggests that no sooner do such organisations become truly influential in the russophone community than they are liable to be closed down.

Kazakhstani authorities try to influence the development of inter-ethnic relations in the country not only by regulating (i.e. condoning or prohibiting) the activities of their citizens but also with initiatives of its own. In December a large forum of the peoples of Kazakhstan was organised in Almaty with much aplomb.[107] Moreover, a special newspaper exclusively devoted to 'inter-ethnic communication' is now published in Almaty.[108] Nazarbaev has presided as a kind of 'godfather' over the party of 'the People's Congress of Kazakhstan'. A stated goal of this party is to give life to the idea of a unified Kazakhstani citizenry – a genuine people of Kazakhstan.[109] The leaders of the party are two prominent Kazakh writers, and most of those who attended the founding congress in October 1991 were ethnic Kazakhs.[110] A movement of 'the Unity of Kazakhstan's People' has also been established,[111] with a very similar programme to that of the the the People's Congress party, and overlapping membership. Both the Party and the Movement have yet to prove that they are capable of building bridges between the various ethnic groups in Kazakhstan.

Real or apparent stability? Many analyses of the political situation in Kazakhstan take as their starting point the view that the country represents an oasis of ethnic and social stability in a region otherwise characterised by growing tension and emigration. The somewhat smug

107. *Iuzhnyi Kazakhstan*, 5 December 1992; *Kazkhstanskaia Pravda*, 9 December 1992; *ibid.*, 15 December 1992.
108. *Kore-inform*. The print-run of the first issue was as low as 5,000, indicating that the owners did not foresee a particularly large circulation.
109 *Programma partii Narodnyi kongress Kazakhstana*, Taldy-Kurgan, 1992; *Narodnyi Kongress*, no. 1, 1993, p. 2.
110. James Critchlow, 'Kazakhstan and Nazarbaev: Political Prospects', *RFE/RL Research Report*, I, 17 January 1992, pp. 31–4.
111. *Kazakhstanskaia Pravda*, 21 November 1992, p. 1.

question of many Kazakh political experts is: What is the secret behind our tranquillity? Some of the answers given are: the Kazakhs' ability to endure hardship; the well-founded trust in the authorities among the great majority of the population; and the realisation that a breakdown of stability in Kazakhstan could lead to the kind of blood-shed caused by inter-ethnic conflicts in many other parts of the former Soviet periphery.[112] Somewhat more original, perhaps, are the reasons given by a Cossack deputy from the Kazakhstani Supreme Soviet. First, he points out that the main Kazakhstani communities – the Kazakhs and the russophones – are approximately equal in size and strength, and neither can hope to prevail over the other; and secondly, the poor communications infrastructure in this country – which is the size of Western Europe – makes the mobilisation of large parts of the population for political action extremely difficult.[113] The first of these arguments can be turned on its head: just because of their equal strength, neither of the groups will easily yield to the other if the worst should happen and tension should start to escalate. In such a situation the Russians might be expected to appeal to the support of Russian authorities across the border.

Many Western experts ask if the impression of a stable Kazakhstan is not in fact deceptive. Bess Brown, for example, sees the govern-ment's crackdown on certain unofficial groups in Almaty as a sign that inter-ethnic tension in the capital may be worse than the authorities are ready to admit.[114] Our Almaty taxi-driver, no less given to social analysis than his colleagues in other countries, claimed that for the Russians in southern Kazakhstan life had become 'abominable'. They do not dare to go out after dusk when Kazakh youth gangs hold sway in the streets. Furthermore, Russian supporters of Nazarbaev have confirmed that intolerance towards Europeans is a serious problem among segments of the Kazakh youth, especially in the larger cities.[115]

Such perceptions may obviously be influenced by personal factors. For example, the evaluation of the inter-ethnic situation by the chair-man of the Slavic cultural centre in Shymkent, where the Russians are

112. Deniz Balgamysh, in *Sovety Kazakhstana*, 17 February 1993, p. 2.
113. *Rossiiskaia Gazeta*, 20 February 1993. See, also, *Moscow News*, no. 40, 1990.
114. Bess Brown, *op. cit.*
115. Author's interview with Gennadii Tolmachëv at Almaty, May 1993.

in a decisive minority, was markedly different from the opinion of his wife. While he personally did not feel any overt discrimination or harassment, she did. This discrepancy was probably a reflection not of sex differences but of the fact that he had been born in Kazakhstan and was determined to stay there (and had therefore started the cultural centre), while she was not only an immigrant but also had a brother in Uzbekistan who fed her hair-raising stories about the ethnic situation there.[116]

An opinion poll among 500 residents of Almaty in June 1993 showed that while few people in the Kazakh capital were optimistic about inter-ethnic relations, even fewer were strongly pessimistic. The results of the poll showed a further gradual shift over time in the attitudes of the population away from both alarmist and over-sanguine positions towards the centre (see Table 9.1).

Table 9.1. EVALUATION OF INTER-ETHNIC
RELATIONS IN KAZAKHSTAN*

	1992	1993
Kazakhstan remains a country of friendship among the peoples	12.5	2.2
Inter-ethnic relations are pretty good	25.5	31.0
The situation is quite tolerable	42.0	52.2
Inter-ethnic relations are tense	14.2	10.6
The situation is explosive	1.7	1.6

Source: *Karavan* (Almaty), 25 June 1993, p. 4.[117]
* Among 500 respondents in Almaty, June 1993.

The most remarkable feature of the inter-ethnic scene in Kazakhstan is the contrast between the extremely high degree of upheaval and suffering in the past and the low degree of violence and tension in the present. Rather than see this as a paradox, we may interpret the latter condition as a consequence of the former one. Explaining Kazakh behaviour under Khrushchev and Brezhnev, Gerhard Simon has claimed that 'the terror of collectivization broke the Kazakhs'

116. Author's interview with Mr and Mrs Podushkin, Shymkent, 16 May 1993.
117. The sample of respondents in the poll was not random. The pollsters had tried to find as many Germans, Greeks and Jews as possible – the groups considered most likely to emigrate.

resistance and increased their willingness to live under the existing conditions and to use them to their own advantage.'[118] While this may be true, experience has also show that a once cowed and bullied slave who is put in a position of power often becomes a spiteful avenger. Vengeance, however, is not what has characterised the policy of the present-day Kazakhstani leadership, which rather seems to be based on a highly pragmatic assessment of the political situation in the post-Soviet successor states: ethnic peace is, in short, a necessary precondition for economic prosperity and international stature. As Nazarbaev himself has put it: 'Recognition of the equality of all the nationalities who are living in Kazakhstan is the way to make the Kazakh nation respected in the world ... Today, nobody wants to have economic relations with unstable regions.'[119] Also Nazarbaev fully realises that by endorsing the cause of special ethnic rights for the Kazakhs, he risks losing the northernmost half of the country.[120] All these factors predispose the Kazakh leadership to civic rather than ethnic approaches to nation-building.

118. Gerhard Simon, *Nationalism and Policy Towards the Nationalities in the Soviet Union*, Boulder CO, 1986/1991, p. 109.

119. *Komsomol'skaia Pravda*, 23 November 1991.

120. Jørn Holm-Hansen, 'Political Rhetoric in Nation-Building in Multi-Ethnic Societies: the Case of Kazakhstan', paper presented to NIAS Central Asia Workshop, Copenhagen 29–31 October 1993.

Part III

10

RUSSIA'S POLICY TOWARDS THE DIASPORA

by Andrei Edemsky and Paul Kolstoe

Terminology

In Russian foreign policy parlance the territory of the former Soviet Union outside Russia has been designated the 'near abroad' (*blizhnee zarubezh'e*). Some observers see the term both as an expression of neo-imperialist thinking and as an indication that Russian policy-makers are not prepared to acknowledge the full independence of the non-Russian Soviet successor states. The term has allegedly been invented in order to set these countries apart from the rest of the world.[1] Indeed, vestiges of imperial thinking are indeed to be found among segments of the Russian political élite, even in the liberal camp, but the term 'near abroad' should not necessarily be associated with it. In fact, most Russian neo-imperialists are loath to think of the Soviet successor states as an 'abroad' in any sense, near or far.

The term 'near abroad' must be understood against the background of the often centuries-old common statehood between Russia and these countries. This community of history has also produced a number of important common problems, such as their strongly integrated economy and defence systems, and the presence of substantial diasporas

---

1. See e.g. a statement by the Presidium of the Parliament of the Republic of Moldova, 16 October 1992: 'Having invented the term of the "near abroad" as a designation for the former colonies which today are independent states, the Russian Federation in reality divides the countries of the world into two categories: independent, and not so independent.' In a similar vein, John Lough has claimed that 'Relations with the "near abroad" countries, as their name implies, are not regarded as being "external"'. John B. K. Lough, 'The Place of Russia's "Near Abroad"', unpublished ms, RMA Sandhurst, 28 January 1993. p. 4. The present authors fail to see this implication.

on each other's territories. Not only Russia but all Soviet successor states are forced by sheer necessity to devote much attention to their relationships with each other.

The Russian policy towards the near abroad contains a number of facets, instruments and objectives. The concerns of the diaspora populations are only one of these, and far from always being the most important. Indeed, Russia's economic and security interests are often pursued quite independently of the diaspora issue. For instance, some of her most important military engagements in the near abroad have been in areas where the Russian demographic presence is minimal, such as South Ossetia and Abkhazia. It falls outside the scope of this book to give a comprehensive analysis of Russia's policy towards the near abroad, but the role of the diaspora issue as an element with in the overall framework of this policy should not forgotten.[2] It is also clear that during 1992–3 the various aspects of Russia's relations with the former Soviet republics, including the concern for the diaspora, were gradually converging into a more coherent policy-concept.

To designate 'Russia' in her relationship to the diaspora, the conventional Russian term 'historic homeland' (*istoricheskaia rodina* – meaning also 'historic mother country')[3] is used. This term does not seem to arouse much controversy. However, the same relationship seen from the opposite end, i.e. that of the diaspora, has not found any similarly accepted term. In the previous chapters, the members of the Russian diaspora have usually been referred to as 'ethnic Russians' or simply 'the Russians'. This defines them in *cultural* terms – through their relationship to the Russian ethnos at large, not through their relationship to the Russian state. Occasionally, these terms are also used in the Russian debate in discussion of Russia's policy towards the diaspora.[4] For several reasons, however, Russian journalists and politicians, especially

---

2. For good overviews of Russia's policy towards the non-Russian Soviet successor states, see John B. K. Lough, 'Defining Russia's Relations with Neighboring States', *RFE/RL Research Report*, II, 20 (14 May 1993), pp. 53–60; and Paul A. Goble, 'Russia and Its Neighbors', *Foreign Policy*, no. 90, spring 1993, pp. 79–88.

3. As a generalised designation for a 'parent country' in its relation to the diaspora, Rogers Brubaker has coined the term 'External National Homeland'. 'National Minorities, Nationalizing States, and External National Homelands', paper prepared for the American Sociological Association Annual Meeting, Miami, 17 August 1993.

4. See, e.g., Yeltsin's statement as quoted in *Izvestiia*, 8 July 1992: 'It is necessary to protect the Russians, and people of Russia (*russkikh, rossiian*), who live in the CIS countries, but they must be protected politically.'

in the liberal camp, often try to avoid the term 'Russians' when discussing Russia's relationship towards them. The reason for this seems to be that they want to take cognisance of the fact that Russia is a multinational state, and her diaspora populations are multinational also. They therefore eschew a term with an implicit ethnic or even nationalistic bias, and try instead to use substitute terms. One of them is 'citizens' (*grazhdane*). In the legal sense the meaning of this word is quite clear and unambiguous: it is an exclusively political concept, signifying simply those individuals who hold a Russian passport, independently of their geographical location, mother tongue or cultural self-perception.

The Russian citizenship law adopted in November 1991 states, as does similar legislation in most other countries, that Russian citizens abroad will enjoy the protection (*pokrovitel'stvo*) of the Russian state.[5] This proviso covers both those Russian citizens who are temporarily travelling abroad and those who are permanent residents of other countries, in both the near and far abroad. However, only a small fraction of the new Russian diaspora actually belong to this group. By the end of 1993, most diasporians had not obtained Russian citizenship, and probably would not do so for the foreseeable future.[6] However, the term *grazhdane* is not infrequently used by Russian politicians at the top level in a metaphorical and ambiguous sense, i.e. as identical in practice with 'the Russian diaspora'.[7]

A related and equally confusing term is '*sootechestvenniki*', literally 'fellow countrymen'. The core of this term is the political concept of the fatherland (*otechestvo*) rather than ethnicity. However, *sootechestvenniki* also include members of other autochthonous ethnic groups of present-day Russia living outside Russia, such as the Tatars in Central Asia and the Ossetians in Georgia. Furthermore, it is not limited to the near abroad but also covers old diaspora groups in Western Europe,

5. See *Vedomosti s"ezda narodnykh deputatov Rossiiskoi Federatsii i Verkhovnogo Soveta Rossiiskoi Federatsii*, no. 6, 1992, pp. 307–21.
6. For further details, see Chapter 11.
7. In May 1991, for instance, Boris Yeltsin stated that 'emigrants [*vykhodtsy*] from Russia live in all republics of the Union, and we will not abandon those of our citizens who live there to the mercy of fate.' This remark, however, was made before the break-up of the Soviet Union – i.e. before the adoption of citizenship laws in the independent Soviet successor states. See *Izvestiia*, 24 May 1991.

the Americas and other countries of the 'far abroad'.[8] One authority defined *sootechestvenniki* as 'persons who at one time were subjects of the Russian empire or citizens of the Soviet Union, together with their relatives in direct line of ascent, who at the present time do not hold Russian citizenship but belong to one of the ethnic groups of Russia, and who consider themselves as being spiritually and culturally-ethnically linked to Russia.'[9]

By this definition, the political relationship of the *sootechestvenniki* to Russia belongs to the past, while the present relationship is a *cultural* one. Nonetheless, as will be shown below, most users of the term maintain that Russia has a responsibility to protect its *sootechestvenniki* in the near abroad, and thus give the term a bearing on the contemporary political situation as well.

Two other terms are also used in the Russian debate on Russian diaspora policy to designate Russian communities living in the 'near abroad': *rosssiiane* and *russkoiazychnye* ('russophones'). *Rossiiane* literally means 'people of Russia', and one would perhaps expect it to be reserved only for permanent inhabitants of Russia.[10] In any case, the term is political (territorial) rather than cultural (ethnic). The inclusion of the russophones among diaspora appellations brings home the fact that for many russified Ukrainians, Belorussians and others in the Soviet successor states the only link to their ethnic homelands – Ukraine, Belarus and so on – is the fifth point in their passport. Culturally they orient themselves towards Russia, even though they do not belong to one of the autochthonous ethnic groups of the Russian Federation.[11] Finally, it could also be mentioned that the term used most frequently in the other Soviet successor states to designate the Russian diaspora communities – namely 'Russian national minorities' – is seldom found in the Russian debate. This term would define the Russians both politically in relation to their country of residence, and culturally in relation to the Russian group as a whole.

The terminological anarchy prevalent in the Russian debate on the diaspora reflects the political confusion on the issue. Everyone knows that 'out there' live millions of people who in some sense are linked

8. Interview with Mikhail Tolstoi, chairman of the Commission on the Russian Diaspora (*rossiiskogo zarubezh'e*) in the Russian Supreme Soviet, in *Delovoi Mir*, 20 March 1993.
9. Professor Igor Blishchenko, in *Izvestiia*, 8 September 1992.
10. See note 4.
11. Konstantin Pleshakov, in *Novoe Vremia*, no. 47, 1992, p. 10.

to Russia, who perhaps attach their hopes to her and who in some sense are her concern; but it has proved extremely hard to define the exact criteria for membership of this group, as well as the kind of relationship it should have with Russia.

There seems to have evolved a broad and loose consensus in Russian political circles that the various diaspora groups in the near abroad should be entitled to some kind of protection from Russia, but the arguments marshalled in favour of this view, and even more the means and ultimate end suggested for it, have varied drastically.

Before the break-up of the Union

The problem of the Russian diaspora was introduced into Soviet politics only in the latter years of the Communist regime, when the central authorities began to play 'the Russian card' to prevent the break-up of the unitary state. As the nationalist opposition gained strength in the non-Russian republics, Mikhail Gorbachev began to express explicit concern for the Russians living in those areas.[12] By contrast, during that period the diaspora question was not high on the agenda of anti-Gorbachev leadership in the Russian Federation. Up till the end of 1991, opposition to the Communist regime was the primary concern of the Yeltsin group, which seemed to have little time or energy to consider the problems that a possible break-up of the Soviet Union might entail for the diasporas. Every initiative of the Gorbachev leadership on the Union question was met by a counter-initiative from the Yeltsinites. For instance, when Gorbachev attempted to cast the Russians in Ukraine in the role of potential fifth-columnists by raising doubts about their future in an independent Ukrainian state, a bilateral treaty between Russia and Ukraine was signed in December 1990.[13] Another example was Yeltsin's statement

---

12. See Gorbachev's speeches in 1990 during his visit to Lithuania and at the USSR Komsomol congress. *Pravda*, 12 January 1990; and *ibid.*, 12 April 1990.
13. Roman Solchanyk, 'Ukraine. the (Former) Center, Russia and "Russia"', *Studies in Comparative Communism*, XXV, 1 (March 1992), pp. 31–45. Already, in August 1990, the 'Democratic Russia' bloc in the Russian Supreme Soviet, together with its counterpart in the Ukrainian parliamentary opposition in the Narodna Rada, had signed a Declaration of Principles of Inter-state Relations between Ukraine and the RSFSR, based on the respective Declarations of State Sovereignty. This served as the basis for the bilateral state treaty then signed on 19 November.

to *Izvestiia* in May 1991, when asked if the civil rights of the Russians in the Baltic states could be guaranteed if the latter became independent:

> First and foremost, tanks and violence cannot serve as guarantees ... The most important and natural guarantee for them will be the retention of solid and multifarious relations between Russia and the other republics. These relations should be built on a reliable legal foundation.[14]

This statement, of course, has to be read in conjunction with the activities of the Soviet army and OMON units in Vilnius and Riga three months earlier.

In its struggle against the Communist Union centre, the Yeltsin entourage at this time sought alliances with the national-democratic leaders in republics whose primary aim was full independence from Moscow, as in the Baltics.[15] During the most difficult times for these regimes, namely 1990–1, Yeltsin had extensive talks with those leaders, giving demonstrative support to their aims, while at the same time refusing to meet the leaders of pro-Union organisations of russophones in those countries.[16]

There are reasons to believe that the leaders of the RSFSR expected to be in opposition to Gorbachev for many years to come, and therefore did not develop their own vision of a post-Soviet society. Probably, the majority of Yeltsin's supporters had no intention of ruining the centre, but rather wanted to make it more democratic and decentralised. One indication of this was a statement by Yeltsin's foreign minister Andrei Kozyrev in June 1991. Outlining his assessment of Gorbachev's plans for a revamped union, he remarked: 'Borders between the republics may be altered but only through negotiations. However, it is not generally important which republic you are a citizen of.'[17] As concerns their policy towards the non-Russian areas of the Union, the Russian democrats had been elaborating a concept of regional policy within the Union framework. Undoubtedly Russian diaspora matters were on the margins of Russian politics.

In the immediate aftermath of the failed coup in August 1991, this attitude was not basically changed. Spokesmen the Yeltsin regime

---

14. *Izvestiia*, 24 May 1991.
15. Riina Kionka, 'Russia Recognizes Estonia's Independence', *Report on the USSR*, III, 5 (1 February 1991), pp. 14–16; Gytis Liulevicius, 'Lithuania Signs Treaty with Russia', *ibid.*, III, 34 (1991), pp. 19–20.
16. *Edinstvo*, (Riga), no. 27, 20–26 August 1990, p. 1.
17. *Literaturnaia Gazeta*, 12 June 1991.

clearly distanced themselves from the russophone leaders in such regions as the Dniester left bank and Eastern Estonia, whom they characterised as dyed-in-the-wool supporters of the *ancien régime* on a par with the Moscow putschists.[18]

After the break-up of the Union

In the winter of 1991 the Russian leadership tried to find a basis for a new identity for Russia in the renewal of the Slavic idea. This concept was embodied in the initial variant of the Commonwealth of Independent States (CIS) which consisted only of the three Slavic successor states. The architect behind this policy was State Secretary Gennadii Burbulis, who thought that in the long run Russia could become the leader of a new alliance of Slavic nations.[19] However, the Slavic CIS foundered; or rather, it was expanded finally into a looser and culturally more heterogeneous structure by the inclusion of Caucasian and Central Asian partners.

While this development probably made the CIS into a more unwieldy policy instrument than its Russian initiators had intended, it nonetheless had some positive effects for the Russian diaspora. Russians in Central Asia were now included in a common political framework with the mainland Russians, and questions concerning the protection of diaspora minorities could now be discussed in CIS forums. On the other hand very few CIS structures were created. Fearful lest the CIS should develop into a new Union of sorts, important Commonwealth members vetoed the establishment of a permanent CIS apparatus.

Contact among the member states was primarily maintained at the level of summit meetings. At one of these meetings, in Minsk in January 1993, it was decided in principle to establish a CIS court to arbitrate in inter-state and inter-ethnic conflicts. However, the CIS has an appallingly bad record of unfulfilled agreements – most of which have merely remained non-committal statements of good will. This appears also to be the case with the inter-ethnic court. In any case, the attention of Russian foreign policy-makers in the first years after

18. See, e.g., statements by Sergei Krasavchenko and Nikolai Medvedev, leaders of a Russian parliamentary commission sent to Moldova and Dniester in September 1991, as reported by *Nezavisimaia Gazeta*, 21 September 1991, p. 3.
19. Cf. Alexander Rahr, '"Atlanticists" versus "Eurasians" in Russian Foreign Policy', *RFE/RL Research Report*, I, 22 (29 May 1992), pp. 17–19.

1991 was directed not towards the 'near' but the 'far' abroad. Their primary aim was to develop relations with Western Europe and North America and to be integrated into the Western world.

Nevertheless, the presence of millions of people in the non-Russian Soviet successor states who are culturally and historically linked with Russia could not be ignored in the long run. The most important aspects of this situation which the Russian leadership had to take into consideration were:

(1) The attitudes towards the diaspora population among the citizens of the Russian Federation. The plight of their co-nationals outside Russia was gradually developing into one of the main concerns of the Russian public.[20] In an opinion poll in September–October 1991, almost 40% of the respondents believed that Russia should act as a guarantor of the rights and freedoms of the Russian-speaking populations in the near abroad (see Table 10.1).

(2) The danger that refugees from the near abroad could be harnessed by the ultra-nationalists in their struggle against the Yeltsin–Gaidar government. The Russian authorities feared that desperate Russian refugees might make common cause with equally disgruntled ex-Soviet troops returning from the same areas and from Eastern Europe. These social elements could coalesce into a strong movement and provide the basis for a new *coup d'état*.

(3) Expectations that the economically motivated return-migration of well-educated and resourceful diaspora Russians would contribute to the hoped-for economic revival of Russia. According to this view, a controlled migration to Russia would be an asset for the country and not a liability.[21]

(4) The possible repercussions which official support for the diaspora Russians might have on the relationship between the Moscow centre and the autonomous units within the Russian Federation. Russian

---

20. Authors' interview with Vladimir Kuznechevskii, head of the Sociological Laboratory Department of *Rossiiskaia Gazeta*, in October 1991. At that time, Kuznechevskii was close to Mikhail Poltoranin, an influential Yeltsin adviser.

21. See, e.g., a statement by Tat'iana Regent, head of the Russian Federal Migration Service, in *Argumenty i Fakty* no. 40, 1992, p. 4; *Izvestiia*, 29 June 1992; and the opinion of Galina Starovoitova, as expressed in *Literaturnaia Gazeta*, 9 October 1991. This viewpoint was possibly less prevalent among the Russian public than among people in government positions.

Table 10.1. ATTITUDES OF THE RUSSIAN PUBLIC TO THE DIASPORA QUESTION, OCTOBER 1991

Question

As a result of the proclamations of independence of the republics, tens of millions of the Russian-speaking population are now living abroad. What, in your opinion, should be the first-priority policy of Presiden Yeltsin with regard to these people?

Answers	%
Russia should act as a guarantor of their rights and freedoms.	39.5
Russia should give them the option of moving to the RSFSR.	12.3
Russia should insist that referendums be conducted in those regions where the Russian-speaking population live.	11.0
It is not necessary to do anything. Let those who live on the territory of other republics solve their own problems.	22.3

Source: *Rossiiskaia Gazeta*, 24 October 1991.

authorities realised that by putting pressure on their neighbours to grant special rights to minorities, or by recognising Russian-dominated secessionist regions such as Dniestria, they would make themselves vulnerable to similar secessionist movements in the various auto-nomous units within the Russian Federation, such as Tatarstan.

In a sense, the Yeltsin administration was caught between the ham-mer and the anvil. On the one hand, it was vulnerable to complaints from the nationalists and Communists both that it had already betrayed the interests of Russians in the near abroad by its part in the process leading up to the collapse of the Soviet Union and that it was continuing in the aftermath to betray their interests by adopting a passive stance on minority protection. On the other hand, any attempt by the Russian leadership to intervene in conflicts in the near abroad involving local russophone populations, with or without the use of military force, would foster an image of Russia trying to act as the policeman of the former Soviet Union. That would inevitably bring back memories of the Great Russian imperialism of bygone days. This was an image to which the Russian nationalists would have no objec-tion, but which would be strongly detrimental to Yeltsin's endeavours to be accepted into the international community of states.

Russia's leaders seemed to be at a loss what to do with the countries in the 'near abroad'. Many of them apparently clung to a hope that these countries would eventually be unable to resist the gravitational pull of Russia. Gennadii Burbulis, for one, believed in March 1992:

'The logic of things will bring [the former Soviet republics] back again our way. Europe will not take them as they are.'[22] Such expectations predisposed them to adopt a passive wait-and-see policy.

Key decision-makers

After 1991, a relatively limited number of important politicians were instrumental in the shaping of the Russian government's policy towards the russophone population in the near abroad: President Yeltsin himself, Foreign Minister Andrei Kozyrev, Presidential Adviser Sergei Stankevich, Vice-President Aleksandr Rutskoi, Chairman of the Committee for Foreign Policy and Foreign Economic Relations of the Russian Parliament Evgenii Ambartsumov, and Deputy Foreign Minister Fëdor Shelov-Kovediaev.

It seems clear that *President Yeltsin* was a pivotal actor in the process. Personal access to him was a key factor in policy-making. He wanted first and foremost to avoid taking any steps that could jeopardise Russia's attempts to be integrated into Western society on a basis of equality and partnership. On the issue of relations with the other Soviet successor states, he regularly maintained a centrist position in discussions within the Russian political élite, and consistently emphasised that problems had to be resolved through negotiation: while the Russian diaspora should be protected by the Russian state, this protection should always be political and moral, not military.[23]

Addressing an important gathering of the top brass of the Russian Army and Navy in mid-June 1992, Yeltsin, referring to events in Moldova, explicitly warned that a 'Yugoslav variant with Russian troops participating cannot be permitted'.[24] Even Yeltsin's declaration during the June war in Dniestria that Russia was 'obliged to react against violence perpetrated against Russians in Moldova' contained the clear message that such measures should only be considered as the

---

22. As quoted in *RFE/RL Research Report*, I, 41 (16 October 1992). Most actions and statements on the part of Western politicians in 1992 and 1993 seem to have confirmed Burbulis's prediction as regards the easternmost former Soviet republics. When it came to the Baltic states and Ukraine, on the other hand, Western leaders were less prone to regard them as Russia's backyards or as 'distant countries of which we know nothing'.

23. *Izvestiia*, 24 May 1991; *ibid.*, 8 July 1992; *Komsomol'skaia Pravda*, 27 May 1992; and *ibid.*, 3 July 1992.

24. *Rossiiskaia Gazeta*, 11 June 1992, pp. 1–2.

last resort.[25] At a press conference in July the same year, he again decisively ruled out a military solution to the Dniester conflict.[26]

However, Yeltsin also largely avoided committing himself publicly to any specific policy solutions. He kept himself above the fray, while his subordinates fleshed out the policy details. He thus left room for other top politicians to participate in the formulation and execution of the policy towards the Russian diaspora.

Andrei Kozyrev's vision of the world was based on a neo-liberal model of international politics. His starting-point was the conviction that the international system had developed after the collapse of the Soviet Union in a way fundamentally different from the bipolar world of the Cold War. According to Kozyrev, the majority of the great powers were linked together in a system of common values centred on the market economy, in which a country's status was defined largely by its level of scientific and technological advancement and by its position in the world market.[27] This economic interdependence led to a situation in which inter-state relations were ruled by the maxim 'The better off my neighbour is, the better off I am.'[28]

Having worked from 1974 to 1990 in the Department of International Organisations in the Soviet Ministry of Foreign Affairs, Kozyrev saw international organisations as playing a vital role in world politics.[29] Thus he believed that the best way to support Russian minorities abroad was to persuade both the West and international organisations to put pressure on Russia's neighbouring states whenever they failed to respect the rights of these minorities. Harbouring such a liberal vision of world politics, Kozyrev consistently advocated negotiated political resolutions. He did not completely exclude the possibility of territorial changes in the former Soviet Union, but he stressed that such changes should be made only in accordance with international norms and in a civilised way.[30]

However, as the Russian leadership, including Kozyrev, came to

---

25. Jeff Checkel, 'Russian Foreign Policy: Back to the Future?', *RFE/RL Research Report*, I, 41 (16 October 1992), pp. 15–29, on p. 19.
26. *Izvestiia*, 8 July 1992.
27. Kozyrev, in *Krasnaia Zvezda*, 20 December 1991.
28. Kozyrev, in *Izvestiia*, 2 October 1991.
29. Checkel, *op. cit.*, p. 21.
30. According to *Le Monde*, he did not rule out the possibility of returning Crimea back to Russia from Ukraine. As a precedent, he pointed to the solution to the Saar problem after World War II. *Le Monde*, 7 June 1993.

see the situation of the Russian diaspora as steadily deteriorating and appeals to international organisations as largely ineffective, Kozyrev's position hardened somewhat. At the VI Congress of People's Deputies held in April 1992 he stated that included in the arsenal of Russian policy-options towards the former Soviet republics was the possibility of withholding both economic aid and preferential trade terms. He remarked that the Western countries have traditionally linked such aid to the observance of human rights and CSCE norms.[31] By the summer of 1992 Kozyrev was no longer ruling out a 'worst-case scenario' in which Russia would use 'forceful methods' to protect Russian minorities abroad.[32]

The presidential adviser *Sergei Stankevich* soon became one of the most vocal proponents of an active Russian policy on the diaspora issue. He was particularly critical of the policy being pursued by the Estonian and Latvian governments towards their Russian minorities, claiming that the citizenship laws in these states were effectively creating apartheid regimes.[33] Stankevich strongly disagreed with the notion that Russia's concern for the Russian-speaking population in the neighbouring states amounted to interference in the internal affairs of independent states. If Russia wanted to attain a role as a fully-fledged state playing an active and distinguished role in the international community, he asserted, she was obliged to shoulder a responsibility for the problems created by her predecessor state, the Soviet Union. In Stankevich's opinion, a neighbouring state's attitude towards the Russian diaspora population should be one of the most important criteria by which Russia decided whether or not to include it among those neighbouring states she regarded as friendly.

The whole range of bilateral relations, including economic relations

31. *Rossiiskaia Gazeta*, 21 April 1992, p. 3. Indeed, the withholding of aid as a reaction to the maltreatment of minorities was among the recommendations made by the influential American expert on post-Soviet affairs, Paul Goble: '[The West] can recognize Russia's trauma and its legitimate interests and work diplomatically and by means of aid with Russia and its neighbors to allow those interests to be pursued in a peaceful way. The West can underscore that any resort to violence against either minorities or neighboring countries will mean both international opprobrium and the end of aid.' Paul Goble, *op. cit.*, p. 87. As will be noted, Goble held this out as a possible sanction also against eventual Russian attempts to approach the diapora question by military means.
32. *Komsomol'skaia Pravda*, 9 June 1992, p. 3.
33. Sergei Stankevich, 'DERZHAVA v poiskakh sebia', *Nezavisimaia Gazeta*, 28 March 1992, p. 4.

and decisions on the pulling-out of Russian troops from the area should all be seen through the prism of minority treatment. In principle, Stankevich supported Kozyrev's desire to have references to international human rights instruments included in bilateral and multinational agreements. However, he maintained also that 'The appeals we have made so far have not been heard. It is necessary to use a tougher tone than has been done so far, without of course crossing the limit of necessary restraint.'[34]

By 1993 Stankevich was openly attacking Kozyrev's policy towards the Baltic states, claiming that it was characterised both by episodic bursts of anger and by hard-edged but isolated and impotent declarations. He maintained that if all other measures failed, Russia should grant citizenship to the disfranchised russophones: 'Russia is entitled to protect her own citizens without having to have recourse to the mediation of foreign human rights activists.' At the same time Stankevich declared that the most important thing was to prevent the outbreak of another Dniester conflict.[35]

During 1992 and 1993, Vice-President *Aleksandr Rutskoi* – a highly decorated Afghan War veteran with close connections both to the army and to the military-industrial complex – issued several calls both for the revival of Russian great-power statehood and for a more active and insistent defence of Russians abroad. It was widely assumed that he was in favour of a restored Union, although in fact he explicitly distanced himself from such ideas.[36] In the spring of 1992 Rutskoi and Sergei Stankevich visited the two hottest spots of regional conflict in the CIS involving Russian populations, Crimea and Dniester, and called on the Russian Supreme Soviet to recognise the sovereignty of the self-proclaimed republics in these areas. Addressing a meeting in Tiraspol, he proclaimed that the Dniester republic 'has existed, exists and will continue to exist'.[37] The fact that Andrei Kozyrev appeared in Chisinau and Moldova shortly afterwards with a completely

34. *ibid.*
35. *Izvestiia*, 8 July 1993; *Novaia Ezhednevnaia Gazeta*, 7 July 1993, p. 2.
36. Aleksandr Rutskoi in *Komsomol'skaia Pravda*, 17 January 1992. See also *Pravda*, 30 January 1992; and *Narodnaia Gazeta*, 29 July 1992.
37. *Izvestiia*, 11 April 1992; *Moskovskie Novosti*, 12 April 1992; *Zhizn'*, April 1992.

different message revealed serious fissures in the Russian foreign-policy establishment.[38]

Evgenii Ambartsumov played the role of a mediator between the Foreign Ministry and the Parliament. On the one hand, he eased the conservative deputies' pressure on Kozyrev's team, while on the other he managed to bring about some changes in official Russian diplomacy. Ambartsumov considered the problem of the Russian minorities to be very important. Like Rutskoi, he categorically rejected charges that he was in favour of empire-restoring, but at the same time he claimed that Russia could not disregard the distress of her *sootechestven-niki*. To his mind this matter, not to mention the explosive Dniester issue, demanded an active Russian policy.[39]

Fëdor Shelov-Kovediaev began his political career in the parliamentary structure. In his capacity as chairman of the Subcommittee on Inter-republican Affairs in the RSFSR Supreme Soviet he was responsible for the negotiations with Estonia and Latvia which led to the conclusion of bilateral treaties in January 1991.[40] Although considered one of the most pro-Western and pro-Baltic members of the Yeltsin team, by November 1991 Shelov-Kovediaev had nonetheless reached the conclusion that the rights of the non-titular nationalities in the two northernmost Baltic countries were at times being violated. However, he strongly insisted that the application of indirect pressure through international political and economic organisations, including the IMF and the World Bank, was the only feasible solution to these problems.[41]

In March 1992 Shelov-Kovediaev was appointed First Deputy Foreign Minister with special responsibility for relations with the 'near abroad'. In the summer of that year he wrote an important strategy

38. A Western researcher speculated that this discrepancy might reflect a 'division of labour' in the Russian leadership: Rutskoi had been assigned the task of the 'tough, bad guy', since Yeltsin himself was reluctant to risk controversial statements that could spoil his good relations with the West. Alexander Rahr, 'Winners and Losers of the Russian Congress', *RFE/RL Research Report*, I, 18 (1 May 1992), pp. 1–7, on p. 6. However, Rutskoi's subsequent fate seemed to make this interpretation less plausible. Rutskoi was increasingly marginalised in the governmental policy-making process, and ever more clearly spoke on behalf not of his president but of the parliamentary opposition.

39. Evgenii Ambartsumov, 'Chtoby nas ne obvinili v predatel'stve', *Literaturnaia Gazeta*, 8 April 1992, p. 11.

40. *Nedelia*, no. 44, 1990, p. 3.

41. Fëdor Shelov-Kovediaev, 'Obespechit' prava rossian, no ne v ushcherbe drugim', *Rossiiskie Vesti*, no. 25, 1991, p. 2.

paper on 'Russia in the New Abroad' in which he outlined his vision of Russia playing a role as an internationally recognised leader in the area of the former Soviet Union with special interests in the region.[42] These interests he defined primarily in terms of security, economy and the safeguarding of democracy. While singling out the situation of national minorities as a main potential trigger for instability, Shelov-Kovediaev conspicuously sidestepped the issue of defending the rights of those russophones living in the Soviet successor states. In 1992, as the plight of the diaspora Russians was being perceived by the Russian public as rapidly worsening, Shelov-Kovediaev was widely denounced as a traitor to the diaspora Russians.[43] He left the Foreign Ministry in September that year.

Institutional actors

The military.   The Russian military leadership experienced severe difficulties in adapting to post-Soviet Union realities. It viewed the idea of Russia's integration into the Western world with scepticism and resented the loss of the Soviet Union's status as a global superpower. It also suffered a serious reduction in its privileges and prestige.

In the draft military doctrine published in a special edition of the General Staff journal *Voennaia Mysl'* in May 1992 a provision was included to the effect that violations of the rights both of Russians outside the Russian Federation and of those identifying themselves ethnically with Russia could not be permitted.[44] This suggested that the officers wanted to used the diaspora problem as part of their process of lobbying for higher military budgets and a way of justifying the military's continued prominence after the disappearance of Cold War superpower confrontation. In late June 1992 the Russian Defence Minister Pavel Grachev declared that only the army was in a position to defend russophones in the CIS.[45] Together with the Vice-President, the Defence Ministry advocated a much more activist and potentially violent stance on the issue of protecting Russian minorities in the near abroad than did the Foreign Ministry. In part

---

42. This summary of Shelov-Kovediaev's paper is based on John Lough, *op. cit.*, 1993, pp. 55ff.
43. *Megapolis-Express*, 26 September 1992, p. 12.
44. Lough, *op. cit.*, 1993, p. 57.
45. Checkel, *op. cit.*, p. 22.

this could be explained by the old adage: 'Where you stand depends on where you sit.' For military men it was natural to think in military terms when trying to find solutions to such problems. Their impact on the formulation of official Russian foreign policy may have been limited, but so also was the ability of the Foreign Ministry or even the President to influence the actions and movements of the military units deployed outside Russia. Although the available information is fragmented and often contradictory, their impact seems to have been verified in Georgia/Abkhazia, and even more so in Dniestria.

At the same time, it is a curious fact that the daily paper of the Defence Ministry, *Krasnaia Zvezda*, seemed to be writing less frequently about Russians in the former Soviet republics than most other major Russian newspapers.[46] Whenever it did so, the articles almost invariably discussed the plight of Russian servicemen in the near abroad but rarely the plight of civilians. To the extent that spokesmen for the Russian military have linked the protection of the Russian minorities to the continued presence of the Russian army in the Soviet successor states, this often seems to reflect concern for the security of the Russian state rather than for the security of Russian minorities. Towards the south and west the Russian state does not yet have any infrastructure of border defence. The infrastructure inherited from the Soviet Army, including almost the entire radar early warning system, is of course located on the outer periphery of the defunct Soviet Union – that is, mostly in the non-Russian successor states. Fearful that Russia should be left defenceless when these installations are no longer under its control, the Russian military are desperately trying to delay this development and at times playing the diaspora card to justify their procrastination. If this interpretation is correct, the Russian military could well become less ostentatiously interested in the diaspora question once the problem of Russia's border security has been solved.

The parliament. The generally conservative orientation of the Russian parliament – i.e. the Supreme Soviet and the Congress of People's Deputies – acted as a brake on the moderate, Western-oriented policy that Yeltsin wanted to pursue. On several occasions the Russian diaspora population was used by certain deputies as an instrument to prod Russia into action of a more aggressive and intrusive kind in the

46. Based on the monitoring of some forty Russian newspapers carried out by the information bureau 'Infoservice', Moscow.

near abroad. For instance, in July 1992 the Supreme Soviet instructed the Russian government to make preparations for temporary economic sanctions against Estonia if that country did not cease its discrimination against 'ethnic *rossiiane*', even though the Russian parliament had no formalised, constitutional right to make foreign policy initiatives of this kind.[47] Rhetoric on the need to protect the rights of Russians outside the Russian Federation, if necessary by force, was turned into a measure of 'true patriotism'. A large part of the legislature, possibly the majority, believed in the possibility of restoring the Soviet Union – an indication of this being their unwillingness to delete references to the Soviet Union from the Russian constitution.

However, certain deputies, some in influential positions, supported the policies of Yeltsin and Kozyrev, and tried to act as a counterweight to their conservative colleagues. The liberal first deputy chairman of the Supreme Soviet, Sergei Filatov, strongly warned against playing the military card on the issue of protecting the Russian minorities.[48] But Filatov was increasingly isolated in the Supreme Soviet structure, and in January 1993 left his parliamentary position to take up a new job as head of the presidential staff.

The activities of three parliamentary committees – on foreign affairs and foreign economic relations, on security and on relations with former Soviet republics – all bore directly upon the diaspora issue. Since all these committees were composed of a mixture of 'democrats' and 'conservatives', they had many lively discussions – but rather unstable attitudes.

The Ministry of Foreign Affairs. The majority of the top diplomats in the Russian Foreign Ministry, including influential figures such as Deputy Foreign Ministers Vitalii Churkin and Sergei Lavrov, supported Kozyrev's strategy of searching for political solutions both to inter-state and inter-ethnic conflicts by bringing them to the arbitration of international organisations. Many Foreign Ministry officials did not recognise the existence of a special Russian diaspora problem, but only a general problem of enforcing internationally accepted human rights. Senior spokesmen for this ministry considered that the problems of Russians in the near abroad were primarily practical. The

47. 'Resolution on human rights in Estonia', *Nezavisimaia Gazeta*, 23 July 1992.
48. 'Cho znachit zashchishchat' russkikh? Vvesti voiska i nachat' voinu?', *Nezavisimaia Gazeta*, 10 September 1992, p. 3.

discrimination they encountered was more often than not at street-level rather than state-orchestrated. The head of the department of human rights and humanitarian cooperation, V. I. Bakhmin, expressed the view in April 1992 that

> ... in the past, settlers from Russia were frequently granted various social privileges. This was to some degree the case in the Baltics, and even more in Central Asia. Now the danger of losing those privileges, together with the feeling of having ended up abroad and complete uncertainty about the future, is a source of psychological unease.[49]

For a long time after the dissolution of the Soviet Union, Russia had no permanent staffs in the former Soviet republics to which the local Russians could turn. Only in the fall of 1992 was money found for the establishment of embassies and consulates in most of the new capitals.[50] Even then many embassies remained drastically understaffed and underequipped, not infrequently operating out of makeshift premises in hotels. These financial problems led to a lack of up-to-date information in Moscow, and hampered the ministry's ability to react swiftly and adequately to any crises involving Russian minorities in the near abroad. For instance, the ministry made plans to send fourteen delegations to study the plight of russophones in the Soviet successor states, but by June 1992, it had been able to finance only five of them.[51]

Political parties and public organisations

A party system similar to those found in Western countries has not so far developed in Russia. The ability of even the largest political parties and public organisations to influence the foreign policy-making process through lobbying and other channels was small. However, although excluded from the corridors of power they did help to shape the general political climate, and thus indirectly contributed to the formulation of policy.

The conservatives and ultra-nationalists within the Russian political spectrum – i.e. those forces not represented in the governmental structure – were extremely active in discussions on the problems of the

49. 'Rossiia i blizhnee zarubezh'e', *Literaturnaia Gazeta*, 29 April 1992, p. 11.
50. *Narodnaia Gazeta*, 26 September 1992.
51. *Izvestiia*, 26 June 1992, p. 6.

diaspora. Indeed it seems fair to say that the further removed from the corridors of power a group was, the more vociferously and aggressively it would defend the rights of the Russians in the near abroad.

Fringe groups such as the national-patriotic front 'Pamiat' very much wanted to take the Russian diaspora under its wing.[52] However, despite the very broad media coverage which this and similar groups received in the West, most of them were clearly without any political clout. Still, one such group, the Liberal-Democratic Party (LDP), did manage during 1991–3 to manoeuvre itself away from a marginal position to occupy a powerful place in the Russian political landscape. Once it had garnered 23% of the vote in the Russian parliamentary elections of December 1993, the statements of its erratic chairman Vladimir Zhirinovskii could no longer be dismissed as the incoherent ravings of a buffoon.

Zhirinovskii repeatedly demanded the re-establishment of the Soviet Union, and sometimes too the somewhat larger *Russian* Empire. He avowed that he would dissolve all the national autonomous formations created by the Communists and reintroduce the tsarist *gubernii*. For example, he would establish a single unitary Baltic *guberniia* to include also parts of the Pskov and Smolensk oblasts as well as the entire oblast of Kaliningrad (Königsberg). Zhirinovskii's reason for this was ethnic: 'In this way a normal population balance with a dominance of Russians will be created.'[53] In November 1991 the authors of this chapter had the opportunity to be present at a conference arranged by the LDP outside Moscow. From our conservations with participants we gained the definite impression that the Russian diaspora was disproportionately well represented. They themselves gave the following reason for this: 'Everybody else has forgotten about us, only Zhirinovskii remembers us.'[54] In the December 1993 elections, the LDP seemed to do even better among Russian citizens in the Soviet successor states than it did among the electorate of the Russian Federation.

Zhirinovskii's solutions to even the most intractable problems were

52. See M. N. Guboglo, 'Russkii faktor' in I. A. Erunov and V. D. Solovei (eds) *Russkoe Delo Segodnia*, Institute of Ethnology and Anthropology, Moscow, 1991, pp. 8ff.
53. Interview with Zhirinovskii, in *Pu'ls Tushina*, 1991, no. 22.
54. See also interview with Zhirinovskii in *Latviias Laiks*, (Riga), 14–20, 1992, p. 3.

radical and simple. His chosen instrument for the restoration of the unitary state was not diplomacy but military might and economic blackmail. However, he frequently contradicted himself and would deny having said things that scores of journalists could report having heard. Thus his past statements will prove a poor guide for determining his future policy course should his political star rise even further.

Paradoxically, despite the high-pitched nationalist rhetoric of many would-be empire-restorers of the extreme right, the impression was often given that ethnic rights, even the collective rights of Russians, were relatively unimportant to them. What they primarily wanted was restoration of the strong unitary and multinational state, such exalted issues completely overshadowed in their minds any interest in either individual human beings or ethnic groups.[55] They emphasised the necessity of defending the Russians in the near abroad by tough means, but they did this primarily because they had found that this particular issue was a vulnerable spot in the armour of the Yeltsin administration, and thus a possible means of destabilising the political situation. Moreover, this tactic had also proved to be effective as a means of pulling politicians and public figures away from the political centre and over towards the right.

In Russian politics the diaspora question has functioned not only as a dividing line between radicals and conservatives but also as a wedge which has broken the liberal-democratic bloc apart. Several of the prominent founding organisations of 'Democratic Russia' left this broad anti-Communist movement in late 1991 or early 1992 over disagreements on this issue. Three of the break-away parties – the Kadet Party, the Russian Christian Democratic Movement (RKhDD) and the Democratic Party of Russia (DPR) – joined together in 1991–2 to form a bloc known as 'Popular Agreement'. The problems of the diaspora soon became prominent in the publications and public statements of all three of these parties. Several hard-hitting articles in the RKhDD paper *Put'* focussed on the nationalising policy of Ukraine.[56] The leader of the DPR, Nikolai Travkin declared on his return from a visit to the Dniester republic in September 1991 that

55. Authors' impressions from conversations with Karem Rash, Eduard Volodin, Aleksandr Prokhanov and Sergei Baburin in Moscow, October 1991 and May 1993.
56. See e.g. Sergei Grigor'ev, 'Ukrainskii vopros v Rossiiskom kontekste', *Put'*, no. 8, 1991, pp. 14–15; *ibid.*, January 1991, p. 10; *ibid.*, March 1991, p. 2; *ibid.*, no. 4, 1992, pp. 4–5.

in his view 'Dniestria has all moral, civil and political right to decide for itself both the issue of status as a state and whom they want to join in future.'[57] In 1992 the bulk of the RKhDD and the Kadet Party members moved even further to the right and linked up with former Communists in the so-called 'red–brown alliance'. Two leaders from these parties, Ilia Konstantinov and Mikhail Astaf'ev, became prominent figures in the National Salvation Front.

Rump Democratic Russia, which in the autumn of 1993 formed the nucleus of the election coalition 'Russia's Choice', continued to function as the main political platform for President Yeltsin. This organisation gave priority to the defence of individual human rights and did not stress the protection of ethnic Russians in particular.

As with the political parties, the input of the Russian academic community into the country's diaspora policy was limited. The leading Russian experts on ethnicity and nationality problems were concentrated in the Institute of Ethnology and Antropology of the Russian Academy of Sciences. During 1992 researchers at this institute published several important monographs and articles on the history and contemporary situation of the diaspora Russians, which contained, on the whole, very balanced and informed analyses.[58] These monographs, however, were purely academic in character and did not purport to offer any policy recommendations. In contrast, reports emanating from the Fund for the Foreign Policy of Russia did exactly that. Headed by the Deputy Director of the Institute of Europe at the Academy of Sciences, Sergei Karaganov, the Fund established itself as a counterpoise to Kozyrev's team. This 'think tank' advocated using all the levers at Russia's disposal – be it economic pressure, military pressure or the presence of local communities of Russians – to advance Russia's interests in the near abroad. Karaganov believed that Russia

57. Nikolai Travkin. 'Nel'zia rezat' po zhivomu', *Demokraticheskaia Gazeta*, 3–9 October 1991. However, there seems to be have been some disagreement in the DPR leadership as to the importance of the diaspora question. In interviews held with the authors at the DPR headquarters in Moscow in October 1991, two leading spokesman, V. Lyzlov and V. Khomiakov, expresses different viewpoints. Lyzlov did not think that the Russians in the non-Russian territories of the former Soviet Union were going through any particularly hard times. This opinion did not carry the day within the party, however.

58. See, e.g., Iu. V. Arutiunian (ed.), *Russkie: Etnosotsiologicheskie Ocherki*, Moscow, 1992; Iu. V. Arutiunian and L. M. Drobizheva, 'Russkie v raspadaiushchemsia soiuze', *Otechestvennaia Istoriia*, no. 3, 1992, p. 5.

should do everything possible to keep the Russian-speaking populations there in place since they could serve in future as important tools
of Russian influence.

> Russia is certainly concerned about the continued existence and positive
> development of the Russian (or russophone) diaspora in all states of the
> former Soviet Union, in the states of the former 'socialist bloc', and in
> all other countries. In this sense, the collapse of the Soviet Union has
> paradoxically given Russia a political, economic and social asset of poten-
> tially significant strength. It is therefore necessary to do everything possi-
> ble (first and foremost by diplomatic means) to guarantee the rights of
> the russophone population in the places where they are living.[59]

The basis for this thinking seemed to be that the leadership of every
state is obliged first and foremost to promote their 'national interests'.
Although it marked a clear break with both Gorbachev's 'new thinking' and Kozyrev's 'neo-new thinking', Karaganov's recipe was nonetheless solidly planted in the realist school of Western political
thinking. Whether or not this kind of *realpolitik* was really in Russia's
interest was another question.

Some hot spots and turning-points

As mentioned, the problems of the diaspora did not figure high on
the official Russian policy agenda in the first years of fledgeling
statehood. Only in the spring and early summer of 1992 did this situation change, primarily because of three factors: the war in Dniestria,
the simultaneous intensification of the Crimean dispute and the fester-
ing question of citizenship for post-war immigrants in Estonia and
Latvia.

Crimea. The bilateral treaty signed by Russia and Ukraine in
December 1990 explicitly recognised the territorial integrity of
the contracting parties.[60] Despite this, the Russian Parliament
instructed its government in January 1992 to look into the legal basis
for the transfer of the peninsula to Ukraine which had taken place in
1954. President Yeltsin distanced himself from the Parliament's

---

59. *Nezavisimaia Gazeta,* 19 August 1992.
60. John Dunlop, 'Russia: confronting a loss of empire' in Ian Bremmer and Ray
    Taras (eds), *Nations and Politics in the Soviet Successor States,* Cambridge, 1993,
    pp. 43–74, pp. 52ff.

endeavours, describing its resolution as rash, but it nevertheless pressed on with the issue. A statement by the Supreme Soviet on 21 May 1992 opened with an assurance that the Russian legislators nourished no territorial pretensions against Ukraine. The Russian legislators averred that they wanted to remain faithful to the principle of the inviolability of borders as these borders existed within the CIS. Even so, they declared that the people of Crimea had 'the full right to decide on the political status of the peninsula in accordance with international norms and on the basis of the will of the population'.[61] While couching their statement in the democratic language of respect for the popular will, the legislators were nonetheless clearly applying a double standard to territorial-legal issues both at home and in the near abroad. Many of the deputies, including the Chairman of the Supreme Soviet, Ruslan Khazbulatov, had on numerous occasions warned in strong language against conducting referendums on independence in ethnic autonomous units within the Russian Federation.[62] The Russian Supreme Soviet therefore seemed prepared to grant Russian communities in the non-Russian Soviet successor states the right to a referendum for secession which it was denying the non-Russians within the Russian Federation.

On the very same day that the Supreme Soviet's statement on Crimea was adopted in Moscow, the Crimean legislators shelved their referendum plans. Undeterred, the Russian parliamentarians continued to pursue the Crimean issue, claiming to have found a loophole in certain historical documents which indicated that the naval port of Sevastopol had not been included in the transfer of jurisdiction over Crimea from Russia to Ukraine in 1954. In July 1993 the Russian Supreme Soviet declared that this city was, and would remain, part of the Russian Federation.[63] The declaration triggered sharp reactions not only from the Ukrainian side but also from the Russian President – a clear sign that Russia was becoming a house divided.

Dniestria. At the VI Congress of People's Deputies held in early April 1992, calls were made for the extension of Russian diplomatic recogni-

61. Address of the Russian Supreme Soviet to the Ukrainian Supreme Soviet, reprinted in *Krymskie Izvestiia*, 26 May 1992.
62. 'Ne rvat' Rossiiu suverenitetami', *Izvestiia*, 13 March 1991; *Nezavismaia Gazeta*, 27 November 1991.
63. Suzanne Crow, 'Russian Parliament Asserts Control over Sevastopol', *RFE/RL Research Report*, II, 31 (30 July 1993), pp. 37–41.

tion to the PMR republic.[64] This move, however, was repulsed, and a very different signal was sent to the region when official diplomatic relations were established between Moscow and Chisinau on 6 April. At the very same time, Russia became directly involved in the Dniester conflict, when she took control of the Tiraspol-based 14th Army on 1 April 1992. This was probably an attempt not to facilitate more active interference in Moldovan politics but to rein in the army so that it did not get 'accidentally' involved if open hostilities broke out.[65] This policy failed, and when Moldovan forces attacked Bendery on 19 June, the 14th Army was actively involved in the defence and recapture of the city. The degree to which the army was acting on its own on the one hand and taking orders from Moscow on the other remains a disputed issue.

Boris Yeltsin's ability to broker a lasting and effective ceasefire on 7 July, when quadripartite negotiations involving Romania, Ukraine, Moldova and Russia had failed to produce any results during the spring, enhanced Russia's influence in the region. So did the actual terms of the ceasefire, which included the deployment of 1,200 soldiers from Moldova, an equal number from the Dniester republican guard and 3,800 from Russia.[66]

To date, the Dniester war is the only conflict in which members of a Russian diaspora community have died in a fight with the authorities of a Soviet successor state.[67] This conflict, in which Slavs and Moldovans were involved on both sides, should more properly be seen as political rather than ethnic.[68] Nonetheless, both sides regularly presented it in ethnic terms only, and the killings which took place clearly brought about a drastic shift in the attitudes of the Russian public on the diaspora question. Before this war, only the rightist Russian press had given active support to diaspora communities in

64. *Rossiiskaia Gazeta*, 8 April 1992.
65. Suzanne Crow, 'Russian Moderates Walk a Tightrope in Moldova', *RFE/RL Research Report*, I, 20 (15 May 1992), p. 11.
66. James M. Greene, 'Russia's "Peacekeeping" Doctrine', unpublished ms., SHAPE, 11 January 1993.
67 Incidents in which Russian mercenaries have died in other conflicts are, in this context, disregarded.
68. Paul Kolstoe and Andrei Edemsky, with Natalia Kalashnikova, 'The Dniester Conflict: Between Irrendentism and Separatism', *Europe-Asia Studies*, XL, 6 (1993), pp. 973–1,000.

Soviet successor states that were trying to achieve autonomy or independence. This cause was now taken up by a much broader spectrum of the Russian media.

Citizenship in Estonia and Latvia. The single event in the history of the diaspora which, more than any other, angered Russian public opinion and led to demands for a tougher policy towards the near abroad was the denial of original citizenship to postwar Russian immigrants in Estonia and Latvia. During 1992 and 1993, no other diaspora issue was accorded so much space in the Russian media or provoked so much bitter and incensed comment.[69]

Hard-pressed by these public sentiments, the Foreign Ministry tried to stick to its policy of moderation. In the autumn of 1991 and early 1992, when even the liberal Russian press was beginning to denounce Baltic legislative practices as tantamount to apartheid,[70] the Russian government refrained from harsh statements on the issue. Its attitude was based on the conviction that the incorporation of these states into the Soviet totalitarian state in 1940 had been unlawful. It was also afraid that any move towards the Baltics which could be seen as an act of aggression would complicate its paramount interest in achieving integration into Europe. Finally, the government hoped that anti-Communist cooperation dating back to the time of common resistance to the Gorbachev regime could somehow be translated into stable partnerships, economic and other. In February 1992 Andrei Kozyrev and the moderates among the Russian legislators succeeded in cajoling the Russian Supreme Soviet into ratifying the year-old Estonian–Russian bilateral agreement, even as, at the very same time, an Estonian citizenship law contravening this agreement was being adopted.

In accordance with his general conviction, Kozyrev actively tried to internationalise the Baltic citizenship issue. At the Copenhagen conference of Baltic countries in March 1992 Kozyrev declared: 'The democratic conviction of the citizens of Russia compels us to express our concern about the activities of some of our Baltic partners, all the more so as the democrats of Russia have stood together with them in the defence of their sovereign rights.' On 7 May the Russian government submitted a memorandum to the Committee of Ministers of the

---

69. Based on the monitoring of about forty Russian newspapers by the information bureau 'Infoservice', Moscow.
70. See, e.g., *Ogonëk*, 1991, no. 52.

Council of Europe accusing the Baltic states of violating both the principles of human rights and the CSCE norms of minority treatment.[71] In September Andrei Kozyrev criticised both Latvia and Estonia from the rostrum of the United Nations General Assembly.[72] The Estonian and Latvian sides were similarly interested in the involvement of the international community in these conflicts, and it seemed that common ground might be found here for their resolution.[73] A host of international human rights experts descended on Latvia and Estonia, producing numerous reports of varying length and thoroughness.[74] Many of them conflicted with each other, and both the Russian and the Baltic sides found enough ammunition in them to sustain their own views.[75] In general, only such excerpts from the reports which confirmed the official position of the state were reproduced in the national press in each country.[76]

The issue of citizenship legislation and minority treatment in the Baltic countries was confounded by the presence in the region of former Soviet army formations which had been taken under Russian command. Both Russia and the Baltic states initially agreed that the troops would have to be pulled out as soon as possible, but the terms and conditions of the withdrawal, as well as the understanding of what was 'possible' in these circumstances, became the subject of endless negotiations. Each side accused the other, with some justification, of trying to link the troop pull-out to the minority issue. The Balts made it clear that they could not afford to be liberal on the citizenship issue as long as foreign troops were stationed in the country, thus intimating that they might be willing to soften their stance once they had left.

71. *RFE/RL Research Report*, I, 41 (16 October 1992), p. 17.
72. *Izvestiia*, 24 September 1992.
73. *Izvestiia*, 21 July 1992; *Nezavisimaia Gazeta*, 22 July 1992; *Kommersant*, 6 November 1991.
74. *Nezavisimaia Gazeta*, 9 December 1992, p. 3; *ibid.*, 26 January 1993.
75. *Rossiiskaia Gazeta*, 28 October 1992.
76. For instance, the opinion of the Norwegian Institute of Human Rights and its director Asbjørn Eide, which were very critical of Estonian and Latvian citizenship legislation, were often reported in the Russian press, but hardly ever in the Baltic press. See e.g. *Komsol'skaia Pravda*, 3 December 1991; *Izvestiia*, 28 October 1992. At times attempts were also made to withhold from the public reports which were not to the liking of the authorities. This was apparently done by Russian authorities with the UN-sponsored Ibrahima report produced by Russia in the autumn of 1992 and by Latvian authorities with the CSCE-sponsored van der Stoel report in April 1993. See *Svenska Dagbladet*, 20 January 1993, and *Izvestiia*, 22 May 1993.

Russian officials, at the same time, moved ever closer to the view that the troops could not be pulled out until the rights of the Russians were guaranteed.

The most explicit and high-level linkage was made by Boris Yeltsin in October 1992.[77] However, only a few days later the Deputy Foreign Minister, Churkin, denied any such linkage in official Russian policy.[78] Since Yeltsin's statements did not seem to influence the withdrawal schedule of the troops, which were moving out at an undiminished pace, it was speculated that they had been mainly intended for internal consumption. In his intensifying battle with the Supreme Soviet, Yeltsin needed a boost to his image both as a genuine patriot and as a defender of Russian interests abroad.

Even Andrei Kozyrev began to link the withdrawal of troops from Latvia and Estonia to human rights performance in these countries. In conversations with his Danish counterpart on 26 October Kozyrev maintained that Russia was prepared to resort to the most far-reaching, tough and radical measures – within the framework of international law. In spite of his sharper rhetoric, Kozyrev came in for increasing criticism, not only from the parliament but also from his chief. At a meeting in the Collegium of the Ministry of Foreign Affairs a few days later, Yeltsin declared:

> The Foreign Ministry ought to concern itself with the lawful rights and liberties of *rossiiane* living in the near abroad. For our diplomats this is a new task. We have to listen to the opinion of the ordinary citizens, who generally think that the russophone population of the Baltics do not have the necessary security. The Foreign Ministry lacks a clear action programme for this.[79]

On 30 November, Yeltsin issued an Order no. 744 'On the Question of the Protection of the Rights and Interests of Russian Citizens [*rossiiskikh grazhdan*] Outside the Russian Federation', and this, on the surface at least, amounted to another public chastisement of the Foreign Ministry for negligence on the diaspora issue.[80] The ministry was told to act more resolutely in defence of the interests of Russian

---

77. In an interview with Russian broadcasters on 7 October. The *Baltic Observer*, 15–21 October 1992, p. 1. On 28 October Yeltsin repeated the essence of this statement.
78. *Izvestiia*, 3 November 1992, p. 4; *Nezavisimaia Gazeta*, 4 November 1992.
79. *Izvestiia*, 28 October 1992.
80. *Rossiiskie Vesti*, no. 108, December 1992.

citizens abroad. However, Yeltsin's practical suggestions for the improvement of the ministry's work were of a most eirenic character. Specifically, the Foreign Ministry was ordered to conclude more bilateral treaties with the countries of the former Soviet Union. Significant also was the fact that Yeltsin stubbornly refused to throw his beleaguered Foreign Minister to the wolves, a signal that in spite of changed Russian rhetoric, the basic thrust of the Russian government's foreign policy (as distinct from that of the parliament) was to exercise restraint and moderation.

Russian state leaders continued to draw the attention of the international community to the issue of the disfranchisement of postwar immigrants in Estonia and Latvia. At the insistence of the Russian President, the issue was discussed at the 47th Session of the United Nations General Assembly in December 1992. The subsequent UN resolution on 'the Human Rights Situation in Estonia and Latvia', was seen in the Russian press as giving support to the Russian position.[81] Russia also voiced its concern at the session of the Council of Baltic Sea States in March 1993,[82] at the Russian–American summit in April, at the Moscow International Symposium on Racism, Xenophobia and Antisemitism in May and in a number of other forums. For a while it was felt that this approach was yielding results. In April 1993 the CSCE High Commissioner on National Minorities, Max van der Stoel, published reports on the minority situation in Estonia and Latvia which contained more detailed recommendations on the citizenship legislation in those countries and implied criticism of it than had appeared in most reports sponsored by international organisations.[83] While these recommendations fell short of what Russian authorities regarded as the optimal solution, they did praise the work of the High Commissioner as constructive.[84] However, although the Estonian

---

81. *Kommersant-daily*, 13 November 1992, p. 3; *Nezavisimaia Gazeta*, 20 November 1992; *Izvestiia*, 20 November 1992; *ibid.*, 18 December 1992, p. 4.

82. *Kommersant-daily*, 17 March 1993.

83. See Max van der Stoel's letters both to Trivimi Velliste, the Estonian Foreign Minister, and to Georgs Andrejevs, the Latvian Foreign Minister, 6 April 1993. CSCE Communication No. 124.

84. 'On the whole, the recommendations and conclusions of the Mission represent a good basis for dealing with problems affecting the Russian-speaking part of the population of Estonia and Latvia. The document is based on a realistic appraisal of the situation, shows balance and compromize, and rightfully refrains from introducing changes and additions as regards principles.' CSCE Communication No. 125/Add. 1, 26 April 1993.

Foreign Minister in his reply also described the recommendations as fair and valuable, neither he nor his Latvian counterpart informed either their parliaments or the public of their contents.[85]

In Moscow the admission of Estonia into the Council of Europe in May 1993 was seen as giving the lie to Kozyrev's search for a Baltic solution through international mediation. Shortly after this admission, in June 1993, the Estonian draft law on aliens was published – a document which was interpreted in Moscow as preparing the way for the expulsion of large batches of Russians. Russia's top leaders, including Yeltsin himself, again resorted to bellicose language, with threats of unilateral action. However, the fact that the Estonian authorities had decided to revise the law at the recommendation of Western experts nonetheless indicated to the Russians that appeals to the international community might still bear fruit.

In spite of the sharp disagreements in Russia on foreign policy questions, a broad consensus developed that the country has not merely a right but also a moral duty to act as defender of the Russian diaspora populations. The validity of this claim is seen as self-evident, and is rarely discussed. Discussions of this issue have focussed rather on the means, the degree of vigour and intrusiveness to be used, and the ultimate objectives of this policy. On these issues sharp controversies have arisen.

Most participants in the debate advocate the protection of the Russian diaspora communities in the Soviet successor states on moral grounds as a concern to be pursued in its own right. For the liberals the crucial question is how to find effective means of supporting the diaspora without creating a dangerous escalation of tension – a situation which could lead to military conflict.[86] Unrisky means could include the establishment of friendship societies for Russian diaspora communities, financial support for Russian cultural centres in the Soviet successor states, subsidies for Russian-language schools abroad

85. Paul Kolstoe's interview with Alex Grigorievs, Bergen, Norway, December 1993. A member of the Latvian parliament till June 1992, Grigorievs managed to get hold of the text and have it published in the Latvian press.
86. See Denis Dragunskii, in *Literaturnaia Gazeta*, 20 November 1991; Otto Lacis, in *Izvestiia*, 7 April 1992; Vladimir Tiurkin, *Rossiiskaia Gazeta*, 23 December 1992, p. 7.

and so on.[87] Such measures were being implemented, to some extent, but not very actively. Russia's dire financial straits put definite limits to these avenues. A growing number of Russian politicians in the democratic camp were also prepared to influence the nationalities issue in the neighbouring states by applying strong diplomatic, political and even economic pressure.

For other participants in the Russian debate the protection of the diaspora was clearly intended as an instrument for achieving certain ulterior objectives. In some groups this objective seemed to be nothing less than the re-establishment of the unitary Soviet or Russian empire. Of course, if this scheme succeeded, the 'Russian diaspora problem' would vanish *ipso facto*. Adherents of this strategy are usually quite uninterested in small incremental steps for the improvement of the lot of the diaspora. On the contrary, anything that could help to ease the anxieties of diasporians might make this lever less effective as a means to preparing the ground for a return to the *status quo ante perestroika*.[88]

On a less grandiose level, the diaspora issue was recommended by some as a means of extorting concessions on specific issues from the countries of residence of the Russian diasporas, or else simply of enhancing Russian influence in these countries generally. As a political instrument, however, the diaspora card will often turn out to be ineffective or even counter-productive. Rather than generating concessions it will often, or even normally, produce resentment and a deeper intransigence on other issues. Prudent policy-makers therefore often prefer other levers.

An important reason why the diaspora issue nevertheless occupied a relatively high place on the Russian foreign policy agenda is that responsible policy-makers were pressed to 'do something' by opposition groups in Russia and to some extent also by the diaspora communities themselves. The effectiveness of this pressure seemed to be proportionate not to the size of the diaspora group in question or even to the amount of harassment or trouble it was experiencing, but rather

87. *Korni* (Riga), April 1992, p. 4; *Golos Rodiny*, no. 15, 1993, p. 2; *Nezavisimaia Gazeta*, 17 March 1993. Even the idea of issuing privatization vouchers to the Russians in the near abroad was broached. See *Krasnaia Zvezda*, 6 November 1992.
88. See, e.g., Sergei Stupar', 'The worse off the Russians are in the Baltics, the better for the anti-Yeltsin opposition in Moscow', *Rossiisskie Vesti*, no. 112, December 1992.

to the formal legislative and political aspects of the treatment they were experiencing. Russians in Central Asia and Transcaucasia might be going through more severe ordeals than those in the Baltic countries, but since the difficulties encountered in the Asian countries were usually not a direct result of official state policies, they were not turned into an issue of inter-state relations to the same degree as the legislative practices of Estonia and Latvia.

Another rationale behind Russia's involvement in the plight of ethnic Russians in the near abroad was the practical need to avert uncontrolled immigration of Russians at a time when Russia was ill-prepared to receive them. If the Russians in the Soviet successor states were to be exposed to systematic or serious discrimination in their countries of residence or see themselves in that light, this might have an immediate impact on Russia if it were to trigger off massive currents of immigration.

International law recognises that the treatment of minorities is not the exclusive domain of nation-states but also a vital concern of the international community. One of the major achievements of the CSCE process since 1975 has been the recognition of this fact, at least in principle, by all European states. International law, however, does *not* envisage any special role for the 'external homelands' of diaspora groups in the monitoring of minority rights. Ideally the international community at large should be the guarantor of minority rights, through its global and regional supra-state organs such as the UN, the Council of Europe, the CSCE and various non-governmental organisations (NGOs). However, in so far as the international community fails to fulfil this function, minority issues invariably seem certain to reappear on the bilateral agendas.

11

ADDRESSING THE DIASPORA PROBLEM: THE WAY AHEAD

Many observers regard the new Russian diaspora as a threat to political stability in the former Soviet Union. This concern is partly the result of the political activities of some of the diasporians themselves – in particular, attempts to reverse the break-up of the Soviet Union. However, the very existence of large Russian communities outside Russia is also sometimes seen as a problem in itself, independent of their actual behaviour. They are seen as cultural anomalies, as mere flotsam of the former empire.

Granted that the Russian diaspora represent a real problem, it is one which can be alleviated in a number of different ways. This chapter explores some possible policy options and tries to assess their potential for stabilising or destabilising the situation. Most of the methods discussed see the ethnically defined 'nation-state' as an ideal and ultimate objective. According to this ideal, there ought to be the maximum of correspondence between the political and *cultural* nation. This objective may be achieved through the marginalisation or even the physical removal of certain minorities. Theoretically, four ways can lead to that goal: genocide, ethnocide, emigration of the minorities and border revisions. In conclusion, this chapter examines one solution which seeks to eliminate the diaspora problem not by eliminating the diaspora as such but by finding rules for the co-existence of all the varied cultural groups that make up a multi-ethnic society.[1]

Genocide and ethnocide

In the present context, genocide is taken to mean the physical extermination of the members of an ethnic group on the grounds that they

---

1. For earlier and partially overlapping discussions of these problems, see Pål Kolstø, 'The New Russian Diaspora: Minority Protection in the Soviet Successor States', *Journal of Peace Research*, XXX, 2 , (1993), pp. 197–217; and Pål Kolstø, 'National Minorities in the Non-Russian Soviet Successor States, *RAND Report DRU-565-FF*, November 1993.

represent an alien and intolerable subsociety within the state.[2] This, of course, is the most drastic of all solutions. Alas, the method did not die with the Third Reich but is still being practised in parts of the world in the 1990s, against Indians in the Amazon, in tribal conflicts in the African interior and in the interior of Europe. The 'ethnic cleansing' in former Yugoslavia contains an element of genocide. This 'option' is not discussed here, not because it is totally unacceptable on moral grounds (which, of course, it is) but because no serious political actors in the former Soviet Union are contemplating it. True, accusations of genocide have abounded whenever tensions in a particular area have led to violent confrontations – notably during the Dniester war.[3] But to make such allegations is to lose sight of the proportions of the problem: the Russian diaspora is not faced with the threat of physical extinction.

Ethnocide is here taken to mean the deliberate dissolution of the collective cultural identity of an ethnic or linguistic minority.[4] By this method the state attempts to make itself culturally homogeneous through the total assimilation of all non-titular ethnic groups into the dominant culture. Many Soviet successor states are indeed encouraging or inducing their populations to adopt the culture of the dominant ethnic group – or, in the case of russified members of the titular nationality, to return to it. It is sometimes claimed that since the bulk of the huge Russian nation resides safely within the confines of the Russian Federation, the assimilation of the Russian diaspora into the titular nationalities of each of the Soviet successor states would not amount to ethnocide: the Russian nation at large would not be affected, and would continue to exist and prosper. However, such a line of reasoning misses the point. The Russian diaspora groups in Moldova, Latvia, Kyrgyzstan and elsewhere are unique communities in their own right.

2. For a discussion of the concept of genocide, see Yves Ternon, 'Reflections on Genocide', in Gérard Chaliand (ed.), *Minority Peoples in the Age of Nation-States*, London, 1989, pp. 126–48.
3. Example from the Dniestrian side: *Dnestrovskaia Pravda*, 4 September 1992, p. 3; from the Moldovan side: *Moldova Suverana*, Digest, 30 October 1992. These examples could easily be multiplied. Russian nationalists sometimes claim that not just the diaspora but the entire Russian nation is threatened by genocide. See, e.g., Valerii Ivanov, 'Russkii vopros v SSSR i puti vozrozhdenia russkoi natsii', *Russkii Vestnik, Vypusk 1* (prilozhenie), Chapter 1: 'Genotsid'.
4. See Françoise Fonval, 'Ethnocide and Acculturation' in Gérard Chaliand (ed.), *Minority Peoples in the Age of Nation-States*, London, 1989, pp. 149–52.

It would be little consolation for individual members of a Russian diaspora community who are forced to give up their cultural identity to know that, in some distant place, other Russians have the chance to retain theirs.

State authorities may apply a wide range of devices and stratagems to deprive minorities of their collective identity. Sometimes legal sanctions but more often economic levers are used. Even though the members of all cultural groups contribute to the state treasury by paying taxes, the money channelled back into society for cultural and educational purposes is geared to the promotion of the titular ethnic culture only. The minorities are free to establish their own private schools, mass media and other cultural facilities, but with no financial support from the state they can ill afford to do so.

No state will ever readily admit that it practises a policy of induced or forced assimilation. Besides, such a policy may produce the very opposite of what it tries to achieve. While state authorities in the modern world are very powerful, they are not omnipotent, and are certainly not in a position to determine the mental processes leading to the formation of different cultural identities among their inhabitants. A heavy-handed and heedless policy of assimilation may provoke a backlash of political disloyalty.

While ethnocide, like genocide, is altogether unacceptable, voluntary assimilation is not. On the contrary, it should be one of the options open to minority groups. Attempts to prevent assimilation through ghettoisation, stigmatisation or apartheid are unacceptable. People should not be forced to keep up the traditions of their forbears if they do not want to. The minorities have been gradually assimilated into the dominant society at all times and on all continents.[5] The extent to which this process is 'voluntary' is often hard to determine. More often than not, it is not a result of a deliberate choice but a net result of many planned and chance circumstances. Usually, a change of mother tongue is the most important ingredient in any assimilation process. Assimilated diaspora groups not only learn the language of the titular nationality but also, within a generation or so, forget their mother tongue. In some instances linguistically acculturated minorities, such as the Scots in Great Britain, retain a strong sense of collective identity, but this is probably possible only for minority groups that have a definite

5. Charles F. Keyes (ed.), *Ethnic Change*, Seattle, 1981; Ernest Gellner, *Nations and Nationalism*, Oxford, 1983/90, pp. 60ff.

territorial base of their own. Only a few of the new Russian diaspora communities belong to that category, and they will probably not be exposed to linguistic assimilation to any serious degree.

Assimilated Russians may continue to have a hazy recollection of the distant origin of their ancestors, but for all practical purposes they will have shed their identity as ethnic Russians. Their identity situation will be comparable to that of most European immigrant groups in the United States, whose only links to their cultural past are often no more than a quaint surname and a collection of faded photos in the attic. Most Russians in the United States, as well as in Western Europe – what we could call 'the old Russian diaspora', – belong to this category.

However, there is every reason to believe that the identity development of the 'new' Russian diaspora will not follow the trajectory of this 'old' diaspora. With a few exceptions,[6] members of the old Russian diaspora in the new world are too few and too scattered to sustain viable, distinct communities. In the Soviet successor states, on the other hand, they are not only much more numerous but may also more easily retain strong ties to the thriving centres of Russian culture in heartland Russia. Finally, the old diaspora had a clear understanding of being emigrants when they left Russia. They might have been compelled to do so for political or other reasons, but they nonetheless made a conscious choice to move out of the Russian orbit. The new Russian diaspora never made any such choice but was plunged into the situation of being a diaspora a long time, sometimes generations, after their original migration.

Return-migration

The options of migration and border revision attempt to eliminate the diaspora problem not by depriving the Russians in the Soviet successor states of their collective identity but by altering the relationship between the demographic and political maps. This is done in the first case by physically moving the diaspora so that it ends up on the 'right' side of existing borders, and in the second case by moving state borders so that they coincide with ethnic boundaries. In contrast to genocide and ethnocide, these options are discussed seriously and openly in the

6. Such as the community of 'third wave' Soviet immigrants at Brighton Beach in New York.

former Soviet Union. Also some Western students of Soviet and post-Soviet affairs have suggested that the ethnic tensions created or aggravated by the dissolution of the Soviet Union cannot be abated without the employment of one or both of these methods. In 1991, for instance, Uri Ra'anan maintained that 'Without some territorial changes, no meaningful approach to the nationalities question . . . is realistic.'[7] In a similar vein Victor Zaslavsky claimed in an important article that 'As the legacy of Soviet nationality policy comes to be recognized, territorial exchanges and organized population transfers might become necessary. These issues should acquire a legitimate place on the agendas of the international community and its organizations.'[8]

Migration and border revision must be characterised as less radical than forced assimilation, but they nonetheless entail substantial changes, political or demographic. At the same time they may also be seen as a logical continuation of the dissolution of the Soviet Union: this dissolution led to the replacement of a multinational state with a number of 'impure' or 'approximate' nation-states, and correction of demographic and territorial 'anomalies' might bring closer the 'pure', ethnically defined nation-state.

Especially in the Baltic states, many representatives of the indigenous population have argued in no uncertain terms that the migration of Russians back to the Russian Federation is the best solution.[9] The argument is partly moral and partly – as an extension of the moral judgement – based on considerations of stability: postwar Russian immigrants to the Baltic region represent an expelled occupation power, and for the former oppressors to be allowed to stay on and live side by side with those who have been oppressed would create intolerable ethnic tensions.

There is unquestionably room for a considerable influx of new settlers in parts of the Russian Federation. According to the Russian mass media, hundreds of villages and hamlets in the Central Non-Black Earth Zone of Russia are more or less deserted, and enormous tracts of land are waiting to be tilled. While no large-scale migration of

7. Uri Ra'anan, 'The end of the multinational Soviet Empire?', in Uri Ra'anan, Maria Mesner, Keith Armes and Kate Martin (eds), *State and Nation in Multi-ethnic Societies*, Manchester, 1991, p. 121.
8. Victor Zaslavsky, 'Nationalism and Democratic Transition in Postcommunist Societies', *Daedalus*, CXXI (Spring 1992), pp. 97–121, on p. 118.
9. *Sovetskaia Molodëzh'* (Riga), 18 September 1991.

Russian from the European parts of the former Soviet Union has yet begun, Russians are already moving out from *other* parts, notably from Central Asia in large numbers. As we have seen, these Russians are departing because of maladjustment, increased ethnic tensions and general discomfiture. While the 'push factor' in such cases is indisputable, this in itself does not fully explain why the Russians seem to be moving out of this area in greater numbers than from the other Soviet successor states. The 'pull-factor' for most Central Asian Russians is also stronger than the average. The technical intelligentsia, to which a fair number of the Central Asian Russian group belong, is in all countries a very mobile social group, and if they should decide to change their place of residence, they will have fewer problems than other social groups in finding new employment. The Baltic Russians, in contrast, are more often blue-collar workers who will not be re-employed so easily.

Generally, the desire to move away is regulated by two factors: the perception of the present situation at the present place of residence and the expectations of improvement at the place of destination. Migration is of course a question not only of leaving but also of arriving somewhere, and the latter factor is likely to cool the enthusiasm of most diaspora Russians for travel. Members of the diaspora born outside the Russian Federation have few, if any, ties to a local community in Russia. For them, 'repatriation' is not a correct description, and many even feel with good reason that they would be leaving the land of their ancestors. To many Russians the idea of 'home' and 'homeland' seems to be closely linked to the soil in which their family members are buried, and the prospect of leaving the graves of their kin behind is abhorrent to them.[10] However, while concern for the family graves is frequently mentioned by Russians in the Soviet successor states as an argument against migration, the strength of this motive may be exaggerated. If this were an overriding value for all Russians, they would never have left heartland Russia in the first place.[11]

Many Russian migrants to Russia must expect both a decreased living standard and a drastically changed life-style. For most city dwellers from the diaspora the prospect of starting a new life as farmers is not

10. See e.g., Valentin Rasputin's fictional treatment of this in *Farewell to Matiora*, Moscow, 1976.
11. Indeed, in *Farewell to Matiora*, Valentin Rasputin showed that this meant less to the younger generation of Russians than it did to their parents and grandparents.

particularly attractive, although some have nonetheless indicated that they are willing to try it.[12] Most of them will first try to settle down in urban areas, but obtaining a job, a flat and a resident permit in Russia's already overcrowded cities will usually be extremely hard. Should they be able to overcome these practical and legal obstacles and settle in large numbers, there could be further undesired ethnic and social repercussions. Russian old-timers might be willing to accept the settlement of Russian immigrants from other successor states, but as a kind of 'compensation', they might demand the expulsion of 'aliens' – non-Russian residents of the Russian republic – or at least no further intake of refugees of other nationalities.[13] In some segments of the Russian public xenophobic attitudes are building up, partly as a reaction to the problems faced by Russians living in the other successor states.[14] In the nationalist newspaper _Russkii Vestnik_ calls have been made for 'sending the "guests" home to where they belong'.[15]

The probable size of the Russian return-migration to Russia in the coming years is a matter of some dispute. Some observers believe that it might take on cataclysmic and uncontrollable proportions,[16] while others caution against exaggerated alarmism.[17] However, a strong conviction that large-scale migration, as distinct from gradual and voluntary migration, will be strongly detrimental and ought to be avoided is shared by most analysts.

Limited migration of Russians from the former Soviet republics

12. '"Vybirayu Rossiiu na zhitel'stvo"', _Komsomol'skaia Pravda_, 16 October 1991.
13. See Nikolai Gritchin, 'U stavropol'tsev gostepriimstva poubavilos', _Izvestiia_, 14 April 1992.
14. See, e.g., _Moskovskie Novosti_, no. 29, 1991, p. 6; ibid., no. 42, 1991; ibid., no. 8, 1992.
15. A. Nadezhdin, 'Kto khoziain na russkoi zemle?', _Russkii Vestnik_, no. 25, 1991, p. 2. Note also interview with Galina Starovoitova in _Moskovskie Novosti_, no. 42, 1991, p. 6.
16. John B. Dunlop, 'Will a Large-Scale Migration of Russians to the Russian Republic Take Place Over the Current Decade?', _Working Papers in International Studies I-93-1_, Hoover Institution, January 1993; 'Sed'maia volna emigratsii', _Izvestiia_, 12 August 1992.
17. See the interview with the director of the Russian Migration Service, Tatiana Regent, in _Megapolis-Express_, 21 October 1992; and articles by the leading Russian expert on migration, Viktor Perevedentsev, in _Nedelia_, nos. 1, 2 and 3, 1992; and _Inzhenernaia Gazeta_, August 1992; _Polis_, no. 2, pp. 69–82; 'Iskhoda ne budet', _Nezavisimaia Gazeta_, 31 July 1992.

would probably be beneficial to Russia. Many diasporians are highly qualified specialists who could contribute much to the building of the Russian economy.[18] All experience shows that in a refugee and migration situation the richest, strongest and best qualified are the first to go.[19] The more socially deprived, on the other hand, lack the energy and the means to migrate. One could say cynically that a limited Russian return-migration would allow Russia to skim the fat of the Russian diaspora and leave the other Soviet successor states with the dregs. A massive return-migration, on the other hand, would undoubtedly place a heavy burden on the resources of the Russian state and society.

A long time passed before a Russian policy on migration crystallised; the relevant legislation was passed only in February 1993. This basically consists of two pieces of legislation, a law on refugees and a law on forced migrants.[20] Those in the latter category are entitled to Russian citizenship and the accompanying benefits while those in the former are not. By the autumn of 1992, 2 million refugees and forced migrants had been registered with migration authorities in the Russian Federation,[21] but only a section of them belonged to the new Russian diaspora, however. Many were Armenians, Meskhet-Turks, Ingushetians or members of other uprooted ethnic groups. The process of integrating the refugees and migrants into Russian society has proceeded slowly. Many find that they are not given the rights to which they are entitled under Russian legislation, such as a residence permit, and job may be difficult to obtain. The migrants are arriving at a time when the labour market in Russia is contracting, and when in many places even qualified labour is not in great demand. Nonetheless, the most serious problem seems to be not work but housing. Even without the arrival of the refugees, millions of people in the Russian Federation are waiting for apartments.

Some close observers believe that the problems encountered by the refugees and forced migrants often result from a callous indifference

18. 'My b nakormili Rossiiu', *Komsomol'skaia Pravda*, 27 December 1991; *Argumenty i Fakty*, no. 40, 1992, *Literaturnaia Gazeta*, 2 December 1992.
19. See, e.g., the discussion between Paul Kolstoe, Tore Lindholm and Vladimir Steshenko in *Poisk*, no. 21, 30 May–5 June 1992.
20. For the text of these laws, see *Rossiiskie Vesti*, 30 March 1993.
21. See Sheila Marnie and Wendy Slater, 'Russia's Refugees', *RFE/RL Research Report*, II, 37 (17 September 1993), pp. 46–53.

to their plight on the part of the responsible authorities.[22] Certainly Russian bureaucracy has for centuries had a reputation for self-serving insensitivity, but there are other explanations for the difficulties of the refugees which may be equally plausible. In the severe economic slump in which at the time of writing Russia finds itself, the country simply does not have the resources needed to give large batches of refugees a decent reception.[23] Therefore, Russia will probably do little to encourage the large-scale migration of ethnic Russians in the foreseeable future.[24]

For reasons of stability, it is a cause for concern that people who are thrown out of their homesteads or put under indirect pressure to leave them often retain for decades a strong desire to go back. (They will refrain from doing so, however, until the political developments which impelled them to leave have been reversed.) In all countries, such refugee groups tend to be attracted by nationalist, irredentist parties. This is true of Algerian French in France (*pieds noirs*), Germans from Silesia, Pomerania and East Prussia, and others.[25] There is reason to believe that at least some of the Russian refugees will react as other European refugee groups have done in earlier times.

What is at stake is not social peace in a particular republic but political stability in the whole of the former Soviet Union. If greater stability in one region is bought at the expense of greater turmoil and less democracy in other regions, little is gained. On the contrary, it can be argued that all inhabitants in this area are in a worse position than before since a dangerous and possibly uncontrollable chain reaction has been set off.

There are probably only two factors that could lead to a massive migration of Russians from the non-Russian Soviet successor states to the Russian Federation:

22. See, e.g., Lidiia Grafova in *Literaturnaia Gazeta*, 14 August 1991; *ibid.*, 18 December 1991; *ibid.*, 15 January 1992.
23. See, e.g., Galina Starovoitova, 'Skol'ko ikh, kuda ikh gonit?', *Literaturnaia Gazeta*, 9 October 1991.
24. See the interview with presidential adviser Sergei Stankevich in *Novaia Ezhednevnaia Gazeta*, 7 July 1993, p. 2.
25. In the West German elections in 1953 and 1955, approximately one-third of all German refugees voted for the irredentist party 'Bund der Heimatvertriebenen und Entrechteten' (BHE). See Werner Kaltefleiter, *Wirtschaft und Politik in Deutschland*, Cologne, 1968, p. 126.

(1) One of these could be a genuine 'economic miracle' taking place in Russia but not in the other Soviet successor states. Many members of the Russian diaspora whom this author has met indicate that they monitor closely the social and economic development in their 'historic fatherland'. As long as the political and social instability in Russia is as great as in their country of residence, if not greater, they see no reason to move there, but if the situation should stabilise, they will go. However, even if the Russian market economy takes off, this does not necessarily mean that more jobs will be created. On the contrary, most economists believe that a successful transition to the market would cause unemployment in Russia to rise dramatically.

(2) Large groups of Russian diasporians have come to feel not only that they are being discriminated against in the other states but also that their physical security is in jeopardy. As a result, they might be willing to leave *en masse*, even if that should entail a risk of being deprived of the most basic necessities of life. The only reliable way to secure a major exodus of Russians from Latvia and Estonia would probably be to expose them to massive intimidation and threats. But it goes without saying that if this were to happen, it would not enhance political stability.

In the immediate postwar period the attitude of the international community to trans-border migration was basically positive. The free movement of people was thought to be conducive to economic growth, and in many countries immigration was seen as a significant element in the nation-building process. However, this perception changed radically in later decades. As Jonas Widgren has remarked, the north now believes that uncontrolled, large-scale migration would have a devastating effect on internal, regional and inter-regional political stability. Conflicts on ethnic and economic grounds could easily spring up. Furthermore, relations between sending and receiving states could deteriorate, leading to war.[26] If this happens with economically motivated migration, it is much more likely with any kind of migration caused by political or ethnic turmoil. And more still, if large sections of the population in the former Soviet Union are uprooted and start to drift, quite a number of them will probably

26. Jonas Widgren, 'International migration and regional stability', *International Affairs* (London), LX, 4 (October 1990), pp. 749–66.

try to enter Western countries – legally or illegally.[27] Anti-immigration feeling in these countries is already running high, and the capacity for absorbing more immigrants is steadily diminishing.

Lidia Grafova of *Literaturnaia Gazeta* has noticed that charitable bodies in the West have shown a greater willingness to help refugees in Russia than the Russian authorities themselves. Her explanation is that 'They understand that if one apartment in the house is burning, the fire will endanger the security of all the tenants. For them Europe is really a common home. By expressing their readiness to help our refugees, the foreigners are possibly, subconsciously, moving to save themselves from us.'[28] While this may be a fairly accurate interpretation of Western intentions, it does not mean that the West is ready to facilitate the transport of entire population groups; its primary concern is to prevent large-scale migration. But if a refugee situation should nonetheless arise, the West might, within its capacity, try to contribute to a 'damage-limitation' exercise in order to secure a modicum of stability; but any attempt to create an unstable political situation within or between the Soviet successor states in the hope that the West will afterwards bail them out of it would be a gross miscalculation.

Border revisions

While border revisions are another possible way of addressing the Russian diaspora question, they could never solve the problem in its entirety. This approach can only be applied where Russians live compactly within a limited area, preferably one contiguous with Russia. (If they constitute less than 50% of the population in that area, a border change might create greater diaspora problems (for other nationalities) than it eliminates.) Two areas where Russians are living outside the Russian Federation fulfil both of these criteria. These are north-eastern Estonia, around the towns of Kohtla-Järve and Narva, and the northern oblasts of Kazakhstan. Some other areas fulfil the criterion of majority compactness but not of contiguity, foremost among these being Crimea. In addition, some areas fulfil the criterion of majority

27. Andrei Kortunov, in *Moskovskie Novosti*, 20 October 1991.
28. Lidiia Grafova, 'Zagovor protiv bezhentsev?', *Literaturnaia Gazeta*, 14 August 1992.

compactness or contiguity, or both, if Russified non-Russians are counted along with the Russians. These include the eastern bank of the Dniester in Moldova and some eastern oblasts in Ukraine. Internal border revisions were fairly common in Soviet history. This reflected the fact that the Soviet republics, the rhetoric notwithstanding, were to all intents and purposes purely administrative units, with less scope for genuine self-government than, for instance, the individual states making up the United States. Now that the republics have achieved independent statehood, any movement of borders has inevitably become a matter potentially with far greater consequences. In 1991, the political map of the Soviet Union was fundamentally altered, but no new borders were drawn. Instead, what used to be internal borders were elevated to the status of international borders. If these were to be redrawn, this would introduce a qualitatively new practice.

It is not surprising that in the post-Soviet debate calls have been made for some of these borders to be changed. The arguments marshalled for such designs have been of different kinds. Most often, the desire has been to make the borders reflect the ethnic distribution of the former Soviet nationalities more accurately. One of the first proponents of such a redrawing of borders after the advent of *perestroika* was the exiled writer Alexander Solzhenitsyn. In his pamphlet 'How are we to organise Russia?', published in 1990, he suggested that the three Slavic republics of Russia, Ukraine and Belarus, should come together to form a new 'Rus' state, and in addition that Russians living in northern Kazakhstan should be allowed to join in.[29] In a later clarification, Solzhenitsyn said that he envisaged referendums at oblast level to provide the legal basis for such territorial transfers.

Solzhenitsyn's proposal provoked a fierce but short-lived controversy in the Soviet press. Almost all leading representatives of the non-Russians joined in a vehement denunciation of his idea, and many Russians had serious objections to it as well.[30] However, the proposal subsequently resurfaced, as it were, in a declaration made by Boris Yeltsin's press secretary, Pavel Voshchanov, on 26 August 1991 in the immediate aftermath of the failed coup. Voshchanov announced that if the other republics were serious about withdrawing completely from the Union, as their latest political declarations indicated, Russia might

29. A. I. Solzhenitsyn, 'Kak nam obustroit' Rossiiu?', *Literaturnaia Gazeta*, 18 September 1990, pp. 3–6.
30. *Literaturnaia Gazeta*, no. 40, 3 October 1990, p. 4.

be forced to raise the question of border revisions. Most observers interpreted this announcement as a *démarche* to Ukraine and Kazakhstan. (Voshchanov explicitly said that he had not referred to the Baltic states since they had already withdrawn completely from the Union.)

Voshchanov's statement was immediately and indignantly denounced in the republican capitals. The President of Kazakhstan echoed the view of most non-Russian leaders when he declared that the result of any attempt to redraw the borders would be war.[31] Partly as a response to Voshchanov's statement, the Ukrainian parliament announced its intention to keep a standing army of 420,000 men (which would be one of the largest in Europe). In Ukraine the Parliament also reconsidered its stance on the nuclear question. Before the Voshchanov controversy that country had pledged that all nuclear weapons deployed on its soil would be transferred to Russia in the shortest possible time in order to make Ukraine a nuclear-free zone, but now the leaders of the republic wanted instead to have the warheads destroyed in their own country – but not necessarily at once: Russia was now seen as a potential security threat, and the Ukrainian leaders wanted for the time being to retain a nuclear capability as a counter-threat.

In October 1991, it was rumoured in Moscow that Boris Yeltsin had discussed the possibility of a pre-emptive nuclear attack against Ukraine.[32] Stanislav Kondrashov claimed in *Izvestiia* that Yeltsin had rejected the idea 'as completely absurd': 'I have studied the question with the military, and technically it is absolutely impossible.'[33] If this is really what Yeltsin said and thought, the Ukrainians certainly had no reason to feel reassured. However, no one seems to have been able to substantiate these rumours.

Many leaders in the new states of the former Soviet Union invoke the Helsinki Final Act as an absolute barrier against border revision, but this is somewhat misleading. The CSCE rules do not exclude the possibility of negotiated border revisions made in accordance with

31. Sophie Quinn-Judge, 'Big Brother Boris', *Far Eastern Economic Review*, 5 September 1991, p. 13.
32. *Nezavisimaia Gazeta*, 24 October; *ibid.*, 7 November 1991.
33. *Izvestiia*, 24 October 1991.

international law and the principle of self-determination.[34] Furthermore, from a formal point of view, the creation of the new states of the former Soviet Union had in fact involved a *violation* of the CSCE ban on enforced, non-negotiated border alterations. Therefore, the subject of border negotiations can hardly be denounced by reference to the CSCE. Nonetheless, it might still be deplored on other grounds, for instance by pointing to the possible destabilisation that might result.

Some Soviet successor states have made territorial pretensions against neighbouring states based not on demographic but on historical arguments. Such are the Latvian and Estonian claims to certain Russian territory which is inhabited almost exclusively by ethnic Russians. And such border transfers would only add to the size of the Russian diaspora community in these states.

In both the Estonian–Russian and the Latvian–Russian bilateral treaties of January 1991 the contracting parties pledged to respect each other's territorial integrity, and the details of a border regime were left for a future bilateral agreement. Nonetheless, in January 1992 the Latvian Parliament claimed the Pytalovo area in western Russia which, under the name of Abrene, had belonged to Latvia during the interwar period.[35] This immediately called forth a strongly worded rejoinder from the Presidium of the Russian parliament, which pointed out that such claims could only lead to tension between the two states.[36]

The Latvian-Russian controversy has not come to boiling point, but a similar dispute with Estonia has developed considerably further. Estonia wants to open negotiations with the Russian Federation with the aim of moving the border some miles eastwards to bring it into accordance with the Tartu peace treaty of 1920. The disputed tracts of land are the area around Ivangorod in the north and the Pechora raion in the south, both of which were transferred from the Estonian

---

34. See e.g. W. Czaplinski, 'Comments' to W. E. Butler, 'The Principle of the Inviolability of European Boundaries', in R. Lefeber, M. Fitzmaurice and E. W. Vierdag (eds), *The Changing Political Structure of Europe*, Dordrecht, 1991, pp. 72ff; Richard Weitz, 'The CSCE's New Look', *RFE/RL Research Report*, I (7 February 1992), p. 29.
35. The *Baltic Independent*, 24–30 April 1992, p. 1.
36. *Rossiiskaia Gazeta*, 13 March 1993.

SSR to the RSFSR in 1945.[37] (In the Pechora raion only 1,000 of the 28,000 inhabitants are Estonians, while 26,000 are Russians.[38] Nevertheless, on 12 September 1991, the Estonian Supreme Council, annulled the Estonian documents, dating from 1945, which confirmed the border regulation, thus clearly signalling that they consider the transfer to have been illegal. On 21 July the next year, the Estonian government issued a statement calling on Russia to pull its border guards back to the 1920 frontier line.[39] This political manoeuvring by Estonia provoked a reaction. On 4 November 1992, the Russian government, without waiting for the conclusion of a bilateral border treaty, declared Russia's current frontiers with the three Baltic states to be the country's official state border.

In a perspective where stability is seen as a desirable end, demands for border revisions which are based on neither ethnicity nor the will of the people can only be considered damaging. At the same time, it is an open question whether border revisions can be seen as likely to enhance stability even if they are based on the will of the people. The most consistent spokesman for such revisions in the Yeltsin entourage was the Special Adviser on Nationality Questions, Galina Starovoitova. While not dismissing historical and demographic border arguments, she maintained that the criterion of the popular will should be paramount in all cases.[40]

Viewed in a moral and democratic perspective, border revisions based on referendums seem almost unassailable. True, Starovoitova might find difficulty in proving that the borders drawn around the Soviet oblasts were any less arbitrary than those around the Union republics. Nonetheless, since these administrative units are much smaller, referendums conducted at this level would certainly mirror the will of the people more accurately. It would also be misleading to label this principle 'nationalistic', because strictly it is not based on the idea

37. See Eenok Kornel, 'Deals with the Estonian-Russian state border are unlawful', *Monthly Survey of Baltic and Post-Soviet Politics*, Sakala Center, Tallinn, November 1991, pp. 14–16; *ibid.*, January 1992, pp. 3–6; *Nezavisimaia Gazeta*, 27 August 1992; *Novoe Vremia*, no. 32, 1992.
38. Most of these Estonians belong to the Setu tribe, who, in contrast to the majority of Estonians, have traditionally been Orthodox Christians and to some degree have developed an identity of their own.
39. 'Weekly Review', *RFE/RL Research Report*, I, 31 (31 July 1992), p. 75.
40. Author's interview with Galina Starovoitova, 4 November 1991. See also *Vecherniaia Moskva*, 28 January 1992.

of the nation-state but leaves the individual to decide whether or not to vote along ethnic lines.

In many places, local Russian diaspora leaders have declared that they are opposed to border revisions. This is the case in Narva.[41] However, the Russian diaspora population at large often, surprisingly, share this view. For instance, in Kazakhstan an opinion poll in September 1991 showed that only 14.4% of the local Russians were in favour of border revisions, while 63.5% were against and 22.8% ventured no opinion.[42] A similar survey in Ukraine in May 1992 showed even less enthusiasm for border changes among the local Russians: 11% would have liked the borders to be re-examined, 74% disliked the idea and 15% did not know.[43] It should be noted that these figures represented Russians from the entire country in question, including areas which would not be directly affected by a border transfer. If the polls had been conducted in the northern oblasts of Kazakhstan or in the Crimea only, the results might have been different. The Ukrainian leadership's strong resistance to the idea of a referendum on independence in the Crimea is an indication of this.

However democratic such referendums on border transfers may be, they become more questionable when seen in the perspective of stability. Certain complicated border questions in Europe have indeed been solved in this way in the twentieth century, and the embers of some ethnic hot spots extinguished, but this practice can only lead to peaceful settlements when all parties involved agree that the popular will is to be respected even when the outcome of the referendum is not their liking. Unambiguous rules for counting votes would also have to be made: how to count blank ballots, whether or not to demand a bottom limit of voter participation for the referendum to be valid etc. If consensus can be reached on these and related issues among only some of the Soviet successor states, and a subsequent referendum shows that the population is divided about equally, tension might well increase rather then be defused. This will also be the result if substantiated charges of election fraud are put forward. And finally, should

41. Author's interview with Vladimir Chuikin, chairman of Narva City Council, 7 November 1991.

42. James Critchlow, 'Kazakhstan: the outlook for Ethnic Relations', *RFE/RL Research Report*, I, 3 (1992), p. 36. See also *Moskovskie Novosti*, no. 50 (15 December), 1991, p. 5.

43. Jaroslaw Martyniuk, 'Roundup: Attitudes toward Ukraine's Borders', *RFE/RL Research Report*, I, 35 (4 September 1992), p. 66.

all these obstacles prove surmountable in one or two instances, the carrying out of actual border revisions in some areas will almost inevitably lead to enhanced pressure for analogous measures to be taken in not-so-analogous situations.

Certainly, not only the principle of referendum-based border revisions but also that of the inviolability of borders may be said to have a certain potential for destabilisation. As long as the will of the population is disregarded, the chances remain that more or less violent demands for self-determination, border revisions etc. may erupt. Such demands could even lead to the introduction of military rule in the disputed area, or in the worst case, in the country as a whole.

Nonetheless, of the two contrasting options of referendum-based border revisions and retention of existing borders the latter should perhaps be considered the lesser evil. It is admittedly ironic that at a time when almost every action of the former Communist leaders is decried by the new political leaders in the former Soviet Union as an act of villainy, the borders which the Communists drew should be treated as sacrosanct.

The dissolution of the Soviet Union into fifteen independent states was certainly based on the idea of the paramount value of the popular will, and by the same token the principle of territorial integrity was seriously undermined. However, it is impossible to implement the notion of the popular will consistently in all cases. It will be reduced to absurdity if applied to smaller and smaller units. If referendums are conducted at oblast level, it will be hard to find valid arguments for not conducting them at *raion* level as well. Still, the line has to be drawn somewhere, both for practical reasons and for reasons of stability. Should the dissolution of the multinational Soviet Union lead to a chain reaction of ever-accelerating fissions, political stability in the area will remain a utopian dream.

Minority protection

There remains a fifth possible way of addressing the problem of the diaspora: minority protection within a politically defined (civic) nation-state. In comparison with the solutions discussed above, this option may be considered far more conservative. It entails no great political or demographic changes, but aims instead to gain acceptance from all parties involved of both the new political map and the existing demographic pattern.

Minority protection cannot replace the need for a strict adherence to the general principles of individual human rights, but must supplement it. Furthermore, any specific regime for minority protection cannot be limited to the protection of one individual ethnic group, such as the diaspora Russians, but must embrace all minorities within a given area. The forms and details of each protection regime may nonetheless differ from place to place. The peculiarities of local history, ethnic composition etc. may also play a certain role, provided that the internationally accepted principles of human rights remain unviolated.

Two different schemes for minority protection may be envisaged: one limited to a certain area where a minority or a group of culturally related minorities constitutes a majority or plurality; and one which covers the entire country in question. The two schemes may co-exist and complement each other. However, territorial autonomy alone will not be a satisfactory solution. The Russian diasporas usually live scattered throughout the entire territory of the other Soviet successor states. To the extent that they are clustered together in small limited areas, this is usually in the larger cities, including the capitals. However, it would be ludicrous to proclaim Riga or Bishkek as autonomous Russian districts in Latvia and Kyrgyzstan. Non-territorial schemes are therefore essential.

Territorial autonomy for ethnic groups may take various forms, ranging from certain specified cultural rights to differing degrees of political self-rule. There are certainly precedents for such arrangements in the former Soviet Union. Indeed, whatever prerogatives and protection the non-Russians enjoyed in the Soviet Union – in culture, education and language policy – they enjoyed them *only* within their 'own' republic. Members of the nationality living in other parts of the Union had no special rights, even if they happened to live in a compact ethnic community. The lesson learnt by the Soviet citizens was that the protection of minority rights is primarily, even 'necessarily', a function of territorial arrangements. They had had no experience of non-territorial schemes of minority protection. The Austro–Marxist idea of cultural (non-territorial) autonomy had been rejected by the future People's Commissar of Nationalities, Josef Stalin, as early as in 1913, and was never revived.[44] This is one reason why so much of the

---

44. I. V. Stalin, *Marksizm i natsional'nyi vopros*, Moscow, 1913/1946, p. 29. Somewhat sanctimoniously, Stalin claimed that Karl Renner's and Otto Bauer's ideas were

post-Soviet debate on minority protection has evolved around the question of territorial autonomy.

The CSCE's Conference on Human Rights at Copenhagen in 1990 seemed to represent a breakthrough for the principle of collective, ethnic autonomy in Europe.[45] In the Final Document from this conference, to which most of the Soviet successor states have acceded, the participating states drew attention to 'local or autonomous administrations corresponding to the specific historical and territorial circumstances' as a possible means of securing the protection of national minorities.[46] Only a year later, however, mindful of the Yugoslavian carnage, the trend in international law changed again. The follow-up expert meeting to the Copenhagen conference, held in Geneva in 1991, refrained from any concrete recommendations concerning autonomies.[47] In CSCE parlance, 'national minority' is a very restrictive concept, covering only nationalities living in a well-defined territory which for some reason is 'theirs'.[48] Diaspora groups are excluded.

It may be argued that territorial-protection regimes for ethnic minorities tend in most cases to strengthen the tribal instinct of the population at the expense of the civic spirit. However, if the Russian diaspora and other post-Soviet minorities are to be persuaded to forgo this option, they must be offered some tangible substitutes, and that will necessitate the creation of effective, viable, non-territorial regimes for the protection of their educational, religious, linguistic and other cultural interests as minorities.

The status of ethnic minorities in the Soviet successor states is influenced by a number of legislative acts including laws on local government, referendums, martial law, migration, elections etc. At

---

inapplicable to Russia since they were based on the principle of the territorial integrity of the state. The Russian Social-Democratic party had proclaimed the principle of self-determination of nations up to and including the right to secession, he pointed out. For a presentation of the ideas of Karl Renner, see Theodor Hanf, 'Reducing conflict through cultural autonomy: Karl Renner's contribution', in Uri Ra'anan, Maria Mesner, Keith Armes and Kate Martin (eds.) *State and Nation in Multi-ethnic Societies*, Manchester, 1991, pp. 33–52.

45. See Lene Johannessen and Kirsten Hvenegård-Lassen, *Minority Rights in Europe – Progress in the CSCE*, Copenhagen, 1992, pp. 10ff.

46. *Document of the Copenhagen Meeting of the Conference on the Human Dimension of the CSCE*, Copenhagen, 1990, p. 41.

47. *Report of the CSCE Meeting of Experts on National Minorities*. Geneva, 1991, pp. 6–7.

48. Johannessen and Hvenegård-Lassen, pp. 6ff.

times, it seems that the relevance of some of these laws to the minority issue is not clearly understood by the minorities themselves. This is apparently the case with the details of the electoral system. Many Soviet successor states have continued the 'winner-takes-all' system which existed in the Soviet Union, retaining one-seat constituencies. While a simple majority system may work satisfactorily in culturally homogeneous societies, it functions as an effective barrier against minority representation in multicultural states.

However, there has been little debate on the electoral system in the new states so far. Certain other aspects of the new legislation, on the other hand, have been intensely controversial. Much attention has been devoted to language legislation, which is certainly an aspect of state policy of immediate concern to minorities (this debate has already been presented in the area-wise chapters of this book, and will not be repeated here). Another bone of contention in many countries consists of laws on 'national minorities'. Often the stipulations of these laws turn out to be declaratory rather than substantial, and the rights, liberties and obligations spelled out are very general. In addition, promises to support the cultural activities of the minorities are not followed up, either because the pledges were never seriously intended or because in the current economic climate the state simply cannot afford them.[49]

The main reason why the legislation on minority rights in the new states still warrants closer scrutiny is that it often gives important indications of the willingness (rather than ability) of the state authorities to protect cultural minorities. While the legal and economic importance of these laws might be limited, the psychological significance is often considerable. This is shown by the heated debates that have often broken out around these laws. In some countries where no such legislation has yet been passed, various organisations representing the minorities are pushing for its adoption.[50]

In some Soviet successor states non-titular groups object to the minority legislation on the grounds that they consider themselves to be indigenous groups on a par with the titular nation and not 'minorities'. This is a major criticism that has been raised against, for instance, the Ukrainian Law on national minorities of June 1992 by

---

49. For an assessment of the laws on national minorities in the European Soviet successor states, see Paul Kolstoe, 'National Minorities in the . . .' *op. cit.* (note 1).
50. See, e.g., *Slaviankie Vesti* (Bishkek), organ of the Slavonic Foundation of Kyrgyzstan, no. 9 (May 1992), p. 3.

Russians in Ukraine.[51] As we saw in Chapter 7, President Kravchuk himself emphasised in 1991 that in contrast, for example, to the Baltic situation, the non-titular ethnic groups in Ukraine, including the Russians, are indeed indigenous. This view is not, however, reflected in Ukrainian legislation.

In some Soviet successor state various kinds of consultative councils for the minorities have been set up. The mandates of these councils often suffer from the same imprecision as do the laws on minorities and their political clout is negligible. As a rule, they are given advisory status only, and the authorities are then free to ignore their recommendation. Some spokesmen for the minorities suspect that the establishment of such organs may be intended primarily as a kind of palliative for the frustration felt by members of the non-titular ethnic groups in those instances where the titular nation is monopolising the political leadership.[52]

All things considered, regimes for the protection of ethnic minorities would seem to be the least destabilising solution to the Russian diaspora problem. It is important that this solution considerably decreases the dangers of unpredictable chain reactions by comparison with the other alternatives discussed. However, a solution to the Russian diaspora problem based on regimes for the protection of minority rights is not without its problems. Western political scientists have pointed out that it is more difficult to find common ground for consensus in government in a culturally heterogeneous society than it is in a society where the members adhere to basically the same preferences and values. Robert A. Dahl has remarked that democracy is 'significantly less frequent in countries with marked subcultural pluralism'.[53] However, this statement should not be understood as an encouragement to create cultural homogeneity in the name of democracy by coercive means.[54] On the contrary, the treatment of minorities (not only ethnic but also

51. 'Zaiavlenie Partii Slavianskogo Edinstva (Ukrainy)', undated leaflet. An identical opinion has been expressed by the 'Rus' society of Russian culture. See *Iug* (Odesa), 18 September 1992: *Vecherniaia Odessa*, 18 September 1992.
52. Boris Tsilevich, *Vremia zhëstkikh reshenii*, Riga, pp. 57ff.
53. Robert A. Dahl, *Democracy and its Critics*, New Haven/London, 1989, pp. 254ff. Dahl uses the term 'polyarchy' rather than 'democracy'. In his vocabulary, however, this is not something different from democracy but rather his attempt to give democracy a precise and operationable content.
54. Clarification made by Robert Dahl during a lecture at the University of Oslo, 8 October 1992.

confessional, ideological etc.) is in a sense the very touchstone of democracy. Moreover, Dahl adds that cultural homogeneity is not strictly necessary to democracy, and points to Switzerland, Austria and the Netherlands as examples of successful democracies with extensive subcultural pluralism.[55] These examples demonstrate that common ground, both for consensus in government and for value systems that are recognisable by all members of society, may be found in a common political (civic) identity for the population rather than a common ethnic one. Certainly a sense of belonging to the larger community of the state is indispensable for any society to function well, but the cohesion of the state does not necessarily have to be based on ethnicity. While the politically defined nation-state has its problems and drawbacks, its strength lies in the fact that it is an inclusive, not an exclusive fellowship.

A paramount concern of any state authority is to secure the political loyalty of all the members of the community towards the state. This is done by inculcating respect for and allegiance to its institutions – the constitution, the elected bodies, the executive, the law-enforcement organs and so on. A vital part of this policy is the cultivation of state symbols such as the flag, the national anthem and national holidays. This is an essential ingredient of the nation-building policy of every state. While this strategy is often confused with nationalism, the proper name for it is patriotism.[56]

These recommendations are not in any way original, and the observant reader will recognise them as more or less identical to President Nazarbaev's political programme. Moreover, it is far from certain that even if consistently implemented (and arguably this is not being done in Kazakhstan) this programme could guarantee ethnic peace in the Soviet successor states. The best defence for it is probably the same as the one Winston Churchill suggested for democracy: it is not a particularly good system, and the only reason why it must be recommended is that all the alternatives are much worse.

In a civic community the sense of belonging and the sense of unity are usually less intense and less unquestionable than in a community based on a common cultural identity, but for that very reason a civic community is to be recommended. As the recent history of Europe has shown, the sense of unity in cultural (ethnic) communities may

---

55. Dahl, *op. cit.*
56. Anthony H. Birch, *Nationalism and National Integration*, London, 1989, p. 4.

become too unconditional. As a result, the loyalty and attachment to the ethnic nation and its leaders may be given priority over respect for human rights. In most parts of the world and certainly in the former Soviet Union, numerous ethnic groups live so intermingled with each other that a pure ethnically defined nation-state can only be brought about by Yugoslav-type solutions.

The optimal solution for most members of the Russian diaspora seems to be their adoption of a political identity as citizens of the successor states and their retention of a cultural identity as Russians. The state authorities of their country of residence should demand their total and unreserved political loyalty, and in return they should unconditionally accept and promote the continued development of their cultural Russianness. Moreover, in all political matter the Russians, like any other national minority, should be treated as fully-fledged citizens with all the consequent rights and obligations. The Russians should unambiguously renounce any politico-territorial changes and settle for the status of an 'integrated minority' with clearly defined minority rights – or, if they prefer, assimilation into the titular group.

For many Russians in the Soviet successor states the idea of becoming an 'ethnic minority' appears utterly outlandish. They point out that they belong to a 150-million-strong nation, one of the largest and most influential in the world. Indeed they do, but today this nation is politically divided among several independent nation-states (a circumstance which does not make it any less great).

Russia could and should give financial support to those cultural organisations, schools etc. that represent the Russian diaspora, and likewise the other Soviet successor states should be encouraged to promote the activities of their diasporas in the other states. In that way the feeling of still belonging to the cultural universe of the 'historic fatherland' could be strengthened. This is the kind of support most often requested by the diasporians themselves.

The hallmark of the civic nation-state and the proof that it functions lie in an inclusive citizenship embracing all permanent residents without distinction. This must surely be a *sine qua non* for the solution of the Russian diaspora question. The non-Russian states should grant citizenship to the Russians without any strings or requirements attached to it different from those which apply to any other permanent residents. At the present time, only Latvia and Estonia deny a section of their Russian residents status as original citizens.

In many Soviet successor states the number of Russians who have registered as citizens is very low. There are obviously several reasons for this. The stipulations and procedures vary from country to country. In some Soviet successor states permanent residents have not been asked whether they want citizenship or not; it is simply taken for granted that they belong to the body politic. In those states where formal registration is required, many Russians seem to postpone the decision until a failure to register proves to be in some way injurious to them economically. This is one aspect of the general political apathy that prevails in the former Soviet Union. Among certain groups it is also an expression of nostalgia for empire. Most of all, however, it seems to reflect the fear of being permanently cut loose from Russia.

Under the Russian citizenship law adopted on 28 November 1991 former citizens of the Soviet Union now permanent residents of a Soviet successor state could receive Russian citizenship on the condition that they applied for it by February 1995 and that they had not already taken up citizenship in their country of residence. This law gave members of the Russian diaspora the chance to postpone a decision on their citizenship till that date, unless the authorities in their country of residence had stipulated a shorter time-limit (as they often did).

Certainly there could be solid reasons for granting the Russians a pause for thought before deciding to join the Russian diaspora permanently. Nonetheless, the stipulations laid down in this Russian citizenship law have the unfortunate side-effect of retarding the establishment of civic nation-states in the former Soviet Union. Moreover, the Russian law did not stipulate that those Russian diasporians who take Russian citizenship would be required to take up permanent residence in Russia. The reason for this was probably that such a stipulation would function as a strong inducement for many of them to move to Russia – and for reasons discussed above, Russian authorities do not want to encourage any such large-scale immigration, but instead want to protect and support the Russians wherever they are.

Some Soviet successor states – namely Estonia and Latvia – have encouraged the Russian authorities to speed up the process of granting Russian citizenship to those ethnic Russians who are permanent residents of their countries.[57] This is somewhat surprising, since these

---

57. See, e.g., Mart Rannut, 'Language & Citizenship Policy in Estonia', paper presented at the Conference on Citizenship and Language Laws in the Newly Independent States of Europe, Copenhagen, 9–10 January 1993.

states will certainly be in an unenviable position if they should end up with hundreds of thousands of permanent residents who are citizens of an overwhelmingly strong and feared neighbour state. This situation must surely lead to increased pressure on the Russians to leave, all the more so as their Russian passports will entitle them to all the benefits and rights of a Russian citizen. For that reason also, the Russian legislators ought to proceed warily on the issue of granting citizenship to the Russian diaspora. Some organisations representing the Russian diaspora communities do encourage their members to apply for Russian citizenship[58] while others try to persuade them to become citizens of their country of residence.

A different question is whether the Soviet successor states should allow their diaspora groups to hold dual citizenship – a system which Russia favours. The existing Russian citizenship law, in principle, grants Russian residents of other states Russian citizenship without their having to relinquish the citizenship they already have, on condition that an agreement on dual citizenship has already been signed with the state in question. The same right is given to the diasporas of other nationalities that are considered indigenous groups of the Russian Federation.[59] Similar legislation has also been passed in other Soviet successor states, namely Ukraine and Turkmenistan.

Political scientists have traditionally regarded dual citizenship as a potentially destabilising rather than stabilising factor in international affairs. The United States and other great powers have frequently used protection of their citizens as a pretext for intervening – militarily on occasions – in the internal affairs of other states. The US experience, however, is not altogether a valid parallel to the post-Soviet situation, simply because of the completely different demographic pattern in the latter case. Not only Russia but almost all Soviet successor states have large diasporas on each other's territory. Possibly a system of dual citizenships lasting for a limited time, which would allow for gradual mental and practical adaption might be a workable compromise. In

---

58. This was, for instance, the position of ROL in Latvia. See *Russkii Put'*, 23 May 1992, p. 1.
59. For the next of the law, see *Vedomosti s"ezda narodnykh deputatov Rossiiskoi Federatsii i Verkhovnogo Soveta Rossiiskoi Federatsii*, no. 6, 1992, pp. 307–21. For a discussion of these problems, see Khronid Liubarskii, 'Grazhdane i "sootechestvenniki"', *Novoe Vremia*, no. 5, 1993, 40–3; 'Dvoinoe grazhdanstvo', *Literaturnaia Gazeta*, 20 July 1992, p. 12.

1974 the brilliant Ukrainian emigré scholar Roman Szporluk discussed how the multinational Ukrainian SSR could become a Ukrainian nation-state. He foresaw two possibilities:

> The first alternative would be to partition the Ukrainian SSR along ethnic-nationality lines: the Donbas and possibly several other *oblasti* would be separated from Ukraine, and the size of the Russian-language element in that smaller Ukraine would be decreased. One imagines that to become acceptable to Ukrainians, this operation would have to reduce the Russian population in that smaller Ukraine to a truly national minority ... The second alternative would maintain the present territorial integrity of the Ukrainian SSR but would define the Ukrainian nationality in a territorial sense: the population of the republic might have the option of considering itself Ukrainian regardless of whether its language of communication is Ukrainian or Russian.[60]

Since the collapse of the Soviet Union the political situation on which these reflections were based has been fundamentally altered, but the ethno-demographic pattern remains basically the same. Szporluk's alternatives are surely just as relevant today as years ago. Lucidly, he spelled out the options which confront the policy-makers in the newly independent states: they have to choose between the ethnic and the territorial nation-state concept. This is true not only in Ukraine, whose two dominant cultures are closely inter-related, but in all Soviet successor states. In fact, we have seen that some of the most serious efforts to create territorial nation-states have taken place in Central Asia, where the cultural distance between the Russians and the indigenous ethnic groups is greatest.[61] As this chapter shows, the leaders of the Soviet successor states vehemently reject Szporluk's first variant, but determination to pursue the second alternative is also sometimes lacking. In this writer's view, it is the better one by far.

60. Roman Szporluk, 'Russians in Ukraine and Problems of Ukrainian Identity in the USSR', in Peter J. Potichnyj (ed.), *Ukraine in the Seventies*, Oakville, 1974, pp. 195–217, on pp. 212–3.
61. The adjectives 'Kazakhstani', 'Kyrgyzstani', 'Uzbekistani', 'Tajikistani' and 'Turkmenistani', as used in this book, are modelled on the more conventional English word 'Pakistani', and used to denote the political and civic aspects of these states – in contrast to 'Kazakh' etc, which pertain to the *cultural* and *ethnic* aspects. They should be seen as the author's modest attempt to contribute to the establishment of a supra-ethnic identity in each of these new nations. This terminology corresponds to a similar distinction in Russian ('Kazakhskii' vs 'Kazakhstanskii'). Unfortunately, for most of the European Soviet successor states, a similar semantic distinction seems to be more difficult to introduce.

SELECT BIBLIOGRAPHY

BOOKS AND MONOGRAPHS

Allworth, Edward (ed.), *Soviet Nationality Problems*. New York, 1971.

— (ed.), *Ethnic Russia in the USSR: The Dilemma of Dominance*. New York, 1980.

— (ed.), *Central Asia: 120 Years of Russian Rule*. London, 1989.

Andersen, Erik André (ed.), *Minoriteternes situation og rettigheder i de baltiske lande*. Copenhagen, 1992.

Arseniev, Nicholas, *Russian Piety*. New York, 1975.

Arutiunian, Iu. V. (ed.), *Russkie. Etnosotsiologicheskie ocherki*. Moscow, 1992.

Azrael, Jeremy R., *Soviet Nationality Policies and Practices*. New York, 1978.

Bagaleia, D. I., *Kolonizatsiia Novorossiiskogo kraia*. Kiev, 1889.

Barghoorn, Frederick C., *Soviet Russian Nationalism*. New York, 1956.

Bennigsen, Alexandre, and S. Enders Wimbush, *Muslims of the Soviet Empire*. London, 1985.

Birch, Anthony H., *Nationalism and National Integration*. London, 1989.

Carrère d'Encausse, Hélène, *Decline of an Empire: The Soviet Socialist Republics in Revolt*. New York, 1980.

——, *La gloire des nations, ou la fin de l'Empire soviétique*. Paris, 1991.

Chaliand, Gérard (ed.), *Minority Peoples in the Age of Nation-States*. London, 1989.

Clem, Ralph S. (ed.), *The Soviet West: Interplay between Nationality and Social Organization*. New York, 1975.

Connor, Walker, *The National Question in Marxist-Leninist Theory and Strategy*. Princeton, 1984.

Dahl, Robert A., *Democracy and its Critics*. New Haven/London, 1989.

Danilevskii, N. Ia., *Rossiia i Evropa*. St. Petersburg, 1888.

Dunlop, John B., 'Will a Large-Scale Migration of Russians to the Russian Republic Take Place over the Current Decade?', Working Papers in International Studies I-93-1, Hoover Institution, January 1993.

Erunov, I. A. and V. D. Solovei (eds), *Russkoe delo segodnia*. Institute of Ethnology and Antropology, Moscow, 1991.

Gellner, Ernest, *Nations and Nationalism*. Oxford, 1983/1990.

Gins, G., *Pereselenie i kolonizatsiia*. St. Petersburg, 1913.

Ginzburg, A. I., *Russkoe naselenie v Turkestane*. Institute of Ethnology and Anthropology, Russian Academy of Sciences, Moscow, 1991.

Goldhagen, Eric (ed.), *Ethnic Minorities in the Soviet Union*. New York, 1968.

Hodnett, Grey, *Leadership in the Soviet National Republics*. Oakville, TX, 1979.

Iakubovskaia, S. I., *Razvitie SSSR kak soiuznogo gosudarstva*. Moscow, 1972.

Ismail-Zade, D. J., *Russkoe krest'ianstvo v Zakavkaz'e*. Moscow, 1982.

Johannessen, Lene, and Kirsten Hvenegård-Lassen, *Minority Rights in Europe – Progress in the CSCE*. Copenhagen, 1992.

Kabuzan, V. M., *Zaselenie Novorossii*. Moscow, 1976.

Kappeler, Andreas, *Russland als Vielvölkerreich*. Munich, 1992.

Karklins, Rasma, *Ethnic Relations in the USSR: The Perspective From Below*. Boston, MA, 1986/1989.

Katz, Zev et al. (eds), *Handbook of Major Soviet Nationalities*. New York, 1975.

Kirch, Aksel, Marika Kirch, and Tarmo Tuisk, *The Non-Estonian Population Today and Tomorrow: A Sociological Overview* (Preprint). Tallinn, December 1992.

Kolarz, Walter, *Russia and Her Colonies*. London, 1952.

Kolstø, Pål. 'National Minorities in the Non-Russian Soviet Successor States.' RAND report DRU-565-FF, November 1993.

Kommunisticheskaia partiia Sovetskogo soiuza v rezoliutsiiakh i resheniiakh. Moscow, 1954 (7th edn).

Kozlov, V. I. *Natsional'nosti SSSR. Etnodemograficheskii obzor*. Moscow, 1982 (2nd edn).

Kozlov, V. I. and A. P. Pavlenko (eds), *Dukhobortsy i Molokane v Zakavkaz'e*. Moscow, 1992.

Kreindler, Isabelle, 'The Changing Status of Russian in the Soviet Union', Hebrew University of Jerusalem, Research Paper no. 37, November 1979.

Kritika fal'sifikatsii natsional'nykh otnoshenii v SSSR. Moscow, 1984.

Lewis, Robert A., Richard H. Rowland, and Ralph S. Clem, *Nationality and Population Change in Russia and the USSR*. New York, 1976.

Lieven, Anatol, *The Baltic Revolution: Estonia, Latvia, Lithuania and the Path to Independence*. New Haven, Conn., 1993.

Malakhov, V., *Ia eto videl, slyshal i pytalsia osmyslit'*, Chisinau, 1992.

Motyl, Alexander J. (ed.), *Thinking Theoretically about Soviet Nationalities*. New York, 1991.

Nahaylo, Bohdan and Victor Swoboda, *Soviet Disunion: A History of the Nationalities Problem in the USSR*. London, 1990.

Natsional'nyi sostav naseleniia SSSR, Moscow, 1991.

Pearson, Raymond, *National Minorities in Eastern Europe 1848–1945*. London, 1983.

Pestrzhetskii, D., *Zaselenie okrain*. St. Petersburg, 1908.

Pipes, Richard, *The Formation of the Soviet Union: Communism and Nationalism 1917–1923*. Cambridge, MA, 1954.

——, *Russia under the Old Regime*. Harmondsworth, 1979.

Ra'anan, Uri, Maria Mesner, Keith Armes and Kate Martin (eds), *State and Nation in Multi-ethnic societies*. Manchester, 1991.

Russkie v Latvii. Istoriia i sovremennost', Riga, 1992.

Simon, Gerhard, *Nationalism and Policy towards the Nationalities in the Soviet Union*. Boulder, CO, 1986/1991.

Smith, Anthony D., *National Identity*. Harmondsworth, 1991.

Smith, Graham (ed.), *The Nationalities Question in the Soviet Union*, London, 1990/1992.

Stalin, I. V., *Sochineniia*, Moscow, 1947.

Taagepera, Rein, and Romuald J. Misiunas, *The Baltic States: Years of Dependence 1940-1990*. London, 1993.

Titma, Mikk and Nancy B. Tuma, 'Migration in the Former Soviet Union', Berichte des Bundesinstituts für ostwissenschaftliche und internationale Studien, Cologne, 1992.

Tsilevich, Boris, *Vremia zhëstkikh reshenii*. Riga, 1993.

Vakar, Nicholas P., *Belorussia: The Making of a Nation*. Cambridge, MA, 1956.

Voslenskii, Mikhail, *Nomenklatura. Gospodstvuiushchii klass Sovetskogo Soiuza*. London, 1984.

Zaslavsky, Victor, *The Neo-Stalinist State*. New York, 1982.

Zelenchuk, V. S., *Naselenie Moldavii*. Kishinëv, 1973.

——, *Naselenie Bessarabii i Podnestrov'ia v XIX v*. Kishinëv, 1979.

Zhilina, A. I., and S. V. Cheshko (eds), *Sovremennoe razvitie etnicheskikh grupp Srednei Azii i Kazakhstana*, Institute of Ethnology and Anthropology, Russian Academy of Sciences, Moscow, 1992.

ARTICLES IN JOURNALS

Arapov, Aleksei, and Iakov Umanskii, '"Russkii vopros" v kontekste mezhnatsional'nykh otnoshenii v Uzbekistane', *Svobodnaia mysl'*, 1992, no. 14, pp. 29-38.

Anderson, Barbara A., and Brian D. Silver, 'Estimating Russification of Ethnic Identity Among Non-Russians in the USSR, *Demography*, XX no. 4 (November 1983), pp. 461-89.

——, 'The Changing Ethnic Composition of the Soviet Union', *Population and Development Review*, XV, no. 4 (December 1989), pp. 609-56.

Armstrong, John A., 'Mobilized and Proletarian Diasporas', *American Political Science Review*, LXX (1976), pp. 393-408.

Arutiunian, Iu. V., and L. M. Drobizheva, 'Russkie v raspadaiushchemsia soiuze', *Otechestvennaia istoriia*, 1992, no. 3, pp. 3-15.

Bernhardt, Rudolf, and Henry Schermers, 'Lithuanian law and international human rights standards', *Human Rights Law Journal*, XIII, nos.5-6 (June 1992), pp. 249-56.

Bilinsky, Yaroslav, 'Soviet Educational Laws of 1958-9 and Soviet Nationality Policy', *Soviet Studies*, XIV (1962-3), pp. 138-57.

Birch, Julian, 'Border Disputes and Disputed Borders in the Soviet Federal System', *Nationalities Papers*, XV, no. 1 (Spring 1987), pp. 43–70.

Brown, Bess, 'Tajik Opposition to be Banned', *RFE/RL Research Report*, II, no. 14 (2 April 1992), pp. 9–12.

——, 'Kazakhstan and Kyrgyzstan on the Road to Democracy', *RFE/RL Research Report*, I, no. 48 (4 December 1992), pp. 20–2.

Brubaker, Rogers, 'East European, Soviet, and Post-Soviet Nationalisms: A Framework for Analysis', *Research on Democracy and Society*, I, (1993), pp. 353–78.

——, 'Political Dimensions of Migration From and Among Soviet Successor States' in Myron Weiner (ed.), *International Migration and Security*, Boulder, CO. 1993, pp. 39–64.

——, 'Nationhood and the national question in the Soviet Union and post-Soviet Eurasia: An institutionalist account', *Theory and Society*, XXIII, no. 1 (February 1994), pp. 47–78.

Bruk, S. I., and V. M. Kabuzan, 'Dinamika chislennosti i rasseleniia russkogo etnosa (1678–1917 gg.)', *Sovetskaia etnografiia*, 1982, no. 4.

——, 'Dinamika chislennosti i rasselenia russkikh posle Velikoi Oktiabrskoi sotsialisticheskoi revoliutsii', *Sovetskaia etnografiia*, no. 5, 1982, pp. 3–20.

Brusnikin, E. M. 'Pereselencheskaia politika tsarizma v kontse XIX veka', *Voprosy istorii*, 1965, no. 1 (January), pp. 28–38.

Bungs, Dzintra, 'Migration to and from Latvia', *Report on the USSR*, I, 37 (14 September 1990), pp. 27–33.

——'Poll Shows Majority in Latvia Endorses Independence', *Report on the USSR*, III (15 March 1991), pp. 22–4.

——'Latvia Adopts Guidelines for Citizenship', *Report on the USSR*, III, 44 (18 October 1991), pp. 17–9.

——'Recent Demographic Changes in Latvia', *RFE/RL Researh Report*, II, 50 (17 December 1993), pp. 44–50.

Butler, W. E., 'The Principle of the Inviolability of European Boundaries' in R. Lefeber, M. Fitzmaurice and E. W. Vierdag (eds), *The Changing Political Structure of Europe*, Dordrecht, 1991.

Carlisle, Donald S., 'Uzbekistan and the Uzbeks', *Problems of Communism*, XL (September-October 1991), pp. 23–44.

Checkel, Jeff, 'Russian Foreign Policy: Back to the Future?', *RFE/RL Research Report*, I, 41 (16 October 1992), pp. 15–29.

Chizhikova, L. N., 'Ob etnicheskikh protsessakh v vostochnykh raionakh Ukrainy', *Sovetskaia etnografiia*, 1968, no. 1, pp. 18–31.

Critchlow, James, 'Kazakhstan and Nazabaev: Political Prospects', *RFE/RL Research Report*, I, 3 (17 January 1992), pp. 31–4.

——,'Kazakhstan: The Outlook for Ethnic Relations', *RFE/RL Research Report*, I, 5 (31 January 1992), pp. 34–9.

——,'Uzbekistan: Underlying Instabilities', *RFE/RL Research Report*, I, 6 (7 February 1992), pp. 8–10.

Crow, Suzanne, 'Russian Parliament Asserts Control over Sevastopol', *RFE/RL Research Report*, II, 31 (30 July 1993), pp. 37–41.

Dreifelds, Juris, 'Latvian National Rebirth', *Problems of Communism*, XXXVIII, 4 (July-August 1989), pp. 77–95.

——,'Immigration and Ethnicity in Latvia', *Journal of Soviet Nationalities*, I (Winter 1990–1), pp. 43–81.

'Estonian political parties on citizenship', *Monthly Review of Baltic and post-Soviet Politics*, Sakala Center, Tallinn, February 1992, pp. 3–6.

Fierman, Bill, 'The View from Uzbekistan', *International Journal of the Sociology of Language*, XXXIII (1982), pp. 71–8.

Girnius, Saulius, 'Migration to and from Lithuania', *Report on the USSR*, I (14 September 1990), pp. 25–7.

Goble, Paul A., 'Russia and Its Neighbors', *Foreign Policy*, 1993, no. 90 (Spring), pp. 79–88.

Gudkov, Leon, 'The Disintegration of the USSR and Russians in the Republics', *Journal of Communist Studies*, IX, no. 1 (March 1993), pp. 75–87.

Guthier, Stephen L., 'The Belorussians: National Identification and Assimilation, 1897–1970 [Part I]', *Soviet Studies*, XXIX, no. 1 (January 1977), pp. 37–61.

Hammer, Darrell P., 'Russian Nationalism and Soviet Politics' in Joseph L. Nogee (ed.), *Soviet Politics: Russia After Brezhnev*, New York, 1985, pp. 122–49.

Hanson, Philip, 'Estonia's Narva Problem, Narva's Estonian Problem', *RFE/RL Research Report*, II, no. 18 (30 April 1993), pp. 17–23.

Harris, Chauncy D., 'The New Russian Minorities: A Statistical Overview', *Post-Soviet Geography*, XXXIV (January 1993), pp. 1–27.

Iordanskii, V., 'Dve grani obshchestvennogo soznaniia: etnicheskaia i natsional'naia', *Mirovaia ekonomika i mezhdunarodnye otnosheniia*, 1993, no. 6, pp. 87–100.

Imart, Guy G., 'Kirgizia-Kazakhstan: A Hinge or a Fault-Line?', *Problems of Communism*, XXXIX (September–October 1990), pp. 1–13.

Jones, Ellen and Fred W. Grupp, 'Modernisation and Ethnic Equalisation in the USSR', *Soviet Studies*, XXXVI, no. 2 (April 1984), pp. 159–84.

Karklins, Rasma, 'Ethnic Politics and Access to Higher Education: The Soviet Case', *Comparative Politics*, XVI, no. 3 (April 1984), pp. 277–94.

Khanazarov, K., 'Protivorechiia sotsial'nogo progressa', *Pozitsiia* (Tashkent), III, no. 2 (March–April 1993), pp. 12–15.

Kholmogorov, A. I., 'International Traits of Soviet Nations (Based on Data From Concrete Sociological Studies in the Baltic Area) [part I]', *Soviet Sociology*, XI (Winter-Spring 1972–3), pp. 211–97.

Kionka, Riina, 'Migration to and from Estonia', *Report on the USSR*, I, 37 (14 September 1990), pp. 20–4.

—, 'Are the Baltic Laws Discriminatory?', *Report on the USSR*, III, 15 (12 April 1991), pp. 21–4.

Kirch, Aksel, 'Russians as a Minority in Contemporary Baltic States', *Bulletin of Peace Proposals*, XXIII, no. 2 (1992), pp. 205–12.

Kolstø, Pål, and Andrei Edemsky with Natalya Kalashnikova, 'The Dniester Conflict: Between Irrendentism and Separatism', *Europe-Asia Studies*, I, no. 6 (1993), pp. 973–1000.

Kolstø, Pål, 'The New Russian Diaspora: Minority Protection in the Soviet Successor States', *Journal of Peace Research*, XXX, no. 2 (March 1993), pp. 197–217.

—, 'Russkaia diaspora: sobstvennaia identichnost'?', *Raduga* (Tallinn), 1993, no. 11, pp. 67–75; and no. 12, pp. 68–74.

Kornel, Eenok, 'Deals with the Estonian-Russian state border are unlawful', *Monthly Survey of Baltic and Post-Soviet Politics*, Sakala Center, Tallinn, November 1991, pp. 14–16.

Krickus, Richard J., 'Latvia's "Russian Question"', *RFE/RL Reseach Report*, II, no. 18 (30 April 1993), pp. 29–34.

Kuzio, Taras, 'Ukrainian Paramilitaries', *Jane's Intelligence Review* (Europe), December 1992, pp. 540–1.

—, 'Ukraine's Young Turks – The Union of Ukrainian Officers', *Jane's Intelligence Review* (Europe), January 1993, pp. 23–6.

Leasure, J. William, and Robert A. Lewis, 'Internal Migration in Russia in the late Nineteenth Century', *Slavic Review*, XXVII, 3 (September 1968), pp. 375–94.

—, 'Internal Migration in Russia in the USSR, 1897–1926', *Demography*, IV, no. 2 (1967), pp. 479–96.

'"Lingvisticheskii" faktor (O neudachnom opyte resheniia iazykovykh problem v Moldove)', *Izvestiia TsK KPSS*, III, no. 5 (1991), pp. 130–4.

Liubarskii, Kronid, 'Grazhdane i "sootechestvenniki"', *Novoe vremia*, 1993, no. 5, pp. 40–3.

Lough, John B. K., 'Defining Russia's Relations with Neighboring States', *RFE/RL Research Report*, II, 20 (14 May 1993), pp. 53–60.

Makarenko, Vadim and Dmitrii Trenin, '"Soiuznye liudi"', *Novoe vremia*, 1991, no. 49, pp. 10–11.

Marnie, Sheila, and Wendy Slater, 'Russia's Refugees', *RFE/RL Research Report*, II, no. 37 (17 September 1993), pp. 46–53.

Marples, David, 'A Sociological Survey of "Rukh"', *Report on the USSR*, II (12 January 1990), pp. 19–22.

Martyniuk, Jaroslaw, 'Ukrainian Independence and Territorial Integrity', *RFE/RL Research Report*, I, no. 13 (1992), pp. 64–8.

—, 'Attitudes toward Language in Ukraine', *RFE/RL Research Report*, I, no. 37 (18 September 1992), pp. 69–70.

Meyer, Jan De, and Christos Rozakis, 'Human Rights in the Republic of Latvia', *Human Rights Law Journal*, XIII nos 5–6 (June 1992), pp. 244–9.

Mihalisko, Kathleen, 'The Other Side of Separatism: Crimea Votes for Autonomy', *Report on the USSR*, III, no. 5 (1991) pp. 36–8.

Miller, John H., 'Cadres Policy in Nationality Areas. Recruitment of CPSU first and second secretaries in the non-Russian republics of the USSR', *Soviet Studies*, XXIX, no. 1 (January 1977), pp. 3–36.

Moiseenko, V., 'Migratsiia naseleniia po dannym vsesoiuznoi perepisi 1926 g.' in *Kuda i zachem edut liudi*, Moscow, 1979, pp. 47–58.

Nahaylo, Bohdan, 'The Birth of an Independent Ukraine', *Report on the USSR*, III (13 December 1991), pp. 1–5.

—, 'Ukraine and Moldova: The View from Kiev', *RFE/RL Research Report*, I, no. 18 (1 May 1992), pp. 39–45.

Panico, Christopher J., 'Turkmenistan Unaffected by Winds of Democratic Change', *RFE/RL Research Report*, II, no. 4, (22 January 1993), pp. 6–10.

Parming, Tönu, 'Population Changes in Estonia, 1935–1970', *Population Studies*, XXVI (March 1972), pp. 53–78.

Pekkanen, Raimo and Hans Danelius, 'Human Rights in the Republic of Estonia', *Human Rights Law Journal*, XIII, no. 5–6 (June 1992), pp. 236–44.

Pipes, Richard, 'Reflections on the Nationality Problems in the Soviet Union', in Nathan Glazer and Daniel P. Moynihan (eds), *Ethnicity. Theory and Practice*, Cambridge, MA, 1975, pp. 453–65.

Pryde, Ian, 'Kyrgyzstan: secularism vs. Islam', *The World Today*, 1992, November, pp. 208–11.

Rahr, Alexander, '"Atlanticists" versus "Eurasians" in Russian Foreign Policy', *RFE/RL Research Report*, I, no. 22 (29 May 1992), pp. 17–19.

Ro'i, Yaacov, 'The Islamic Influence on Nationalism in Soviet Central Asia', *Problems of Communism*, XXXIX (July–August 1990), pp. 49–64.

Rumer, Boris Z., 'The Gathering Storm in Central Asia', *Orbis*, XXXVII, no. 1 (Winter 1993).

Rywkin, Michael, 'Central Asia and the Price of Sovietization', *Problems of Communism*, XIII (January–February 1964), pp. 7–15.

Saarikoski, Vesa, 'Russian Minorities in the Baltic States', in Pertti Joenniemi and Peeter Vares (eds), *New Actors on the International Arena: The Foreign Policies of the Baltic Countries*, Tampere Peace Research Institute, Research Report, 1993, no. 50, pp. 132–49.

Schwartz, Lee, 'Regional Population Redistribution and National Homelands in the USSR', in Henry R. Huttenbach (ed.), *Soviet Nationality Policies. Ruling Ethnic Groups in the USSR*, London, 1990, pp. 121–61.

Schwarz, Solomon M. 'Revising the History of Russian Colonialism', *Foreign Affairs* (April 1952), pp. 488–93.

Segbers, Klaus, 'Migration and Refugee Movements from the USSR: Causes and Prospects', *Report on the USSR*, III, no. 46 (15 November 1991), pp. 6–14.

Sheehy, Ann, 'The Estonian Law on Aliens', *RFE/RL Research Report*, II, no. 38 (24 September 1993), pp. 7–11.

Sillaste, Galina, 'Nicheinye liudi', *Narodnyi deputat*, 1993, no. 7, p. 52.

Socor, Vladmir, 'Why Moldova does Not Seek Reunification with Romania', *RL/RFE Research Report*, I, no. 5 (1992), pp. 27–33.

——, 'Russian Forces in Moldova', *RFE/RL Research Report*, I, no. 34 (1992), pp. 38–43.

Solchanyk, Roman, 'The Referendum in Ukraine: Preliminary Results', *Report on the USSR*, III, no. 13 (29 March 1991).

——, 'Centrifugal Movements in Ukraine on the Eve of the Independence Referendum', *Report on the USSR*, III (29 November 1991), pp. 8–13.

——, 'Ukraine, The (Former) Center, Russia and "Russia"', *Studies in Comparative Communism*, XXV no. 1 (March 1992), pp. 31–45.

——, 'The Crimean Imbroglio: Kiev and Simperopol', *RFE/RL Research Report*, I, no. 33 (21 August 1992), pp. 13–6.

——, 'The Politics of Language in Ukraine', *RFE/RL Research Report*, II, no. 10 (5 March 1993), pp. 1–4.

Stewart, Susan, 'Ukraine's Policy toward Its Ethnic Minorities', *RFE/RL Research Report*, II, no. 6 (10 September 1993), pp. 55–62.

Szporluk, Roman, 'Nationalities and the Russian Problem in the USSR: an Historical Outline', *Journal of International Affairs*, XXVII (no. 1 1973), pp. 22–40.

——, 'Russians in Ukraine and Problems of Ukrainian Identity in the USSR', in Peter J. Potichnyj (ed.), *Ukraine in the Seventies*. Oakville, TX, 1974, pp. 195–217.

——, 'Dilemmas of Russian Nationalism', *Problems of Communism*, XXXVIII (July–August 1989), pp. 15–35.

——, 'The Strange Politics of Lviv: An Essay in Search of an Explanation' in Zvi Gitelman (ed.), *The Politics of Nationality and the Erosion of the USSR*, London, 1992, pp. 215–31.

Taagepera, Rein, 'Ethnic Relations in Estonia', *Journal of Baltic Studies*, XXIII, no. 2 (Summer 1992), pp. 121–32.

Tatur, Sergei, 'Vmeste podnimat' Uzbekistan', *Zvezda Vostoka*, 1991, no. 1, pp. 3–17.

Vardys, V. Stanley, 'Lithuanian National Politics', *Problems of Communism*, XXXVIII (July–August 1989), pp. 53–76.

Vasil'eva, Ol'ga, 'Novaia natsiia? Russkie v SSSR kak natsional'noe men'shinstvo', *XX vek i mir*, 1991, no. 7 (July), pp. 15–9.

Vetik, Raivo, 'Ethnic Conflict and Accomodation in Post-Communist Estonia, *Journal of Peace Research*, XXX, no. 3 (August 1993), pp. 271–80.

Vidrin, Dmitro, 'Rosiiani v Ukraini: Pid chas referendumu, do i pislia', *Politologichni chitanniia*, 1992, no. 1, pp. 237–49.

Widgren, Jonas, 'International migration and regional stability', *International Affairs* (London), LX, no. 4 (October 1990), pp. 749–66.

Wilson, Andrew, 'The Growing Challenge to Kiev from the Donbas', *RFE/RL Research Report*, II, 33 (20 August 1993), pp. 8–13.

Wixman, Ronald, 'Territorial Russification and Linguistic Russianization in Some Soviet Republics', *Soviet Geography*, XXII, 10 (December 1981), pp. 667–75.

Zaslavsky, Victor, and Yuri Luryi, 'The Passport System in the USSR and Changes in Soviet Society', *Soviet Union/Union Sovietique*, VI, part 2 (1979), pp. 137–53.

Zaslavsky, Victor, 'Nationalism and Democratic Transition in Postcommunist Societies', *Dædalus*, CXXI, no. 2 (Spring 1992), pp. 97–121.

NEWSPAPERS

ESTONIAN
Digest
Estoniia
The Baltic Independent
The Estonian Independent
Molodëzh 'Estonii
Vechernii Kur'er

LATVIAN
Atmoda/Baltiiskoe vremia
Diena, with Saturday supplement
   Subbotnyi den'
Dünaburg
Edinstvo
Korni
Lad'ia
Latviias laiks (Russian edition)
Russkii put'
Sovetskaia Molodëzh/SM-segodnia
The Baltic Observer
Za Rodinu

LITHUANIAN
Ekho Litvy
Golos Litvy

Interdvizhenie Litvy
Respublika

RUSSIAN
Argumenty i fakty
Delovoi mir
Demokraticheskaia gazeta
Den'
Emigratsiia
Federatsiia
Glasnost'
Golos
Inzhenernaia gazeta
'Iug'
Izvestiia
Literaturnaia gazeta
Literaturnaia Rossiia
Kazach'i vedomosti
Kommersant
Kommersant-daily
Komsomol'skaia pravda
Krasnaia zvezda
Kul'tura
Kuranty
Megapolis-Express

Moskovskii komsomolets
Moskovskii literator
Moscow News/Moskovskie novosti
Narodnaia gazeta
Narodnaia pravda
Nedelia
Nezavisimaia gazeta
Novaia ezhednevnaia gazeta
Poisk
Polis
Pravda
Pul's Tushina/Russkii pul's
Put'
Rabochaia tribuna
Rossiia
Rossiiskaia gazeta
Rossiiskie vesti
Russkii vestnik
Sovetskaia Rossiia
Smena
Trud
Vecherniaia Moskva
Zhizn'

MOLDOVAN
Desteptarea (Probuzhdenie)
Dnestrovskaia pravda
Dnestrovskii meridian
Moldova Suverana (Russian edition)
Tara (Russian edition)
Trudovoi Tiraspol
Vechernii Kishinëv
Vocea poporului (Russian edition)

BELORUSSIAN
My i vremia
Respublika
Sovetskaia Belorussiia

UKRAINIAN
Flag Rodiny
Golos Ukrainy
Iug
Kievskii sotsial-demokrat
Kievskie vedomosti
Krims'kii visnik

Krymskaia pravda
Krymskie izvestiia
Neskorena natsiia
Nezavisimost'
Pravda Ukrainy
Respublika Krym
Slava i chest'
Svobodnyi Krym
Vecherniaia Odessa

AZERBAIJANI
Bakinskii rabochii

GEORGIAN
Novaia gazeta
Svobodnaia Gruziia

TAJIKISTANI
Narodnaia gazeta
Slovo Tajikistana

UZBEKISTANI
Molodëzh' Uzbekistana
Narodnoe slovo
Pravda Vostoka
Tashkentskaia pravda

KYRGYZSTANI
Chuiskie izvestiia
Res publica
Slavianskie vesti
Sovetskaia Kirgiziia/Slovo
 Kyrgyzstana
Svobodnye gory

KAZAKHSTANI
Aziia
Aziia Dauysy (Russian edition)
Iuzhnyi Kazakhstan
Karavan
Kazakhstan
Kazakhstanskaia pravda
Kore-inform
Narodnyi kongress
Novoe pokolenie
Russkii vestnik (Almaty)
Sovety Kazakhstana
[Znamia truda]

DOCUMENTS, UNPUBLISHED MSS.

Papers from the conference 'The New Russian Diaspora', Lielupe, Latvia, 13–15 November 1992:

Aasland, Aadne, 'Russian Ethnic Identity in Latvia – A Sociological Survey'.

Brusina, Ol'ga, 'Russkie v Srednei Azii: "Kolonizatory" ili natsional'noe men'shinstvo?'.

Kasatkina, Natalia, 'Istoriia russkoi diaspory Litvy (1940–1981)'.

Krumina, Irina, 'Politicheskaia aktivnost' russkikh v Latvii: Istoriia i perspektivy'.

Lukianchikova, Miroslava, 'Usloviia stanovleniia novoi russkoi diaspory v Moldove'.

Pol'skii, Spartak, 'Russkaia diaspora v Belarusi. Etnopoliticheskoe polozhenie'.

Simon, Gerhard, 'Russkie za predelami Rossii. Stalinskoe nasleelie'.

Antane, Aina, 'Some Aspects of Cultural Autonomy of Minorities in Latvia 1920–1934 and Today', paper presented at the symposium 'National Identity in the Baltic States and Croatia/Slovenia', Oslo, 5–6 September 1991.

Brubaker, Rogers, 'National Minorities, Nationalizing States, and External National Homelands', paper prepared for the American Sociological Association Annual Meeting, Miami, 17 August 1993.

'Citizenship and Language Laws in the Newly Independent States of Europe', Copenhagen, 9–10 January 1993, seminar papers.

'Country reports on human rights practices for 1992, Report submitted by the U.S. Department of State', February 1993.

'Deklaratsiia namerenii obshchestvenno-politicheskogo dvizheniia "Demo-kraticheskii Krym"', mimeograph.

'Deklaratsiia o nezavisimosti Respubliki Moldova', Chisinau, 27 August 1991.

'Document of the Copenhagen Meeting of the Conference on the Human Dimension of the CSCE', Copenhagen, 1990.

Eide, Asbjørn, 'Human Rights Aspects of the Citizenship Issues in Estonia and Latvia. Based on available material and visit 3–7 February 1992. At the Request of the European Bank for Reconstruction and Development. Progress Report', 11 March 1992.

Fall, Ibrahima, 'Summary of the Report on a Fact-Finding Mission to Latvia', 27 November 1992.

Greene, James M. 'Russia's "Peacekeeping" Doctrine', SHAPE, 11 January 1993.

Grigorievs, Alex, 'The Baltic Predicament', Chr. Michelsen Institute, Bergen, Norway, December 1993.

'Gromodiani Ukraini! Na referendumi 1 grudnia, golosuite TAK'. RUKH election pamphlet, November 1991.

Helsinki Watch: 'New Citizenship Laws in the Republics of the Former USSR', vol. IV, issue 7, 1992.

——, 'Violations by the Latvian Department of Citizenship and Immigration', vol. V, issue 19, October 1993.

Krieken, Peter van, 'Baltics: Citizenship and Languages', Stockholm, February 1993.

Lough, John B.K., 'The Place of Russia's "Near Abroad"', RMA Sandhurst, 28 January 1993.

'Obrashchenie meditsinskikh rabotnikov Respubliki Moldovy', an appeal signed by delegates to the 1st conference of the Pirogov Association of Medical Workers, Chisinau, 27 September 1992.

'Programma partii Narodnyi kongress Kazakhstana', Taldy-Kurgan 1992.

'Programmnye printsipy partii slavianskogo edinstva' (Ukrainy).

'Report of the CSCE Meeting of Experts on National Minorities', Geneva, 1991.

'Russians in Estonia: Problems and Prospects', Report Prepared by the Staff of the Commission on Security and Cooperation in Europe, September 1992.

Stoel, Max van der, CSCE High Commissioner on National Minorities, letters to the Estonian, Latvian, and Lithuanian Governments, 6 April 1993.

'Summary confirming the violation of human rights in the Nistrian pseudo-republic of Moldova', 5 August 1992, signed by Alexandru Arseni, chairman of the Committee on Human Rights and National Relations in the Moldovan parliament.

'Ustav Iuzhno-Kazakhstanskogo slavianskogo kul'turnogo tsentra', 11 December 1991.

'Ustav natsional'noi assotsiatsii "Russkaia kul'tura" Respubliki Uzbekistan', Tashkent, 1992.

'Ustav predstavitel'noi assamblei' (Estonia).

'Ustav Russkoi obshchiny Latvii', Riga, 23 March 1991.

'Ustav Slavianskogo Fonda v Kyrgyzstane', adopted on 18 July 1991.

'Zaiavlenie Parlamenta Republiki Moldova o pravovom statuse lits, prinadlezhashchim k etnicheskim, iazykovym i religioznym men'shinstvam', Chisinau, 26 May 1992.

LAW TEXTS

Laws on citizenship

Russia. Adopted on 28 November 1991. *Vedomosti s"ezda narodnykh deputatov*

Rossiiskoi Federatsii i Verkhovnogo Soveta Rossiiskoi Federatsii, 1992, no. 6, pp. 307–21.

Estonia. 1938 citizenship reenacted with amendments 22 February 1992. See reprint in *Estoniia*, 7 June 1993.

Latvia. Resolution concerning restoration of the rights of citizens of the Republic of Latvia, adopted 15 October 1991; 'Draft law on Citizenship, Republic of Latvia', November 1991. Passed on only one reading in the Supreme Council and never adopted. Reproduced in 'Citizenship and Language Laws in the Newly Independent States of Europe, Seminar documents', Copenhagen 9–10 January 1993. Several new drafts produced during 1993, but none of them have as yet been adopted.

Lithuania. Law on Citizenship of the Republic of Lithuania, adopted 3 November 1989. Amended 5 December 1991.

Belorussia. 'Zakon respubliki Belarus' o grazhdanstve respubliki Belarus', adopted 18 October 1991, typescript.

Ukraine. 'Zakon Ukrainy o grazhdanstve Ukrainy', adopted 8 October 1991. *Vidomosti Verkhovnoi Radi Ukraini*, 1991, no. 50, pp. 1443–51 (law no. 791).

Moldova. 'Zakon respubliki moldova o grazhdanstve respubliki Moldova', adopted 5 June 1991, typescript.

Azerbaijan. 'Zakon Azerbaijanskoi SSR o grazhdanstve Azerbaijanskoi SSR', adopted 26 June 1990, typescript.

Georgia, 'Zakon respubliki Gruziia o grazhdanstve Gruzii', adopted 25 March 1993, typescript.

Turkmenistan. 'Zakon Turkmenistana o grazhdanstve Turkmenistana', adopted 30 September 1992. Typescript.

Uzbekistan. Adopted on 2 July 1992. *Pravda Vostoka*, 28 July 1992.

Kyrgyzstan. *Sovetskaia Kirgiziia*, 4 September 1990. Superseded by the Constitution of 5 May 1993.

Kazakhstan. 'Zakon o grazhdanstve respubliki Kazakhstan', adopted 20 December 1991. *Vedomosti Verkhovnogo Soveta Kazakhskoi SSR*, 1991, no. 52, pp. 81–96.

Language laws

Estonia. Language Law of the Estonian SSR, adopted on 18 January 1989, see reprint in *Estoniia*, 7 June 1993.

Latvia. *Zakon Latviiskoi SSR o iazykakh*, Riga, 1989. Adopted 5 May 1989. Revised version adopted 31 March 1992, see *Diena*, 24 April 1992. Additions to the code on Administrative violations concerning the Official State Language, adopted 1 July 1992.

Lithuania. 'Decree on language', adopted 25 January 1989.

Ukraine. 'Zakon o iazykakh v Ukrainskoi SSR', adopted 28 October 1989. *Vedomosti Verkhovnoi Radi Ukraini*, 1989, law no. 631, pp. 59–67.

Moldova. *Zakonodatel'nye akty Moldavskoi SSR o pridanii moldavskomu iazyku statuse gosudarstvennogo i vozvrate emu latinskoi grafiki*, Chisinau, 1990. Adopted 31 August and 1 September 1989.

Kyrgyzstan. Adopted on 23 September 1989. *Vedomosti Verkhovnogo Soveta Kirgizskoi SSR*, Frunze, 1989, no. 17 (949), pp. 547–53. Today for all practical purposes obsolete.

Kazakhstan. 'Zakon Kazakhskoi SSR o iazykakh v Kazakhskoi SSR', adopted 22 September 1989. Mimeograph. To be superseded by a new law in April 1994.

Laws on national minorities

Estonia. 'Law on Ethnic Rights of the Citizens of the Estonian SSR', adopted 15 December 1989.

Lithuania. 'Lithuanian law on ethnic minorities', adopted on 23 November 1989, amended 29 January 1991. Printed in 'Citizenship and Language Laws in the Newly Independent States of Europe', Copenhagen, 9–10 January 1993, seminar papers. Another citizenship law based on rather different principles was finally adopted on 22 July 1994.

Latvia. 'Zakon Latviiskoi Respubliki o svobodnom razvitii natsional'nykh i etnicheskikh grupp Latvii i ikh prave na kul'turnuiu avtonomiu', Riga 1991. Adopted 19 March 1991.

Ukraine. 'Zakon o natsional'nykh men'shinstvakh v Ukraine', adopted 25 June 1992. *Vidomosti Verkhovnoi Radi Ukraini*, no. 36 1992, pp. 1187–1189.

Laws on aliens

Estonia. Adopted 8 July 1993. *Molodëzh' Estonii*, 15 June 1993 (draft); *Estoniia*, 23 July 1993 (adopted version).

Lithuania. 'Law on the legal status of Foreigners in the Republic of Lithuania', adopted 4 September 1991. *Parliamentary Record* no. 5, pp. 5–10.

Georgia', 'Zakon respubliki Gruziia o pravovom polozhenii inostrantsev', adopted 3 June 1993, typescript.

International treaties

Russian-Latvian bilateral agreement. 'Dogovor ob osnovakh mezhgosudarst-vennykh otnoshenii Rossiiskoi Sovetskoi Federativnoi Sotsialisticheskoi Respubliki i Latviiskoi Respubliki, *Diena*, 25 January 1991 (*prilozhenie*).

Russian-Estonian bilateral agreement. 'Dogovor ob osnovakh mezhgosudarst-vennykh otnoshenii Rossiiskoi Sovetskoi Federativnoi Sotsialisticheskoi Respubliki i Estonskoi Respubliki', mimeograph.

Russian-Kazakhstani bilateral agreement. *Sovety Kazakhstana*, 23 July 1992.

INDEX